Implementing, Managing, and Maintaining a Microsoft® Windows Server™ 2003 Network Infrastructure (70-291)

Textbook

Greg Bott

PUBLISHED BY
Microsoft Press
A Division of Microsoft Corporation
One Microsoft Way
Redmond, Washington 98052-6399

Library of Congress Cataloging-in-Publication Data

Bott, Greg, 1966-
    ALS Implementing, Managing, and Maintaining a Microsoft Windows Server 2003
    Network Infrastructure / Greg Bott.
      p. cm.
    Includes bibliographical references and index.
    ISBN 0-07-294488-9
    (McGraw-Hill)
    ISBN 0-7356-2030-x
    (Microsoft Press)
    1. Computer networks--Planning. 2. Computer networks--Management. 3. Microsoft
Windows server. I. Title.

  TK5105.5B658 2004
  004.6--dc22   2003071054

Printed and bound in the United States of America.

4 5 6 7 8 9   QWT   8 7 6 5

Distributed in Canada by H.B. Fenn and Company Ltd.

A CIP catalogue record for this book is available from the British Library.

Microsoft Press books are available through booksellers and distributors worldwide. For further information about international editions, contact your local Microsoft Corporation office or contact Microsoft Press International directly at fax (425)
936-7329. Visit our Web site at www.microsoft.com/mspress. Send comments to *moac@microsoft.com*.

Active Directory, BackOffice, Microsoft, Microsoft Press, MS-DOS, MSN, Outlook, Windows, the Windows logo, Windows
Media, Windows NT, and Windows Server are either registered trademarks or trademarks of Microsoft Corporation in the
United States and/or other countries. Other product and company names mentioned herein may be the trademarks of their
respective owners.

The example companies, organizations, products, domain names, e-mail addresses, logos, people, places, and events depicted
herein are fictitious. No association with any real company, organization, product, domain name, e-mail address, logo,
person, place, or event is intended or should be inferred.

This book expresses the author's views and opinions. The information contained in this book is provided without any
express, statutory, or implied warranties. Neither the authors, Microsoft Corporation, nor its resellers or distributors will be
held liable for any damages caused or alleged to be caused either directly or indirectly by this book.

Program Managers: Hilary Long, Linda Engelman
Project Editor: Julie Miller
Technical Editor: Owen Fowler
Copy Editors: Ginny Bess, Christina Palaia (BookMasters, Inc.)
Indexer: Nancy Guenther (BookMasters, Inc.)
Instructional Designer: Emily Springfield

Sub Assy Part No. X10-36038
Body Part No. X10-23990

CONTENTS AT A GLANCE

CONTENTS

ABOUT THIS BOOK

Welcome to *Implementing, Managing, and Maintaining a Microsoft Windows Server 2003 Network Infrastructure (70-291)*, a part of the Microsoft Official Academic Course (MOAC) series. Through lectures, discussions, demonstrations, textbook exercises, and classroom labs, this course teaches students the skills and knowledge necessary to configure, manage, and troubleshoot a Windows Server 2003 network infrastructure. The nine chapters in this book walk you through key concepts of Windows Server 2003 network management such as Dynamic Host Configuration Protocol (DHCP), Domain Name System (DNS), Routing and Remote Access, and Software Update Services (SUS).

TARGET AUDIENCE

This textbook was developed for information technology professionals who plan to implement, administer, and support Windows Server 2003 networks, as well as individuals preparing to take the 70-291 exam.

PREREQUISITES

This textbook requires that students meet the following prerequisites:

- 12–18 months of hands-on experience supporting, administering, or implementing a Windows network.
- A strong familiarity with the networking concepts

THE TEXTBOOK

The textbook content has been crafted to provide a meaningful learning experience to students in an academic classroom setting.

Key features of the Microsoft Official Academic Course textbooks include the following:

- Learning objectives for each chapter that prepare the student for the topic areas covered in that chapter.
- Chapter introductions that explain why the content is important.
- An inviting design with screen shots, diagrams, tables, bulleted lists, and other graphical formats that makes the book easy to comprehend and supports a number of different learning styles.
- Clear explanations of concepts and principles, and frequent exposition of step-by-step procedures.

- A variety of readeraids that highlight a wealth of additional information, including:

  ❑ Note – Real-world application tips and alternative procedures, and explanations of complex procedures and concepts

  ❑ Important – Explanations of essential setup steps before a procedure and other instructions

  ❑ More Info – Cross-references and additional resources for students

- Short, optional, hands-on exercises that break up lectures and provide a warm-up for more complex lab exercises.

- End-of-chapter review questions that assess knowledge and can serve as homework, quizzes, and review activities before or after lectures. (Answers to the textbook questions are available from your instructor.)

- Chapter summaries that distill the main ideas in a chapter and reinforce learning.

- Case scenarios, approximately two per chapter, provide students with an opportunity to evaluate, analyze, synthesize, and apply information learned during the chapter.

- Comprehensive glossary that defines key terms introduced in the book.

THE SUPPLEMENTAL COURSE MATERIALS CD-ROM

This book comes with a Supplemental Course Materials CD-ROM, which contains a variety of informational aids to complement the book content:

- An electronic version of this textbook (eBook). For information about using the eBook, see the section titled "eBook Setup Instructions" later in this introduction.

- The Microsoft Press Readiness Review Suite built by MeasureUp. This suite of practice tests and objective reviews contains questions of varying complexity and offers multiple testing modes. You can assess your understanding of the concepts presented in this book and use the results to develop a learning plan that meets your needs.

- An eBook of the *Microsoft Encyclopedia of Networking*, Second Edition.

- Microsoft PowerPoint slides based on textbook chapters, for note-taking.

- Windows System Resource Manager, a feature of Microsoft Windows, that allows administrators to control how CPU and memory resources are allocated to applications, services, and processes. For more information or to install Windows System Resource Manager, open the Readme.htm in the \WSRM folder.

- Microsoft Word Viewer and Microsoft PowerPoint Viewer.

■ A second CD contains a 180-day evaluation edition of Windows Server 2003, Enterprise Edition.

NOTE The 180-day evaluation edition of Windows Server 2003, Enterprise Edition provided with this book is not the full retail product; it is provided only for the purposes of training and evaluation. Microsoft Technical Support does not support this evaluation edition.

Readiness Review Suite Setup Instructions

The Readiness Review Suite includes a practice test of 300 sample exam questions and an objective review with an additional 125 questions. Use these tools to reinforce your learning and to identify areas in which you need to gain more experience before taking the exam.

▶ **Installing the Practice Test**

1. Insert the Supplemental Course Materials CD into your CD-ROM drive.

   NOTE If AutoRun is disabled on your machine, refer to the Readme.txt file on the Supplemental Course Materials CD.

2. On the user interface menu, select Readiness Review Suite and follow the prompts.

eBook Setup Instructions

The eBook is in Portable Document Format (PDF) and must be viewed using Adobe Acrobat Reader.

▶ **Using the eBooks**

1. Insert the Supplemental Course Materials CD into your CD-ROM drive.

   NOTE If AutoRun is disabled on your machine, refer to the Readme.txt file on the CD.

2. On the user interface menu, select Textbook eBook and follow the prompts. You also can review any of the other eBooks provided for your use.

   NOTE You must have the Supplemental Course Materials CD in your CD-ROM drive to run the eBook.

THE LAB MANUAL

The Lab Manual is designed for use in a combined lecture and lab situation, or in a separate lecture and lab arrangement. The exercises in the Lab Manual correspond to textbook chapters and are intended for use in a classroom setting under the supervision of an instructor.

The Lab Manual presents a rich, hands-on learning experience that encourages practical solutions and strengthens critical problem-solving skills:

- Lab Exercises teach procedures by using a step-by-step format. Questions interspersed throughout Lab Exercises encourage reflection and critical thinking about the lab activity.

- Lab Review Questions appear at the end of each lab and ask questions about the lab. They are designed to promote critical reflection. (Answers to all Lab Manual questions are available from your instructor.)

- Lab Challenges are review activities that ask students to perform a variation on a task they performed in the Lab Exercises, but without detailed instructions.

- A Troubleshooting Lab, which appears after a number of regular labs and consists of mid-length review projects based on true-to-life scenarios. This lab challenges students to "think like an expert" to solve complex problems.

- Labs are based on realistic business settings and include an opening scenario and a list of learning objectives.

Students who successfully complete the Lab Exercises, Lab Review Questions, Lab Challenges, and Troubleshooting Lab in the Lab Manual will have a richer learning experience and deeper understanding of the concepts and methods covered in the course. They will be better able to answer and understand the testbank questions, especially the knowledge application and knowledge synthesis questions. They will also be much better prepared to pass the associated certification exams if they choose to take the exam.

NOTATIONAL CONVENTIONS

The following conventions are used throughout this texbook and the Lab Manual:

- Characters or commands that you type appear in **bold** type.

- Terms that appear in the glossary also appear in **bold** type.

- Italic in syntax statements indicates placeholders for variable information. *Italic* is also used for book titles and terms defined in the text.

- Names of files and folders appear in Title caps, except when you are to type them directly. Unless otherwise indicated, you can use all lowercase letters when you type a filename in a dialog box or at a command prompt.

- Filename extensions appear in all lowercase.

- Acronyms appear in all uppercase.

- `Monospace` type represents code samples, examples of screen text, or entries that you might type at a command prompt or in initialization files.

- Square brackets [ ] are used in syntax statements to enclose optional items. For example, [*filename*] in command syntax indicates that you can type a filename with the command. Type only the information within the brackets, not the brackets themselves.

- Braces { } are used in syntax statements to enclose required items. Type only the information within the braces, not the braces themselves.

KEYBOARD CONVENTIONS

- A plus sign (+) between two key names means that you must press those keys at the same time. For example, "Press ALT+TAB" means that you hold down ALT while you press TAB.

- A comma (,) between two or more key names means that you must press the keys consecutively, not at the same time. For example, "Press ALT, F, X" means that you presss and release each key in sequence. "Press ALT+W, L" means that you first press ALT and W at the same time, and then you release them and press L.

COVERAGE OF EXAM OBJECTIVES

This title is intended to support your efforts to prepare for the 70-291 exam. The following table correlates the exam objectives with the textbook chapters and Lab Manual lab exercises.

> **NOTE** The Microsoft Learning Web site describes the various MCP certification exams and their corresponding courses. It provides up-to-date certification information and explains the certification process and the course options. See http://www.microsoft.com/learning/mcpexams/default.asp for up-to-date information about MCP exam credentials about other certification programs offered by Microsoft.

Table 1-1   Textbook and Lab Manual Coverage of Exam Objectives

Objective	Textbook Chapter	Lab Manual Content
Implementing, Managing, and Maintaining IP Addressing		
Configure TCP/IP addressing on a server computer.	Chapter 1	Lab 1, Exercise 1-4
Manage DHCP.		
■ Manage DHCP clients and leases.	Chapter 1	Lab 1, Exercise 1-4
■ Manage DHCP Relay Agent.	Chapter 1	Lab 1, Exercise 1-7
■ Manage DHCP databases.	Chapter 2	Lab 2, Exercise 2-1, Lab 2, Exercise 2-2
■ Manage DHCP scope options.	Chapter 1	Lab 1, Exercise 1-6
■ Manage reservations and reserved clients.	Chapter 1	Lab 1, Exercise 1-5
Troubleshoot TCP/IP addressing.		
■ Diagnose and resolve issues related to Automatic Private IP Addressing (APIPA).	Chapter 1 and Chapter 2	Lab 1, Exercise 1-1
■ Diagnose and resolve issues related to incorrect TCP/IP configuration.	Chapter 2	Lab 2, Exercise 2-5

Table 1-1   Textbook and Lab Manual Coverage of Exam Objectives

Objective	Textbook Chapter	Lab Manual Content
Troubleshoot DHCP.		
■ Diagnose and resolve issues related to DHCP authorization.	Chapter 1	Lab 1, Exercise 1-3
■ Verify DHCP reservation configuration.	Chapter 1	Lab 1, Exercise 1-5
■ Examine the system event log and DHCP server audit log file to find related events.	Chapter 2	Lab 2, Exercise 2-3
■ Diagnose and resolve issues related to configuration of DHCP server and scope options.	Chapter 2	Lab 2, Exercise 2-5
■ Verify that the DHCP Relay Agent is working correctly.	Chapter 1	Lab 1, Exercise 1-7
■ Verify DHCP database integrity.	Chapter 1	Lab 1, Exercise 1-7

Implementing, Managing, and Maintaining Name Resolution

Install and configure the DNS Server service.	Chapter 3	Lab 3, Exercise 3-1
■ Configure DNS server options.	Chapter 3	Lab 3, Exercise 3-1
■ Configure DNS zone options.	Chapter 3	Lab 3, Exercise 3-2
■ Configure DNS forwarding.	Chapter 3	Lab 3, Exercise 3-4
Manage DNS.		
■ Manage DNS zone settings.	Chapter 3	Lab 3, Exercise 3-2
■ Mange DNS record settings.	Chapter 3	Lab 3, Exercise 3-3
■ Manage DNS server options.	Chapter 4	Lab 4, Exercise 4-4
Monitor DNS. Tools might include System Monitor, Event Viewer, Replication Monitor, and DNS debug logs.	Chapter 4	Lab 4, Exercise 4-3

Implementing, Managing, and Maintaining Network Security

Implement secure network administration procedures.		
■ Implement security baseline settings and audit security settings by using security templates.	Chapter 5	Lab 5, Exercise 5-2
■ Implement the principle of least privilege.	Chapter 5	
Monitor network protocol security. Tools might include the IP Security Monitor MMC snap-in and Kerberos support tools.	Chapter 6	Lab 6, Exercise 6-2

Table 1-1   **Textbook and Lab Manual Coverage of Exam Objectives**

Objective	Textbook Chapter	Lab Manual Content
Troubleshoot network protocol security. Tools might include the IP Security Monitor MMC snap-in, Event Viewer, and Network Monitor.	Chapter 6	Lab 6, Exercise 6-4
Implementing, Managing, and Maintaining Routing and Remote Access		
Configure Routing and Remote Access user authentication.	Chapter 8	Lab 8, Exercise 8-3
■ Configure remote access authentication protocols.	Chapter 8	Lab 8, Exercise 8-3
■ Configure Internet Authentication Service (IAS) to provide authentication for Routing and Remote Access clients.	Chapter 8	Lab 8, Exercise 8-3
■ Configure Routing and Remote Access policies to permit or deny access.	Chapter 8	Lab 8, Exercise 8-4
Manage remote access.		
■ Manage packet filters.	Chapter 8	Lab 8, Exercise 8-6
■ Manage Routing and Remote Access routing interfaces.	Chapter 8	Lab 8, Exercise 8-2
■ Manage devices and ports.	Chapter 8	Lab 8, Exercise 8-2
■ Manage routing protocols.	Chapter 8	Lab 8, Exercise 8-2
■ Manage Routing and Remote Access clients.	Chapter 8	Lab 8, Exercise 8-3, Lab 8, Exercise 8-4
Manage TCP/IP routing.		
■ Manage routing protocols.	Chapter 8	Lab 8, Exercise 8-2
■ Manage routing tables.	Chapter 8	Lab 8, Exercise 8-2
■ Manage routing ports.	Chapter 8	Lab 8, Exercise 8-2, Lab 8, Exercise 8-6
Implement secure access between private networks.	Chapter 8	Lab 8, Exercise 8-2
Troubleshoot user access to remote access services.		
■ Diagnose and resolve issues related to remote access VPNs.	Chapter 8	Lab 8, Exercise 8-3
■ Diagnose and resolve issues related to establishing a remote access connection.	Chapter 8	Lab 8, Exercise 8-3
■ Diagnose and resolve user access to resources beyond the remote access server.	Chapter 8	
Troubleshoot Routing and Remote Access routing.		
■ Troubleshoot demand-dial routing.	Chapter 8	
■ Troubleshoot router-to-router VPNs.	Chapter 8	

Table 1-1   **Textbook and Lab Manual Coverage of Exam Objectives**

Objective	Textbook Chapter	Lab Manual Content
Maintaining a Network Infrastructure		
Monitor network traffic. Tools might include Network Monitor and System Monitor.	Chapter 9	Lab 9, Exercise 9-3
Troubleshoot connectivity to the Internet.	Chapter 9	Lab 9, Exercise 9-4
Troubleshoot server services.		
■ Diagnose and resolve issues related to service dependency.	Chapter 9	Lab 9, Exercise 9-5
■ Use service recovery options to diagnose and resolve service-related issues.	Chapter 9	Lab 9, Exercise 9-5

THE MICROSOFT CERTIFIED PROFESSIONAL PROGRAM

The MCP program is the best way to prove your proficiency with current Microsoft products and technologies. The exams and corresponding certifications are developed to validate your mastery of critical competencies as you design and develop, or implement and support, solutions using Microsoft products and technologies. Computer professionals who become Microsoft certified are recognized as experts and are sought after industry-wide. Certification brings a variety of benefits to the individual and to employers and organizations.

> **MORE INFO**   For a full list of MCP benefits, go to *http://www.microsoft.com/ learning/mcp/mcp/benefits.asp.*

Certifications

The MCP program offers multiple certifications, based on specific areas of technical expertise:

- **Microsoft Certified Professional (MCP)**   In-depth knowledge of at least one Windows operating system or architecturally significant platform. An MCP is qualified to implement a Microsoft product or technology as part of a business solution for an organization.

- **Microsoft Certified Systems Engineer (MCSE)**   Qualified to effectively analyze the business requirements for business solutions and design and implement the infrastructure based on the Windows and Windows Server 2003 operating systems.

- **Microsoft Certified Systems Administrator (MCSA)**   Qualified to manage and troubleshoot existing network and system environments based on the Windows and Windows Server 2003 operating systems.

- **Microsoft Certified Database Administrator (MCDBA)**   Qualified to design, implement, and administer Microsoft SQL Server databases.

MCP Requirements

Requirements differ for each certification and are specific to the products and job functions addressed by the certification. To become an MCP, you must pass rigorous certification exams that provide a valid and reliable measure of technical proficiency and expertise. These exams are designed to test your expertise and ability to perform a role or task with a product, and are developed with the input of industry professionals. Exam questions reflect how Microsoft products are used in actual organizations, giving them "real-world" relevance.

- Microsoft Certified Professional (MCP) candidates are required to pass one current Microsoft certification exam. Candidates can pass additional Microsoft certification exams to validate their skills with other Microsoft products, development tools, or desktop applications.

- Microsoft Certified Systems Engineer (MCSE) candidates are required to pass five core exams and two elective exams.

- Microsoft Certified Systems Administrator (MCSA) candidates are required to pass three core exams and one elective exam.

- Microsoft Certified Database Administrator (MCDBA) candidates are required to pass three core exams and one elective exam.

ABOUT THE AUTHORS

The textbook, Lab Manual, pretest, testbank, and PowerPoint slides were written by instructors and developed exclusively for an instructor-led classroom environment.

Greg Bott is the author of the textbook. He is a husband, father, writer, golden retriever owner, and consultant. He resides in Dallas, Texas, where he has owned and operated his own consulting firm for six years. Greg's professional computer experience comes from working as a consultant for Price Waterhouse, as a program manager at Microsoft Corporation, and solving problems for a diverse client base. He is a Software Engineering Master's degree candidate at the University of Texas and has presented at technical conferences such as Fusion, Tech Ed Dallas, and Tech Ed Amsterdam. He has addressed audiences across the United States, South Korea, China, and Singapore. He has written several Microsoft Official Curriculum courses and contributed to the *Microsoft Windows 2000 Server Security Operations Guide* and co-authored the *Microsoft ASP.Net Security Operations Guide*.

Michael Hall is the co-author of the Lab Manual and the author of the testbank, pretest, and slides. He is the Director of Technical Training and a network administrator for the Georgia Department of Technical and Adult Education. He resides in Powder Springs, Georgia, with his wife and three daughters. In addition to his duties with the Georgia Department of Technical and Adult Education, he operates a technical consulting business that focuses on network design and implementation as well as courseware development and training. He has a Master's degree from Kennesaw State University and maintains several technical certifications from both Microsoft and Cisco Systems.

Tony Smith is the co-author of the Lab Manual and is a collaborating writer and technical editor of several technical manuals, books, and publications. He resides in Story, Wyoming, with his wife and three children. He is the owner of a technical consulting firm and for the past 10 years he has focused his efforts on assisting community colleges, universities, and state education programs in technical program development and the instruction of technology courses. He maintains several technical certifications from vendors including Microsoft, Novell, and Cisco. He has two master's degrees: one in Educational Program Curriculum and Development and the second in Science and Technology Programs Development. He is actively involved in technical consulting with corporations including Self-Test Software, MeasureUp, and Microsoft as a technical contributor and writer.

FOR MICROSOFT OFFICIAL ACADEMIC COURSE SUPPORT

Every effort has been made to ensure the accuracy of the material in this book and the contents of the CD-ROM. Microsoft Learning provides corrections for books through the World Wide Web at the following address:

http://www.microsoft.com/learning/support/

If you have comments, questions, or ideas regarding this book or the companion CD-ROM, please send them to Microsoft Learning using either of the following methods:

Postal Mail:

Microsoft Learning
Attn: *Implementing, Managing, and Maintaining a Microsoft Windows Server 2003 Network Infrastructure (70-291)* Editor
One Microsoft Way
Redmond, WA 98052-6399

E-mail: moac@microsoft.com

Please note that product support is not offered through the above addresses.

EVALUATION EDITION SOFTWARE SUPPORT

The 180-day evaluation edition of Windows Server 2003, Enterprise Edition provided with this textbook is not the full retail product and is provided only for training and evaluation purposes. Microsoft and Microsoft Technical Support do not support this evaluation edition. It differs from the retail version only in that Microsoft and Microsoft Technical Support do not support it, and it expires after 180 days.

For online support information relating to the full version of Windows Server 2003 Enterprise Edition that might also apply to the evaluation edition, go to *http://support.microsoft.com*. For information about ordering the full version of any Microsoft software, call Microsoft Sales at (800) 426-9400 or visit *http://www .microsoft.com*.

> **CAUTION** The evaluation edition of Windows Server 2003, Enterprise Edition should not be used on a primary work computer.

CHAPTER 1
IMPLEMENTING DHCP

Upon completion of this chapter, you will be able to:

- Describe the purpose of the **Dynamic Host Configuration Protocol (DHCP)** and how it streamlines network administration.

- Explain the **Internet Protocol (IP)** address **DHCP lease** process.

- Authorize a **DHCP server** and explain how unauthorized DHCP servers are prevented from distributing incorrect addresses to **DHCP clients**.

- Explain the purpose of **multicasting**.

- Configure a DHCP server by defining a **scope** and a **superscope**, creating **DHCP client reservations**, and configuring **DHCP options**.

- Explain the purpose of, and configure, a **DHCP relay agent**.

Transmission Control Protocol/Internet Protocol (TCP/IP) hosts must be correctly configured to communicate with other TCP/IP hosts on a network. Each host must have an Internet Protocol (IP) address and a **subnet mask**, and if communicating outside the local subnet, each must also have a **default gateway**. Each IP address must be valid and unique within the host's **internetwork**. This requirement presents a challenge for network administrators. To ensure that each host has a unique IP address, the process of assigning, changing, and reassigning addresses must be carefully monitored. If it is done manually, accurate and timely records must be kept of each host that note where the host is located and what IP address and subnet mask have been assigned to it. This quickly becomes a daunting, tedious task. Organizations with large numbers of workstations requiring IP addresses would have great difficulty managing IP addressing manually. Dynamic Host Configuration Protocol (DHCP) simplifies the problem by automating the assigning, tracking, and reassigning of IP addresses.

BRIEF HISTORY OF DHCP

Since the advent of TCP/IP, several solutions have been developed to address the challenge of configuring TCP/IP settings for organizations with a large number of workstations. **Reverse Address Resolution Protocol (RARP)** was designed for diskless workstations that had no means of permanently storing their TCP/IP settings. RARP, as its name suggests, is essentially the opposite of **Address Resolution Protocol (ARP)**. ARP clients broadcast an IP address to discover the corresponding **Media Access Control (MAC) address** (an address unique to a piece of hardware). RARP clients broadcast the MAC address (as shown in Figure 1-1). (*Broadcasting* is a communication method for sending information to all components on a network of computers simultaneously.) A RARP server then responds by transmitting the IP address assigned to the client computer.

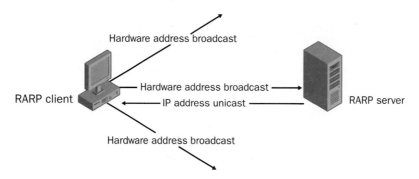

Figure 1-1   A workstation that uses RARP receives an IP address from a RARP server in response to a broadcast message containing the client's hardware address.

Because RARP failed to provide other much-needed settings to the client, such as a subnet mask and a default gateway, it gave way to another solution, the **Bootstrap Protocol (BOOTP)**.

BOOTP, which is still in use today, enables a TCP/IP workstation to retrieve settings for all the configuration parameters it needs to run, including an IP address, a subnet mask, a default gateway, and **Domain Name System (DNS)** server addresses. Using Trivial File Transfer Protocol (TFTP), a workstation also can download an executable boot file from a BOOTP server. The major drawback of BOOTP is that an administrator still must specify settings for each workstation on the BOOTP server. A better way to administer TCP/IP would be to automatically assign unique IP addresses while preventing duplicate address assignment and while providing other important settings such as the default gateway, subnet mask, DNS, **Windows Internet Naming Service (WINS)** server, and so on. Ideally, this would be accomplished without having to manually list every device on the network. Enter DHCP.

DHCP is based heavily on BOOTP, but rather than push preconfigured parameters to expected clients, DHCP can dynamically allocate an IP address from a pool of addresses and then reclaim it when it is no longer needed. Because this process is dynamic, no duplicate addresses are assigned by a properly configured DHCP server and administrators can move computers between subnets without manually configuring them. In addition, a large number of standard configuration and platform-specific parameters can be specified and dynamically delivered to the client.

WHAT IS DHCP?

DHCP is an open, industry-standard protocol that reduces the complexity of administering networks based on TCP/IP. It is defined by the **Internet Engineering Task Force (IETF)** Requests for Comments (RFCs) 2131 and 2132.

> **MORE INFO   RFCs 2131 and 2132**   RFCs 2131 and 2132 DHCP is an IETF standard based on the BOOTP protocol and is defined in RFCs 2131 and 2132, which can be looked up at http://www.rfc-editor.org/rfcsearch.html.

IP addressing is complex, in part because each *host* (a computer, printer, or other device with a network interface) connected to a TCP/IP network must be assigned at least one unique IP address and subnet mask in order to communicate on the network. Additionally, most hosts will require additional information, such as the IP addresses of the default gateway and the DNS servers. DHCP frees system administrators from manually configuring each host on the network. The larger the network, the greater the benefit of using DHCP. Without dynamic address assignment, each host has to be configured manually and IP addresses must be carefully managed to avoid duplication or misconfiguration.

Managing IP addresses and host options is much easier when configuration information can be managed from a single location rather than coordinating information across many locations. DHCP can automatically configure a host while it is booting on a TCP/IP network, as well as change settings while the host is connected to the network. All of this is accomplished using settings and information from a central DHCP database. Because settings and information are stored centrally, you can quickly and easily add or change a client setting (for example, the IP address of an alternate DNS server) for all clients on your network from a single location. Without a centralized database of configuration information, it is difficult to maintain a current view of the host settings or to change them.

All Microsoft Windows Server 2003 products (the Standard Edition, Enterprise Edition, Web Edition, and Datacenter Edition) include the DHCP Server service, which is an optional installation. All Microsoft Windows clients automatically install the DHCP Client service as part of TCP/IP, including Windows Server 2003, Microsoft Windows XP, Microsoft Windows 2000, Microsoft Windows NT 4, Microsoft Windows Millennium Edition (Windows Me), and Microsoft Windows 98.

In brief, DHCP provides four key benefits to those managing and maintaining a TCP/IP network:

- **Centralized administration of IP configuration**   DHCP IP configuration information can be stored in one location and enables the administrator to centrally manage all IP configuration information. A DHCP server tracks all leased and reserved IP addresses and lists them in the DHCP console. You can use the DHCP console to determine the IP addresses of all DHCP-enabled devices on your network. Without DHCP, not only would you have to manually assign addresses, you would also have to devise a method of tracking and updating them.

- **Dynamic host configuration**   DHCP automates the host configuration process for key configuration parameters. This eliminates the need to manually configure individual hosts when TCP/IP is first deployed or when IP infrastructure changes are required.

- **Seamless IP host configuration**   The use of DHCP ensures that DHCP clients get accurate and timely IP configuration parameters, such as the IP address, subnet mask, default gateway, IP address of the DNS server, and so on, without user intervention. Because the configuration is automatic, troubleshooting of misconfigurations, such as mistyped numbers, is largely eliminated.

- **Flexibility**   Using DHCP gives the administrator increased flexibility, allowing the administrator to more easily change IP configurations when the infrastructure changes.

- **Scalability**   DHCP scales from small to large networks. DHCP can service networks with 10 clients as well as networks with thousands of clients. For very small, isolated networks, **Automatic Private IP Addressing (APIPA)** can be used. (APIPA is discussed later in this chapter.)

HOW DHCP WORKS

The core function of DHCP is to assign addresses. As discussed previously, the key aspect of this process is that it is dynamic. What this means to the network administrator is that the network can be configured to allocate an IP address to any device that is connected anywhere on the network. This allocation of addresses is achieved by sending application layer messages to, and DHCP server and receiving application layer messages from, a DHCP server. All DHCP messages are carried in **User Datagram Protocol (UDP)** datagrams using the well-known port numbers 67 (at the server) and 68 (at the client).

> **MORE INFO**   **The Application Layer**   The application layer is part of the Open Systems Interconnection (OSI) reference model defined by the International Organization for Standardization (ISO) and the Telecommunication Standards Section of the International Telecommunications Union (ITU-T). The model is used for reference and teaching purposes. It divides computer networking functions into seven layers. From top to bottom, the seven layers are application, presentation, session, transport, network, data-link, and physical. For more information about the OSI reference model, see the Network+ Certification Training Kit, Second Edition (Microsoft Press, 2001).

Before learning how address allocation works, you should understand some terminology: DHCP clients, servers, and leases. These terms are defined in the following sections.

DHCP Clients and Servers

A computer that obtains its configuration information from DHCP is known as a *DHCP client*. DHCP clients communicate with a DHCP server to obtain IP addresses and related TCP/IP configuration information. The IP addresses and configuration information that the DHCP server makes available to the client are defined by the DHCP administrator.

DHCP Leases

A *DHCP lease* defines the duration for which a DHCP server loans an IP address to a DHCP client. The lease duration can be any amount of time between 1 minute and 999 days, or it can be unlimited. The default lease duration is eight days.

DHCP Message Types

The application layer messages in DHCP server/client communication must be one of the following eight types:

- **DHCPDISCOVER** Sent by clients via broadcast to locate a DHCP server. Per RFC 2131, the DHCPDISCOVER message may include options that suggest values for the network address and lease duration.

- **DHCPOFFER** Sent by one or more DHCP servers to a DHCP client in response to DHCPDISCOVER, along with offered configuration parameters.

- **DHCPREQUEST** Sent by the DHCP client to signal its acceptance of the offered address and parameters. The client generates a DHCP-REQUEST message containing the address of the server from which it is accepting the offer along with the offered IP address. Because the client has not yet configured itself with the offered parameters, it transmits the DHCPREQUEST message as a broadcast. This broadcast notifies the server that the client is accepting the offered address and also notifies the other servers on the network that the client is rejecting their offers.

- **DHCPDECLINE** Sent by a DHCP client to a DHCP server, informing the server that the offered IP address has been declined. The DHCP client will send a DHCPDECLINE message if it determines that the offered address is already in use. After sending a DHCPDECLINE, the client must begin the lease or renewal process again.

- **DHCPACK** Sent by a DHCP server to a DHCP client to confirm an IP address and to provide the client with those configuration parameters that the client has requested and the server is configured to provide.

- **DHCPNACK** Sent by a DHCP server to a DHCP client to deny the client's DHCPREQUEST. This might occur if the requested address is incorrect because the client was moved to a new subnet or because the DHCP client's lease expired and cannot be renewed. After receiving a DHCPNACK message, the client must begin the lease or renewal process again.

- **DHCPRELEASE** Sent by a DHCP client to a DHCP server to relinquish an IP address and cancel the remaining lease. This message type is sent to the server that provided the lease.

- **DHCPINFORM** Sent from a DHCP client to a DHCP server to ask only for additional local configuration parameters; the client already has a configured IP address. This message type is also used to detect unauthorized DHCP servers.

How Clients Obtain an Initial Lease

A DHCP client performs the initial lease process in the following situations:

■ The very first time the client boots

■ After releasing its IP address

■ After receiving a DHCPNACK message, in response to the DHCP client attempting to renew a previously leased address

If successful, the initial lease process is accomplished using a series of exchanges between a DHCP client and DHCP server that utilize four messages: DHCP-DISCOVER, DHCPOFFER, DHCPREQUEST, and DHCPACK. This message exchange process is illustrated in Figure 1-2.

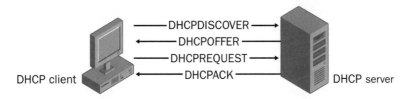

Figure 1-2   Messages exchanged with a DHCP server to obtain a lease

Locating a Server

The client broadcasts a DHCPDISCOVER message to find a DHCP server. Because the client does not already have an IP address or know the IP address of the DHCP server, the DHCPDISCOVER message is sent as a local area broadcast, with 0.0.0.0 as the source address and 255.255.255.255 as the destination address. The DHCP-DISCOVER message is a request for the location of a DHCP server and IP addressing information. The request contains the client's MAC address and computer name so that the DHCP servers know which client sent the request.

Receiving Address Offers

All DHCP servers that receive the DHCPDISCOVER message, and have a valid configuration for the client, broadcast a DHCPOFFER message with the following information:

■ Source (DHCP server) IP address

■ Destination (DHCP client) IP address

■ An offered IP address

■ Client hardware address

■ Subnet mask

■ Length of lease

■ A server identifier (the IP address of the offering DHCP server)

As depicted in Figure 1-3, the DHCPDISCOVER and DHCPOFFER messages are broadcast.

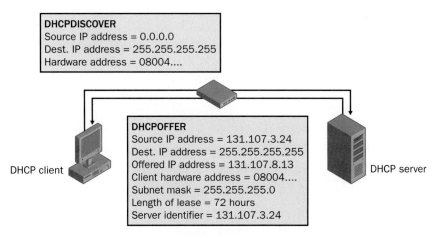

Figure 1-3   DHCPDISCOVER and DHCPOFFER messages are broadcast.

After broadcasting its DHCPDISCOVER message, the DHCP client waits 1 second for an offer. If an offer is not received, the client will not be able to initialize, and the client will rebroadcast the request three times (at 9-, 13-, and 16-second intervals, plus a random offset between 0 milliseconds and 1 second). If an offer is not received after four tries, the client continuously retries in five-minute intervals. If DHCP fails, Windows XP, Windows Server 2003, Windows 98, Windows Me, and Windows 2000 clients can use APIPA to obtain a dynamically assigned IP address and subnet mask. Windows XP and Windows Server 2003 can also use an alternate configuration, which dynamically assigns predefined settings if a DHCP server cannot be located. APIPA and alternate configurations are described in the "Automatic Client Configuration" section later in this chapter.

Responding to Address Offers

After the client receives an offer from at least one DHCP server, it broadcasts a DHCPREQUEST message to all DHCP servers. The broadcast DHCPREQUEST message contains the following information:

- The IP address of the DHCP server chosen by the client

- The requested IP address for the client

- A list of requested parameters (subnet mask, router, DNS server list, domain name, vendor-specific information, WINS server list, NetBIOS node type, NetBIOS scope)

When DHCP servers whose offers were not accepted receive the DHCPREQUEST message, they retract their offers.

Receiving Acknowledgement

The DHCP server with the accepted offer sends a successful acknowledgement to the client in the form of a DHCPACK message. This message contains a valid lease for an IP address, including the renewal times (T1 and T2, which are discussed in the following section, "How DHCP Renews a Lease") and the duration of the lease (in seconds).

How DHCP Renews a Lease

Because the IP lease has a finite lifetime, the client must periodically renew the lease after obtaining it. As Figure 1-4 illustrates, Windows DHCP clients attempt to renew the lease either at each reboot or at regular intervals after the DHCP client has initialized.

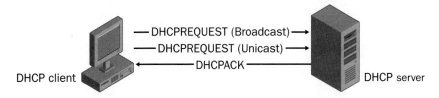

Figure 1-4   DHCP messages exchanged during lease renewal

As Figure 1-4 shows, a lease renewal involves just two DHCP messages—DHCP-REQUEST (either broadcast or unicast) and DHCPACK. If a Windows DHCP client renews a lease while booting, these messages are sent through broadcast IP packets. If the lease renewal is made while a Windows DHCP client is running, the DHCP client and the DHCP server communicate using unicast messages. (In contrast with broadcast messages, *unicast messages* are point-to-point messages between two hosts.)

When a client obtains a lease, DHCP provides values for the configuration options that were requested by the DHCP client and are configured on the DHCP server. By reducing the lease time, the DHCP administrator can force clients to regularly renew leases and obtain updated configuration details. This can be useful when the administrator wants to change the scope's configuration or wants to keep more addresses available to DHCP clients by reclaiming them more quickly. A *DHCP scope* is a range of IP addresses that are available to be leased or assigned to DHCP clients by the DHCP service. A scope may also include one or more options. An *option* is a specific configuration item, such as a subnet mask or a default gateway IP address, that the DHCP administrator wants the DHCP server to provide to the DHCP client.

> **NOTE**   **When to Increase or Decrease DHCP Lease Times**   If your TCP/IP network configuration doesn't change often or if you have more than enough IP addresses in your assigned IP **address pool**, you can increase the DHCP lease considerably beyond its default value of eight days. However, if your network configuration changes frequently or if you have a limited pool of IP addresses that is almost used up, keep the reservation period short—perhaps one day. The reason is that if the pool of available IP addresses is used up, machines that are added or moved might be unable to obtain an IP address from a DHCP server and thus would be unable to participate in network communication.

A DHCP client first attempts to reacquire its lease at half the lease time, which is known as *T1*. The DHCP client obtains the value of T1 from the DHCPACK message that confirmed the IP lease. If the lease reacquisition fails at T1, the DHCP client attempts a further lease renewal at 87.5 percent of the lease time, which is known as *T2*. Like T1, T2 is specified in the DHCPACK message. If the lease is not reacquired before it expires (if, for example, the DHCP server is unreachable for an extended period of time), as soon as the lease expires, the client immediately releases the IP address and attempts to acquire a new lease.

Changing Subnets and DHCP Servers

If the DHCP client requests a lease through a DHCPREQUEST message that the DHCP server cannot fulfill (for example, when a portable computer is moved to a different subnet), the DHCP server sends a DHCPNACK message to the client. This informs the client that the requested IP lease will not be renewed. The client then begins the acquisition process again by broadcasting a DHCPDISCOVER message. Figure 1-5 illustrates the sequence of DHCP messages that occurs when a client boots in a new subnet.

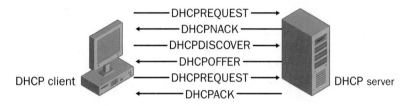

Figure 1-5   DHCP messages exchanged when a DHCP client boots in a new subnet

When a Windows DHCP client boots in a new subnet, it broadcasts a DHCPREQUEST message to renew its lease. The DHCP renewal request is broadcast on the subnet so all DHCP servers that provide DHCP addresses will receive the request. This DHCP server responding on the new subnet is different from the server that provided the initial lease. When the DHCP server receives the broadcast, it compares the address the DHCP client is requesting with the scopes configured on the server and the subnet. If it is not possible to satisfy the client request, the DHCP server issues a DHCPNACK message, and the DHCP client then begins the lease acquisition process again.

If the DHCP client is unable to locate any DHCP server when rebooting, it issues an ARP broadcast for the default gateway that was previously obtained, if one was provided. If the IP address of the gateway is successfully resolved, the DHCP client assumes that it remains located on the same network from which it obtained its current lease and continues to use its lease. Otherwise, if the IP address of the gateway is not resolved, the client assumes that it has been moved to a network that has no DHCP services currently available (such as a home network), and it configures itself using either APIPA or an alternate configuration. Once it configures itself, the DHCP client tries to locate a DHCP server every 5 minutes in an attempt to renew its lease.

Using the DHCP Relay Agent

DHCP relies heavily on broadcast messages. Broadcast messages are generally limited to the subnet in which they originate and are not forwarded to other subnets. This poses a problem if a client is located on a different subnet from the DHCP server. A DHCP relay agent is either a host or an IP router that listens for DHCP (and BOOTP) client messages being broadcast on a subnet and then forwards those DHCP messages to a DHCP server. The DHCP server sends DHCP response messages back to the relay agent, which then broadcasts them onto the subnet for the DHCP client. Using DHCP relay agents eliminates the need to have a DHCP server on every subnet.

To support and use the DHCP service across multiple subnets, routers connecting each subnet should comply with the DHCP/BOOTP relay agent capabilities described in RFC 1542. To comply with RFC 1542 and provide relay agent support, each router must be able to recognize BOOTP and DHCP protocol messages and relay them appropriately. Because routers typically interpret DHCP messages as BOOTP messages, a router with only BOOTP relay agent capability relays DHCP packets and any BOOTP packets sent on the network.

The DHCP relay agent is configured with the address of a DHCP server. The DHCP relay agent listens for DHCPDISCOVER, DHCPREQUEST, and DHCPINFORM messages that are broadcast from the client. The DHCP relay agent then waits a previously configured amount of time and, if no response is detected, sends a unicast message to the configured DHCP server. The server then acts on the message and sends the reply back to the DHCP relay agent. The relay agent then broadcasts the message on the local subnet, allowing the DHCP client to receive it. This is depicted in Figure 1-6.

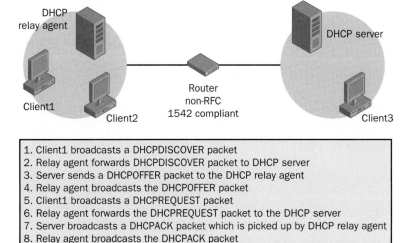

1. Client1 broadcasts a DHCPDISCOVER packet
2. Relay agent forwards DHCPDISCOVER packet to DHCP server
3. Server sends a DHCPOFFER packet to the DHCP relay agent
4. Relay agent broadcasts the DHCPOFFER packet
5. Client1 broadcasts a DHCPREQUEST packet
6. Relay agent forwards the DHCPREQUEST packet to the DHCP server
7. Server broadcasts a DHCPACK packet which is picked up by DHCP relay agent
8. Relay agent broadcasts the DHCPACK packet

Figure 1-6   DHCP messages are forwarded by a DHCP relay agent

Automatic Client Configuration

In most cases, DHCP clients find a server either on a local subnet or through a relay agent. To allow for the possibility that a DHCP server is unavailable, Windows Server 2003, Windows XP, Windows 2000, and Windows 98 provide APIPA. APIPA is a facility of the Windows TCP/IP implementation that allows a computer to determine IP configuration information without a DHCP server or manual configuration.

APIPA avoids the problem of IP hosts being unable to communicate if for some reason the DHCP server is unavailable. Figure 1-7 illustrates different IP address assignment outcomes when a DHCP client attempts to find a DHCP server. In the case where a DHCP server is not found and APIPA is configured and enabled, an APIPA address is assigned. APIPA is useful for small workgroup networks where no DHCP server is implemented. Because autoconfiguration does not support a default gateway, it works only with a single subnet and is not appropriate for larger networks.

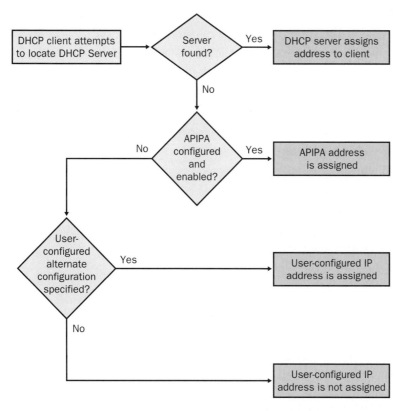

Figure 1-7 How IP addresses are assigned using APIPA or an alternate configuration

If the DHCP client is unable to locate a DHCP server and is not configured with an alternate configuration (as shown in Figure 1-8), the computer configures itself with an IP address randomly chosen from the Internet Assigned Numbers Authority (IANA)–reserved class B network 169.254.0.0 and with the subnet mask 255.255.0.0. The autoconfigured computer then tests to verify that the IP address it has chosen is not already in use by using a gratuitous ARP broadcast. If the chosen IP address is in use, the computer randomly selects another address. The computer makes up to 10 attempts to find an available IP address.

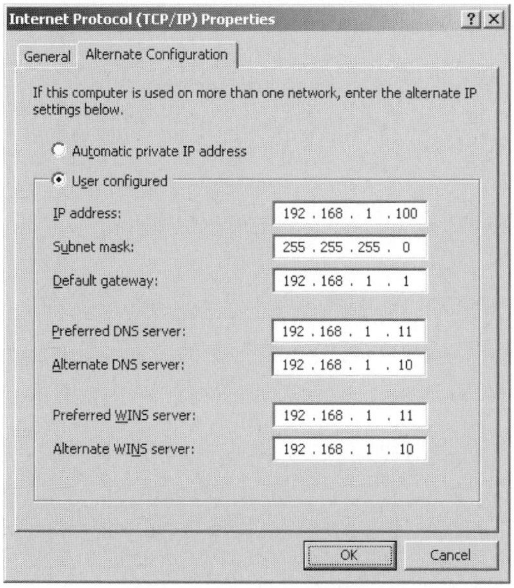

Figure 1-8 Alternate Configuration properties page

Once the selected address has been verified as available, the client is configured to use that address. The DHCP client continues to check for a DHCP server in the background every 5 minutes, and if a DHCP server is found, the configuration offered by the DHCP server is used.

Windows XP and Windows Server 2003 clients can be configured to use an alternate configuration, which the DHCP client uses if a DHCP server cannot be contacted. The alternate configuration includes an IP address, a subnet mask, a default gateway, DNS, and WINS server addresses.

One purpose of the alternate configuration is as a solution for portable computers that move between a corporate, DHCP-enabled network and a home network where static IP addressing is used. For example, Janice has a portable computer she uses at work and at home. At work, her portable computer obtains IP address information using DHCP, but she does not use a DHCP server at home. Janice can use alternate configuration to hold her home IP address, subnet mask, default gateway, and DNS server information so that when she connects her portable computer to her home network, it is configured automatically.

If you use DHCP with an alternate configuration, and the DHCP client cannot locate a DHCP server, the alternate configuration is used to configure the network adapter. No additional discovery attempts are made except under the following conditions:

- The network adapter is disabled and then enabled again
- Media (such as network cabling) is disconnected and then reconnected
- The TCP/IP settings for the adapter are changed, and DHCP remains enabled after these changes

If a DHCP server is found, the network adapter is assigned a valid DHCP IP address lease.

▶ Displaying the Alternate Configuration Tab

To display the Alternate Configuration tab shown in Figure 1-9, the network adapter must be configured to obtain an IP address automatically. To view the Alternate Configuration tab, follow these steps:

1. Open the Control Panel, and double-click Network Connections.

2. In the Network Connections window, right-click Local Area Connection, and then click Properties.

3. In the Local Area Connection Properties page, click Internet Protocol (TCP/IP), and then click Properties.

4. In the Alternate Configuration tab, specify your IP address settings.

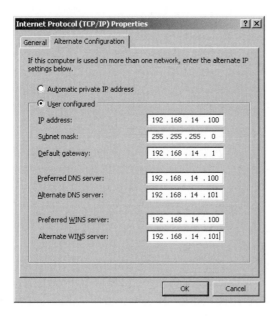

Figure 1-9 The Alternate Configuration tab of the Internet Protocol (TCP/IP) properties page

AUTHORIZING A DHCP SERVER

In implementations of DHCP prior to Windows 2000, any user could create a DHCP server on the network, an action that could lead to conflicts in IP address assignments. For example, if a client obtains a lease from an incorrectly configured DHCP server, the client might receive an invalid IP address, which prevents it from communicating on the network. This can prevent users from logging on. In Windows Server 2000 and Windows Server 2003, an *unauthorized DHCP* server (also referred to as a *rogue* DHCP server) is simply a DHCP server that has not been explicitly listed in the **Active Directory** directory service as an authorized server. You must authorize a DHCP server in Active Directory before the server can issue leases to DHCP clients.

DHCP Server Authorization Process

At the time of initialization, the DHCP server contacts Active Directory to determine whether it is on the list of servers that are currently authorized to operate on the network. One of the following actions then occurs:

■ If the DHCP server is authorized, the DHCP Server service starts.

■ If the DHCP server is not authorized, the DHCP Server service logs an error in the system event log, does not start, and, of course, will not respond to client requests.

Let's examine two scenarios. In the first scenario, the DHCP server is part of a domain and is authorized. In the second scenario, the DHCP server is not in a domain and, consequently, not authorized. These scenarios are roughly represented by the right and left sides of Figure 1-10, respectively.

In the first scenario, the DHCP server initializes and determines if it is part of the directory domain. Since it is, it contacts the directory service to verify that it is authorized. The directory service confirms the server is authorized. After receiving this confirmation, the server broadcasts a DHCPINFORM message to determine if other directory services are available and repeats the authorization process with each directory service that responds. After this is completed, the server begins servicing DHCP clients accordingly.

In the second scenario, the server is *not* a part of a domain. When the server initializes, it checks for DHCP member servers. If no DHCP member servers are located, the server begins servicing DHCP clients and continues to check for member servers by sending a DHCPINFORM message every 5 minutes. If a DHCP member server is located, the server shuts down its DHCP service and, of course, stops servicing DHCP clients.

Active Directory must be present to authorize DHCP servers and block unauthorized servers. If you install a DHCP server on a network without Active Directory, no authorization will take place. If you subsequently add Active Directory, the DHCP server will sense the presence of Active Directory; however, if it has not been authorized, the server will shut itself down. DHCP servers are not authorized by default; they must be explicitly authorized.

Protecting Against Improper Use of Workgroup DHCP Servers

When a DHCP server that is not a member server of the domain (such as a member of a workgroup) initializes, the following happens:

- The server broadcasts a DHCPINFORM message on the network.

- Any other server that receives this message responds with a DHCPACK message and provides the name of the directory domain it is part of.

- If a workgroup DHCP server detects another member DHCP server of a domain on the network, the workgroup DHCP server assumes itself to be unauthorized on that network and shuts itself down.

- If the workgroup DHCP server detects the presence of another workgroup server, it ignores it; this means multiple workgroup servers can be active at the same time as long as there is no directory service.

Even when a workgroup server initializes and becomes authorized (because no other domain member server or workgroup server is on the network), it continues to broadcast DHCPINFORM every 5 minutes. If an authorized domain member DHCP server initializes later, the workgroup server becomes unauthorized and stops servicing.

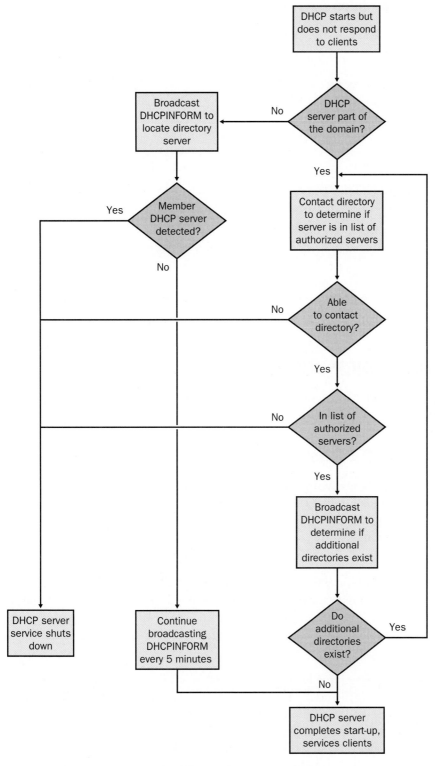

Figure 1-10   The DHCP initialization and authorization process

▶ **Authorizing the DHCP Server Service**

To authorize a DHCP server in Active Directory, perform the following steps:

1. Open the DHCP console from the Administrative Tools menu.

2. In the console tree, right-click DHCP, and then click Manage Authorized Servers.

3. In the Manage Authorized Servers dialog box, select Authorize.

4. In the Authorize DHCP Server dialog box, type the name or IP address of the DHCP server to be authorized, and then click OK.

5. The computer will list the IP and full computer name and then ask for confirmation. Click OK to continue.

When authorization is complete, the arrow on the server icon in the DHCP console changes from red to green. You may need to refresh the console.

Practice authorizing a DHCP server by doing Exercise 1-1, "Installing and Authorizing a DHCP Server," now.

NOTE   **Who Can Authorize DHCP Servers**   To authorize a DHCP server, a user must be a member of the Enterprise Admins group, which exists in the root domain of the forest.

CONFIGURING A DHCP SCOPE

Scopes determine which IP addresses are allocated to clients. You can configure as many scopes on a DHCP server as needed for your network environment.

What Is a DHCP Scope?

A DHCP scope, as mentioned previously, is a set of IP addresses and associated configuration information that can be supplied to a DHCP client. A scope must be defined and activated before DHCP clients can use the DHCP server for dynamic TCP/IP configuration.

A DHCP administrator can create one or more scopes on one or more Windows Server 2003 servers running the DHCP Server service. However, because DHCP servers do not communicate scope information with each other, the administrator must be careful to define scopes so that multiple DHCP servers are not assigning the same IP address to multiple clients or assigning addresses that are statically assigned to existing IP hosts.

The IP addresses defined in a DHCP scope must be contiguous and are associated with a subnet mask. If the addresses you want to assign are not contiguous, you must create a scope encompassing all the addresses you want to assign and then exclude specific addresses or address ranges from the scope. You can create only one scope per subnet on a single DHCP server. To allow for the possibility that some IP addresses in the scope might have been already assigned and are in use, the DHCP administrator can specify an *exclusion*—one or more IP addresses in the scope that are not handed out to DHCP clients.

Address Pools

Once a DHCP scope is defined and exclusion ranges are applied, the remaining addresses form what is called an *available address pool* within the scope. Pooled addresses can then be dynamically assigned to DHCP clients on the network.

Exclusion Ranges

An *exclusion range* is a limited sequence of IP addresses within a scope range that are to be excluded from DHCP service offerings. Where exclusion ranges are used, they ensure that any addresses within the defined exclusion range are not offered to clients of the DHCP server. You should exclude all statically configured IP addresses in the range.

▶ **Configuring a DHCP Scope**

To configure a DHCP scope, follow these steps:

1. Open the DHCP console from the Administrative Tools menu.

2. In the console tree, left-click, then right-click the DHCP server on which you want to create the new DHCP scope, and then click New Scope.

3. In the New Scope Wizard, click Next, type a name and description for the scope, and then click Next. You can use any name that you want, but it should be descriptive enough so that you can identify the purpose of the scope on your network. (For example, you could use a name such as "Administration Building Client Addresses.")

4. On the IP Address Range page, type the range of addresses that can be leased as part of this scope. (For example, use a range of IP addresses from a starting IP address of 10.1.1.50 to an ending address of 10.1.1.150.) Because these addresses are given to clients, they must all be valid addresses for your network and not currently in use. The default subnet mask that corresponds to your IP address range is provided. If you want to use a different subnet mask, type the new subnet mask, and then click Next.

5. On the Add Exclusions page, in the Start box, type the beginning of the IP address range you want to exclude, and in the End box, type the end of the IP address range you want to exclude. To exclude a single IP address, in the Start box, type the IP address.

6. Click Add and repeat step 5 until you have specified all the IP addresses to exclude. You should exclude any addresses statically assigned. Click Next.

7. On the Lease Duration page, type the number of days, hours, and minutes before an IP address lease from this scope expires. As discussed earlier, this determines how long a client can hold a leased address without renewing it. The default lease duration is eight days. Click Next.

8. On the Configure DHCP Options page, click Yes, I Want To Configure These Options Now to use the wizard to configure the most common DHCP options, such as the IP address of default gateways, DNS servers, and WINS settings. Click Next.

9. On the Router (Default Gateway) page, type the IP address for the default gateway that should be used by clients that obtain an IP address from this scope. Click Add to place the default gateway address in the list, and then click Next.

10. On the Domain Name And DNS Servers page, if you are using DNS servers on your network, type your organization's domain name in the Parent domain box.

11. On the Domain Name And DNS Servers page, type the name of your DNS server, and then click Resolve to ensure that your DHCP server can contact the DNS server and determine its address.

12. On the Domain Name And DNS Servers page, click Add to include the server in the list of DNS servers that are assigned to the DHCP clients. Click Next.

13. On the WINS Servers page, type the IP address of the WINS server(s) on your network and click Add. If you do not know the IP address, in the Server name box, type the name of the WINS server and click Resolve. After adding the WINS servers, click Next.

Practice
configuring a
DHCP scope by
doing Exercise
1-2,
"Configuring a
DHCP Scope,"
now.

14. On the Activate Scope page, click Yes, I Want To Activate This Scope Now to activate the scope and allow clients to obtain leases from it, and then click Next.

15. On the Completing The New Scope Wizard page, click Finish.

Multicast Addressing

The Microsoft DHCP server has been extended to allow the assignment of multicast addresses, in addition to unicast addresses. A proposed IETF standard defines multicast address allocation. The proposed standard benefits network administrators by allowing multicast addresses to be assigned in the same fashion as unicast addresses, enabling complete utilization of the existing infrastructure.

Multicast address allocation is often used with conferencing or audio applications, which usually require users to specially configure multicast addresses. Unlike IP broadcasts, which must be readable by all computers on the network, a multicast address points to a group of computers, using the concept of group membership to identify those to whom the message is to be sent.

The multicast address allocation feature has two parts: (1) the server-side implementation to hand out multicast addresses and (2) the client-side application programming interfaces (APIs) that applications can use to request, renew, and release multicast addresses. To use multicast addresses, the administrator first configures the multicast scopes and the corresponding multicast IP ranges on the server through a snap-in. The multicast addresses are then managed like normal IP addresses. The client can call the APIs to request a multicast address from a scope. The underlying implementation uses DHCP protocol-style packet formats between the client and the server.

CONFIGURING A DHCP RESERVATION

Use reservations for DHCP-enabled hosts that need to have static IP addresses on your network. Examples of hosts that require static IP addresses are e-mail servers and application servers. File and print servers may also require static or reserved IP addresses if they are accessed by their IP addresses.

What Is a DHCP Reservation?

Reservations enable permanent address lease assignment by the DHCP server. Where reservations are used, they ensure that a specified hardware device on the subnetwork can always use the same IP address. Reservations must be created within a scope and must not be excluded from the scope. Excluded addresses are not available for assignment to clients even if reserved for a client. An IP address is set aside, or reserved, for a specific network device that has the MAC address associated with that IP address. Therefore, when creating a reservation, you must know the MAC address for each device for which you are reserving an address. For Windows 98, Windows 2000, Windows XP, and Windows Server 2003, the MAC address can be obtained by typing **ipconfig /all** at the command line, which will result in output similar to the following:

```
Ethernet adapter :
Description . . . . . . . . : DEC DC21140 PCI Fast Ethernet Adapter
Physical Address. . . . . . : 00-03-FF-F6-FF-FF
DHCP Enabled. . . . . . . . : Yes
IP Address. . . . . . . . . : 169.254.150.72
Subnet Mask . . . . . . . . : 255.255.0.0
Default Gateway . . . . . . :
DHCP Server . . . . . . . . : 255.255.255.255
Primary WINS Server . . . . :
Secondary WINS Server . . . :
Lease Obtained. . . . . . . : 07 12 03 6:11:42 PM
Lease Expires . . . . . . . :
```

The MAC address in this example is 00-03-FF-F6-FF-FF.

▶ **How to Configure a DHCP Reservation**

To configure a DHCP reservation, follow these steps:

1. Open the DHCP console.

2. In the console tree, click Reservations.

3. On the Action menu, click New Reservation.

   Figure 1-11 shows an example of a completed New Reservation properties page.

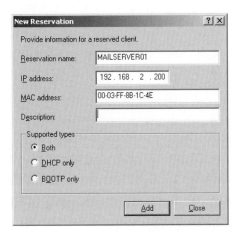

Figure 1-11   The DHCP New Reservation properties page

4. In the New Reservation dialog box, provide the following information and then click Add:

    a. Reservation name (for example, **MailServer01**)

    b. IP address

    c. MAC address

    d. Description (optional)

    e. Supported types (DHCP Only, BOOTP Only, Both).

You can restrict the type of client that may utilize this reservation to DHCP or BOOTP or allow both. Some older client computers that are running a non-Microsoft operating system may use the older BOOTP instead of DHCP. Also, Windows 2000 Remote Installation Services (RIS) clients use the BOOTP when they initialize. Click Both, unless you want the client computers to be limited to a specific protocol to receive an IP address.

5. To add the client reservation to the scope, click Add.

6. Repeat the two previous steps for any other client reservations that you want to add, and then click Close.

Practice configuring a DHCP reservation by doing Exercise 1-3, "Configuring a DHCP Reservation," now.

CONFIGURING DHCP OPTIONS

DHCP options are additional client-configuration parameters that a DHCP server can assign when serving leases to DHCP clients. DHCP options are configured using DHCP console and can apply to scopes and reservations. For example, IP addresses for a router or default gateway, WINS servers, or DNS servers are commonly provided for a single scope or globally for all scopes managed by the DHCP server. Many DHCP options are predefined through RFC 2132, but the Microsoft DHCP server also allows you to define and add custom options. Table 1-1 describes some of the options that can be configured.

Table 1-1   DHCP Scope Options

Option	Description
Router (default gateway)	The addresses of any default gateway or router. This router is commonly referred to as the default gateway.
Domain name	A DNS domain name defines the domain to which a client computer belongs. The client computer can use this information to update a DNS server so that other computers can locate the client.
DNS and WINS servers	The addresses of any DNS and WINS servers for clients to use for network communication.

User and Vendor Classes

DHCP options can be assigned to all scopes, one specific scope, and to a specific machine reservation. There are four types of DHCP options in Windows Server 2003:

- **Server options**   Server options apply to all clients of the DHCP server. Use these options for parameters common across all scopes on the DHCP server.

- **Scope options**   Scope options apply to all clients within a scope and are the most often used set of options. Scope options override server options.

- **Class options**   Class options provide DHCP parameters to DHCP clients based on type—either **vendor classes** or **user classes**.

- **Client options**   Client options apply to individual clients. Client options override all other options (server, scope, and class).

User classes are created at the discretion of the DHCP administrator. Vendor classes are defined by the machine's vendor and cannot be changed. Figure 1-12 shows the use of a vendor class to apply the 002 Microsoft Release DHCP Lease On Shutdown option to computers running Windows 2000. Using vendor and user classes, an administrator can then configure the DHCP server to assign different options, depending on the type of client receiving them. For example, an administrator can configure the DHCP server to assign different options based on type of client, such as desktop or portable computer. This feature gives administrators greater flexibility in configuring clients. If client class options are not used, default settings are assigned.

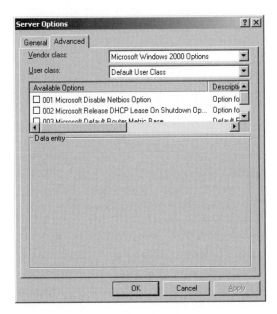

Figure 1-12   The DHCP Server Options properties page

> **MORE INFO**   *Vendor Class and Vendor Options*   *The vendor class and vendor options are described in RFC 2132 and can be looked up at http://www.rfc-editor.org/rfcsearch.html.*

CONFIGURING A DHCP RELAY AGENT

When the DHCP client and the DHCP server are on the same subnet, the DHCP-DISCOVER, DHCPOFFER, DHCPREQUEST, and DHCPACK messages are sent by means of MAC-level and IP-level broadcasts. When the DHCP server and DHCP client are not on the same subnet, the connecting router or routers must support the forwarding of DHCP messages between the DHCP client and the DHCP server, or a BOOTP/DHCP relay agent must be installed on the subnet. The BOOTP and DHCP protocols rely on network broadcasts to perform their work. Routers in normal routed environments do not automatically forward broadcasts from one interface to another.

Two methods enable you to work around this limitation. First, if the routers separating the DHCP server and clients are RFC 1542 compliant, the routers can be configured for BOOTP forwarding. Through BOOTP forwarding, routers forward DHCP broadcasts between clients and servers and inform servers on the originating subnet of the DHCP requests. This process allows DHCP servers to assign addresses to the remote clients from the appropriate scope.

The second way to allow remote communication between DHCP servers and clients is to configure a DHCP relay agent on the subnet containing the remote clients. DHCP relay agents intercept DHCPDISCOVER packets and forward them to a remote DHCP server whose address has been preconfigured. A *DHCP relay agent* is either a router or a host computer configured to listen for DHCP/BOOTP broadcast messages and direct them to a specific DHCP server or servers. Using relay agents eliminates the necessity of having a DHCP server on each physical network segment or having RFC 2131–compliant routers. Relay agents not only direct local DHCP client requests to remote DHCP servers, but also return remote DHCP server responses to the DHCP clients. Although the DHCP relay agent is configured through Routing And Remote Access, the computer hosting the agent does not need to be functioning as an actual router between subnets. RFC 2131–compliant routers (supercedes RFC 1542) contain relay agents that allow them to forward DHCP packets.

How Relay Agents Work

Figure 1-13 and the following numbered list shows how a DHCP client on Subnet 2 obtains a DHCP address lease from the DHCP server on Subnet 1.

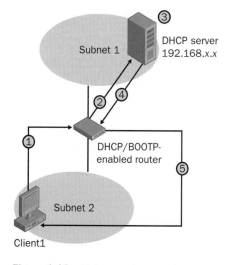

① Broadcast DHCPDISCOVER reaches relay agent (router)

② Fills in gateway address field, sends DHCPDISCOVER to DHCP server

③ Selects address from scope based on gateway address field

④ Sends DHCPOFFER to gateway address field

⑤ Router relays DHCPOFFER to DHCP client

Figure 1-13   Using a relay agent

1. The DHCP client broadcasts a DHCPDISCOVER message on Subnet 2 as a UDP datagram over UDP port 67, which is the port reserved and shared for BOOTP and DHCP server communication.

2. The relay agent, in this case a DHCP/BOOTP relay–enabled router, examines the gateway IP address field in the DHCP/BOOTP message header. If the field has an IP address of 0.0.0.0, the relay agent fills it with its own IP address and forwards the message to Subnet 1, where the DHCP server is located.

3. When the DHCP server on Subnet 1 receives the DHCPDISCOVER message, it examines the gateway IP address field for a DHCP scope to determine whether it can supply an IP address lease. If the DHCP server has multiple DHCP scopes, the address in the gateway IP address field identifies the DHCP scope from which to offer an IP address lease.

   For example, if the gateway IP address field has an IP address of 192.168.45.2, the DHCP server checks its DHCP scopes for a scope range that matches the Class C IP network that includes the gateway IP address of the computer. In this case, the DHCP server checks to see which scope includes addresses between 192.168.45.1 and 192.168.45.254. If a scope exists that matches this criterion, the DHCP server selects an available address from the matched scope to use in an IP address lease offer (DHCPOFFER) response to the client.

4. The DHCP server sends a DHCPOFFER message directly to the relay agent identified in the gateway IP address field.

5. The router relays the address lease offer (DHCPOFFER) to the DHCP client as a broadcast since the client's IP address is still unknown.

   After the client receives the DHCPOFFER, a DHCPREQUEST message is relayed from client to server, and a DHCPACK message is relayed from server to client, according to RFC 1542.

▶ **Installing a DHCP Relay Agent**

To install a DHCP relay agent, follow these steps:

1. On the Administrative Tools menu, open Routing And Remote Access.

2. In the console tree, expand the server icon, and then click IP Routing.

3. In the details pane, right-click General, and then click New Routing Protocol.

4. In the New Routing Protocol dialog box, click DHCP Relay Agent, and then click OK.

5. Open the Properties dialog box for the DHCP relay agent. In the Server Address box, type the IP address of a DHCP server, and then click Add.

Using Superscopes

A *superscope* is an administrative grouping of scopes that is used to support *multinets*, or multiple logical subnets (subdivisions of an IP network) on a single network segment (a portion of the IP internetwork bounded by IP routers). Multinetting commonly occurs when the number of hosts on a network segment grows beyond the capacity of the original address space. By creating a logically distinct second scope and then grouping these two scopes into a single superscope, you can double your physical segment's capacity for addresses. (In multinet scenarios, routing is also required to connect the logical subnets.) In this way, the DHCP server can provide clients on a single physical network with leases from more than one scope.

> **NOTE** **Superscopes Only Contain List of Member Scopes** Superscopes contain only a list of member scopes or child scopes that can be activated together; they are not used to configure other details about scope use.

▶ **Creating a Superscope**

To create a superscope, you must first create a scope. After you have created a scope, you can create a superscope by completing the following steps:

1. Open the DHCP console.

2. In the console tree, select the applicable DHCP server.

3. From the Action menu, select New Superscope.

    This menu command appears only if at least one scope that is not currently part of a superscope has been created at the server.

4. On the Welcome To The New Superscope Wizard page, click Next.

5. On the Superscope Name page, in the Name box, type the name of your superscope, and then click Next.

6. On the Select Scopes page, in the Available Scopes box, select one or more scopes from the list to add to the superscope, and then click Next.

7. On the Completing The New Superscope Wizard page, click Finish.

Superscope Configurations for Multinets

The next sections show how a simple DHCP network consisting originally of one physical network segment and one DHCP server can be extended by means of superscopes to support multinet configurations.

Superscope Supporting Local Multinets   Figure 1-14 illustrates multinetting on a single physical network (Subnet A) with a single DHCP server.

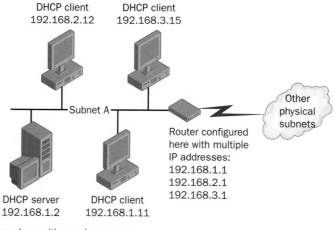

Figure 1-14   Multinetting on a single network segment

To support this scenario, you can configure a superscope that includes as members the original scope (Scope 1) and the additional scopes for the logical multinets you need to support (Scopes 2 and 3).

> **NOTE   Connecting Two Logical Subnets**   When supporting two logical subnets on one physical segment, use a router to connect traffic from one subnet to another.

Superscope Supporting Remote Multinets   Figure 1-15 illustrates a configuration used to support multinets on a physical network (Subnet B) that is separated from the DHCP server. In this scenario, a superscope defined on the DHCP server, along with a relay agent configured on the router, combines subnets A and B into a multinet, where hosts on both subnets can communicate with the DHCP Server in Subnet A.

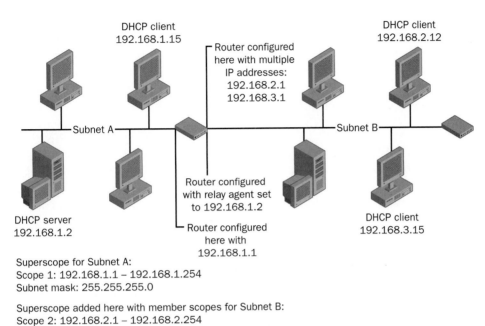

Superscope for Subnet A:
Scope 1: 192.168.1.1 – 192.168.1.254
Subnet mask: 255.255.255.0

Superscope added here with member scopes for Subnet B:
Scope 2: 192.168.2.1 – 192.168.2.254
Scope 3: 192.168.3.1 – 192.168.3.254
Subnet mask: 255.255.255.0

Figure 1-15   Routed multinetting

Superscopes Supporting Two Local DHCP Servers   Without superscopes, two DHCP server computers issuing leases on a single segment would create address conflicts. Figure 1-16 illustrates such a scenario.

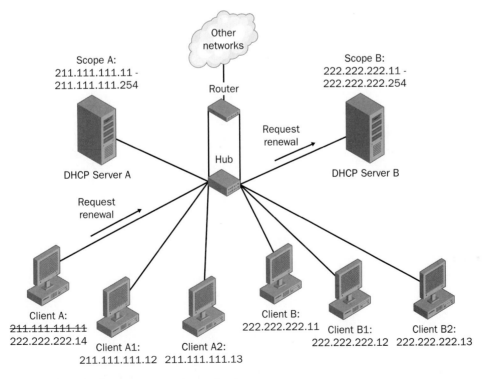

Figure 1-16   Conflicts in a two-server subnet

In this configuration, DHCP Server A manages a different scope of addresses from that of DHCP Server B, and neither has any information about addresses managed by the other. A problem arises when a client that has previously registered with Server A, for example, releases its name during a proper shutdown and later reconnects to the network.

When the client (Client A) reboots, it tries to renew its address lease. However, if Server B responds to Client A's request before Server A does, Server B rejects the foreign address renewal request with a DHCPNACK message. As a result of this process, Client A's address resets, and Client A is forced to seek a new IP address. In the process of obtaining a new address lease, Client A might be offered an address that places it on an incorrect logical subnet.

Figure 1-17 shows how you can avoid these problems and manage two scopes predictably and effectively by using superscopes on both DHCP servers. In this configuration, both servers are still located on the same physical subnet. A superscope is included on both Server A and Server B that includes both scopes defined on the physical subnet as members. To prevent the servers from issuing leases in each other's scopes, each server excludes the full scope range belonging to the other server. This is illustrated in Figure 1-17.

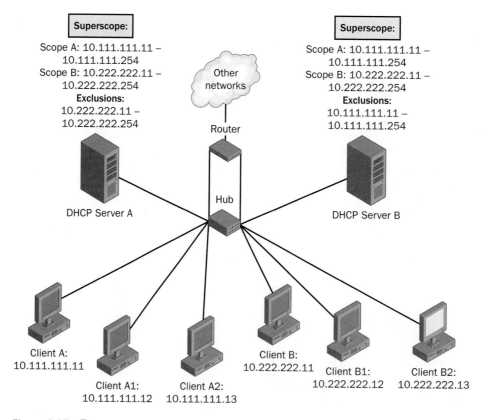

Figure 1-17   Two servers using a superscope

SUMMARY

- DHCP is a simple, standard protocol that makes TCP/IP network configuration much easier for the administrator by dynamically assigning IP addresses and providing additional configuration information to DHCP clients automatically.

- Additional configuration information is provided in the form of options and can be associated with reserved IPs, to a vendor or user class, to a scope, or to an entire DHCP server.

EXERCISES

IMPORTANT   *Complete All Exercises*   If you plan to do any of the textbook exercises in this chapter, you must do all of the exercises to return the computer to its original state in preparation for the subsequent Lab Manual labs.

Exercise 1-1: Installing and Authorizing a DHCP Server

1. Click Start, and then click Manage Your Server.

2. On the Manage Your Server page, click Add Or Remove A Role.

3. On the Preliminary Steps page, click Next.

4. On the Server Role page, click DHCP Server, and then click Next.

5. On the Summary Of Selections page, click Next.

6. On the Welcome To The New Scope Wizard page, click Cancel. (You will create a scope in Exercise 1-2.)

7. On the Cannot Complete page, click Finish.

8. Click Start, point to Administrative Tools, and then click DHCP.

9. In the DHCP console, left-click and then right-click the DHCP server that you want to authorize, and then click Authorize.

10. Open the Event Viewer and examine the System log. Locate an information event whose source is DhcpServer, which indicates that the DHCP server has been successfully authorized

11. In the DHCP console, right-click the server you authorized, and then click Unauthorize. Click Yes to confirm the removal of the DHCP server from the directory and then refresh the console.

Exercise 1-2: Configuring a DHCP Scope

1. Open the DHCP console.

2. In the DHCP console, right-click the DHCP server for which you want to configure a scope, and then click New Scope.

3. On the Welcome page, click Next.

4. On the Scope Name page, type a name and description for the scope, and then click Next.

5. On the IP Address Range page, enter the following information and then click Next.

    a. Starting IP address: **10.1.1.50**

    b. Ending IP address: **10.1.1.100**

    c. Subnet mask: **255.255.0.0**

6. On the Add Exclusions page, exclude 10.1.1.70 through 10.1.1.75 from the range, and then click Next.

7. On the Lease Duration page, set the lease duration to **4 days** and click Next.

8. On the Configure DHCP Options page, click Yes, I Want To Configure These Options Now, and then click Next.

9. On the Router (Default Gateway) page, enter **10.1.1.1** as the router, and then click Next.

10. On the Domain Name and DNS Servers page, in the Parent domain box, type **contoso.com**, and in the IP address box, type **10.1.1.200**. Click Add, and then click Next.

11. On the WINS Servers page, in the IP address box, type **10.1.1.200**. Click Add, and then click Next.

12. On the Activate Scope box, click No, I Will Activate This Scope Later, click Next, and then click Finish.

13. In the DHCP console, examine the scope that you have just created.

Exercise 1-3: Configuring a DHCP Reservation

1. In the DHCP console, expand the scope you created in Exercise 1-2. Right-click Reservations, and then click New Reservation.

2. On the New Reservation properties page, type the following values, click Add, and then click Close.

    a. Reservation Name: **MailServer01**

    b. IP address: **10.1.1.71**

    c. MAC address: **00-53-45-0F-00-0A**

Exercise 1-4: Removing DHCP

In this exercise, you will undo the configuration changes you made in the previous exercises.

1. Click Start and then click Manage Your Server.

2. On the Manage Your Server page, click Add Or Remove A Role.

3. On the Preliminary Steps page, click Next.

4. On the Server Role page, click DHCP Server and then click Next.

5. Select the Remove The DHCP Server Role check box and then click Next.

6. On the DHCP Server Role Removed page, click Finish.

REVIEW QUESTIONS

1. Under what circumstances should network administrators use DHCP?

2. Place the following DHCP message types in the order in which a successful initial IP address assignment procedure uses them.

    a. DHCPACK

    b. DHCPOFFER

    c. DHCPREQUEST

    d. DHCPDISCOVER

3. How does a DHCP client respond when its attempt to renew its IP address lease fails and the lease expires?

4. You have configured a scope with an address range of 192.168.0.11 through 192.168.0.254. However, your DNS server on the same subnet has already been assigned a static address of 192.168.0.200. With the least administrative effort, how can you allow for compatibility between the DNS server's address and DHCP service on the subnet?

5. Within your only subnet, you want 10 specific DHCP clients (out of 150 total on the network) to use a test DNS server that is not assigned to any other computers through DHCP. How can you best achieve this objective?

CASE SCENARIOS

Case Scenario 1-1: Obtaining an IP Address

Last month, a server was configured for DHCP and was functioning normally. Five days ago, a test server on the same network segment was promoted to be the first domain controller on the network. Today several users on the same subnet as the original DHCP server have complained that they are unable to obtain an IP address using DHCP. What is the most likely reason users are unable to obtain an IP address?

a. The user's IP address leases have expired.

b. A DHCP relay agent is missing or incorrectly configured.

c. There are duplicate IP addresses on the network.

d. The DHCP server must be authorized and is not.

Case Scenario 1-2: Maximizing Lease Availability

You are configuring DHCP scope options for Contoso, Ltd. The company has a limited number of IP addresses available for clients, and it wants to configure DHCP to maximize lease availability. Choose all of the following actions that will accomplish this objective:

a. Set long lease durations for IP addresses.

b. Set short lease durations for IP addresses.

c. Configure a DHCP option to automatically release an IP address when the computer shuts down.

d. Create DHCP reservations for all portable computers.

CHAPTER 2
MANAGING AND MONITORING DHCP

Upon completion of this chapter, you will be able to:

- Describe the importance and best practices of managing a **Dynamic Host Configuration Protocol** (DHCP) server.

- Manage a DHCP database by performing the following tasks: backing up and restoring, compacting a DHCP database, and reconciling a DHCP database.

- Monitor a DHCP database by creating and viewing a DHCP audit log, creating a DHCP performance baseline, viewing **DHCP server** and **scope** statistics, and creating DHCP performance alerts.

After you successfully install and configure DHCP on a Microsoft Windows Server 2003 server, you must manage and monitor the server on an ongoing basis. The more volatile your environment (volatility results from adding, removing, or repurposing servers), the more important it is that you manage and monitor your DHCP servers. Your network's level of volatility determines both the frequency of management and monitoring that you will have to do.

The purpose of managing and monitoring a DHCP server is to help prevent problems, to ensure the server is performing the functions for which you deployed it, and to verify that the server is performing its functions at an acceptable level of performance. Effective monitoring enables you to identify and remedy trends that may eventually lead to downtime or loss of performance. This chapter looks at how you manage and monitor a DHCP server.

MANAGING DHCP

DHCP plays a key role in an organization's network infrastructure. As discussed in Chapter 1, "Implementing DHCP," organizations use DHCP to provide mandatory connection settings (Internet Protocol [IP] address and subnet mask). DHCP servers also provide IP addresses of important resources such as **Domain Name System (DNS)** servers and **Windows Internet Naming Service (WINS)** servers. Without an accessible DHCP server, most clients completely lose network connectivity. Therefore, like any key resource in your organization, you must carefully manage the DHCP server. Proper management of a DHCP server helps prevent server downtime and aids in quick recovery after a server failure. Table 2-1 lists DHCP administrative tasks and when they are most often performed.

Table 2-1   **DHCP Administrative Tasks**

Administrative Task	When the Task Is Performed
Configure or modify scopes	At installation or when adding clients outside of current scopes
Configure or modify options	When adding or modifying network service servers
Configure the DHCP relay agent	When adding new subnets
Back up the DHCP database	Every hour, by default
Restore the DHCP database	When the database is corrupt
Compact the DHCP database	When it is necessary to manage DHCP database growth
Reconcile DHCP scopes	When inconsistencies are found

UNDERSTANDING DNS DYNAMIC UPDATES

Windows Server 2003 DNS supports the **DNS dynamic update** protocol **(RFC [Request for Comments]** 2136), which enables DNS clients to dynamically update their resource records in DNS **zones**. You can specify that the DHCP server in your network dynamically update DNS when it configures a **DHCP client** computer. This reduces the administration time that is necessary when manually administering zone records. You use the dynamic update feature in conjunction with DHCP to update resource records when a computer releases or updates its IP address.

On the DHCP server, you specify the DNS zone(s) that the DHCP server is responsible for automatically updating. On the DNS server, you specify the DHCP server as the only computer that is authorized to update the DNS entries.

If you use multiple Windows Server 2003 DHCP servers on your network and you configure your zones to allow secure dynamic updates only, you must use Active Directory Users And Computers to add your DHCP servers to the built-in DnsUpdateProxy security group. This enables your DHCP servers to perform updates on behalf of your DHCP clients.

You should include dynamic DNS updates from DHCP servers if

■ The DNS client operating system is not Microsoft Windows 2000, Microsoft Windows XP, or Windows Server 2003.

- Assigning the permissions, which enable each computer, group, or user to update the respective DNS entries, becomes unmanageable.

- Allowing individual DNS clients to update DNS entries presents security risks that could potentially allow unauthorized computers to impersonate authorized computers.

Client computers running Windows 2000 or later attempt to update **address (A) resource records** directly, but they utilize the DHCP server to dynamically update their **pointer (PTR) resource records**, as shown in Figure 2-1 (note that steps 3 and 4 may be reversed). A records associate host names to IP addresses, while PTR records associate IP addresses to host names. When both are present, a DNS server may perform forward and reverse lookups.

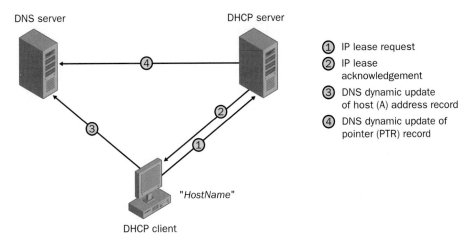

Figure 2-1   Dynamic update process for Windows 2000 or later clients

DHCP-enabled client computers running earlier versions of Microsoft operating systems are unable to update or register their DNS resource records directly. These DHCP clients must use the DHCP service provided with Windows Server 2003 to register and update both their A and PTR resource records. Figure 2-2 shows this process.

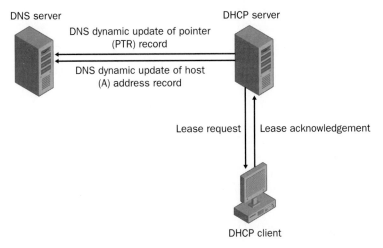

Figure 2-2   Dynamic update process for clients that run pre–Windows 2000 Microsoft operating systems

You can modify this default behavior in various ways by configuring DNS update settings on the DHCP server. This is discussed in the next section.

Configuring DNS Dynamic Update Settings on the DHCP Server

To enable dynamic update, on the properties page of the DHCP server, select Enable DNS Dynamic Updates According To The Settings Below. This option and the Dynamically Update DNS A And PTR Records Only If Requested By The DHCP Clients option are both selected by default. When the defaults are selected and a DHCP client requests the DHCP server to update its PTR resource record, the DHCP server carries out only that request. To configure the DHCP server to update both the A and PTR resource records, use the DHCP Manager console to display the properties of the DNS server and modify the settings in the DNS tab as shown in Figure 2-3. To update DNS for clients running earlier versions of the Windows operating system, such as Microsoft Windows 98 and Windows NT 4, select the Dynamically Update DNS A And PTR Records For DHCP Clients That Do Not Request Updates option, which is also shown in Figure 2-3.

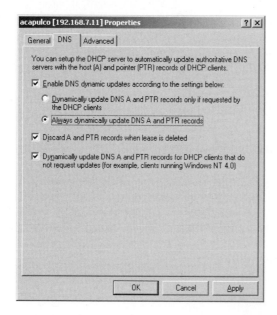

Figure 2-3   Enabling the DHCP server to update DNS A and PTR records

> **NOTE**   *Configuring Scope Properties*   DNS dynamic updates also are configured at the scope level by using the Scope Properties dialog box or for a host with a reserved IP address in the properties dialog box for that reservation.

If you are unable to secure dynamic updates, you may want to disable DNS dynamic updates. To prevent the DHCP server from attempting dynamic updates on behalf of Windows 2000, Windows XP, or Windows Server 2003 clients, clear the Enable DNS Dynamic Updates According To The Settings Below check box.

Generally, there is no reason to maintain a deleted client's DNS information. Selecting the Discard A And PTR Records When Lease Is Deleted check box removes the client's resource records from DNS when the DHCP address leases are deleted.

Practice configuring DNS dynamic updates by doing Exercise 2-1, "Configuring DNS Dynamic Update," now.

The final dynamic update setting you can configure in the DNS tab determines whether the DHCP server provides dynamic DNS update service on behalf of DHCP clients that are not capable of performing dynamic updates, such as computers running Microsoft Windows NT 4. By default, Windows Server 2003 DHCP servers do not attempt to perform dynamic updates on behalf of these clients. To enable the Windows Server 2003 DHCP server to perform updates on behalf of these clients, select Dynamically Update DNS A And PTR Records For DHCP Clients That Do Not Request Updates.

Using Secure Dynamic Updates

Although dynamic updates allow clients to update DNS resource records, this is not a secure method. A more secure way of updating DNS resource records is using secure dynamic updates. The server attempts the update only if the client can prove its identity and has the proper credentials to make the update. Secure dynamic updates are available only through Active Directory directory service and when Active Directory–integrated DNS is enabled. (For more information, see Chapter 3, "Implementing Name Resolution Using DNS".)

Configuring Secure Dynamic Update   By default, **Active Directory–integrated zones** only allow secure dynamic updates, and this setting can be modified when you create the zone. If you created the zone as a standard primary zone, and then you converted it into an Active Directory–integrated zone, it preserves the primary zone dynamic update configuration, which can be changed using the DNS console.

▶ **Configuring Secure Dynamic Updates**

This procedure uses the DNS console to verify a zone is using secure dynamic updates. To verify the dynamic update setting, follow these steps:

1. In the DNS console, right-click the zone that you want to configure for secure dynamic updates, and then click Properties.

2. In the Dynamic Updates drop-down list box, verify that Secure Only (see Figure 2-4) is selected.

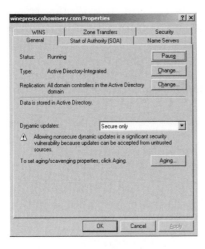

Figure 2-4   DNS zone configured for secure updates only

By default, when the DHCP Client service registers resource records for a DNS name, it first attempts a standard dynamic update. If the dynamic update fails, the client attempts to negotiate a secure dynamic update. You also can configure the client to always attempt a standard dynamic update or secure dynamic update by adding the UpdateSecurityLevel registry entry to the following subkey:

```
HKEY_LOCAL_MACHINE\SYSTEM\CurrentControlSet\Services\Tcpip\Parameters
```

The value of UpdateSecurityLevel can be set to the decimal values 0, 16, or 256, which configure security as follows:

- **0**   Specifies the use of secure dynamic update when a standard dynamic update is refused. This is the default value.

- **16**   Specifies the use of standard dynamic update only.

- **256**   Specifies the use of secure dynamic update only.

Using the DnsUpdateProxy Security Group   Using secure dynamic updates can lead to situations in which records cannot be updated. When using secure dynamic updates, the registering client, and only the registering client, can modify that name. For example, consider a DHCP server that registered a record for a pre–Windows 2000 client. Later, that client is upgraded to Windows XP and now has the capability to update its own DNS resource records. Because secure dynamic updates require the owner (which is the DHCP server) of a resource record to update that record, the newly upgraded client is unable to update its own record. Similarly, if your secondary DHCP server registers a name and then goes offline, that name cannot be dynamically updated until the secondary server comes back online.

To remedy these issues, Windows Server 2003 Active Directory provides a built-in security group called *DnsUpdateProxy*. Objects created by this group are not secure. As a result, initially the object has no owner, so a DHCP server or client that did not create it, even in zones requiring secure updates, can update it. However, as with all records, as soon as the first DHCP server or client that is not a member of the DnsUpdateProxy security group modifies such a record, that server or client then becomes its owner. At this point, only the owner can update the record in zones requiring secure updates. Thus, if every DHCP server registering resource records for older clients is a member of this group, and the clients themselves are not members of the group, the problems discussed earlier are eliminated. To avoid problems, consider adding DHCP servers to the DnsUpdateProxy security group.

Adding Computer Objects to the DnsUpdateProxy Security Group   You can add computer objects to the DnsUpdateProxy security group through the Active Directory Users And Computers console.

▶ **Adding a DHCP Server to the DnsUpdateProxy Security Group**

To add a DHCP server to the DnsUpdateProxy security group, follow these steps:

1. Click Start, point to All Programs, point to Administrative Tools, and click Active Directory Users And Computers.

2. Expand contoso.com, and then click the Users container folder.

3. Right-click DnsUpdateProxy, and then click Properties.

4. In the Members tab, click Add.

5. In the Enter The Object Names To Select box, type the names of the member servers or domain controllers that host DHCP.

6. Click Check Names, and then close the property sheet by clicking OK.

> **NOTE** **Adding DHCP Servers to the DnsUpdateProxy Security Group** If you are using multiple DHCP servers for fault tolerance and secure DNS dynamic updates are required for zones serviced by these DHCP servers, be sure to add each of the computers operating a Windows Server 2003 DHCP server to the DnsUpdateProxy security group.

Security Concerns Although adding all DHCP servers to this special built-in group, DnsUpdateProxy, helps resolve some concerns about maintaining secure DNS updates, this solution also introduces some additional security risks.

For example, any DNS domain names registered by the computer running the DHCP server are not secure. The A resource record for the DHCP server is an example of such a record. To protect against this risk, you can manually specify a different owner for any DNS records associated with the DHCP server.

However, a more significant issue arises if the DHCP server that is a member of the DnsUpdateProxy security group is installed on a domain controller. In this case, the service location (SRV), the host (A), and the **canonical name (CNAME) resource records** that are registered by the Netlogon service for the domain controller are not secure. To minimize this problem, you should not install a DHCP server on a domain controller when using dynamic updates.

> **CAUTION** **Adding DHCP Servers to the DnsUpdateProxy Security Group** For Windows Server 2003, the use of secure dynamic updates can be compromised by running a DHCP server on a domain controller when the Windows Server 2003 DHCP service is configured to perform registration of DNS records on behalf of DHCP clients. To avoid this problem, deploy DHCP servers and domain controllers on separate computers.

Troubleshooting Dynamic Update

On occasion, you might have problems with dynamic update or secure dynamic update. This section helps you identify and solve dynamic update problems.

If dynamic updates do not correctly register a name or an IP address, one or more of the following actions should aid you in diagnosing and solving the problem:

- Check the system event log on the client for specific errors.

- Force the client to renew its registration by typing **ipconfig /registerdns** at the command prompt.

- Check to see whether or not dynamic updates are enabled for the zone that is authoritative for the name that the client attempts to update.

- To rule out other problems, check to see if the dynamic update client lists the primary DNS server for the zone as its preferred DNS server. To determine the preferred DNS server for the client, check the IP address configured in the **Transmission Control Protocol/Internet Protocol (TCP/IP)** properties of the network connection for the client, or, at the command prompt, type **ipconfig /all**.

- If the client lists a preferred server other than the primary DNS server for the zone, dynamic updates can still function correctly; however, other problems might cause the failure, such as a network connectivity problem between the two servers or a prolonged recursive lookup for the primary server of the zone.

- If the zone is Active Directory–integrated, any DNS server that hosts an Active Directory–integrated copy of the zone can process the updates.

- Check to see if the resource record's **access control list (ACL)** is configured to enable dynamic updates. If the zone is configured for secure dynamic updates, the update can fail if the record's security settings do not permit this client to make changes to the record, or the update can fail if this client does not own the name that it is updating. To determine whether the update failed for one of these reasons, check Event Viewer on the client.

Enabling secure dynamic updates can also prevent a client from creating, modifying, or deleting records depending on the ACL for the zone and the name. By default, secure dynamic updates prevent a client from creating, deleting, or modifying a record if the client is not the original creator of the name. For example, if two computers have the same name and both try to register their names in DNS, dynamic updates fail for the client that registers second.

If a client fails to update a name in a zone that is configured for secure dynamic updates, one of the following conditions might have caused the failure:

- The system time on the DNS client and the system time on the DNS server are not synchronized.

- You have modified the UpdateSecurityLevel registry entry to prevent the use of secure dynamic updates on the client.

- A zone is locked. A DNS server locks a zone before doing a large zone transfer. When the zone is locked, a client cannot update a name.

- The client does not have the appropriate rights to update the resource record. You can confirm this by checking the ACL associated with the updated name. If the client does not have the appropriate rights to update the resource record, check to see that the DHCP server registered the name of the client and that the DHCP server is the owner of the corresponding dnsNode object. If so, you might consider placing the DHCP server in the DnsUpdateProxy security group. However, recall that any object created by a member of the DnsUpdateProxy security group is not secure.

CHAPTER 2: MANAGING AND MONITORING DHCP

MANAGING A DHCP DATABASE

Your network is constantly changing. New servers are added and existing servers are changing roles or are removed from the network altogether. As discussed already, it is because your network is constantly changing that you must both monitor and manage the DHCP service to ensure it is meeting the needs of the organization. Specifically, you must manage the DHCP database by performing the following database functions:

- Backup and restore
- Reconciliation
- Compacting the database
- Removing the database

What Is a DHCP Database?

The DHCP server database is a *dynamic database*, which is a data store that is updated as DHCP clients are assigned or as they release their TCP/IP configuration parameters. Because the DHCP database is not a distributed database like the DNS server database, maintaining the DHCP server database is less complex. DNS is stored hierarchically across many different servers with each server containing a part of the overall database. DHCP, in contrast, is contained in a few files on one server.

The DHCP server database in the Windows Server 2003 family uses the Joint Engine Technology (JET) storage engine. When you install the DHCP service, the files shown in Table 2-2 are automatically created in the %systemroot%\System32\Dhcp directory.

Table 2-2 **DHCP Service Database Files**

File	Description
Dhcp.mdb	The DHCP server database file.
Temp.edb	A file used by the DHCP database as a temporary storage file during database index maintenance operations. This file sometimes resides in the %systemroot%\System32\Dhcp directory after a system failure.
J50.log and J50#####.log	A log of all database transactions. The DHCP database uses this file to recover data when necessary.
J50.chk	A *checkpoint file* indicates the location of the last information that was successfully written from the transaction logs to the database. In a data recovery scenario, the checkpoint file indicates where the recovery or replaying of data should begin. The checkpoint file is updated when data is written to the database file (Dhcp.mdb).
Res*.log	Reserved log files that are used to record the existing transactions if the system runs out of disk space.

> **CAUTION   Removing or Altering Database Files**   The J50.log file, J50#####.log
> file, Dhcp.mdb file, and Dhcp.tmp file should not be removed or altered. Altering
> these files may cause your DHCP server to fail.

There is no limit to the number of records a DHCP server stores. The size of the
database is dependent upon the number of DHCP clients on the network. The DHCP
database grows over time because clients join and leave the network. Microsoft
suggests that a DHCP server service no more than 10,000 clients and 1,000 scopes.

The size of the DHCP database is not directly proportional to the number of active
client lease entries. Over time, some DHCP client entries become obsolete or
deleted. Space is not reclaimed and therefore some space remains unused.

To recover the unused space, the DHCP database is compacted. Dynamic database
compaction occurs on DHCP servers as an automatic background process during
idle time or after a database update.

Backing Up and Restoring DHCP Server Configuration

Windows Server 2003 DHCP servers support automatic and manual backups. To
provide fault tolerance in the case of a failure, it is important to back up the DHCP
database. This enables you to restore the database from the backup copy if the
hardware fails. When you perform a backup, the entire DHCP database is saved,
including the following:

- Scopes, including **superscopes** and **multicast** scopes
- Reservations
- Leases
- Options, including server options, scope options, reservation options,
  and **class** option

> **CAUTION   Security Credentials**   Note that security credentials are not
> included in this list. Neither automatic nor manual processes back up security
> credentials. You must reconfigure them after restoring the DHCP database.

Automatically Backing Up a DHCP Database
By default, the DHCP service automatically backs up the DHCP database and
related registry entries to a backup directory on the local drive. This occurs every
60 minutes. By default, automatic backups are stored in the %systemroot%\System32
\Dhcp\Backup directory. The administrator can also change the backup location.
Automatic backups use only automatic restores (automatic restores are performed
by the DHCP service when corruption is detected).

Manually Backing Up a DHCP Database
You can also back up the DHCP database manually. By default, manual backups
are stored in the %systemroot%\System32\Dhcp\Backup\ directory. The administrator can also change the backup location. Manual backups use only manual
restores. You can manually back up the DHCP database while the DHCP service is
running. The backup destination must be on the local disk; remote paths are not

Practice backing up the DHCP database manually by doing Exercise 2-2, "Manually Backing Up a DHCP Database," now

allowed, and the backup directory is created automatically (if it does not already exist). The administrator can then copy the backed up DHCP files to an offline storage location (such as a tape or a disk).

Automatically Restoring the DHCP Database

When the DHCP service starts, if the original DHCP database is unable to load, the DHCP service automatically restores from a backup directory on the local drive.

If the DHCP database fails, the administrator can choose to either restore from the backup directory on the local drive or, if that's not available, restore from the offline backup location.

If the server hardware fails and the local backup is unavailable, the administrator can restore only from the offline backup location.

Manually Restoring a DHCP Database

You can restore the database from the backup directory on the local drive. If restoring the DHCP database from the backup directory on the local drive is unsuccessful, you must restore the DHCP database from an offline storage location.

▶ Configuring a DHCP Database Backup Path

To configure a DHCP database backup path, follow these steps:

1. In the DHCP console, in the console tree, select the appropriate DHCP server.

2. On the Action menu, click Properties.

3. In the Advanced tab, in the Backup Path field, type the appropriate backup path, and then click OK.

▶ Manually Backing Up a DHCP Database

To manually back up a DHCP database to the backup directory on a local drive, follow these steps:

1. In the DHCP console, in the console tree, select the appropriate DHCP server.

2. On the Action menu, click Backup.

3. In the Browse For Folder dialog box, select the appropriate folder to back up to, and then click OK.

▶ Manually Restoring a DHCP Database

To manually restore a DHCP database from the backup directory on a local drive, follow these steps:

1. In the DHCP console, in the console tree, select the appropriate DHCP server.

2. On the Action menu, click Restore.

3. In the Browse For Folder dialog box, select the folder where the backup resides, and then click OK.

4. In the DHCP dialog box, click Yes to stop and then restart the service.

5. If the status of the service does not update, press F5 to refresh the DHCP console.

Reconciling a DHCP Database

Reconciling is the process of verifying DHCP database values against DHCP registry values. You should reconcile your DHCP database in the following scenarios:

- The DHCP database values are configured correctly, but they are not displayed correctly in the DHCP console.

- After you have restored a DHCP database, but the restored DHCP database does not have the most recent values.

For example, assume your existing database was deleted and you have to restore an older version of the database. If you start DHCP and open the console, you will notice that the scope and options display, but the active leases do not. Reconciliation populates the client lease information from the registry to the DHCP database.

How a DHCP Database Is Reconciled

When you reconcile a server or a scope, the DHCP service uses both the summary information in the registry and the detailed information in the DHCP database to reconstruct the most current view of the DHCP service. You can choose to reconcile all scopes on the server by selecting the DHCP server, or you can reconcile one scope by selecting the appropriate scope.

Before using the Reconcile feature to verify client information for a DHCP scope from the registry, the server computer needs to meet the following criteria:

- You must restore the DHCP server registry keys, or they must remain intact from previous service operations on the server computer.

- You must generate a fresh copy of the DHCP server database file in the %systemroot%\System32\Dhcp folder on the server computer.

▶ **Generating a Fresh Copy of the DHCP Server Database**

You can generate a fresh copy of the DHCP server database by following these steps:

1. Verify you have a backup copy of the DHCP database, including all required files and subdirectories.

2. Stop the DHCP server.

3. Delete all the database files in the current database path folder.

4. Restart the DHCP server.

When the registry and database meet the previous criteria, you can restart the DHCP service. Upon opening the DHCP console, you might notice that scope information is present, but that there are no active leases displayed. To regain your active leases for each scope, use the Reconcile feature.

▶ **Reconciling All Scopes in a DHCP Database**

To reconcile all scopes in a DHCP database, follow these steps:

1. In the DHCP console, in the console tree, select the DHCP server.

2. On the Action menu, click Reconcile All Scopes.

3. In the Reconcile All Scopes dialog box, click Verify.

4. In the DHCP dialog box, click OK.

▶ **Reconciling One Scope in a DHCP Database**

To reconcile one scope in a DHCP database, follow these steps:

1. In the DHCP console, select the appropriate scope in the console tree.

2. On the Action menu, click Reconcile.

3. In the Reconcile dialog box, click Verify.

4. In the DHCP dialog box, click OK.

When viewing properties for individual clients displayed in the list of active leases, you might notice client information displayed incorrectly. When the scope clients renew their leases, the DHCP Manager corrects and updates this information.

Practice reconciling a DHCP database by doing Exercise 2-3, "Reconciling a DHCP Database."

Compacting a DHCP Database

To recover unused space, the DHCP database must be compacted. Windows Server 2003 dynamically compacts the database in an automatic background process during idle time after a database update. Although dynamic compacting greatly reduces the need for performing offline compaction, it does not fully eliminate it. Offline compaction reclaims the space more efficiently. You should perform it at least once a month for large, volatile networks that have 1,000 or more DHCP clients. For smaller networks, manual compaction is required only every few months.

Windows Server 2003 includes the Jetpack.exe utility, which manually compacts the DHCP and other Jet databases (such as WINS). Use Jetpack.exe to compact a Jet database periodically whenever the database grows beyond 30 megabytes or more in size. As mentioned previously, for Windows Server 2003, the DHCP Server service performs dynamic Jet compaction of the DHCP database while the server is online. This reduces, but does not eliminate the need to use Jetpack.exe for offline compaction.

Consider the following command that uses Jetpack.exe:

```
jetpack dhcp.mdb tmp.mdb
```

The syntax for this command is

```
Jetpack.exe <database name> <temp database name>
```

Practice compacting a DHCP database by doing Exercise 2-4, "Manually Compacting a DHCP Database." now

Using this command, Jetpack.exe uses Tmp.mdb for compaction. Tmp.mdb is a temporary database used by Jetpack.exe to compact Dhcp.mdb. Dhcp.mdb is the DHCP database file. Jetpack.exe compacts the DHCP database by copying database information to Tmp.mdb, deleting the original DHCP database file, Dhcp.mdb, and then renaming the temporary database file to the original file name, Dhcp.mdb.

Enabling Server-Based Conflict Detection

The Windows Server 2003 DHCP server provides the ability to enable server-based conflict detection, which pings an IP address before leasing it to ensure the IP address is not already in use. Windows Server 2003, Windows XP, and Windows 2000 automatically verify that the IP address offered by the DHCP server is available before accepting it, so conflict detection is useful only for pre–Windows 2000 clients. Server-Based Conflict Detection can be enabled on the Advanced tab of the DHCP server properties page. To avoid unnecessary network traffic, leave it disabled unless the assignment of duplicate IP addresses to pre–Windows 2000 clients becomes an issue.

Removing the DHCP Role

Removing the DHCP role from a server is also known as *decommissioning*. When you remove DHCP, the DHCP files are deleted from the server, except for the program files that are in use. To remove the program files, you must restart the system.

▶ **Removing the DHCP Role**

To remove or uninstall DHCP, follow these steps:

1. On the Start menu, click Manage Your Server.

2. On the Manage Your Server page, click Add Or Remove A Role.

3. On the Preliminary Steps page, click Next.

4. On the Server Role page, click DHCP Server, and then click Next.

5. On the Role Removal Confirmation page, click Remove The DHCP Server Role, and then click Next.

6. On the DHCP Server Role Removed page, click Finish.

Best Practices for Managing a DHCP Database

When backing up and restoring a DHCP database, apply the following best practices:

■ Manually back up the DHCP database to a location other than %systemroot% \System32\Dhcp\Backup, which is the default location for the automatic backup. If you store a manually created copy of the DHCP database in the same location as the copy that is created automatically, the DHCP service will not function properly.

■ Maintain a copy of the backed up DHCP database offline (for example, keep a copy on a tape or a disk). Because the DHCP service automatically backs up a copy of the DHCP database to a location on the local drive, you can lose both the original DHCP database and the backup DHCP database if the hardware fails.

MONITORING A DHCP DATABASE

Monitoring the DHCP service requires you to collect and view data about the DHCP service. You need to monitor both the DHCP clients and the DHCP server. You also might want to monitor related services, such as DNS and WINS. This section focuses on what is involved in monitoring the DHCP server.

Establishing a Performance Baseline

Effectively monitoring DHCP server performance requires quantifying acceptable and unacceptable performance of the DHCP server. To identify a drop in DHCP performance early, you already must have identified "normal" DHCP performance. Identifying normal performance for your environment and DHCP server requires that you establish a performance baseline. A *baseline* is the level of system performance that you decide is acceptable. You should establish or create the baseline when the server is handling a typical workload. When you have a performance baseline, it is easy to identify performance issues because you can compare metrics of key resources as they currently are against the performance baseline. Significant deviations from the baseline often indicate system problems.

Baselines are also valuable when planning for changes and additions to the network. Using performance baselines and data collected over time enables you to assess the throughput of a DHCP server, given a certain number of users. Based on the data from DHCP monitoring, you can extrapolate the result of adding additional users and estimate what additional resources are necessary, if any.

When monitoring a computer configured as a DHCP server, consider other functions the server may be performing, including the following:

- Is it a domain controller, a file and print server, or a mail server in addition to being a DHCP server?

- What is the total utilization of the server's resources? How would adding the DHCP server role impact the server's overall performance?

- Consider the time of day at which you are collecting data: Is it during peak logon times?

- Are other scheduled processes, such as backups, running at the same time?

- How many users accessed the server for functions other than DHCP while you were collecting data for your baseline?

The DHCP service uses memory, processor, disk, and network subsystems. Although these subsystems are important for the DHCP service to perform optimally, you can obtain the greatest benefit by monitoring the performance of the network subsystem.

Location of DHCP Data

Four tools provide DHCP data: the DHCP console, DHCP audit log, Event Viewer, and Performance console. Each tool provides information, as described in table Table 2-3.

Table 2-3   **DHCP Data Tools**

Tool	Description	Examples of Information Provided
DHCP console statistics	Use the DHCP console to display DHCP server statistics, which is data collected at either the server level or the scope level since the DHCP service was last started.	■ DHCP service start and stop times ■ Number of IP addresses available in a scope ■ Number of leases in use in a scope ■ Number of clients in use
DHCP audit log/Event Viewer	These two tools do the exact same thing. They provide information about DHCP events. Information includes significant occurrences either in the system or in an application that requires notification to the user or an additional entry to a log.	■ When the service is stopped or started, and by whom ■ DHCP service errors ■ DHCP service authorizations
Performance console	This tool provides DHCP performance data. The DHCP service includes a set of performance counters that the administrator can use to monitor various types of server activity.	■ Number of leases renewed for a period of time ■ Number of DHCPACK or DHCPNACK packets for a period of time ■ Amount of disk space that the DHCP database uses ■ Number of IP address conflicts

Using DHCP Statistics to Monitor a DHCP Server

DHCP statistics represent data collected at the server level or the scope level since the most recent start of the DHCP service.

Statistics provide a real-time view that you can use to check the status of your DHCP server or scopes. You can get statistics for a particular scope or at the server level; the latter shows the aggregate of all the scopes that the server manages.

Using the DHCP console, you can view the DHCP statistics, for both a server and a scope, as listed in Table 2-4.

Table 2-4   **DHCP Statistics**

DHCP Statistics	Description	Server Statistics	Scope Statistics
Start Time	When the DHCP service was started	X	
Up Time	Period of time the DHCP service has been active	X	
Discovers	Number of client DHCPDISCOVERs received	X	

(continued)

Table 2-4   **DHCP Statistics**

DHCP Statistics	Description	Server Statistics	Scope Statistics
Offers	Number of client DHCPOFFERs sent	X	
Requests	Number of client DHCPREQUESTs received	X	
Acks	Number of client DHCPACKs sent	X	
Nacks	Number of client DHCPNACKs sent	X	
Declines	Number of client DHCPDECLINEs received	X	
Releases	Number of client DHCPRELEASEs received	X	
Total Scopes	Total number of scopes on the DHCP server	X	
Total Addresses	Total number of IP addresses configured for clients	X	X
In Use	Number of IP addresses currently leased	X	X
Available	Number of IP addresses available for lease	X	X

Viewing DHCP Statistics

You can view DHCP statistics for both a server and a scope. For greater ease in viewing DHCP statistics, you can enable DHCP server statistics to refresh automatically, which also enables the DHCP scope statistics to refresh automatically.

▶ **Enabling Automatic Refresh of DHCP Statistics**

To enable automatic refresh of DHCP statistics, follow these steps:

1. In the DHCP console, in the console tree, select the appropriate DHCP server.

2. On the Action menu, click Properties.

3. In the General tab, select the Automatically Update Statistics Every check box, configure the Hours and Minutes fields appropriately, and then click OK.

▶ **Viewing DHCP Server Statistics**

To view DHCP server statistics, follow these steps:

1. In the DHCP console, in the console tree, select the appropriate DHCP server.

2. On the Action menu, click Display Statistics. Figure 2-5 is displayed.

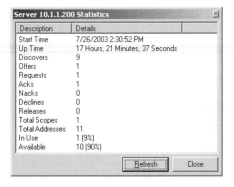

Figure 2-5   DHCP server statistics

▶ **Viewing DHCP Scope Statistics**

To view DHCP scope statistics, follow these steps:

1. In the DHCP console, in the console tree, select the appropriate DHCP scope.

2. On the Action menu, click Display Statistics. Figure 2-6 is displayed.

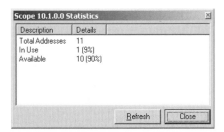

Figure 2-6   DHCP scope statistics

Using the DHCP Audit Log to Monitor a DHCP Server

Logging DHCP server data enables you to gather information about the DHCP Server service operations on the network. You can view a single day's log file for information, or you can collect log files on a separate server for analysis of DHCP server data over a longer period. This information is helpful when deciding whether you need to add more DHCP servers or when troubleshooting problems with DHCP servers. It is important that you understand the audit log process because there are times when logging will cease and log files will be overwritten. Understanding the process will enable you to gather the DHCP statistics necessary to maintain optimal performance of your DHCP server.

A DHCP audit log gives the administrator a day-to-day collection of DHCP events. DHCP audit logs provide you with the information that you may need for monitoring your DHCP server. You can use DHCP audit logs to view activity for one specified day, or you can collect the log files to analyze DHCP server activity over longer periods.

DHCP Audit Log File

A *DHCP audit log file* is a log of service-related events, such as the following:

- The starting and stopping of the service

- The verification of authorizations

- Leasing, renewal, and denial of IP addresses

When you enable logging, the DHCP server creates log files named DhcpSrvLog-*day*.log, where *day* is a three-letter abbreviation that represents the day the log was created; for example, a log created on Sunday would be named DhcpSrvLog-Sun .log. The DHCP server stores these files in the DHCP database directory. Figure 2-7 shows a sample log file.

```
ID,Date,Time,Description,IP Address,Host Name,MAC Address
24,07/27/03,00:00:13,Database Cleanup Begin,,,
25,07/27/03,00:00:13,0 leases expired and 0 leases deleted,,,,
25,07/27/03,00:00:13,0 leases expired and 0 leases deleted,,,,
24,07/27/03,07:47:01,Database Cleanup Begin,,,
25,07/27/03,07:47:01,0 leases expired and 0 leases deleted,,,,
25,07/27/03,07:47:01,0 leases expired and 0 leases deleted,,,,
55,07/27/03,07:47:25,Authorized(servicing),,contoso01.com,,
10,07/27/03,07:52:25,Assign,10.1.1.90,Bott98,0003FF4398CA,
24,07/27/03,08:47:03,Database Cleanup Begin,,,
25,07/27/03,08:47:03,0 leases expired and 0 leases deleted,,,,
25,07/27/03,08:47:03,0 leases expired and 0 leases deleted,,,,
24,07/27/03,09:47:05,Database Cleanup Begin,,,
25,07/27/03,09:47:05,0 leases expired and 0 leases deleted,,,,
25,07/27/03,09:47:05,0 leases expired and 0 leases deleted,,,,
24,07/27/03,10:47:07,Database Cleanup Begin,,,
25,07/27/03,10:47:07,0 leases expired and 0 leases deleted,,,,
25,07/27/03,10:47:07,0 leases expired and 0 leases deleted,,,,
24,07/27/03,11:47:09,Database Cleanup Begin,,,
25,07/27/03,11:47:09,0 leases expired and 0 leases deleted,,,,
25,07/27/03,11:47:09,0 leases expired and 0 leases deleted,,,,
24,07/27/03,12:47:11,Database Cleanup Begin,,,
25,07/27/03,12:47:11,0 leases expired and 0 leases deleted,,,,
25,07/27/03,12:47:11,0 leases expired and 0 leases deleted,,,,
24,07/27/03,13:47:13,Database Cleanup Begin,,,
25,07/27/03,13:47:13,0 leases expired and 0 leases deleted,,,,
25,07/27/03,13:47:13,0 leases expired and 0 leases deleted,,,,
24,07/27/03,14:47:15,Database Cleanup Begin,,,
25,07/27/03,14:47:15,0 leases expired and 0 leases deleted,,,,
25,07/27/03,14:47:15,0 leases expired and 0 leases deleted,,,,
24,07/27/03,15:47:17,Database Cleanup Begin,,,
25,07/27/03,15:47:17,0 leases expired and 0 leases deleted,,,,
25,07/27/03,15:47:17,0 leases expired and 0 leases deleted,,,,
```

Figure 2-7   Sample DHCP audit log file

The log files are comma-delimited text files that contain log entries representing a single line of text. A DHCP audit log file includes the fields shown in Table 2-5.

Table 2-5   **DHCP Audit Log File Fields**

Field	Description
ID	A DHCP server event ID code
Date	The date on which this entry was logged on the DHCP server
Time	The time at which this entry was logged on the DHCP server
Description	A description of this DHCP server event
IP Address	The IP address of the DHCP client
Host Name	The host name of the DHCP client
MAC Address	The Media Access Control (MAC) address that the network adapter hardware of the client uses

The DHCP server's audit log files use reserved event ID codes to provide information about the type of server event or activity logged. Table 2-6 describes the DHCP event ID codes that might appear in the log file.

Table 2-6   **DHCP Event IDs and Descriptions**

Event ID	Description
00	The log started.
01	The log stopped.
02	The log temporarily paused because of low disk space.
10	A client leased a new IP address.
11	A client renewed a lease.
12	A client released a lease.
13	An IP address was found in use on the network.
14	A lease request was not satisfied because the address pool of the scope was exhausted.
15	A lease was denied.
20	A client leased a Bootstrap Protocol (BOOTP) address.

How DHCP Audit Logging Works

The following process describes how audit logging starts, performs, and ends during a 24-hour day:

1. A new log file is created when one of the following events occurs: the DHCP server is started, or the local time passes 12:00 A.M.

2. Depending on whether the audit log file has been modified in the previous 24 hours, the following actions occur:

   a. If the file previously existed without modification for more than a day, it is overwritten.

   b. If the file existed but was modified within the previous 24 hours, it is not overwritten. Instead, new logging activity is appended to the end of the existing file. This is the case when either the system or the DHCP Server service is restarted.

3. The server writes a header message in the audit log file, which indicates that logging has started.

4. During audit logging, the DHCP server performs various logical disk checks to ensure disk space used by the log stays within boundaries set in the registry. Disk checks are performed at intervals of events and when the server computer reaches 12:00 A.M. in its local clock. By default, disks are considered full when the amount of free disk space falls below 20 megabytes or the current audit file is larger than one-seventh (1/7) of the maximum allotted space for the combined total space of all audit log files stored on the computer. The default maximum space is 70 megabytes.

5. If the disk check finds the disk is full, logging ceases, but disk checks continue. If more disk space becomes available, logging resumes.

6. At 12:00 A.M., the current day's log file is closed and the logging process begins again.

> **NOTE** **Keeping Log Files Older Than Seven Days** To keep the audit log information for a period greater than a week, remove audit log files from the directory before the next week's audit log overwrites it.

▶ Enabling and Configuring DHCP Audit Logging

To enable and configure DHCP audit logging, follow these steps:

1. In the DHCP console, in the console tree, select the appropriate DHCP server.

2. On the Action menu, click Properties.

3. In the General tab, verify that the Enable DHCP Audit Logging option is selected.

4. In the Advanced tab, in the Audit Log File Path field, type the appropriate audit log file path, and then click OK.

5. In the DHCP dialog box, click Yes to stop and then restart the service.

Practice viewing DHCP audit logging by doing Exercise 2-5, "Configuring and Viewing the DHCP Audit Log."

Viewing the DHCP Audit Log

Because DHCP audit logging is enabled by default, as soon as DHCP is installed and configured, you can view the DHCP audit logs to view the information that you need to monitor your DHCP server. Using Windows Explorer, go to the directory where you are storing the audit log file, and double-click the appropriate log file.

> **NOTE** **Where the DHCP Service Stores Logs** By default, the DHCP service stores audit logs in the %systemroot%\System32\Dhcp folder. An audit log file contains the event IDs and their meanings in the file. Audit logs are named DhcpSrvLog-day.log where *day* is the three-letter abbreviation for the day of the week. For example, the audit log for Wednesday is DhcpSrvLog-Wed.log.

Using the Performance Console to Monitor DHCP

There is an administrative utility, called the Performance console, that you can use to monitor DHCP server performance. When you open the Performance console, the console tree has two nodes. The first node is System Monitor, and the second node is Performance Logs And Alerts.

System Monitor

You can add performance objects and counters to any one of the System Monitor's three graphical views: graph, histogram, and report. To view any of the views individually, right-click the desired view and then click New Window From Here. You also can view logged data. If you add a counter that has more than one instance, you have the option to select the instance. For example, if the computer you are monitoring has two network interfaces, when you select the Network Interface performance object, you have the option of selecting one or both of the interfaces for monitoring. A *performance object* is a logical collection of counters that is associated with a resource or service that can be monitored. A *performance counter* is a data item that is associated with a performance object. For each counter selected,

System Monitor presents a value corresponding to a particular aspect of the performance defined for the performance object. A *performance object instance* is a term used to distinguish between multiple performance objects of the same type on a computer.

Common Performance Counters   Table 2-7 provides a sampling of common performance counters, along with explanations of what the data might mean. (The performance object is the DHCP server.)

Table 2-7   **Common Performance Counters**

Performance Counter	What Data Is Collected	What the Data Means	What to Look for After a Baseline Is Established
Packets received/ second	This is the number of message packets that the DHCP server receives per second.	A large number indicates heavy, DHCP-related message traffic to the server.	Monitor for sudden increases or decreases, which could reflect problems, such as loss of connectivity, on the network.
Requests/second	This is the number of DHCP request messages that the DHCP server receives per second from clients.	A sudden or unusual increase in this number indicates a large number of clients trying to renew their leases with the DHCP server. This might indicate that scope lease durations are too short.	Monitor for sudden increases or decreases, which could reflect problems, such as loss of connectivity, on the network.
Active queue length	This is the current length of the internal message queue of the DHCP server. This number equals the number of unprocessed messages that the server has queued.	A large number might indicate that the DHCP server cannot keep up with the load of requests presented.	Monitor for both sudden increases and gradual increases, which could reflect increased load or decreased server capacity.
Duplicates dropped/second	This is the number of duplicated packets that the DHCP server drops per second.	This number can be affected by multiple DHCP relay agents or network interfaces that are forwarding the same packet to the server. A large number indicates that the server is not responding fast enough or that the relay agent's boot threshold time is not set high enough.	Monitor this counter for any activity that indicates that more than one request is being transmitted on behalf of clients. A large number indicates that either the client is timing out too quickly or the server is not responding fast enough.

Creating DHCP Performance Alerts

The counters that are available for the DHCP server performance object are also available for creating alerts. If you know the acceptable level that a counter can rise above or fall below before an issue occurs, you can create an alert to both notify you and run a program or script. An *alert* is a feature that detects when a predefined counter value either rises above or falls below a specified setting. The specified setting on the counter is the *alert threshold*. For example, if in your baseline the DHCP active queue length is nearly always less than three, set an alert threshold for six or seven. A sudden increase in DHCP active queue length may indicate that the request load is too great for the DHCP server.

Practice creating alerts by doing Exercise 2-6, "Creating Alerts for a DHCP Server," now

Best Practices for Creating DHCP Alerts

When you create alerts for a DHCP server, follow these recommended guidelines:

- Define the acceptable level that a DHCP counter can rise above or fall below before creating an alert. To do this, you log the DHCP counter for a specific time period to create a baseline. Using this baseline, you can ascertain the normal operating range for a given DHCP counter and then create alerts to notify you when the activity for this DHCP counter is outside of the normal operating range.

- Use scripts with your alerts. Use DHCP Netsh commands in a script to respond to the alert.

> **MORE INFO   Using Netsh Commands**   For more information on using Netsh commands, see Microsoft Knowledgebase article 242468, "How to Use the Netsh.exe Tool and Command-Line Switches." To find this article, go to http://support.microsoft.com and enter the article number in the Search The Knowledge Base text box.

Best Practices for Monitoring DHCP

Consider the following best practices when monitoring the performance of a DHCP server:

- **Create a baseline of performance data on the DHCP server.**   You can compare the baseline with counters that can indicate if the server hosting DHCP is overloaded, or if the network is failing to send DHCP requests to the server.

- **Check the standard counters for server performance (such as processor utilization, paging, disk performance, and network utilization).**   Because DHCP often is installed on a server that also hosts other services or applications, it is important to understand the total application and service load on the server and how the load on the server might affect the operation of the DHCP Server service.

- **Review DHCP server counters, such as Acks/sec, to look for significant drops or increases that indicate a change in DHCP traffic.**   A sudden increase in activity could result from the addition of new DHCP clients, or it could reflect a change to a shorter **DCHP lease**. A sudden decrease in activity could indicate a lengthening of the DHCP lease, a failure of the network to transmit DHCP requests, or a failure of the DHCP server to process the requests.

USING AUTOMATIC PRIVATE IP ADDRESSING

As discussed in Chapter 1, "Implementing DHCP," **Automatic Private IP Addressing (APIPA)** is an addressing feature for simple networks that consist of a single network segment. Whenever a computer running Windows Server 2003 has been configured to obtain an IP address automatically, and when no DHCP server or alternate configuration is available, the computer uses APIPA to assign itself a private IP address in the range of 169.254.0.1 to 169.254.255.254.

To determine whether APIPA is currently enabled and active, type **ipconfig /all** at a command prompt. The resulting text identifies your IP address and other information. If the Autoconfiguration Enabled line reads Yes and the IP address is in the 169.254.0.1 to 169.254.255.254 range, APIPA is active.

This automatic-addressing feature works only for computers on a network segment that cannot obtain an IP address through other means. If a DHCP server later becomes available to a **host** that has assigned itself an APIPA address, the computer changes its IP address to one obtained from the DHCP server. Computers using APIPA addresses can communicate only with other computers using APIPA addresses on the same network segment; they are not directly reachable from the Internet. Note also that through APIPA, you cannot configure a computer with a DNS server address, a default gateway address, or a WINS server address. If you want a computer to obtain an address automatically but want to specify such an address when no DHCP server is available, you can specify it by using an alternate configuration. For more information about alternate configurations, see Chapter 1, "Implementing DHCP."

APIPA is available on any computer running Windows 98, Microsoft Windows Millennium Edition (Me), Windows 2000, Windows XP, or Windows Server 2003.

Disabling APIPA

If you want to ensure that APIPA will not be used, you can either configure an alternate address in the connection's IP properties or disable the automatic-addressing feature by editing the registry. Note that to disable APIPA for one adapter and to disable APIPA for all adapters requires you to edit different registry keys.

▶ **Disabling APIPA on a Single Adapter**

To disable APIPA on a single adapter by editing the registry, complete the following steps:

1. Use the registry editor Regedit.exe to add the registry entry IPAutoconfigurationEnabled with a value of 0 (REG_DWORD data type) in the following subkey:

   ```
   HKEY_LOCAL_MACHINE\SYSTEM\CurrentControlSet\Services\Tcpip\Parameters\
   Interfaces\interface
   ```

2. Restart the computer.

▶ **Disabling APIPA on Multiple Adapters**

To disable APIPA for multiple adapters by editing the registry, complete the following steps:

1. Set the value of the IPAutoconfigurationEnabled entry to 0 (REG_DWORD data type) in the following registry subkey:

   `HKEY_LOCAL_MACHINE\SYSTEM\CurrentControlSet\Services\Tcpip\Parameters`

2. Restart the computer.

Troubleshooting APIPA

For computers running any version of the Windows operating system since Windows 98, APIPA addresses are default addresses. That is, they are assigned to connected hosts whose network configuration has not been altered since the operating system was installed. In certain small networks, you might want to leave the computers with these default APIPA addresses to simplify network communication and administration. If so, you can run the Ipconfig /all command on networked computers to determine whether the address assigned to each computer's local area connection falls within the APIPA range of 169.254.0.1 to 169.254.255.254.

If the Ipconfig /all command does not reveal an APIPA address, the output instead reveals one of three scenarios: no address with or without an error message, an all-zeros address, or a nonzero IP address outside of APIPA range.

When no IP address has been assigned to a host, an error message might provide the specific cause. For example, the Ipconfig /all output might inform you that the media (in other words, the network cable) has been disconnected. At this point, you can check the network cable attachments and then run the Ipconfig /renew command to obtain a new IP address through the APIPA feature. Should this strategy fail to provide the host with a new IP address, you should proceed to diagnose hardware problems such as faulty cables, hubs, and switches.

Sometimes the Ipconfig /all command output does not provide an explicit cause for the computer's failure to obtain an IP address. If so, suspect problems with the network adapter. Verify that the computer in question has a network adapter properly installed, along with the most recent version of the appropriate driver. Then run the Ipconfig /renew command to attempt to obtain an IP address again. If problems persist, you should proceed to diagnose hardware issues.

An all-zeros address typically means that TCP/IP has successfully initialized on the computer, but has not yet obtained an address from a DHCP server. For example, if your computer has successfully obtained an IP address from a DHCP server and you type **ipconfig /release** to release the address, your IP address will display 0.0.0.0.

For properly functioning computers in an environment not deliberately using APIPA for network configuration, a nonzero IP address outside of APIPA range is expected. Common examples of this type of address include the blocks of IP addresses reserved by IANA for private networks (10.0.0.0 through 10.255.255.255, 172.16.0.0 through 172.31.255.255, and 192.168.0.0 through 192.168.255.255).

SUMMARY

- You can configure DHCP to dynamically update DNS. If you choose to dynamically update DNS resource records, you should consider using secure dynamic updates.

- Because DHCP is a key component in your organization, you must manage and monitor it.

- DHCP management consists of backing up and restoring the database as well as reconciling, compacting, and, in some cases, removing the database.

- You can monitor DHCP by using Performance Monitor, the DHCP audit log file, Event Viewer, and DHCP server and scope statistics.

- APIPA is useful for providing addresses to single-segment networks that do not have a DHCP server.

EXERCISES

IMPORTANT   Completing All Exercises   If you plan to do any of the textbook exercises in this chapter, you must do all of the exercises in the chapter to return the computer to it's original state for the associated Lab Manual labs. Note that the following exercises require DNS and DHCP to be installed, which is the state of the student computers after the completion of Lab Manual Lab 1.

Exercise 2-1: Configuring DNS Dynamic Update

To configure DNS dynamic update, follow these steps:

1. Open the DNS console.
2. Right-click the zone for which you want to configure dynamic updates, and then click Properties.
3. In the General tab, in the Dynamic Updates list, select Nonsecure And Secure, and then click OK.

Exercise 2-2: Manually Backing Up a DHCP Database

To back up the DHCP database at the source server, complete the following steps:

1. Open the DHCP console.
2. In the console tree, select the DHCP server you want to back up.
3. On the Action menu, select Backup.

   The Browse For Folder dialog box opens.
4. Select the folder that will contain the backup DHCP database, and then click OK.

   You must choose a local drive for the DHCP database backup folder.

Exercise 2-3: Reconciling a DHCP Database

To reconcile a DHCP database, follow these steps:

1. Open the DHCP console.

2. Perform one of the following, and then click Verify:

   a. To reconcile a particular scope, right-click that scope, and click Reconcile.

   b. To reconcile all scopes, right-click the DHCP server, and then click Reconcile All Scopes.

3. If the reconciliation is successful, a DHCP dialog box appears stating that the database is consistent.

Exercise 2-4: Manually Compacting a DHCP Database

To manually compact a DHCP database, follow these steps:

1. At a DHCP server computer, open a command prompt.

2. To change to the DHCP directory, at the command prompt, type **cd%systemroot%\system32\dhcp**, and then press Enter.

3. To stop the DHCP service, at the command prompt, type **net stop dhcpserver**, and press Enter.

4. To compact the DHCP database, at the command prompt, type **jetpack dhcp.mdb tmp.mdb**, and press Enter.

   A message is displayed stating how long it took to compact the database, that the database was moved from the temporary file to Dhcp.mdb, and that the process completed successfully.

5. To start the DHCP service, at the command prompt, type **net start dhcpserver**, and press Enter.

Exercise 2-5: Configuring and Viewing the DHCP Audit Log

To configure and view the DHCP audit log, follow these steps:

1. Open the DHCP console.

2. In the console tree, click the DHCP server for which you want to enable audit logging.

3. On the Action menu, click Properties.

4. In the General tab, select the Enable DHCP Audit Logging check box, and then click OK.

5. In the Advanced tab, in the Audit Log File Path box, type **c:\textbook\exercises\chapter02**.

6. You are asked if you want to restart the DHCP service to apply the changes. Select Yes.

7. Navigate to the **c:\Textbook\Exercises\Chapter02** folder, and double-click DhcpSrvLog-*day*.log (where *day* is the three-letter abbreviation of today's log).

Exercise 2-6: Creating Alerts for a DHCP Server

To create an alert for a DHCP server, follow these steps:

1. In the Performance console, under Performance Logs And Alerts, select Alerts.

2. On the Action menu, click New Alert Settings.

3. In the New Alert Settings dialog box, in the Name box, type **DHCP Renew Alert**, and then click OK.

4. In the General tab, in the DHCP Renew Alert dialog box, in the Comment field, type **Alert When DHCP Client Renews IP Lease**, and then click Add.

5. In the Add Counters dialog box, in the Performance Object field, select DHCP Server, add the counter Acks/sec, and then click Close.

6. In the General tab, in the DHCP Renew Alert dialog box, in the Limit field, type **1**.

7. In the General tab, in the DHCP Renew Alert dialog box, in the Interval field, type **5**.

8. In the Action tab, select Send A Network Message To, and then type **Administrator**.

   When the alert is tripped, a dialog box will appear.

9. In the Schedule tab, under Start Scan, verify that Manually (Using The Shortcut Menu) is selected, and then click OK.

REVIEW QUESTIONS

1. You have a Windows NT 4 client for which you want to enable dynamic updates. You want the DHCP server to automatically update both the A record and PTR record. Which action will accomplish this?

   a. Take no action. Updating of the A record and PTR record happens automatically by default.

   b. In the DNS tab of the DHCP server properties dialog box, select Dynamically Update DNS A And PTR Records For DHCP Clients That Do Not Request Updates.

   c. In the DNS tab of the DHCP server properties dialog box, select Always Dynamically Update DNS A And PTR Records.

   d. Register the client as a dynamic host with the DHCP server.

2. You have not modified the default settings for DNS on the DHCP client or server. Which of the following client record or records will the DHCP server update in DNS? (Assume the clients are running Windows XP.)

   a. The PTR resource record

   b. The A resource record

   c. Both the PTR and A resource records

   d. Neither the PTR nor the A resource record

3. For a zone in which only secure dynamic updates are allowed, you have configured your DHCP server to perform dynamic updates on behalf of Windows NT 4 clients. Other dynamic DNS settings on the DHCP server have the default settings. After you migrate the clients to Windows XP, you find that their A resource records are no longer being updated. What is the most likely explanation for this problem?

4. True or False: If a DNS zone accepts only secure dynamic updates and the DHCP server is a member of the DnsUpdateProxy security group, the resource records created by the Netlogon service for the domain controller lack security? Explain your answer.

5. Automatic and manual backups of the DHCP database are successfully performed. You want to restore the following: all of the scopes, reservations, leases, options, and security credentials. What should you do?

   a. Restore from the automatic backup.

   b. Restore from the manual backup.

   c. Restore from an offline backup.

   d. Restore from the automatic or manual backup, and reconfigure security credentials manually.

6. You just completed a restoration of the DHCP database. You start the DHCP console to verify a successful restoration. You notice the scope and options are displayed, but active leases are not. What should you do to repopulate the active leases?

   a. The restoration failed. Perform the restoration again.

   b. The restoration failed because the backup was corrupt. Locate a valid backup and use it to restore the DHCP database.

   c. Using the DHCP console, perform reconciliation.

   d. Delete the Tmp.mdb file, and restart the DHCP service.

7. You are monitoring a DHCP server and you want to save the audit log that was created last Tuesday. Today is Monday. What should you do?

   a. Do nothing; the DHCP server automatically saves the log after writing to it.

   b. Remove the log file from the directory.

   c. Change the location of the log files.

   d. On Wednesday, stop and start the DHCP Server service.

8. You want to determine how many IP addresses are available for lease across all scopes. What tool should you use for this?

   a. System Event Log

   b. DHCP scope statistics

   c. DHCP server statistics

   d. DHCP audit log

CASE SCENARIOS

Case Scenario 2-1: Monitoring DHCP Requests

You have been monitoring DHCP server activity by using System Monitor. You have been viewing the Discovers/sec counter. You observe a sudden increase in the number of DHCP requests. Which of the following statements could explain the sudden increase?

a. A large number of clients are initializing simultaneously and attempting to locate a DHCP server.

b. A large number of clients are shutting down simultaneously and releasing their IP address leases.

c. Scope leases are too short, forcing an increase in DHCPNACK messages.

d. Two new DHCP servers have been initialized on the network and are querying the directory service for the enterprise root.

Case Scenario 2-2: Monitoring DHCP Network Traffic

Recently, users have complained that the network is slow at different periods throughout the week. You suspect heavy DHCP traffic is a contributing cause. When DHCP traffic is heavier than normal, you want notification of it. How can you accomplish this?

CHAPTER 3
IMPLEMENTING NAME RESOLUTION USING DNS

Upon completion of this chapter, you will be able to:

- Describe the process of **name resolution** and why it is important to your organization.

- Install and configure the **Domain Name System (DNS)**.

- Describe and configure **primary zones, secondary zones, in-addr.arpa zones**, and **stub zones**.

- Create an **Active Directory–integrated zone**, and explain the benefits of doing so.

- Describe the different types of **DNS servers** and the functions they perform.

- Explain the benefits of delegating a **zone**, and create a delegated zone.

- Describe the process of a **zone transfer**.

This chapter introduces fundamental concepts related to DNS name resolution in Microsoft Windows Server 2003. The chapter also explains key DNS concepts, such as the **DNS namespace**, **DNS zones**, types of DNS servers, DNS **resource records**, and DNS **resolvers**. Also discussed is the process of configuring DNS servers, the types and process of DNS queries, and forwarding. Because DNS plays such a key role in Windows Server 2003, it is critical that you have a strong grasp of its concepts, processes, and methods of configuration. Without DNS, your network will most likely not function—clients won't be able to resolve names to **Internet Protocol (IP)** addresses. In addition, **Active Directory** directory service clients use DNS to locate domain controllers; therefore, it is important that you understand key DNS concepts and how to properly configure DNS for your network.

OVERVIEW OF THE NAME RESOLUTION PROCESS

For network devices, such as computers and printers, to communicate on the Internet or within your organization's network, they must be able to locate one another. In a Windows Server 2003 network, the primary means of locating network devices and network services is through the use of DNS.

For example, in order for ComputerA to communicate with ComputerB using **Transmission Control Protocol/Internet Protocol (TCP/IP)**, ComputerA must obtain the IP address of ComputerB. The process of obtaining an IP address for a computer name (for example, "ComputerA") is called *name resolution*. DNS and Windows Internet Naming System (WINS) name resolution are separate software processes of translating between names that are easy for users to understand and numerical IP addresses, which are difficult for users but necessary for TCP/IP communications.

OVERVIEW OF DNS

Before the growth of the ARPANET into what we now know as the Internet, text files handled name resolution. The text file listed each name of the host and its corresponding IP address (the HOSTS.txt file). Whenever a new host was added to the network, the HOSTS.txt file was updated with the host name and IP address. Periodically, all ARPANET users would then download and use the updated HOSTS.txt file. Because the HOSTS.txt file was flat, rather than hierarchical, every host name on the ARPANET had to be unique. There was no method for creating namespaces such as domains.

Another problem was the size of the database and the inability to distribute the workload that resulted from parsing this file across multiple computers. Every HOSTS.txt file listed every available host, which meant that every computer that parsed the HOSTS.txt file did 100 percent of the work to resolve client names into IP addresses. Clearly, this was inefficient, and a better name resolution system had to be devised.

In 1984, when the number of hosts on ARPANET reached 1,000, DNS was introduced. Because DNS is designed as a distributed database with a hierarchical structure, it can serve as the foundation for host name resolution in a TCP/IP network of any size, including the Internet. The distributed nature of DNS enables the name resolution workload to be shared among many computers. Today, most internetworking software, such as electronic mail programs and Web browsers, uses DNS for name resolution.

Benefits of DNS

Although DNS is most commonly associated with the Internet, private networks also use DNS because of the following benefits:

- **Scalability** Because DNS is capable of distributing workload across several databases or computers, it can scale to handle any level of name resolution required.

- **Constancy** Host names remain constant even when associated IP addresses change, which makes locating network resources much easier.

- **Ease of use**   Users access computers using easy-to-remember names such as www.microsoft.com rather than a numerical IP address, such as 192.168.1.100.

- **Simplicity**   Users need to learn only one naming convention to find resources on either the Internet or an intranet.

What Is DNS?

To understand the importance of DNS and how it functions within a Windows Server 2003 networking environment, you must understand the following components of DNS:

- Domain namespace

- DNS zones

- Types of DNS name servers

- DNS resource records

The following sections discuss each of these components.

Domain Namespace

The *domain namespace* is a hierarchical, tree-structured namespace, starting at an unnamed root used for all DNS operations. In the DNS namespace, each **node** and **leaf object** in the domain namespace tree represents a named domain. Each domain can have additional child domains. Figure 3-1 illustrates the structure of an Internet domain namespace.

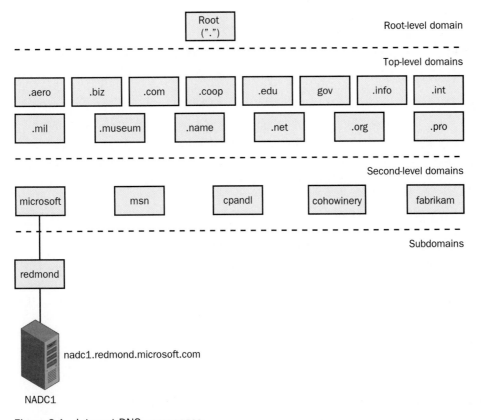

Figure 3-1   Internet DNS namespace

The DNS namespace has a hierarchical structure, and each **DNS domain** name is unique. In Figure 3-1, at the top of the Internet DNS namespace is the root domain. The root domain is represented by "." (a period). Under the DNS root domain, the **top-level domains**, or first-level domains, are organizational types such as .org, .com, and .edu. There are three types of top-level domains:

- **Generic**   See Table 3-1 for examples of generic, top-level domain names.

- **Country code**   Examples of country code domain names are .uk, .jp, and .us.

- **Infrastructure domain**   .arpa is the infrastructure domain name.

The Internet public created generic domains. Individual countries use code domains as necessary. The Internet Assigned Numbers Authority (IANA) assigns top-level domains. Table 3-1 lists the top-level domain names and their uses.

Table 3-1   **Generic Top-Level Domain Names**

Domain Name	Use
.aero	Exclusively reserved for the aviation community
.biz	A top-level domain that is aimed at large and small companies around the world
.com	Commercial organizations, such as microsoft.com for the Microsoft Corporation
.coop	A top-level domain for cooperatives
.edu	Educational institutions, now mainly four-year colleges and universities, such as wustl.edu for Washington University in St. Louis.
.gov	Agencies of the U.S. federal government, such as fbi.gov for the U.S. Federal Bureau of Investigation
.info	An unrestricted domain aimed at providing information for worldwide consumption
.int	Organizations established by international treaties, such as nato.int for NATO
.mil	U.S. military, such as af.mil for the U.S. Air Force
.museum	A domain restricted to museums and related organizations and individuals
.name	A global domain for use by individuals that possibly develops into a global digital identity for users
.net	Computers of network providers, organizations dedicated to the Internet, Internet service providers (ISPs), and so forth, such as internic.net for the Internet Network Information Center (InterNIC)
.org	A top-level domain for groups that do not fit anywhere else, such as non-governmental or nonprofit organizations (for example, w3.org, which is the World Wide Web Consortium)
.pro	A top-level domain for professionals, such as doctors, lawyers, and accountants

DNS uses the **fully qualified domain name (FQDN)** to map a host name to an IP address. An *FQDN* describes the exact relationship between a host and its DNS domain. For example, computer1.sales.microsoft.com represents a host name, computer1, in the sales domain, in the Microsoft second-level domain, and in the .com top-level domain. Figure 3-2 illustrates an FQDN.

Figure 3-2   Breakdown of an FQDN

Second-level DNS domains are registered to individuals or organizations, such as microsoft.com, the Microsoft Corporation domain; or wustl.edu, which is Washington University in the St. Louis domain; or gov.au, the domain for the Australian government. Second-level DNS domains can have many subdomains, and any domain can have hosts. A *host* is a specific computer or other network device within a domain, such as computer1 in the sales subdomain of the microsoft.com domain.

One benefit of the hierarchical structure of DNS is that it is possible to have two hosts with the same host names that are in different locations in the hierarchy. For example, two hosts named computer1—computer1.sales.microsoft.com and computer1.cpandl.microsoft.com—can both exist without conflict because they are in different locations in the namespace hierarchy.

As previously noted, another benefit of the DNS hierarchical structure is that workload for name resolution is distributed across many different resources.

DNS zones, name servers, and resource records are discussed later in this chapter.

INSTALLING DNS

To enjoy the benefits of DNS, you must, of course, install DNS. Before you install DNS, it is recommended that you configure your computer to use a static IP address. If the DNS server is assigned its IP address from Dynamic Host Configuration Protocol (DHCP), its IP address may change. If the DNS server's IP address changes, queries sent by DNS clients configured with the old IP address will fail. Windows Server 2003 provides several wizards and other tools to install DNS quickly and easily. One method of installing DNS is by using the Manage Your Server page. The Manage Your Server page enables you to add or remove server roles, such as file server, print server, DHCP server, and DNS server. The following procedure explains how to use the Manage Your Server page to add the DNS server role.

▶ **Adding the DNS Server Role**

To add the DNS server role, follow these steps:

1. Click Start, point to Control Panel, point to Administrative Tools, and then click Manage Your Server.

   The Manage Your Server page starts automatically by default when you log on.

2. On the Manage Your Server page, click Add Or Remove A Role.

3. On the Preliminary Steps page, click Next.

4. On the Server Role page, click DNS Server, and then click Next.

5. On the Summary Of Selections page, click Next.

6. On the Welcome To The Configure A DNS Server Wizard page, click Next.

7. On the Select Configuration Action page, click Configure Root Hints Only (Recommended For Advanced Users Only), and then click Next.

8. On the Completing The Configure A DNS Server Wizard page, click Finish.

9. On the This Server Is Now A DNS Server page, click Finish.

Practice adding a DNS server role by doing Exercise 3-1, "Adding the DNS Server Role," now.

DNS ZONES

For administrative purposes, DNS domains can be organized into zones. A zone is a collection of host name–to–IP address mappings for hosts in a contiguous portion of the DNS namespace, as shown in Figure 3-3. A zone can hold the resource records for one domain, or it can hold the resource records for multiple domains. A zone can host more than one domain only if the domains are contiguous—that is, connected by a direct parent-child relationship. One reason to divide a namespace into zones is to delegate authority for different portions of it. One very large domain could be difficult to administer.

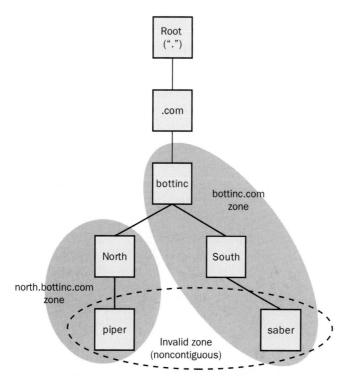

Figure 3-3   Two valid zones and one **noncontiguous namespace**, invalid zone

For each DNS domain name included in a zone, the zone becomes the authoritative source for information about that domain. When a zone is authoritative over a portion of the namespace, it means that it hosts the resource records for that portion of the namespace. It does not mean, however, that the server can update or modify the zone.

Zones are classified by where they are stored, whether they are writable, and by what information they receive and return. Zones can be stored either in text files or in Active Directory.

DNS servers are classified by the type of zones they host. A DNS server can host primary zones, secondary zones, stub zones, or no zones. A DNS server is called the **primary name server** for the primary zones it hosts and a **secondary name server** for the secondary zones it hosts. A caching-only server hosts no zones.

In brief, zone data is maintained on a DNS name server and is stored in one of two ways:

- As a flat zone file containing lists of mappings
- In an Active Directory database

With regard to types of queries, each zone can be either a **forward lookup zone** or a **reverse lookup zone**. In turn, a forward or reverse lookup zone can be one of three types:

- Primary
- Secondary
- Stub

When you configure a DNS server, you can configure it either with several zone types or with none at all, depending on the type of role that the DNS server has in the network.

By using different zones, you can configure your DNS solution to best meet your needs. For example, it is recommended that you configure a primary zone and a secondary zone on separate DNS servers to provide fault tolerance should one server fail. You can configure a stub zone if the zone is maintained on a separate DNS server.

The next two sections discuss the different ways in which zone data is stored: in standard zones and in Active Directory–integrated zones.

Standard Zones

There are numerous options for optimal configuration of the DNS server, based on network topology, administrative needs, and size of the namespace. Typical DNS server operation involves three standard zones (primary, secondary, and in-addr.arpa). Windows Server 2003 provides a fourth option, stub zones. Each of the standard zones is discussed in the following sections.

Standard Primary Zones

A standard primary zone hosts a read/write copy of the DNS zone in which resource records are created and managed. Only one server can host and load the master copy of the zone, no additional primary servers for the zone are permitted, and only the server hosting the primary zone is allowed to accept dynamic updates and process zone changes. When setting up DNS servers to host the zones for a domain, the primary server normally is located where it will be accessible for administering the zone file.

Practice adding a primary zone by doing Exercise 3-2, "Adding a Standard Primary Forward Lookup Zone," now.

Standard Secondary Zones

A copy of the zone file may be stored on one or more servers to balance network load, provide fault tolerance, or avoid forcing queries across a slow, wide area network (WAN) link. A standard secondary zone is a read-only copy of the standard primary DNS zone. Performing a zone transfer, which is done by simply copying the zone file from the primary server to a secondary server, creates a secondary zone. When a secondary zone is created, you must specify the IP address of one or more master DNS servers from which you want to copy the zone. These copies are referred to as secondary zone database files. The secondary zone database files are updated regularly from the primary zone database.

in-addr.arpa Zones

Most queries sent to a DNS server are *forward queries*; that is, they request an IP address based on a DNS name. DNS also provides a reverse lookup process, which enables a host to determine another host's name based on its IP address. For example, a query contains the equivalent of "What is the DNS domain name of the host at IP address 192.168.100.1?"

To answer this query, the **in-addr.arpa domain** is consulted in combination with the IP address in question. As you read the IP address from left to right, the network portion is some number of bits on the left, and the host portion is some number of bits on the right, based on the subnet mask. For example, 192.168.100.2, with a default subnet mask of 255.255.255.0, means the network portion is 192.168.100, and the host portion is 2. Because the higher-level portion of the address is on the right, it must be reversed when building the domain tree. In short, because FQDNs go from specific to general, and IP addresses go from general to specific, to facilitate reverse lookup, the IP address is reversed when concatenated with the in-addr.arpa domain. For example, the reverse lookup zone for the subnet 192.168.100.0 is 100.168.192.in-addr.arpa. The in-addr.arpa domain tree makes use of the **pointer (PTR) resource record**, which is used to associate the IP address with the host name. This lookup should correspond to an address (A) resource record for the host in a forward lookup zone.

Reverse lookup queries often are used by network applications for verification rather than identification or as a tool for monitoring and troubleshooting the DNS service.

> **NOTE**   **in-addr.arpa and IPv4-Based Networks**   The in-addr.arpa domain is used only for Internet Protocol version 4 (IPv4)-based networks. In the DNS console for Windows Server 2003, the DNS server's New Zone Wizard uses this domain when it creates a new reverse lookup zone. Internet Protocol version 6 (IPv6)-based reverse lookup zones are based on the domain ip6.arpa.

Reverse DNS zones have the same start of authority (SOA) and **name server (NS) resource records** as forward lookup zones. You also can configure reverse lookup zones to be standard primary or secondary zones or to be Active Directory–integrated. Active Directory–integrated reverse lookup zones replicate in the same manner as Active Directory–integrated forward lookup zones.

Stub Zones

A DNS server running Windows Server 2003 also supports a new type of zone called a stub zone. A *stub zone* is a copy of a zone that contains only those resource records necessary to identify the authoritative DNS servers for that zone. A stub zone is a pointer to the DNS server that is authoritative for that zone, and it is used to maintain or improve DNS resolution efficiency.

The stub zone contains a subset of zone data consisting of an SOA, an NS, and an A record. Like a standard secondary zone, resource records in the stub zone cannot be modified; they must be modified at the primary zone.

Stub zones enable a DNS server to perform recursion by using the stub zone's list of name servers without needing to query the Internet or internal root server for the DNS namespace. Using stub zones throughout your DNS infrastructure enables you to distribute a list of the authoritative DNS servers for a zone without using secondary zones. However, stub zones do not serve the same purpose as secondary zones and should not be considered when addressing redundancy and load sharing.

Active Directory–Integrated Zones

Storing zones in Active Directory is a Microsoft proprietary method of managing, securing, and replicating DNS zone information. An *Active Directory–integrated zone* is a DNS zone contained within Active Directory. Zones stored in text files are typically referred to as standard, or *file-backed zones*, and zones stored in Active Directory are referred to as *Active Directory–integrated zones*. Storing a zone in Active Directory has the following benefits:

- **Fault tolerance**   Information is stored on multiple servers.

- **Security**   DNS zones stored in Active Directory can take advantage of increased security by modifying the **discretionary access control list (DACL)**. The DACL enables you to specify which users and groups may modify the DNS zones.

- **Zones are multimaster**   This means that zones can be updated in more than one location. All domain controllers where the zone is stored can modify the zone. Changes to the zone are then replicated to the other domain controllers that contain the zone file.

- **Efficient replication**   Zone transfers are replaced by more efficient Active Directory replication. This can be especially important over networks with slow links because Active Directory compresses replication data that passes between sites.

- **Secondary zones**   Zones stored in Active Directory can also be transferred to standard secondary servers to create secondary zones in the same way that file-backed zones are transferred.

Windows Server 2003 provides a more efficient method of replicating DNS zone information than does Microsoft Windows 2000 Server. In Microsoft Windows 2000, updates to Active Directory zones are replicated to all domain controllers in that domain, whether or not they are DNS servers. With Windows Server 2003, Active Directory–integrated zones can be replicated three different ways:

Practice changing standard primary zones into Active Directory-integrated zones by doing Exercise 3-3, "Changing a Zone to Active Directory-Integrated," now.

- To all domain controllers in the domain (this is the same as Windows 2000)

- To all domain controllers that are DNS servers in the local domain

- To all domain controllers that are also DNS servers in the entire forest

You can create two types of Active Directory–integrated zones: forward lookup zones and reverse lookup zones. These are discussed in the following sections.

Forward Lookup Zones

An Active Directory–integrated *forward lookup zone* is similar to a standard primary zone. Outside of Active Directory, primary and secondary servers are necessary because they follow a single-master update model. Only one server contains a writable copy of the zone database. However, Active Directory–integrated zones follow a multimaster update model, meaning all Active Directory–integrated zones contain a read/write copy of the zone and can make changes to the zone information. Therefore, primary and secondary distinctions are not necessary. A forward lookup zone stores records to answer forward queries such as the one shown in Figure 3-4.

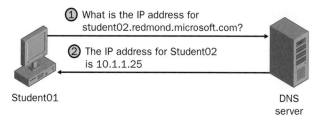

Figure 3-4 Forward lookup query

Reverse Lookup Zones

Practice creating reverse lookup zones by doing Exercise 3-4, "Creating a Reverse Lookup Zone," now.

A *reverse lookup zone* is used for resolving an IP address to a name and is similar to the standard in-addr.arpa zone. The reverse lookup zone is stored and updated in the same manner as the Active Directory–integrated forward lookup zone. A reverse lookup zone stores records to answer reverse lookup queries such as the one posed in Figure 3-5.

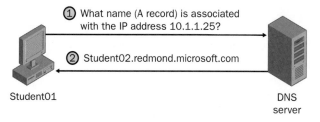

Figure 3-5 Reverse lookup zone

ROOT HINTS

DNS servers resolve DNS queries using local authoritative or cached data. But if the server does not contain the requested data and is not authoritative for the name in a query, it may perform **recursive resolution** or return a referral to another DNS server depending on whether the client requested recursion. The DNS Server service must be configured with the **root hints** to resolve queries for names that it is not authoritative for or for which it contains no delegations. Root hints contain the names and IP addresses of the DNS servers authoritative for the root zone. You can use the DNS console to manage the list of root servers as shown in Figure 3-6.

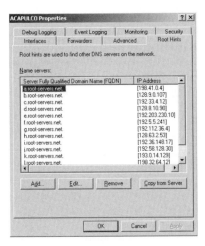

Figure 3-6 DNS root hints property page

By default, DNS servers use a root hints file, Cache.dns. The Cache.dns file is stored in the %systemroot%\System32\Dns folder on the server computer. When the server starts, Cache.dns is preloaded into server memory. By using root hints to find root servers, a DNS server is able to complete recursive queries. This process is designed to enable any DNS server to locate the servers that are authoritative for any other DNS domain name used at any level in the namespace tree.

When the Configure A DNS Server Wizard is used to configure a DNS server, it sends an NS query for the root domain (.) to the preferred and alternative DNS servers for the server. The query response is placed into the root hints of the DNS server. If no root servers are detected, the wizard sends the same query to the DNS servers specified in the Cache.dns file that correspond to the root servers on the Internet. If no root servers are detected, the wizard prompts the user to either make the server a root server or to manually specify root hints. Updating root hints enables the server to function more efficiently. You should update root hints whenever a new server is added or changed.

▶ **Updating Root Hints on the DNS Server**

To update root hints on the DNS server, follow these steps:

1. Open the DNS management console.

2. Right-click the applicable DNS server, and then click Properties.

3. Click the Root Hints tab.

4. Modify the server root hints as follows:

   ❑ To add a root server to the list, click Add, and then specify the name and IP address of the server to be added to the list of root servers.

   ❑ To modify a root server in the list, click Edit, and then specify the name and IP address of the server to be modified in the list.

   ❑ To remove a root server from the list, select it from the list, and then click Remove.

In addition to manually adding or deleting the list of root servers, you also can use the Copy From Server button, as shown previously in Figure 3-6. This enables you to specify the IP address of another DNS server from which your DNS server can copy the root hints.

You also can use the Dnscmd command to add or delete a server from root hints. Dnscmd is discussed in Chapter 4, "Managing and Monitoring DNS." In the following example, the server at 10.1.1.200 is added to the list of root servers at the name server ns1.eu.reskit.com:

```
C:\Windows>dnscmd ns1.eu.reskit.com. /RecordAdd /roothints @  ns 10.1.1.200
Command completed successfully.
```

> **MORE INFO**   **The Dnscmd Command**   Dnscmd is not installed by default; it must be added. Along with other tools, the Dnscmd command can be installed from the Microsoft Windows Server 2003 Installation CD from the following location: \Support\Tools\Suptools.msi.

In Windows Server 2003, for the DNS Server service running on a domain controller, root hints are stored in the domain-wide application directory partition.

> **NOTE**   **Using Root Hints When Operating Internal Root Servers**   If you have an internal DNS root in your DNS infrastructure, configure the root hints of internal DNS servers to point to only the DNS servers hosting your root domain and not the DNS servers hosting the Internet root domain. This will prevent your internal DNS servers from sending private information over the Internet when resolving names.

Removing the Root DNS Zone

A DNS server running Windows Server 2003 follows these specific steps in its name-resolution process: the DNS server first queries its cache, then checks its zone records, then sends requests to forwarders, and then tries resolution by using root servers.

By default, a Microsoft DNS server connects to the Internet to process DNS requests that require root resolution. When you use the Dcpromo tool to promote a server to a domain controller, the domain controller requires DNS. If you install DNS during the promotion process, a root zone is created. This root zone indicates to your DNS server that it is a root Internet server. Therefore, your DNS server does not use forwarders or root hints in the name-resolution process and may cause name resolution to fail. In order to fix this, remove the root zone on the DNS server.

▶ **Removing the DNS Root Zone**

1. Click Start, point to Administrative Tools, and then click DNS.

2. Expand *servername*, where *servername* is the name of the server, and then expand Forward Lookup Zones.

3. Right-click the "." zone, and then click Delete.

DNS SERVER TYPES

DNS server types are determined by the type of zone or zones they host and by the functions they perform. A DNS server may host either a primary or secondary zone or both. At the same time, a server may also be a *master name server*, which is a server that is responsible for updating other servers. If the server doesn't host any zones, it is a caching-only server. These four types of servers are supported in Windows Server 2003 and are discussed in the following sections.

Primary Name Server

Primary name servers contain one or more primary zones. When a change is made to the zone data, such as adding resource records to the zone, the changes must be made on the primary server for that zone. Changes are then propagated to secondary name servers. The primary name server also services client queries.

Secondary Name Server

The secondary name server hosts one or more secondary zone databases. Because a zone transfer is used to create a secondary zone, the primary name server and zone already must exist to create a secondary name server.

Master Name Server

A name server is a master name server when it is responsible for sending updated copies of the database to other name servers. A master name server can host either a primary or secondary copy of a zone database. This means that a master server can be either a primary name server or a secondary name server. In Figure 3-7:

- ns1.contoso.com is the primary and master server for ns2.contoso.com.

- ns2.contoso.com is a secondary server, receives updates from ns1, and is a master server to ns3.

- ns3.contoso.com is a secondary server and receives updates from ns2.

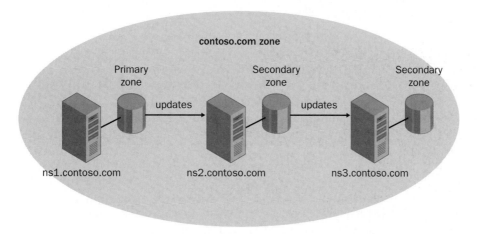

Figure 3-7   Primary and secondary zones acting as master name servers

Caching-Only Server

Caching-only servers do not host any zones and are not authoritative for a particular domain. Caching-only DNS servers start with an empty cache and add resource record entries as the server fulfills client requests. This information is then available from its cache when answering subsequent client queries. A caching-only DNS server is valuable at a site when DNS functionality is needed locally but when creating a separate domain or zone is not desirable.

DNS RESOURCE RECORDS

A *resource record* is information that is related to a DNS domain; for example, the host record defining a host IP address. Resource records are represented in binary form in packets when queries and responses are made using DNS. In DNS zone files, however, resource records are represented as text entries. Most resource records are represented as single-line text entries. If an entry is going to span more than one line, you can use parentheses to encapsulate the information. In many implementations of DNS, only the SOA record can be multiple lines in length. For readability, blank lines and comments often are inserted in the zone files and are ignored by the DNS server. Comments always start with a semicolon (;), and they end with a carriage return.

Resource records have the following syntax:

```
Owner [TTL] Class Type RDATA
```

Table 3-2 describes the common set of information in resource records.

Table 3-2 Typical Resource Record Fields

Name	Description
Owner	Identifies the host or the DNS domain to which this resource record belongs.
TTL (Time to Live)	A 32-bit integer representing the maximum time, in seconds, that a DNS server or client caches this resource record before it is discarded. This field is optional, and if it is not specified, the client uses the minimum TTL in the SOA record.
Class	Defines the protocol family in use, which is IN for the Internet system.
Type	Identifies the type of resource record. For example, A indicates that the resource record stores host address information.
RDATA (Resource Record Data)	Contains RDATA. The RDATA field is a variable-length field that represents the information being described by the resource record. For example, in an A resource record, the data contained in this field is the 32-bit IP address that represents the host identified by the owner.

Resource Record Types

The DNS database consists of resource records that relate different information about the names in the database. A resource record for a DNS name can identify a single resource within the network, such as the network host that uses that name, or that there is a service running on that network host, such as electronic mail.

Different types of resource records provide DNS data about computers on a TCP/IP network. The most common resource records are described in Table 3-3 and in detail in the following sections. This discussion includes resource records specific to Windows 2000 and Windows Server 2003 DNS implementations.

Table 3-3 **Resource Record Types**

Description	Class	TTL	Type	Data
Start of Authority	Internet (IN)	60 minutes	SOA	Owner name, primary name server FQDN, serial number, refresh interval, retry interval, expire time, and minimum TTL
Host	Internet (IN)	TTL of the SOA in the same zone	A	Owner name (host DNS name) and host IPv4 address
Name Server	Internet (IN)	TTL of the SOA in the same zone	NS	Owner name and DNS server name
Mail Exchanger	Internet (IN)	TTL of the SOA in the same zone	MX	Owner name, Mail Exchanger (MX) server DNS name, and preference number
Canonical Name (an alias)	Internet (IN)	TTL of the SOA in the same zone	CNAME	Owner name (alias name) and host DNS name

Start of Authority (SOA) Resource Record

Every zone contains an SOA resource record at the top of the zone file. An SOA resource record indicates the starting point or original point of authority for information stored in a zone. It contains all the zone-specific information for the DNS server to use when maintaining the zone. The SOA resource record is the first resource record that is created when creating a new zone.

The RDATA field for the SOA resource record contains the fields shown in Table 3-4.

Table 3-4 **RDATA Fields for the SOA Resource Record**

RDATA Fields	Description
Authoritative server	Contains the name of the primary DNS server authoritative for the zone.
Responsible person	Shows the e-mail address of the administrator who is responsible for the zone. This field takes a period (.) instead of an at (@) sign.
Serial number	Shows how many times the zone is updated. When a zone's secondary server contacts its master server to determine whether it needs to initiate a zone transfer, the zone's secondary server compares its own serial number with that of the master. If the serial number of the master server is higher, the secondary server initiates a zone transfer.
Refresh	Shows how often the secondary server for the zone checks to see whether the zone data is changed.
Retry	After sending a zone transfer request, shows how long (in seconds) the zone's secondary server waits before sending another request.
Expire	After a zone transfer, shows how long (in seconds) the zone's secondary server continues to respond to zone queries before discarding its own zone as invalid.

(continued)

Table 3-4   **RDATA Fields for the SOA Resource Record**

RDATA Fields	Description
Minimum TTL	Applies to all the resource records in the zone whenever a TTL value is not specified in a resource record or is shorter than the minimum TTL specified in the zone's SOA record. Whenever a DNS client queries the server, the server sends back resource records containing a record-specific TTL or the minimum TTL. Negative responses are cached for the minimum TTL of the SOA resource record of the authoritative zone.

The following output is an example of an SOA resource record:

```
na.contoso.com.  IN  SOA (
    nadc1.na.contoso.com.; authoritative server for the zone
    administrator.na.contoso.com. ; zone admin e-mail
                                 ; (responsible  person)
    5099        ; serial number
    3600        ; refresh (1 hour)
    600         ; retry (10 mins)
    86400       ; expire (1 day)
    60      )   ; minimum TTL (1 min)
```

Name Server (NS) Resource Record

The name server (NS) resource record identifies a DNS server that is authoritative for a zone. The name of the DNS server that is authoritative for a zone is stored in the RDATA field. NS records are used to indicate both primary and secondary DNS servers for the zone specified in the SOA resource record and to indicate the DNS servers for any delegated zones. If a zone has multiple authoritative servers (for example, a primary server and one or more secondary servers), you need to have an NS record for each server. The Windows Server 2003 DNS Server service automatically creates the first NS record for a zone when the zone is created. You can add additional NS records by using DNS Manager or the Dnscmd command-line tool.

> **NOTE**   *Zones and NS Records*   *Every zone must contain at least one NS record.*

For example, if the administrator for contoso.com delegates authority for the na.contoso.com. subdomain to the nadc1.na.contoso.com server, the following line is added to the contoso.com and na.contoso.com zones:

```
na.contoso.com.  IN  NS  nadc1.na.contoso.com.
```

Host Address (A) Resource Record

The host address (A) resource record maps a FQDN to an IP address. For example, the following A resource record is located in the zone na.contoso.com and maps the FQDN of a server to its IP address:

```
nadc1.na.contoso.com.   IN   A  172.16.48.1
```

The A resource record contains the following fields:

- The Owner, TTL, Class, and Type fields, which are described in Table 3-2, "Typical Resource Record Fields," earlier in this chapter.

- The RDATA field is the IP address of the owner.

PTR Resource Record

The PTR resource record performs the reverse function of the A resource record by mapping an IP address to an FQDN. For example, the following PTR resource record maps the IP address 172.16.48.1 of nadc1.na.contoso.com to its FQDN:

```
1.48.16.172.in-addr.arpa.   IN   PTR   nadc1.na.contoso.com.
```

PTR resource records contain the following fields:

Practice locating DNS resource records by doing Exercise 3-5, "Locating DNS Resource Records," now.

- The Owner, TTL, Class, and Type fields, which are described in Table 3-2, "Typical Resource Record Fields," earlier in this chapter.

- The RDATA field is the host name of the host with the IP address contained in the Owner field.

Canonical Name (CNAME) Resource Record

The canonical name (CNAME) resource record creates an alias for a specified FQDN. You can use CNAME records to hide the implementation details of your network from the clients that connect to it.

For example, if you want to put a File Transfer Protocol (FTP) server named ftp1.na.contoso.com on your na.contoso.com subdomain, but you know that in six months you might move it to a computer named ftp2.na.contoso.com and you do not want your users to have to know about the change, do the following: create an alias called ftp.na.contoso.com that points to ftp1.na.contoso.com. When you move your computer, you need change only the CNAME record to point to ftp2.na.contoso.com. For example, the following CNAME resource record creates an alias for ftp1.na.contoso.com:

```
ftp.na.contoso.com.   IN   CNAME   ftp1.na.contoso.com.
```

After a DNS client queries for the name for ftp.na.contoso.com, the DNS server finds the CNAME resource record, resolves the query for ftp1.na.contoso.com, and returns both the A and CNAME resource records to the client.

> **NOTE   CNAME and Aliases in a Zone**   If a CNAME resource record is present at a node (DNS name), no other resource records for the same name should be present in the zone. This ensures that the data for a CNAME and its aliases cannot be different. According to **Request for Comments (RFC)** 2181, an alias can have only one canonical name.

CNAME resource records contain the following fields:

- The Owner, TTL, Class, and Type fields. The Owner field for CNAME records is the alias.

- The RDATA field is the name of the host to which the alias points.

Mail Exchanger (MX) Resource Record

The mail exchanger (MX) resource record specifies a server that is willing to act as a mail server for a DNS name. The mail server identified by an MX record is a host that either processes or forwards mail for a DNS domain name. Processing the mail means either delivering it to the addressee or passing it to a different type of mail transport. Forwarding the mail means sending it to its final destination server, sending it by using Simple Mail Transfer Protocol (SMTP) to another mail exchange server that is closer to the final destination, or queuing it for a specified amount of time.

To improve the reliability of the mail service for a domain, you can designate secondary mail servers that can store mail for a domain. If the primary mail server stops responding, the secondary servers can hold the mail and then forward it when the mail server comes back into service. An SMTP *smart host* (a host capable of using MX records) uses multiple mail servers, provided you configure multiple MX resource records.

The following example shows MX resource records for the mail servers for the domain na.contoso.com:

```
@ IN  MX   5  mailserver1.na.contoso.com.
@ IN  MX  10  mailserver2.na.contoso.com.
@ IN  MX  20  mailserver3.na.contoso.com.
```

MX resource records contain the following fields:

- The Owner, TTL, Class, and Type fields, which are described in Table 3-2, "Typical Resource Record Fields," earlier in this chapter.

- The following data is stored in the RDATA field of the MX resource record:

  - The fourth field in the MX record is the mail server preference value. The preference value specifies the preference given to the MX record among other MX records. Records with lower priority numbers (which are higher priority) are preferred. Thus, when a mail client needs to send mail to a certain DNS domain, it first contacts a DNS server for that domain and retrieves all the MX records. It then contacts the mailer with the lowest preference value.

    MORE INFO   **Mail Routing and the Domain System**   For more information about how mail is routed in the domain system, see RFC 974, which can be looked up at http://www.rfc-editor.org/rfcsearch.html.

  - The final field is the name of the mail server to contact.

For example, suppose Holly Holt sends an e-mail message to loviatt@na.contoso .com on a day that mailserver1 is down, but mailserver2 is working. Her e-mail client tries to deliver the message to mailserver1 because it has the lowest preference value, but it fails because mailserver1 is down. In this case, Holly's e-mail client chooses mailserver2 because its preference value is the second lowest. If mailserver2 is operating, the mail is successfully delivered to mailserver2.

To prevent mail loops, if the e-mail client is on a host that is listed as an MX for the destination host, the e-mail client can deliver only to an MX with a lower preference value than its own host. If a mail server receives multiple MX records with equal priority, the choice of which MX record to use depends on implementation.

Service Locator (SRV) Resource Record

Service locator (SRV) resource records enable you to specify the location of servers that provide a specific network service over a specific protocol and in a specific domain. SRV records allow you to have several servers offering a network service and to move services between servers without changing the client configuration. For example, if you have two application servers in your domain, you can create SRV resource records in DNS that specify which hosts serve as application servers. Client applications that support SRV records will use DNS to retrieve the SRV resource records for the application servers.

Active Directory is an example of an application that relies on SRV resource records. An example of an application that supports SRV resource records is the Windows 2000 and Windows Server 2003 Net Logon service. On Windows 2000, Microsoft Windows XP, and Windows Server 2003, client computers use SRV resource records to locate domain controllers for a domain and join an Active Directory domain.

The format for an SRV record is as follows:

```
_Service_Protocol.Name [TTL] Class SRV Priority Weight Port Target
```

Table 3-5 outlines the SRV resource record fields.

Table 3-5   SRV Resource Record Fields

Field Name	Description
Service	Specifies the name of the service, such as http or telnet.
Protocol	Specifies the protocol, such as Transmission Control Protocol (TCP) or User Datagram Protocol (UDP).
Name	Specifies the domain name to which the resource record refers.
TTL	Uses a 32-bit integer to represent the maximum time, in seconds, that a DNS server or client caches this entry before it is discarded. This field is optional, and if it is not specified, the client uses the minimum TTL in the SOA record.
Class	Defines the protocol family in use, which is usually IN for the Internet system. The other value defined in RFC 1034 is CH for the Chaos system, which was used experimentally at the Massachusetts Institute of Technology.

Table 3-6 describes the data stored in the RDATA field of the SRV resource record.

Table 3-6   SRV Record RDATA Fields

Field Name	Description
Priority	Specifies the priority of the host. Clients attempt to contact the host with the lowest priority number.
Weight	Performs load balancing. When the Priority field is the same for two or more records in the same domain, clients must try records with higher weights more often, unless the clients support some other load-balancing mechanism.
Port	Shows the port for the service on this host.
Target	Shows the FQDN for the host providing the service.

The following example shows SRV records for two domain controller servers:

```
_ldap._tcp.contoso.com. IN  SRV 0  0  80  dc1.contoso.com.
_ldap._tcp.contoso.com. IN  SRV 10 0  80  dc2.contoso.com.
```

This example does not specify a TTL. Therefore, the DNS client uses the minimum TTL specified in the SOA resource record.

If a computer needs to locate a Lightweight Directory Access Protocol (LDAP) server in the contoso.com domain, the DNS client sends an SRV query for the following name:

```
_ldap._tcp.contoso.com.
```

The DNS server replies with the SRV records listed in the previous example. The DNS client then chooses between DC1 and DC2 by looking at their priority values. Because DC1 has the lowest priority value, the LDAP client chooses DC1. In this example, if the priority values were the same but the weight values were different, the client would choose a domain controller randomly with a probability proportional to the Weight field value.

Next, the DNS client requests the A record for DC1.contoso.com, and the DNS server sends the A record. Finally, the client attempts to contact the domain controller using the IP address in the A record.

Computers running Windows 2000, Windows XP, and Windows Server 2003 support RFC 2782, a DNS resource record for specifying the location of services (DNS SRV).

Other Resource Record Types

Table 3-7 shows additional resource records and the RFCs that define them. Many of these resource records are considered experimental and are rarely used. Windows Server 2003 family provides support for the definition, storage, and retrieval of these resource records. For more information about each resource record type, see the corresponding RFC. (See http://www.rfc-editor.org/rfcsearch.html for more information about each RFC.)

Table 3-7   Other Resource Record Types Supported by Windows Server 2003

Record Type	RFC
AAAA	1886
AFSDB	1183
HINFO	1035
ISDN	1183
KEY	2535
MB	1035
MG	1035
MINFO	1035
MR	1035
NXT	2535
OPT	2671
RP	1183

(continued)

Table 3-7   **Other Resource Record Types Supported by Windows Server 2003**

Record Type	RFC
RT	1183
SIG	2535
TXT	1035
WKS	1035
X25	1183

Resource Records Not Defined in RFCs

In addition to the resource record types listed in the RFCs, Windows Server 2003 uses the resource record types shown in Table 3-8.

Table 3-8   **Resource Record Types Not Defined in RFCs but Supported by Windows Server 2003**

Name	Description
WINS	The WINS resource record contains the IP addresses of the WINS servers that a DNS server must query to resolve A record queries. A Microsoft Windows NT, Windows 2000, or Windows Server 2003 DNS server can use a WINS server to look up the host portion of a DNS name that does not exist in the DNS zone that is authoritative for the name. If a DNS server is authoritative for a zone but does not contain the necessary A record, the DNS server queries only WINS.
WINSR	The WINS reverse lookup (WINSR) resource record is used in a reverse lookup zone to find the host portion of the DNS name for a specified IP address. A DNS server sends a NetBIOS adapter status query to the IP address specified in the query if the zone authoritative for the queried IP address does not contain the record and does contain the WINSR resource record.
ATMA	The Asynchronous Transfer Mode address (ATMA) resource record, which is defined by the ATM Forum, is used to map DNS domain names to ATM addresses.

Delegation and Glue Records

Delegation and glue records are resource records that you add to a zone to delegate a subdomain to a separate zone hosted on a different DNS server. A *delegation record* is represented by the NS record in the parent zone that lists the authoritative DNS server hosting the child zone for the delegated subdomain. A *glue record* is the A record in the parent zone for the authoritative DNS server hosting the child zone for the delegated subdomain.

For example, the DNS server that hosts the zone for the domain contoso.com will delegate authority for the subdomain na.contoso.com to the DNS server ns2.na .contoso.com, which is where a zone for the domain na.contoso.com is hosted. To create this delegation, the following records are added to the parent zone contoso.com:

```
na.contoso.com.     IN  NS  ns2.na.contoso.com
ns2.na.contoso.com. IN  A   172.16.54.1
```

When a DNS client submits a query for a name in the child zone to the DNS server that is authoritative for the parent zone, the authoritative DNS server for the parent zone checks its zone. The delegation resource records tell it which DNS server is authoritative for the child zone. The authoritative DNS server for the parent zone can then return a referral containing the delegation records to the DNS client.

A glue record is necessary in this example because ns2.na.contoso.com is a member of the delegated domain na.contoso.com. However, if it was a member of a different domain, such as microsoft.com, the DNS client can perform standard name resolution to resolve the name of the authoritative DNS server to an IP address, in which case a glue record is not required. Separate domain configurations are less common.

Incorrect delegations are a major source of name resolution failure for DNS because an incorrect delegation removes a branch of the DNS namespace tree, and the other nodes in the tree cannot locate the DNS names in and under the branch. For this reason, it is recommended that you verify delegations periodically and that administrators responsible for parent and child zones communicate any modifications that can affect delegation.

Wildcard Resource Records

In some DNS designs, you might need to use a large number of resource records in a zone; however, you might find it difficult to manually add the records. In such cases, you can define a wildcard DNS resource record.

The following is an example of a wildcard address from the contoso.com domain:

```
*    IN   A    172.16.54.1
```

If the preceding A record is in DNS, all queries for a host in the contoso.com domain not explicitly defined in the zone file receive a reply for 172.16.54.1. Windows 2000 and Windows Server 2003 DNS support wildcard resource records.

UNDERSTANDING THE DNS QUERY PROCESS

When a DNS client needs to look up a name to obtain its corresponding IP address, it forms a DNS query that contains the following information:

- DNS domain name stated as an FQDN
- Query type—specifies resource records to be returned (A, SRV, and so on)
- DNS domain name class, which is IN for the Internet system

The query is first passed to the local DNS resolver client service for resolution. If the query cannot be resolved locally, it is sent to the primary DNS server.

If the query does not match an entry in the cache, the resolution process continues with the client querying a DNS server to resolve the name. Queries from clients or servers can take one of two forms: iterative or recursive.

Iterative Queries

An **iterative query** is a DNS query sent to a DNS server in which the querying host requests it to return the best answer it can provide using its own information and without seeking further assistance from other DNS servers. For example, in Figure 3-8, a host queries the primary DNS server, which checks its records and refers the client to Server A. Server A checks its names cache, does not find an answer, and sends a referral to Server B instead. The host receives the response and submits a query to Server B, which responds with a referral to Server C. The host queries Server C and receives a response.

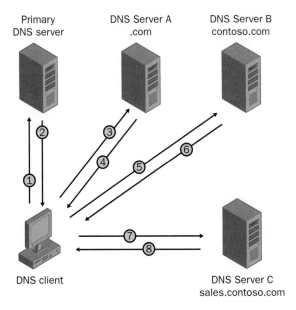

Figure 3-8 The iterative query process

As shown in Figure 3-8, the querying host is responsible for issuing additional queries until it obtains a definitive answer. In the example that follows, the host issues three queries before receiving the requested information. The process is as follows:

1. The first step of the query process is to convert a name request into a query and then pass it to the DNS Client service for resolution that uses locally cached information. If the query can be answered from the local cache, the process is complete. Otherwise, the client submits an iterative query to its primary DNS server.

2. The primary DNS server checks to see if it has authority for that domain. In this example, it does not have authority, but it does contain information that points to the .com top-level domain DNS servers. The primary server responds with a referral to .com top-level domain servers.

3. The DNS client submits an iterative query to DNS Server A.

4. DNS Server A responds with a referral to DNS Server B.

5. The client submits an iterative query to DNS Server B for sales.contoso.com.

6. DNS Server B responds with a referral to DNS Server C.

7. The client submits an iterative query to DNS Server C.

8. DNS Server C is authoritative for the sales.contoso.com domain and responds with a definitive answer to the client query (in this case, the A record for sales.contoso.com).

Iteration is used in the following situations:

■ The client requests the use of recursion, but recursion is disabled on the DNS server.

■ The client does not request the use of recursion when querying the DNS server.

■ An iterative request from a client tells the DNS server that the client expects the best answer the DNS server can provide immediately, without contacting other DNS servers.

Recursive Queries

A *recursive query* is a DNS query sent to a DNS server in which the querying host asks the DNS server to provide a definitive answer to the query, even if that means contacting other servers to provide the answer. When sent a recursive query, the DNS server iteratively queries other DNS servers to obtain an answer. In Figure 3-9, the querying host issues only one query before receiving the requested information.

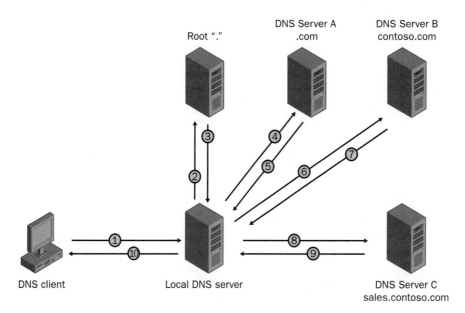

Figure 3-9   The recursive query process

To centralize the workload and reduce network traffic, host computers typically issue recursive queries to DNS servers. A network of 1,000 clients iteratively querying DNS servers is clearly less efficient than centralizing queries to a handful of DNS servers. Centralizing queries means each client sends a single recursive query rather than each client sending multiple iterative queries. DNS servers generally issue iterative queries against other DNS servers if they are unable to answer a recursive query from cached information. By using recursive queries, the workload of resolving DNS names can be concentrated to a few servers and thereby achieve much greater efficiency. Figure 3-9 illustrates the client submitting a recursive query and receiving a definitive answer. The process is as follows:

1. The first step of the query process is to convert a name request into a query and then pass it to the DNS Client service for resolution using locally cached information. If the query can be answered from the local cache, the process is complete. Otherwise, the query is passed to the local DNS server.

2. The local name server checks to see if it has authority for that domain. In this example, it does not have authority, but it does contain root hints. The local name server uses the root hints to begin a search for the name server that has authority for the domain sales.contoso.com. It then queries the root name server.

3. The root name server sends IP addresses of name servers for the .com top-level domain back to the local DNS server.

4. The local DNS server submits an iterative query to DNS Server A (.com) for sales.contoso.com.

5. DNS Server A responds with a referral to the contoso.com name server, DNS Server B.

6. The local DNS server submits another iterative query to DNS Server B, contoso.com.

7. DNS Server B responds with the IP address for the authoritative server, DNS Server C.

8. The local DNS server submits an iterative query to DNS Server C.

9. DNS Server C responds with a definitive answer (in this case, the A record).

10. The local DNS server responds to the DNS client with a definitive answer. The client can now establish a TCP/IP connection with sales.contoso.com. From the client's perspective, one request was submitted to and fulfilled by the local DNS server. The information obtained by the local DNS server is cached to answer subsequent queries.

Recursive Query Timings   By default, DNS servers use timings for retry intervals and time-out intervals. These are as follows:

■ A recursion retry interval of 3 seconds. This is the length of time the DNS service waits before retrying a query made during a recursive lookup.

■ A recursion time-out interval of 15 seconds. This is the length of time the DNS service waits before failing a recursive lookup that has been retried.

Under most circumstances, these parameters do not need adjustment. However, if you are using recursive lookups over a slow-speed WAN link, you might be able to improve server performance and query completion by making slight adjustments to these settings.

Disabling the use of recursion on a DNS server is generally done when DNS clients are limited to resolving names to a specific DNS server, such as one located on your intranet. Recursion also might be disabled when the DNS server is incapable of resolving external DNS names, and clients are expected to failover to another DNS server for resolution of these names.

You can disable the use of recursion by configuring the Advanced properties in the DNS console, as shown in Figure 3-10.

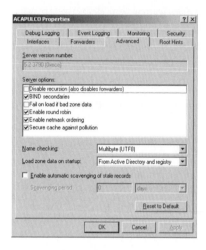

Figure 3-10   DNS Advanced properties page

> **NOTE**   **Disabling Recursion on a DNS Server**   If you disable recursion on the DNS server, you will not be able to use forwarders on the same server.

Query Responses

The two previous examples of DNS queries illustrate the process ending with a positive response returned to the client. However, queries can return other answers as well. Following are the most common answers:

- **An authoritative answer**   An authoritative answer is a positive answer returned to the client and delivered with the authority bit set in the DNS message to indicate the answer was obtained from a server with direct authority for the queried name.

- **A positive answer**   A positive answer can consist of the queried resource record or a list of resource records (also known as a resource record set) that fits the queried DNS domain name and record type specified in the query message. Positive answers may or may not be authoritative.

- **A referral answer**   A referral answer contains additional resource records not specified by the name or type in the query. This type of answer is returned to the client if the recursion process is not supported. The records are meant to act as helpful reference answers that the client can use to continue the query using iteration.

  A referral answer contains additional data, such as resource records, that are other than the type queried. For example, if the queried host name was "www" and no A resource records for this name were found in this zone, but a CNAME resource record for "www" was found instead, the DNS server can include that information when responding to the client.

If the client is able to use iteration, it can make additional queries using the referral information in an attempt to fully resolve the name.

■ **A negative answer**   A negative answer from the server can indicate that one of two possible results was encountered while the server attempted to process and recursively resolve the query fully and authoritatively:

❑ An authoritative server reported that the queried name does not exist in the DNS namespace.

❑ An authoritative server reported that the queried name exists but no records of the specified type exist for that name.

The resolver passes the query response back to the requesting program and caches the response.

Name Server Caching

As DNS servers make recursive queries on behalf of clients, they temporarily cache resource records. Cached resource records contain information obtained from DNS servers that are authoritative for DNS domain names learned while making iterative queries to search and fully answer a recursive query performed on behalf of a client. Later, when other clients place new queries that request resource record information matching cached resource records, the DNS server can use the cached resource record information to answer them. Caching provides a way to speed the performance of DNS resolution for subsequent queries of popular names, while substantially reducing DNS-related query traffic on the network.

When information is cached, a TTL value applies to all cached resource records. As long as the TTL for a cached resource record does not expire, a DNS server can continue to cache and use the resource record again when answering queries by its clients that match these resource records. Caching TTL values used by resource records in most zone configurations are assigned the minimum (default) TTL, which is set in the zone's SOA resource record. By default, the minimum TTL is 3,600 seconds (1 hour) but can be adjusted, or, if needed, individual caching TTLs can be set at each resource record.

DELEGATING ZONES

Initially, a zone stores information about a single DNS domain name. As other domains are added, you must make a decision about whether or not the domain will be part of the same zone. If you choose to add the subdomain, you may

■ Manage the subdomain as part of the original zone

■ Delegate management of the subdomain to a different zone

For example, Figure 3-11 shows the contoso.com domain, which contains domain names for Contoso, Ltd. When the contoso.com domain is first created at a single server, it is configured as a single zone for all of the Contoso DNS namespace. If, however, the contoso.com domain needs to use subdomains, those subdomains must be included in the zone or delegated away to another zone.

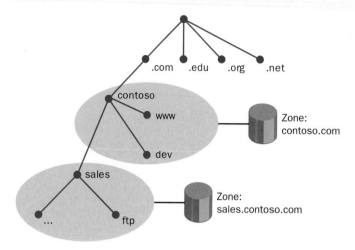

Figure 3-11   Using a subdomain to segment a zone

In this example, the contoso.com domain shows a new subdomain—the sales.contoso .com domain—delegated away from the contoso.com zone and managed in its own zone. However, the contoso.com zone needs to contain a few resource records to provide the delegation information that references the DNS servers that are authoritative for the delegated sales.contoso.com subdomain.

If the contoso.com zone does not use delegation for a subdomain, the data for the subdomain remains part of the contoso.com zone. For example, the subdomain dev.contoso.com is not delegated away but is managed by the contoso.com zone.

As previously discussed, namespaces can be divided into one or more zones. Zones can be stored, distributed, and replicated to other DNS servers. Before creating additional zones, determine if any of the following needs are true for your organization:

- Your organization has a need to delegate management of part of your DNS namespace to another location or department.

- You want to provide a more fault-tolerant DNS environment.

- You want to improve DNS name resolution performance by dividing one large zone into small zones, thereby distributing workload among several servers.

- Your organization has opened a new branch office or site and you need to extend the DNS namespace by adding numerous subdomains.

If any of these reasons are true for your organization, you could benefit from delegating zones. When structuring zones, use a plan that reflects the structure of your organization. Also, be aware that for each new zone you create, you will need delegation records in other zones that point to the authoritative DNS servers for the new zone. This is necessary both to transfer authority and to provide correct referral to other DNS servers and clients of the new servers being made authoritative for the new zone.

Figure 3-12 shows delegation from a parent zone to a new zone created for a subdomain, sales.contoso.com.

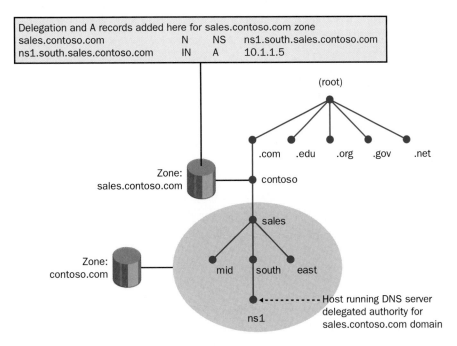

Figure 3-12   Delegating a subdomain to a new zone

In Figure 3-12, an authoritative DNS server computer for the newly delegated sales.contoso.com subdomain is named based on a derivative subdomain included in the new zone (ns1.south.sales.contoso.com). To make this server known to others outside of the newly delegated zone, two resource records are needed in the microsoft.com zone to complete delegation to the new zone:

- An NS resource record is necessary to effect the delegation. This resource record is used to advertise that the server named ns1.south.sales.contoso .com is an authoritative server for the delegated subdomain.

- An A resource record (glue record) is needed to resolve the name of the server specified in the NS resource record to its IP address. The process of resolving the host name in this resource record to the delegated DNS server in the NS resource record is sometimes referred to as *glue chasing*.

UNDERSTANDING ZONE TRANSFERS

Zone transfers are the complete or partial transfer of all data in a zone from the primary DNS server hosting the zone to a secondary DNS server hosting a copy of the zone. The copy of the zone hosted on a secondary DNS server is initially created using a zone transfer. When changes are made to the zone on a primary DNS server, the primary DNS server notifies the secondary DNS servers that changes have occurred and the changes are replicated to all the secondary DNS servers for that zone using zone transfers.

In the original DNS specifications, only one form of zone transfer was available, which was known as *full zone transfer*. RFC 1995 discusses an additional type of zone transfer, known as the *incremental zone transfer*. Windows Server 2003 supports incremental zone transfers. This section describes both types of zone transfers, as well as the notification process known as *DNS Notify*.

The following events trigger zone transfers:

- A transfer is manually initiated using the console at the secondary server.
- The zone refresh interval expires.
- The DNS Server service is started at the secondary server.
- The master server notifies the secondary server of a zone change or changes.

Zone transfers are always initiated at the secondary server for a zone and sent to their configured master servers, which act as their source for the zone. Master servers can be any other DNS server that loads the zone, such as either the primary server for the zone or another secondary server. When the master server receives the request for the zone, it can reply with either an incremental (IXFR) or full (AXFR) transfer of the zone to the secondary server.

In a full zone transfer, the primary DNS server hosting the primary zone transfers a copy of the entire zone database to the secondary DNS server hosting a copy of the zone. Whether a full or incremental transfer, the process shown in Figure 3-13 is followed:

1. When the value of the Refresh field in the SOA resource record for the zone hosted on the secondary DNS server expires, the secondary DNS server queries the primary DNS server for the SOA record of the primary zone.

2. The primary DNS server for the zone replies to the query with the SOA resource record.

3. The secondary DNS server for the zone compares the serial number in the returned SOA record to the serial number in the SOA record for the local copy of the zone. If the serial number sent by the primary DNS server for the zone is higher than the serial number for its local zone, the zone needs to be updated, and the secondary DNS server sends an AXFR request (a request for a full zone transfer) to the primary DNS server.

4. The primary DNS server receives the request for the zone transfer and sends the full zone database to the secondary DNS server, essentially re-creating the copy of the zone while maintaining any zone settings.

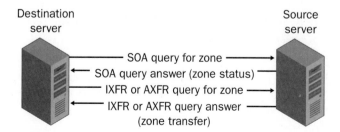

Figure 3-13   The zone transfer process

If the primary DNS server for the zone does not respond to the request for a zone transfer sent from the secondary DNS server, the secondary DNS server continues to retry after the interval specified in the Retry field in the SOA resource record for the zone. If there is still no answer after the interval specified in the Expire field in the SOA resource record for the zone expires, the secondary DNS server discards its zone.

Incremental Zone Transfer

Incremental zone transfers were designed to reduce the amount of network traffic generated by full zone transfers. Rather than sending a copy of the entire zone file, an incremental zone transfer sends only records that have changed since the last zone update. Both Windows 2000 and Windows Server 2003 support incremental zone transfers.

Although an incremental zone transfer saves network bandwidth, it uses additional disk space on the server to record the version history. The primary DNS server for the zone maintains a recent version history of the zone, which observes any record changes that occurred in the most recent version updates of the zone. To conserve disk space, DNS servers store only the most recent updates. The Windows Server 2003 DNS Server service stores these updates in a log file that resides in the %systemroot%\System32\Dns folder. The log file is named by using the name of the zone file with .log appended. For example, if the zone file for the contoso.com domain is stored in the file Contoso.com.dns, the log file is named Contoso.com.dns.log.

An incremental zone transfer uses the following process:

1. Initially, when a secondary server is first configured, it sends a full zone transfer request (AXFR) to its master DNS server. The master (source) server responds by sending a full copy of the zone to the secondary (destination) server.

2. Each zone delivery has a version indicated by a serial number in the properties of the SOA resource record and a refresh interval (by default, 900 seconds). The refresh interval indicates at what interval the secondary server should request another copy of the zone from the source server.

3. After the interval expires, the destination server submits an SOA query to request an incremental zone transfer.

4. The source server answers the query by sending its SOA record, which contains the aforementioned serial number.

5. The destination server compares the serial number from the SOA record to its current local serial number. If the numbers are equal, no transfer is requested, and the refresh interval is reset.

6. If the value of the serial number in the SOA response is higher than its current local serial number, records on the source are newer than the local records and an IXFR query is sent to the source server. This query contains the local serial number so the source server can determine which records the destination server needs.

7. Depending on several factors, the source server responds with either an incremental or full transfer of the zone. The primary DNS server for a zone is not required to perform an incremental zone transfer. It can choose to perform a full zone transfer under the following conditions:

    ❑ The primary DNS server does not support incremental zone transfers.

    ❑ The primary DNS server does not have all the necessary data for performing an incremental zone transfer.

    ❑ An incremental zone transfer uses more network bandwidth than a full zone transfer.

8. When the secondary DNS server receives an incremental zone transfer, it creates a new version of the zone and begins replacing outdated resource records with the updated resource records from the source server, applying oldest to newest. When all the updates are completed, the secondary DNS server replaces its old version of the zone with the new version of the zone.

DNS Notify

Windows-based DNS servers support DNS Notify, an update to the original DNS protocol specification that permits a means of initiating notification to secondary servers when zone changes occur (RFC 1996). Servers that are notified can then initiate a zone transfer as described previously to request zone changes from their master servers and update their local replicas of the zone. This process improves consistency of zone data.

The list of secondary DNS servers that a primary DNS server will notify is maintained in the *notify list*, which is a list of the IP addresses for those secondary servers. When the zone is updated, the primary DNS server for the zone notifies only DNS servers on the notify list. For secondary DNS servers to be notified by the DNS server acting as their configured source for a zone, each secondary server must first have its IP address in the notify list of the source server. In Windows Server 2003 DNS, you can use the DNS Notify dialog box, accessed through the DNS console, shown in Figure 3-14, to set the notify list.

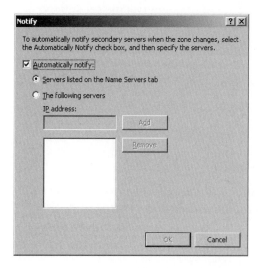

Figure 3-14   The DNS Notify dialog box

▶ **Creating a Notify List for a Zone**

To create a notify list for a zone, follow these steps:

1. Click Start, point to Administrative Tools, and then click DNS.

2. In the console tree, click the applicable zone.

3. On the Action menu, click Properties.

4. In the Zone Transfers tab, click Notify.

5. Verify that the Automatically Notify check box is checked.

6. Select the method to be used for creating a list for notifying other DNS servers when changes to the zone occur. Your options are as follows:

   a. Use the Servers Listed On The Name Servers tab option to permit only those servers that appear by IP address in the Name Servers tab to be included in the notify list.

   b. Select The Following Servers option if you want to specify a different notify list to be used instead.

7. If you selected The Following Servers option in the previous step, add or remove server IP addresses to form the notify list as needed:

   a. To add a server to the notify list, type its IP address in the IP Address field, and then click Add.

   b. To remove a server from the notify list, click the server IP address in the list box, and then click Remove.

In addition to notifying the listed servers, the DNS console permits you to use the contents of the notify list as a means to restrict or limit zone transfer access to only those secondary servers specified in the list. This can help prevent an undesired attempt by an unknown or unapproved DNS server to pull, or request, zone updates.

When the zone on a primary DNS server is updated, the following events occur:

- The Serial Number field in the SOA record is updated to indicate that a new version of the zone is written to a disk.

- The primary DNS server sends a notify message to the DNS servers that are specified in its notify list.

- A secondary DNS server for the zone that receives the notify message responds by sending an SOA-type query back to the notifying primary DNS server to determine if the zone on the primary DNS server is a later version than the copy of the zone currently stored on the secondary DNS server.

- If a notified secondary DNS server determines that the serial number specified in the SOA record of the zone on the primary DNS server is higher than the serial number specified in the SOA record for its current zone copy (the zone contains more recent updates), the notified secondary DNS server requests a zone transfer (AXFR or IXFR).

> **NOTE   DNS Notification in Active Directory–Integrated Zones**   For replication of Active Directory–integrated zones, DNS notification is not needed. This is because DNS servers that load a zone from Active Directory automatically poll the directory (as specified by the SOA resource record's refresh interval) to update and refresh the zone. In these cases, configuring a notify list can actually degrade system performance by causing unnecessary, additional transfer requests for the updated zone.

UNDERSTANDING FORWARDING

A **forwarder** is a DNS server on a network used to forward DNS queries for external DNS names to DNS servers outside of that network. A *conditional forwarder* forwards queries according to specific domain names.

Standard Forwarding

As discussed previously, a DNS server on a network is designated as a forwarder by having the other DNS servers in the network forward the queries they cannot resolve locally to that DNS server. By using a forwarder, you can manage name resolution for names outside of your network, such as names on the Internet, and you improve the efficiency of name resolution for the computers in your network. For example, to use forwarders to manage the DNS traffic between your network and the Internet, configure the firewall used by your network to allow only one DNS server to communicate with the Internet. When you have configured the other DNS servers in your network to forward queries they cannot resolve locally to that DNS server, it will act as your forwarder.

Because external network traffic is going through a single DNS server, that server builds up a large cache of DNS data, which, over time, decreases Internet traffic and provides faster response times to clients.

Without having a specific DNS server designated as a forwarder, all DNS servers can send queries outside of a network using their root hints. As a result, a lot of internal, and possibly critical, DNS information can be exposed on the Internet. In addition to this security and privacy issue, this method of resolution can result in a large volume of external traffic that is costly and inefficient for a network with a slow Internet connection or a company with high Internet service costs.

A DNS server configured to use a forwarder will behave differently than a DNS server that is not configured to use a forwarder. A DNS server configured to use a forwarder behaves as follows:

1. When the DNS server receives a query, it attempts to resolve this query by using the primary and secondary zones that it hosts and by using its cache.

2. If the query cannot be resolved using this local data, it will forward the query to the DNS server designated as a forwarder.

3. The DNS server will wait briefly for an answer from the forwarder before attempting to contact the DNS servers specified in its root hints.

4. Rather than send the standard iterative query, when a DNS server forwards a query to a forwarder, by default, it sends a recursive query to the forwarder.

Conditional Forwarding

Conditional forwarding enables a DNS server to forward queries to other DNS servers based on the DNS domain names in the queries. With conditional forwarding, a DNS server could be configured to forward all the queries it receives for names ending with research.wingtiptoys.com to a specific DNS server's IP address or to the IP addresses of multiple DNS servers.

For example, when two companies, fabrikam.com and wingtiptoys.com, merge or collaborate, they may want to allow clients from the internal namespace of one company to resolve the names of the clients from the internal namespace of another company.

The administrators from one organization (fabrikam.com) may inform the administrators of the other organization (wingtiptoys.com) about the set of DNS servers that they can use to send DNS queries for name resolution within the internal namespace of the first organization. In this case, the DNS servers in the wingtiptoys.com organization will be configured to forward all queries for names ending with fabrikam.com to the designated DNS servers.

> **NOTE** **Authoritative DNS Servers' Forwarding Behavior** Authoritative DNS servers cannot forward queries according to domain names for which they are authoritative. For example, the authoritative DNS server for the zone widgets.microsoft.com cannot forward queries according to the domain name widgets.microsoft.com. If the DNS server were allowed to do this, it would nullify the server's capability to respond to queries for the domain name widgets.microsoft.com. The DNS server authoritative for widgets.microsoft.com can forward queries for DNS names that end with hr.widgets.microsoft.com, if hr.widgets.microsoft.com is delegated to another DNS server.

The conditional forwarder setting consists of the following:

- The domain names for which the DNS server will forward queries
- One or more DNS server IP addresses for each domain name specified

▶ **Configuring Forwarding**

To configure forwarding, follow these steps:

1. Open DNS.
2. In the console tree, click the applicable DNS server.
3. On the Action menu, click Properties.
4. In the Forwarders tab, for conditional forwarding, enter a domain name; for normal forwarding, choose All Other DNS Names.
5. Under Selected Domain's Forwarder IP Address list, type the IP address of a forwarder, and then click Add.

Forwarding Sequence

Each domain name used for forwarding on a DNS server is associated with the IP addresses of one or more DNS servers. A DNS server configured for forwarding will use its forwarders list after it has determined that it cannot resolve a query using its authoritative data (primary or secondary zone data) or cached data. If the server cannot resolve a query using forwarders, it may attempt recursion to the root hint servers.

The order of the IP addresses listed determines the sequence in which the IP addresses are used. After the DNS server forwards the query to the forwarder with the first IP address associated with the domain name, it waits a short period for an answer from that forwarder (according to the DNS server's time-out setting) before resuming the forwarding operation with the next IP address associated with the domain name. It continues this process until it receives an affirmative answer from a forwarder or until it has tried all addresses in the list.

When a DNS server configured to use conditional forwarding receives a query for a domain name, it compares that domain name with its list of domain name conditions and uses the longest domain name condition that corresponds to the domain name in the query. For example, a DNS server receives a query for www.qualitycontrol .research.wingtiptoys.com.

It compares that domain name with both wingtiptoys.com and research.wingtiptoys .com. The DNS server determines that research.wingtiptoys.com is the domain name that more closely matches the original query.

Forward-Only Server

A DNS server can be configured to not perform recursion after the forwarders fail; if it does not get a successful query response from any of the servers configured as forwarders, it sends a negative response to the DNS client.

The option to prevent recursion can be set for each conditional forwarder in Windows Server 2003. For example, a DNS server can be configured to perform recursion for the domain name research.wingtiptoys.com, but not to perform recursion for the domain name wingtiptoys.com.

> **NOTE   Disabling Recursion**   If you disable recursion in the Advanced tab in DNS server properties, you will not be able to use forwarders on the same server.

CONNECTING LOCAL NETWORKS TO THE INTERNET

Although it is possible to configure DNS servers inside your firewall to use the same DNS names as are used to access them from outside your firewall, this is not recommended. The recommended practice is to use a different namespace for your internal network, such applying the suffix ".local" to your domain name (for example contoso.local), than for your external namespace (for example, contoso.com).

We'll look at three ways that DNS names are resolved when the above recommen- dation is used: resolving a DNS name internal to the organization, resolving a DNS name external to the organization without using a proxy server, and resolving an external DNS name using a proxy server. In the following scenarios, Contoso, Ltd. has configured its external network to use contoso.com and its internal network uses contoso.local. The two zones are separated by a firewall and outside the firewall, DNS servers are provided by Contoso's ISP.

Resolving Internal Names

A client needs to access an internal Web site, *web.contoso.local*. The resolution process is as follows (see Figure 3-15):

1. The client sends a query for web.contoso.local to the internal DNS server.

2. The internal DNS server resolves web.contoso.local to an IP address and sends the result to the client.

   The client initiates a connection to web.contoso.local.

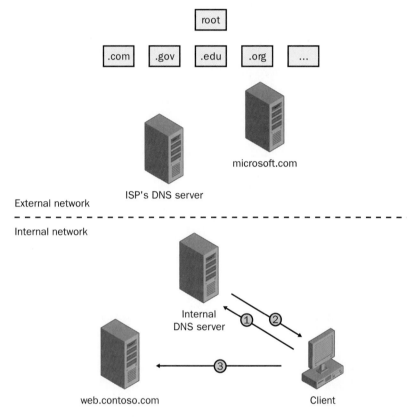

Figure 3-15 Resolving internal names

Resolving External Names Without a Proxy Server

Contoso's internal DNS servers are configured to forward requests for Internet addresses to the external DNS servers provided by the ISP. In this scenario, a client needs to access support.microsoft.com. The resolution process is as follows (see Figure 3-16).

1. The client sends the query for support.microsoft.com to the internal DNS server.

2. The internal DNS server forwards the query to the external DNS server provided by the ISP.

3. The external DNS server, not authoritative for this domain, checks its cache. If no entry exists for support.microsoft.com, it forwards the query to the top-level root domain.

4. The top-level root server replies to the external DNS server with a list of .com servers.

5. The external DNS server forwards the query for microsoft.com to a .com server.

6. The .com server replies to the external DNS server with the address of microsoft.com.

7. The external DNS server forwards the query for support.microsoft.com to the microsoft.com server.

8. The microsoft.com server replies to the external DNS server with the address of support.microsoft.com.

9. The external DNS server forwards the address to the internal DNS server.

10. The internal DNS server forwards requested information to the client.

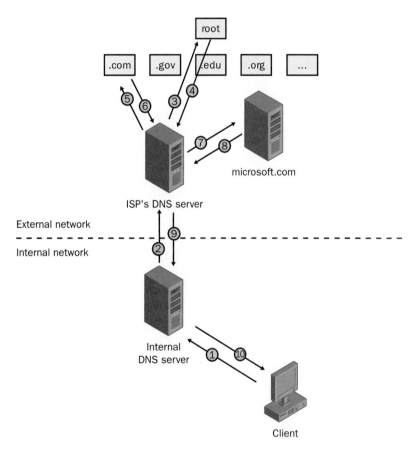

Figure 3-16   Resolving external names

Resolving External Names Using a Proxy

To resolve support.microsoft.com using a proxy server, the query process is as follows (see Figure 3-17).

1. The proxy client sends a request for microsoft.com to the proxy server.

2. The proxy server determines this is an external address and forwards the request to its assigned external DNS server.

3. The external DNS server checks its cache for the address and, not finding it, sends a request to the top-level domain .com server.

4. The top-level domain .com server sends the address of the .com domain to the external DNS server.

5. The external DNS server forwards the request for microsoft.com to the .com domain.

6. The .com domain sends the address of microsoft.com to the external DNS server.

7. The external DNS server forwards the request to the microsoft.com DNS server.

8. The microsoft.com DNS server resolves the query and replies to the external DNS server.

9. The external DNS server forwards the reply to the proxy server.

10. After the proxy server receives the reply from the external DNS server, it queries microsoft.com directly for the address of support.microsoft.com.

11. The microsoft.com DNS server replies to the request and sends information to the proxy server.

12. The proxy server sends the response to the client.

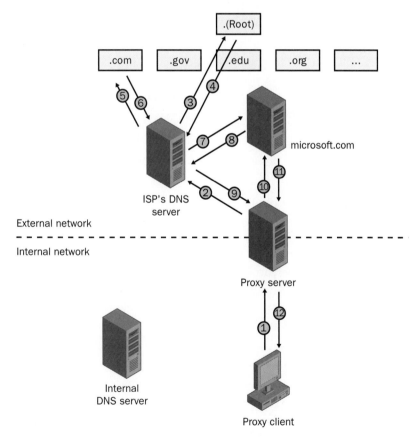

Figure 3-17   Resolving external names using a proxy

SUMMARY

- DNS names and the DNS protocol are required for Active Directory domains and for compatibility with the Internet.

- The DNS namespace is hierarchical and based on a unique root that can have any number of subdomains. An FQDN is the name of a DNS host in this namespace that indicates the host's location relative to the root of the DNS domain tree. An example of an FQDN is host1.subdomain.microsoft.com.

- A DNS zone is a contiguous portion of a namespace for which a server is authoritative. A server can be authoritative for one or more zones, and a zone can contain one or more contiguous domains. A DNS server is authoritative for a zone if it hosts the zone, either as a primary or secondary DNS server. Each DNS zone contains the resource records it needs to answer queries for its portion of the DNS namespace.

- There are several types of DNS servers: primary, secondary, master name, and caching-only.

  - A DNS server that hosts a primary DNS zone is said to act as a primary DNS server. Primary DNS servers store original source data for zones. With Windows Server 2003, you can implement primary zones in one of two ways: as standard primary zones, in which zone data is stored in a text file, or as an Active Directory–integrated zone, in which zone data is stored in the Active Directory database.

  - A DNS server that hosts a secondary DNS server is said to act as a secondary DNS server. Secondary DNS servers are authoritative backup servers for the primary server. The servers from which secondary servers acquire zone information are called masters.

  - A master server can be the primary server or another secondary server.

  - A caching-only server forwards requests to other DNS servers and hosts no zones, but builds a cache of frequently requested records.

- Recursion is one of the two process types for DNS name resolution. A DNS client will request that a DNS server provide a complete answer to a query that does not include pointers to other DNS servers, effectively shifting the workload of resolving the query from the client to the DNS server. For the DNS server to perform recursion properly, the server needs to know where to begin searching for names in the DNS namespace. This information is provided by the root hints file, Cache.dns, which is stored on the server computer.

- A DNS server on a network is designated as a forwarder by having the other DNS servers in the network forward the queries they cannot resolve locally to that DNS server. Conditional forwarding enables a DNS server to forward queries to other DNS servers based on the DNS domain names in the queries.

EXERCISES

> **IMPORTANT**   **Completing All Exercises**   If you plan to do any of the textbook exercises in this chapter, you must do all of the exercises in the chapter to return the computer to its original state for the associated Lab Manual labs.

Exercise 3-1: Adding the DNS Server Role

In this exercise, you will use the Manage Your Server page to add the DNS server role.

1. Click Start, point to Control Panel, point to Administrative Tools, and then click Manage Your Server.

   Manage Your Server starts automatically by default when you log on.

2. On the Manage Your Server page, click Add Or Remove A Role.

3. On the Preliminary Steps page, click Next.

4. On the Server Role page, click DNS Server, and then click Next.

5. On the Summary Of Selections page, click Next.

6. On the Welcome To The Configure A DNS Server Wizard page, click Next.

7. On the Select Configuration Action page, click Configure Root Hints Only (Recommended For Advanced Users Only), and then click Next.

8. On the Completing The Configure A DNS Server Wizard page, click Finish.

9. On the This Server Is Now A DNS Server page, click Finish.

Exercise 3-2: Adding a Standard Primary Forward Lookup Zone

In this exercise, you will use the DNS console to add a standard primary forward lookup zone.

1. Click Start, point to Administrative Tools, and then click DNS.

2. In the console tree, click, then right-click *ComputerName* (where *Computer-Name* is the name of your computer), and then click New Zone.

3. On the Welcome To The New Zone Wizard page, click Next.

4. On the Zone Type page, click Primary Zone and clear the Store The Zone In Active Directory (Available Only If DNS Server Is A Domain Controller) option, and then click Next.

5. On the Forward Or Reverse Lookup Zone page, click Forward Lookup Zone, and then click Next.

6. On the Zone Name page, in the Zone Name box, type ***computername*.contoso.com**, and then click Next.

7. On the Zone File page, verify that Create A New File With This File Name is selected and *computername*.contoso.com.dns is displayed in the box, and then click Next.

8. On the Dynamic Update page, verify Do Not Allow Dynamic Updates is selected, and then click Next.

9. On the Completing The New Zone Wizard page, click Finish.

Exercise 3-3: Changing a Zone to Active Directory–Integrated

In this exercise, you will change a standard zone to an Active Directory–integrated primary zone.

1. Click Start, point to Administrative Tools, and then click DNS.

2. In the console tree, expand *ComputerName* (where *ComputerName* is the name of your computer), expand Forward Lookup Zones, right-click *computername*.contoso.com, and then click Properties.

3. In the General tab, click Change.

4. In the Change Zone Type window, select the Store The Zone In Active Directory (Available Only If DNS Server Is A Domain Controller), and then click OK.

5. When you are asked if you want this zone to become Active Directory–integrated, click Yes.

6. To close the *computername*.contoso.com Properties window, click OK.

7. In the console tree, click Forward Lookup Zones, and in the details pane, note that the type of zone for *computername*.contoso.com is now Active Directory–Integrated Primary.

Exercise 3-4: Creating a Reverse Lookup Zone

In this exercise, you will create a reverse lookup zone.

1. Click Start, point to Administrative Tools, and then click DNS.

2. In the console tree, expand *ComputerName* (where *ComputerName* is the name of your computer), right-click Reverse Lookup Zones, and then click New Zone.

3. On the Welcome To The New Zone Wizard page, click Next.

4. On the Zone Type page, verify the Primary Zone option is enabled and verify that the Store The Zone In Active Directory (Available Only If DNS Server Is A Domain Controller) option is selected, and then click Next.

5. On the Active Directory Zone Replication Scope page, verify that To All Domain Controllers In The Active Directory Domain Contoso.com is selected, and then click Next.

6. On the Reverse Lookup Zone Name page, in the Network ID box, type **10.1.1**, and then click Next.

7. On the Dynamic Update page, verify that Allow Only Secure Dynamic Updates (Recommended For Active Directory) is selected, and then click Next.

8. On the Completing The New Zone Wizard page, click Finish.

9. In the console tree, click Reverse Lookup Zones, and in the details pane, verify a zone named 10.1.1.*x* Subnet (where *x* is the number of your computer) with a type Active Directory–Integrated Primary is displayed.

Exercise 3-5: Locating DNS Resource Records

Exercise 3-5 teaches you how to use the DNS console to identify three different types of resource records.

1. Click Start, point to Administrative Tools, and then click DNS.

2. In the console tree, expand Forward Lookup Zones, and then click *domain*.contoso.com (where *domain* is the name of your domain).

3. Locate the SOA, NS, and A records in the details pane.

Exercise 3-6: Removing the DNS Server Role

To prepare for the labs associated with this chapter (Lab Manual Lab 3), this exercise shows you how to remove the DNS server role.

1. Click Start, point to Administrative Tools, and then click Manage Your Server.

   The Manage Your Server page starts automatically by default when you log on.

2. On the Manage Your Server page, click Add Or Remove A Role.

3. On the Preliminary Steps page, click Next.

4. On the Server Role page, click DNS Server, and then click Next.

5. On the Role Removal Confirmation page, click the Remove The DNS Server Role check box, and then click Next.

6. On the DNS Server Role Removed page, click Finish.

REVIEW QUESTIONS

1. Describe the process by which secondary servers determine whether a zone transfer should be initiated.

2. What is the difference between an IXFR query and an AXFR query?

3. You discover that an administrator has adjusted the default TTL value for your company's primary DNS zone to 5 minutes. Which of the following is the most likely effect of this change?

   a. Primary servers initiate a zone transfer every 5 minutes.

   b. DNS clients have to query the server more frequently to resolve names for which the server is authoritative.

   c. Secondary servers initiate a zone transfer every 5 minutes.

   d. DNS hosts reregister their records more frequently.

4. Relative to file-backed zones, storing DNS zones in Active Directory results in which of the following?

   a. Less frequent transfer of information

   b. Increased need for administration

   c. Less saturation of network bandwidth

   d. Ability to perform secure dynamic updates

5. You want to consolidate DNS traffic between your network and the Internet. How could you use a forwarder to accomplish this?

6. What are some reasons a source server might respond with an AXFR to an IXFR request?

7. True or False: A primary server always initiates a zone transfer?

CASE SCENARIOS

Case Scenario 3-1: Minimizing DNS Traffic and Administration

Contoso, Ltd., has a branch office connected to corporate headquarters with a slow WAN link. The company wants to minimize the amount of traffic generated by the local DNS server on this link and minimize DNS administration in the branch office.

How would you configure the DNS server to meet these requirements?

   a. Disable round-robin and netmask ordering.

   b. Reduce the refresh interval in the SOA resource record for the primary zone.

   c. Do not configure any forward or reverse zones, but configure the server to use a forwarder.

   d. Configure the forward lookup zone with a WINS lookup record, and decrease the cache time-out value.

Case Scenario 3-2: Troubleshooting Access to External Resources

You are the network administrator for Contoso, Ltd. Users are complaining that they cannot access resources external to the local network. You eliminate connectivity issues to the DNS server and narrow the problem to name resolution. Using Ping.exe, you are able to successfully resolve local hosts but cannot resolve names external to the local network. Which of the following is the most likely cause of this issue?

   a. The local DNS server is not authoritative for the Internet DNS domains.

   b. Iterative queries are disabled on the DNS servers.

   c. Recursive queries are disabled on the DNS servers.

   d. DNS root hints are missing or incorrectly configured.

CHAPTER 4
MANAGING AND MONITORING DNS

Upon completion of this chapter, you will be able to:

- Use management tools to configure the **Domain Name System (DNS)** including Nslookup, DNSLint, and Dnscmd.

- Define DNS and **Windows Internet Naming Service (WINS)** integration and explain how host names and the **network basic input/output system (NetBIOS)** names fit into DNS and WINS integration.

- Configure options available on the Advanced tab of the DNS Server Properties dialog box.

- Explain how outdated **resource records** are aged and scavenged and initiate the aging and scavenging process.

- Display and purge the DNS **resolver** cache.

- Secure DNS objects in **Active Directory** directory service.

- Use the Event Log, DNS debug log, and Active Directory replication monitor to monitor and troubleshoot DNS.

DNS is a key service in Microsoft Windows Server 2003 networks. If DNS fails, clients often lose connectivity to the Internet or to other clients and Active Directory fails. Effective management and monitoring procedures mitigate the possibility of **DNS server** failure.

This chapter introduces you to the tools, concepts, and procedures necessary to manage and monitor DNS **name resolution**. Topics in this chapter include securing DNS, monitoring and troubleshooting DNS with tools such as the DNS Events Log and DNS debug log, and using tools such as Nslookup, the Replication Monitor, and Dnscmd.

USING DNS MANAGEMENT TOOLS

Several tools are useful for managing and monitoring DNS services. These tools include the following:

- The DNS console, which is part of Administrative Tools. The DNS console is the primary tool for configuring DNS. It is shown in Figure 4-1.

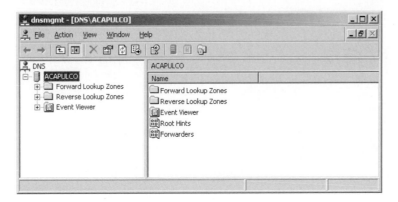

Figure 4-1   The DNS console

- Nslookup, which can be used to query **DNS zone** information to verify existing and proper configuration of resource records.

- DNSLint, which is a tool that verifies the consistency of a particular set of DNS records on multiple DNS servers.

- Logging features, such as the DNS server log, which you can view with the DNS console or Event Viewer. File-based logs also can be used temporarily as an advanced debugging option to log and trace selected service events.

- Dnscmd, which enables you to use the command line to perform most of the tasks you can perform using the DNS console.

Using the DNS Console to Monitor DNS Servers

You can use the DNS console to manually or automatically test DNS servers by submitting two different types of queries:

- A simple query, or **iterative query**. The DNS resolver (client) on the server computer queries the local DNS servers, which are located on the same computer.

- A **recursive query** to other DNS servers. The DNS resolver (client) on the server computer queries the local DNS server, but instead of submitting an iterative query, it submits a recursive query. Specifically, the client asks the server to use recursion to resolve a name server (NS)–type query for the root of the DNS **domain namespace**. This type of query typically requires additional recursive processing and can be helpful in verifying that server **root hints** or zone delegations are properly set.

These settings are accessed by clicking the Monitoring tab in the DNS server properties window. You can perform the test by clicking the Test Now button or specify an interval for performing the test.

Results of both manual and automatic tests are displayed in the Test Results list box shown in Figure 4-2. This information includes the following:

■ The date and time when each query was submitted

■ Additional status results of the specific test used, such as whether the simple or recursive query failed or succeeded

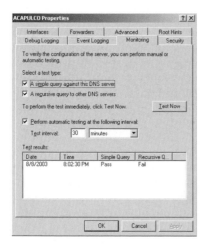

Figure 4-2   Test Results list box

Querying DNS with Nslookup

Nslookup is a command-line tool provided with **Transmission Control Protocol/ Internet Protocol (TCP/IP)** available in Windows Server 2003 that performs DNS queries and enables examination of the content of zone files on local and remote servers. Nslookup often is used to verify the configuration of DNS zones and to diagnose and solve name resolution problems.

Nslookup can be run at the command prompt (in command prompt mode) or as a program that accepts serial commands and queries (in interactive mode). To look up a single host name, you would typically enter a single command at the command prompt. For example, executing the following command at the command prompt returns the Internet Protocol (IP) addresses associated with the **fully qualified domain name (FQDN)** www.microsoft.com (output results will vary):

```
C:\>nslookup www.microsoft.com
Server:  bottincdc1.bottinc.com
Address:  192.168.0.100

Non-authoritative answer:
Name:    www.microsoft.akadns.net
Addresses:  207.46.134.155, 207.46.134.190, 207.46.249.222, 207.46.249.27
            207.46.249.190
Aliases:  www.microsoft.com
```

To resolve the query, the Nslookup utility submits the name to the DNS server specified for the primary connection on the local client computer. This DNS server can then answer the query from its cache or through recursion.

If you submit a query for a host name that does not exist, you receive the following response:

```
C:\>nslookup thisdoesnotexist.bottinc.com
Server:  bottincdc1.bottinc.com
Address:  192.168.0.100

*** bottincdc1.bottinc.com can't find thisdoesnotexist.bottinc.com:
    Non-existent domain
```

If you troubleshoot a specific DNS server instead of the one specified for the primary connection on the local client computer, you can specify that DNS server using the Nslookup command. For example, the following command executed at the command prompt queries the DNS server at 207.46.138.20 for the name www.microsoft.com:

```
C:\>nslookup www.microsoft.com 207.46.138.20
```

You can also use Nslookup to resolve IP addresses to host names. For example, the following command executed at the command prompt returns the FQDN associated with the address 207.46.249.222, as shown in this output:

```
C:\>nslookup 207.46.249.222
Server:  localhost
Address:  127.0.0.1

Name:    www.microsoft.com
Address:  207.46.249.222
```

Nslookup Syntax

Use the following syntax for Nslookup in the command prompt mode:

```
nslookup [-opt  ...] [{Host| [Server]}]
```

The Nslookup command uses the following syntax:

- **-opt**   Specifies one or more Nslookup subcommands as a command-line option.

- **Host**   Looks up information for *Host* using the current default DNS name server (NS), if no other server is specified. To look up a computer not in the current **DNS domain**, append a period to the name.

- **Server**   Specifies to use this server as the DNS name server. If you omit *Server*, the default DNS name server is used.

Using Interactive Mode

When issuing multiple Nslookup commands, it is generally more efficient to use Nslookup in interactive mode. To enter interactive mode, open a command prompt, type **nslookup**, and press ENTER.

In interactive mode, Nslookup accepts commands that allow the program to perform a variety of functions, such as displaying the specific contents of messages included in DNS exchanges, simulating a **zone transfer**, or searching for records of a specific type on a given server. These commands can be displayed by typing the **help** or **?** command, as shown in Figure 4-3.

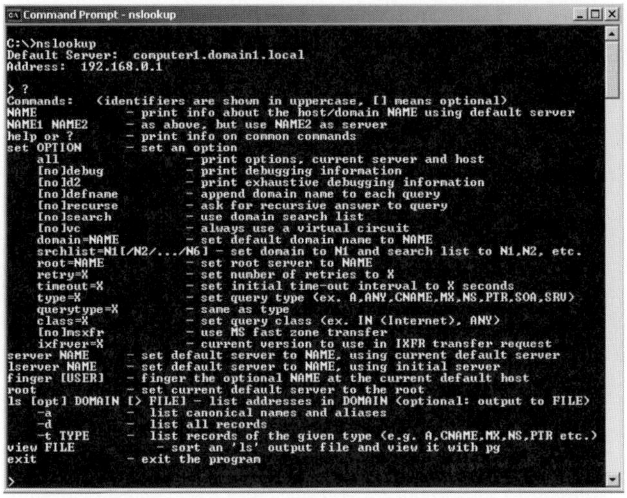

Figure 4-3   Nslookup commands

Exploring Nslookup Options

When you are in interactive mode, you can also use the Set command to configure Nslookup options that determine how the resolver carries out queries. One option is to use the Debug command. By default, Nslookup is set to Nodebug. Typing **set debug** while in interactive mode enters debug mode, which enables Nslookup to display the DNS response messages communicated from the DNS server as shown in Figure 4-4.

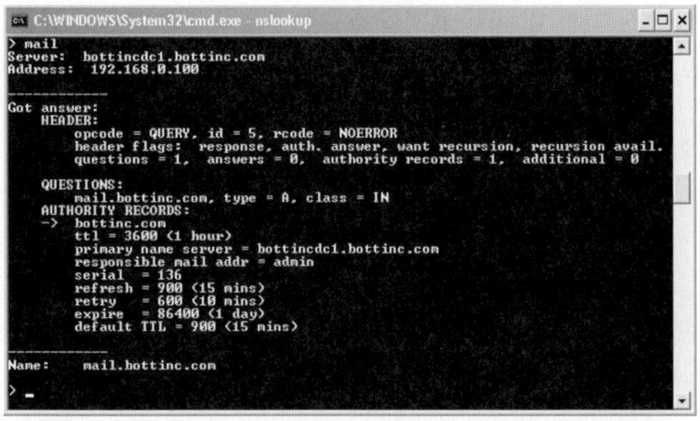

Figure 4-4   Nslookup in debug mode

> **NOTE**   **Nslookup Commands Are Case-Sensitive**   Nslookup commands entered while in interactive mode are case-sensitive and must be typed in lowercase.

You can view the options currently configured for Nslookup by running the Set All command, as shown in Figure 4-5.

Figure 4-5   Displaying Nslookup options

Table 4-1 describes the most common options configured with the Set command.

Table 4-1   Command-Line Options Available with the Set Command

Option	Purpose	Example (Interactive Mode)
set all	Shows the configuration status of all options.	`>set all`

set [no]debug	Puts Nslookup in debug mode. With debug mode turned on, more information is printed about the packet sent to the server and the resulting answer.	`>set debug`
		Or
		`>set nodebug`

set [no]d2	Puts Nslookup in verbose debug mode so you can examine the query and response packets between the resolver and the server.	`>set d2`
		Or
		`>set nod2`

set domain= *<domain name>*	Tells the resolver which domain name to append for unqualified queries (for example, sales is an unqualified query as opposed to sales.fabrikam.com), including all queried names not followed by a trailing dot.	`>set domain=bottinc.com`
set timeout= *<time-out value>*	Tells the resolver what time-out value to use, in seconds. This option is useful for slow links on which queries frequently time out and the wait time must be lengthened.	`>set timeout=5`
set type= *<record type>* or set querytype= *<record type>* or set q=*<record type>*	Tells the resolver which type of resource records to search for (for example, address [A], pointer [PTR], or service locator [SRV] records). If you want the resolver to query for all types of resource records, type **set type=all**.	`>set type=A` `>set q=MX`

The next section describes how to perform common tasks using Nslookup in interactive mode.

Looking Up Different Data Types

By default, names queried for in Nslookup return only matching host address (A) resource records. To look up different data types within the domain namespace, use the Set Type command or Set Querytype (Set Q) command at the command prompt. For example, to query for mail exchanger (MX) resource records only instead of A resource records, type **set q=mx**, as shown here:

```
C:\>nslookup
Default Server:  bottincdc1.bottinc.com
Address:  192.168.0.100

> set q=mx
> microsoft.com
Server:  bottincdc1.bottinc.com
Address:  192.168.0.100

Non-authoritative answer:
microsoft.com    MX preference = 10, mail exchanger = maila.microsoft.com
microsoft.com    MX preference = 10, mail exchanger = mailb.microsoft.com
microsoft.com    MX preference = 10, mail exchanger = mailc.microsoft.com

maila.microsoft.com      internet address = 131.107.3.124
maila.microsoft.com      internet address = 131.107.3.125
mailb.microsoft.com      internet address = 131.107.3.122
mailb.microsoft.com      internet address = 131.107.3.123
mailc.microsoft.com      internet address = 131.107.3.121
mailc.microsoft.com      internet address = 131.107.3.126
>
```

> **NOTE**   **Querying a Record of Any Type**   To query for a record of any type, execute the Nslookup command Set q=any.

The first time a query is made for a remote name, the answer is authoritative, but subsequent queries are nonauthoritative. This pattern appears for the following reason: the first time a remote host is queried, the local DNS server contacts the DNS server that is authoritative for that domain. The local DNS server then caches that information so that subsequent queries are answered nonauthoritatively out of the local server's cache.

Querying Another Name Server Directly

To query another name server directly, use the Server or Lserver commands to switch to that name server. The Lserver command uses the local server to get the address of the server to switch to, whereas the Server command uses the current default server to get the address.

After you execute either of these commands, all subsequent lookups in the current Nslookup session are performed at the specified server until you switch servers again. The following syntax illustrates what you would type to initiate a server switch:

```
C:\> nslookup
Default Server:  nameserver1.contoso.com
Address:  10.0.0.1

> server nameserver2
Default Server:  nameserver2.contoso.com
Address:  10.0.0.2
```

Using Nslookup Subcommand Ls to View Zone Data

You can use the Nslookup subcommand Ls to list information for a DNS domain. When you issue an Nslookup command with the Ls subcommand, you effectively are requesting a zone transfer. The syntax for the Ls command is as follows:

```
ls [- a | d | t type] domain [> filename]
```

Table 4-2 lists valid options.

Table 4-2   Nslookup Ls Options

Option	Purpose	Example
-t *QueryType*	Lists all records of a specific type	>ls -t cname contoso.com
-a	Lists aliases of computers in the DNS domain (equivalent to -t CNAME)	>ls -a contoso.com
-d	Lists all records for the DNS domain (equivalent to -t ANY)	>ls -d contoso.com
-h	Lists central processing unit (CPU) and operating system information for the DNS domain (equivalent to -t HINFO)	>ls -h contoso.com
-s	Lists well-known services of computers in the DNS domain (equivalent to -t WKS)	>ls -s contoso.com

The following output demonstrates the use of the Ls command in interactive mode.

```
>ls contoso.com
[nameserver1.contoso.com]
nameserver1.contoso.com. NS server = ns1.contoso.com
nameserver2.contoso.com  NS server = ns2.contoso.com
nameserver1          A    10.0.0.1
nameserver2          A    10.0.0.2
>
```

By default, the DNS Server service allows zone information to be transferred only to servers listed in the **name server (NS) resource records** of a zone. Although this is a secure setting, consider increasing security by allowing zone transfers only to specified IP addresses. You also have the option to allow zone transfers to any server. This is not recommended and can expose your DNS data to an attacker attempting to map your network for a larger attack. The following error message is returned if zone transfer security has been set:

```
*** Can't list domain <example>.: Query refused
```

Using DNSLint

DNSLint is a command-line DNS tool included with Windows Server 2003 that verifies the consistency of a particular set of DNS records on multiple DNS servers. It also can help diagnose and fix problems caused as a result of missing or incorrect DNS records. DNSLint compiles results into a Hypertext Markup Language (HTML) file named, by default, DNSLint.html. The file is stored in the same directory from which you executed the DNSLint command.

For example, DNSLint can help when clients experience problems resolving **NetBIOS names** or when verifying that the SRV records (which clients might use to find WINS servers) are available and accurate. DNSLint can help ascertain whether DNS is contributing to the problem.

You also can use DNSLint to troubleshoot DNS-related Active Directory replication issues. Specifically, use DNSLint to determine the following:

■ Whether all DNS servers that are supposed to be authoritative for the root of an Active Directory forest actually have the necessary DNS records to successfully synchronize **directory partition replicas** among domain controllers in an Active Directory forest. DNSLint identifies which DNS records are missing from each authoritative DNS server.

■ Whether a particular Active Directory domain controller can resolve the necessary DNS records to successfully synchronize partition replicas among domain controllers in an Active Directory forest. DNSLint identifies which DNS records cannot be resolved by the domain controller that is tested.

MORE INFO   Using DNSLint to Troubleshoot Active Directory Replication
Issues   See Microsoft Knowledge Base Article 321046, "HOW TO: Use
DNSLint to Troubleshoot Active Directory Replication Issues." To find this article,
go to http://support.microsoft.com and enter the article number in the Search
The Knowledge Base text box.

In another scenario, you are able to send e-mail, but not receive it. One likely cause of this is incorrect DNS configuration. To determine whether DNS is misconfigured, use DNSLint to verify the DNS records on the DNS servers that are used to resolve the e-mail server's IP address.

DNSLint Syntax and Functions

The syntax for DNSLint is as follows:

```
dnslint /d domain_name | /ad [LDAP_IP_address] | /ql input_file
        [/c [smtp,pop,imap]] [/no_open] [/r report_name]
        [/t] [/test_tcp] [/s DNS_IP_address] [/v] [/y]
```

DNSLint performs one of three functions and then generates an HTML report.

■ **/d**   The /d (domain name test) switch is used to test a particular DNS domain name. This switch is used to help diagnose "lame delegation" issues and other related DNS issues. *Lame delegation* occurs when either a zone is delegated to a server that has not been properly configured to be authoritative for the zone or a server that is authoritative for the zone has an NS record that points to another that is not authoritative for the zone.

■ **/ad**   The /ad (Active Directory replication test) switch is used to test the DNS records that are responsible for Active Directory forest replication. Figure 4-6 shows the result section of the DNSLint report run using the Dnslint /ad /s localhost /v command.

Figure 4-6   DNSLint result section

- **/ql**   The /ql (Query List test) switch is used to test the DNS records specified in a text input file.

> **MORE INFO**   **Using DNSLint**   *See Microsoft Knowledge Base Article 321045, "Description of the DNSLint Utility." To find this article, go to http://support .microsoft.com and enter the article number in the Search The Knowledge Base text box.*

The following procedure describes how to use the autocreate parameter with the /ql switch to generate an input file you can customize.

▶ **Creating an Input File for DNSLint**

To create the DNSLint report, follow these steps:

1. Open the command prompt.

2. Navigate to the directory containing Dnslint.exe.

3. At the command prompt, type **dnslint /ql autocreate**.

   When the autocreate parameter is added to the /ql switch, a sample query text file is generated.

4. At the command prompt, type **notepad in-dnslint.txt**.

5. In Microsoft Notepad, in the seventh line from the bottom of the file, change the line from dns1.cp.msft.net to *ComputerName.* **northwindtraders.msft**.

6. In Notepad, in the last four lines of the file, change any instances of Microsoft.com to the name of the domain that you are querying.

7. In Notepad, in the last five lines of the file, change any instances of 207.46.197.100 to the IP address of the DNS server that you are querying.

8. In Notepad, save the file as Dnslintquery.txt in the same directory in which In-dnslint.txt is located, and then close Notepad.

9. At the command prompt, type **dnslint /ql dnslintquery.txt /v**.

   The /ql switch requests queries from the specified list (Dnslintquery.txt). The /v switch requests a verbose response.

10. When the HTML report opens, verify the contents, and then close the report.

11. Close the command prompt.

Using Dnscmd

You can use the Dnscmd command-line tool to perform most of the tasks that you can do from the DNS console. This tool can be used to script batch files, to help automate the management and updates of existing DNS server configurations, or to perform setup and configuration of DNS servers. For example, you can do the following:

■ Create, delete, and view zones and records.

■ Reset server and zone properties.

■ Perform zone maintenance operations, such as updating the zone, reloading the zone, refreshing the zone, writing the zone back to a file or to Active Directory, and pausing or resuming the zone.

■ Clear the cache.

■ Stop and start the DNS service.

■ View statistics.

Dnscmd is provided as a command-line tool for managing DNS servers. To use Dnscmd, you must install Windows Support Tools.

▶ **Installing Windows Support Tools**

To install Windows Support Tools, follow these steps:

1. Insert the Windows Server 2003 CD into your CD-ROM drive.

2. Go to the \Support\Tools folder.

3. Double-click Suptools.msi.

4. On the Welcome To The Windows Support Tools Setup Wizard page, click Next.

5. On the End User License Agreement page, click I Agree, and then click Next.

6. On the User Information page, provide your name and the name of your organization, and then click Next.

7. On the Destination Directory page, type the path to where Windows Support Tools should be installed, and then click Install Now.

8. On the Completing The Windows Support Tools page, click Finish.

▶ **Displaying a Complete List of Zones**

To display a complete list of the zones configured on a DNS server by using Dnscmd, at the command prompt, type **dnscmd [*ComputerName*] /enumzones**.

Executing Dnscmd using localhost results in the following:

```
C:\>dnscmd localhost /enumzones
Enumerated zone list:
        Zone count = 5
 Zone name                      Type      Storage        Properties
 .                              Cache     AD-Legacy
 _msdcs.contoso01.com           Primary   AD-Forest      Secure
 1.1.10.in-addr.arpa            Primary   AD-Legacy      Secure Rev
 computer01.contoso.com         Primary   AD-Legacy
 contoso01.com                  Primary   AD-Domain      Secure

Command completed successfully.
```

▶ **Displaying Specific Zone Information**

To display information about a specific zone that is configured on a DNS server by using Dnscmd, at the command prompt, type the following:

dnscmd [*ComputerName*] /zoneinfo [*zone*]

Executing the following command results in output similar to what follows:

```
C:\>dnscmd localhost /zoneinfo contoso01.com
Zone query result:
Zone info:
        ptr                 = 00083050
        zone name           = contoso01.com
        zone type           = 1
        update              = 2
        DS integrated       = 1
        data file           = (null)
        using WINS          = 0
        using Nbstat        = 0
        aging               = 0
        refresh interval    = 168
        no refresh          = 168
        scavenge available  = 3529116
        Zone Masters
        NULL IP Array.
        Zone Secondaries
        NULL IP Array.
        secure secs         = 3
        directory partition = AD-Domain      flags 00000015
        zone DN             = DC=contoso01.com,cn=MicrosoftDNS, DC=DomainDnsZones,
                              DC=contoso01,DC=com
   Command completed successfully.
```

Practice displaying DNS zone information by doing Exercise 4-1, "Displaying DNS Zone Information Using Dnscmd," now.

INTEGRATING DNS ZONES WITH WINS

DNS and WINS integration is the process in which DNS uses WINS to resolve names to IP addresses. DNS is used to resolve host names and services to IP addresses, and WINS is used to resolve NetBIOS names to IP addresses. You can manually configure NetBIOS name-to-IP-address mappings on the DNS server, or you can configure the DNS server to forward the name queries to the WINS server for resolution. Integrating DNS with WINS allows DNS clients to use the existing NetBIOS name entries in WINS for host name lookup. The DNS service provides the capability to use WINS servers to look up names that are not found in the DNS namespace by checking the NetBIOS namespace that WINS manages.

When you configure WINS lookup for a forward lookup zone, a WINS resource record pointing to the WINS server you specify on the WINS tab is added to the zone database. When you configure WINS-R lookup for a reverse lookup zone, a corresponding WINS-R resource record is added to the zone database.

Practice integrating DNS and WINS by doing Exercise 4-2, "Integrating DNS and WINS," now.

Host and NetBIOS names can be the same in Microsoft Windows 2000 or Windows Server 2003, which allows DNS and WINS to work together to resolve names. In some circumstances, it may be advantageous for organizations to use the existing WINS database for host name lookups rather than configuring every client in the WINS database to be in the DNS database.

MANAGING DNS USING ADVANCED DNS SERVER PROPERTIES

Advanced DNS server properties refer to the settings that can be configured in the Advanced tab of the DNS Server Properties dialog box (shown in Figure 4-7). These properties relate to server-specific features, such as disabling recursion, handling resolution of multihomed hosts, and achieving compatibility with non-Microsoft DNS servers.

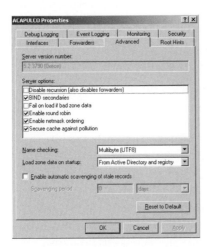

Figure 4-7   The Advanced tab of the DNS Server Properties dialog box

The server installation settings include six server options, which are either on or off, and three other server features with various selections for configuration. Table 4-3 shows the default settings for all nine features.

Table 4-3   **Default DNS Installation Settings**

Property	Setting
Disable Recursion	Off
BIND Secondaries	On
Fail On Load If Bad Zone Data	Off
Enable Round Robin	On
Enable Netmask Ordering	On
Secure Cache Against Pollution	On
Name Checking	Multibyte (UTF-8)
Load Zone Data On Startup	From Active Directory And Registry
Enable Automatic Scavenging Of Stale Records	Off (requires configuration when enabled)

In most situations, these installation defaults are acceptable and do not require modification. However, when needed, you can use the DNS console to modify these advanced parameters and accommodate special deployment needs and situations.

You can restore these default settings at any time using the Advanced tab. Simply click Reset To Default.

The following sections describe the available installation options in more detail.

Disable Recursion

The Disable Recursion server option is disabled by default (meaning that recursion is enabled). When the Disable Recursion option is enabled, the DNS Server service does not answer queries for which it is not authoritative or which it has not already answered and placed in its cache. Instead, the DNS Server service provides the client with *referrals*, which are resource records that allow a DNS client to perform iterative queries to resolve an FQDN. Do not disable recursion on a server if any other name servers use it as a **forwarder**. Disable recursion when you want to create an authoritative-only name server and prevent cache pollution. Since the server does not query other servers, it does not maintain a cache and is very difficult to spoof (pollute the cache).

BIND Secondaries

The BIND Secondaries option controls whether fast transfer format is used during a DNS zone transfer. Berkeley Internet Name Domain (BIND) is a common implementation of DNS written and ported to most available versions of the UNIX operating system. *Fast transfer format* is an efficient means of transferring zone data that provides data compression and allows multiple records to be transferred per individual Transmission Control Protocol (TCP) message. Fast zone transfer is always used among Windows-based DNS servers, so the BIND Secondaries option does not affect communications among Windows servers. However, only BIND versions 4.9.4 and later can handle these fast zone transfers.

For BIND versions earlier than 4.9.4, DNS servers running Windows Server 2003 can be configured to transfer a zone using the slower, uncompressed transfer format. When you select the BIND Secondaries check box in the Advanced tab of the Server Properties dialog box, no fast transfers are made.

If you know your DNS server will be performing zone transfers with DNS servers using BIND version 4.9.4 or later, you should disable this option to allow fast zone transfers to occur. (BIND 9.1 was released January 17, 2001.)

Fail On Load If Bad Zone Data

DNS servers running on Windows Server 2003 will, by default, load a zone even if that zone contains errors. In that scenario, errors are logged and ignored. Enabling Fail On Load If Bad Zone Data prevents a zone with errors from being loaded.

Reordering Results Sets

Multihomed computers (computers with either more than one network interface card or one network interface card with more than one IP address) typically have registered multiple host address (A) resource records for the same host name. When a client attempts to resolve the host name of a multihomed computer by contacting a DNS server, the DNS server returns a *response list*, or answer list, to the client that contains the resource records matching the client query. Upon receiving the response list from the DNS server, a DNS client attempts to contact the target host with the first IP address in the response list. If this attempt fails, the client then attempts to contact the second IP address, and so on. The Enable Netmask Ordering option and the Enable Round Robin option are both used to change the order of resource records returned in this response list.

Enable Round Robin

Round robin is a load balancing mechanism used by DNS servers to share and distribute network resource loads. If multiple resource records satisfy a query, you can use round robin to rotate the order of resource record types returned to the client.

By default, DNS uses round robin to rotate the order of resource record data returned in query answers in which multiple resource records of the same type exist for a queried DNS domain name. This feature provides a simple method for load balancing client use of Web servers and other frequently queried multihomed computers. The capability to perform round-robin rotation on all types of resource records is a new feature introduced in Windows Server 2003.

> **NOTE**   **Netmask Ordering Priority**   Local subnet priority (netmask ordering) supersedes the use of round-robin rotation for multihomed computers. When enabled, however, round robin is used as a secondary method to sort multiple records returned in a response list.

Round Robin Example   The Web server named server1.contoso.com has three network adapters and three distinct IP addresses. In the stored zone (either in a database file or in Active Directory), the three A resource records mapping the host name to each of its IP addresses appear in this fixed order:

```
server1   IN   A   10.0.0.1
server1   IN   A   10.0.0.2
server1   IN   A   10.0.0.3
```

The first DNS client—Client1—that queries the server to resolve this host's name receives the list in this default order. However, when a second client—Client2—sends a subsequent query to resolve this name, the list is rotated as follows:

```
server1    IN   A   10.0.0.2
server1    IN   A   10.0.0.3
server1    IN   A   10.0.0.1
```

Disabling Round Robin   When you clear the Enable Round Robin check box, round robin is disabled for the DNS server. If round robin is disabled for a DNS server, the order of the response for these queries is based on a static ordering of resource records in the answer list as they are stored in the zone (either its zone file or Active Directory).

Enable Netmask Ordering   Netmask ordering is a method DNS uses to give ordering and preference to IP addresses on the same network when a requesting client queries for a host name that has multiple A resource records. This is designed so that the client program will attempt to connect to a host using the closest (and, therefore, presumably fastest) IP address available.

When returning more than one IP address to a client when Netmask Ordering is enabled, IP addresses most closely matching the client's subnet mask are placed at the top of the response list. The Enable Netmask Ordering option is selected by default. For example, a multihomed computer, server1.contoso.com, has three A resource records for each of its three IP addresses in the contoso.com zone. These three records appear in the following order in the zone—either in the zone file or in Active Directory:

```
server1    IN   A   192.168.1.27
server1    IN   A   10.0.0.14
server1    IN   A   172.16.20.4
```

When a DNS client resolver at IP address 10.4.3.2 queries the server for the IP addresses of the host server1.contoso.com, the DNS Server service notes that the originating IP network address (10.0.0.0) of the client matches the network (class A) ID of the 10.0.0.14 address in the answer list of resource records. The DNS Server service then reorders the addresses in the response list as follows:

```
server1    IN   A   10.0.0.14
server1    IN   A   192.168.1.27
server1    IN   A   172.16.20.4
```

If the **network ID** of the IP address of the requesting client does not match any of the network IDs of the resource records in the answer list, the list is not reordered.

In a network that uses IP subnetting (nondefault subnet masks), a DNS server first returns IP addresses that match both the client's network ID and subnet ID before returning any IP addresses that match only the client's network ID.

For example, a multihomed computer, server1.contoso.com, has four A resource records corresponding to each of its four IP addresses in the contoso.com zone. Two of these IP addresses are for distinct and separate networks. The other two IP addresses share a common IP network address, but because custom netmasks of

255.255.248.0 are used, the IP addresses are located in different subnets. These example resource records appear in the following order in the zone, either in the zone file or in Active Directory:

```
server1    IN   A   192.168.1.27
server1    IN   A   172.16.22.4
server1    IN   A   10.0.0.14
server1    IN   A   172.16.31.5
```

If the IP address of the requesting client is 172.16.22.8, both of the IP addresses that match the same IP network as the client, the 172.16.0.0 network, are returned to the client at the top of the response list. However, in this example, the 172.16.22.4 address is placed ahead of the 172.16.31.5 address because it more closely matches the network ID of the client.

The reordered answer list returned by the DNS service is as follows:

```
server1    IN   A   172.16.22.4
server1    IN   A   172.16.31.5
server1    IN   A   192.168.1.27
server1    IN   A   10.0.0.14
```

> **NOTE** **LocalNetPriority Setting and Netmask Ordering**   Netmask ordering is often referred to as the LocalNetPriority setting. This name originates from the corresponding LocalNetPriority option used with the Dnscmd command-line utility.

Secure Cache Against Pollution

By default, the Secure Cache Against Pollution option is enabled. This setting allows the DNS server to protect its cache against referrals that are potentially polluting or nonsecure. When the setting is enabled, the server caches only those records with a name that corresponds to the domain for which the original queried name was made. Any referrals received from another DNS server along with a query response are simply discarded.

For example, if a query is originally made for the name example.microsoft.com, and a referral answer provides a record for a name outside the microsoft.com domain name tree (such as msn.com), that name is discarded if the Secure Cache Against Pollution option is enabled. This setting helps prevent unauthorized computers from impersonating another network server.

When this option is disabled, however, the server caches all the records received in response to DNS queries—even when the records do not correspond to the queried-for domain name.

Name Checking

By default, the Name Checking drop-down list box in the Advanced tab of the DNS Server Properties dialog box is set to Multibyte (UTF-8). Thus, the DNS service, by default, verifies that all domain names handled by the DNS service conform to the UCS Transformation Format (UTF). *Unicode* is a 2-byte encoding scheme, compatible with the traditional 1-byte **American Standard Code for Information Interchange (ASCII)** format, that allows for binary representation of most human languages. Table 4-4 lists and describes the four name-checking methods.

Table 4-4   **Name-Checking Methods**

Method	Description
Strict RFC **(American National Standards Institute [ANSI])**	Uses strict checking of names. These restrictions, set in **Request for Comments (RFC)** 1123, include limiting names to uppercase and lowercase letters (A–Z, a–z), numbers (0–9), and hyphens (-). The first character of the DNS name can be a number.
Non RFC (ANSI)	Permits names that are nonstandard and that do not follow RFC 1123 Internet host naming specifications.
Multibyte (UTF-8)	Permits recognition of characters other than ASCII, including Unicode, which is normally encoded as more than one octet (8 bits) in length.
	With this option, multibyte characters can be transformed and represented using UTF-8 support, which is provided with Windows Server 2003.
	Names encoded in UTF-8 format must not exceed the size limits stated in RFC 2181, which specifies a maximum of 63 octets per label and 255 octets per name. Character count is insufficient to determine size because some UTF-8 characters exceed one octet in length. This option allows for domain names using non-English alphabets.
All Names	Permits any naming conventions.

Despite the flexibility of the UTF-8 name-checking method, you should consider changing the Name Checking option to Strict RFC when your DNS servers perform zone transfers to non-Windows servers that are not UTF-8-aware. Although DNS server implementations that are not UTF-8-aware might be able to accept the transfer of a zone containing UTF-8-encoded names, these servers might not be capable of writing back those names to a zone file or reloading those names from a zone file.

You should use the other two name-checking options, Non RFC and All Names, only when a specific application requires them.

Load Zone Data On Startup

By default, the Load Zone Data On Startup property is set to the From Active Directory And Registry option. Thus, by default, DNS servers in Windows Server 2003 initialize with the settings specified in the Active Directory database and the server registry.

You can also load zone data using two other settings: From Registry and From File. The From Registry option forces the DNS server to initialize by reading parameters stored in the Windows registry. The From File option forces the DNS server to initialize by reading parameters stored in a boot file. The boot file must be a text file named Boot located on the local computer in the %systemroot%\System32 \Dns folder.

When a boot file is used, settings in the file are applied to the server, overriding the settings stored in the registry on the DNS server. However, for parameters that are not configurable using boot file directives, registry defaults (or stored reconfigured server settings) are applied by the DNS Server service.

> **MORE INFO**   **DNS Boot File Structure**   *See the Microsoft Knowledge Base Article 194513, "The Structure of a Domain Name System Boot File." To find this article, go to http://support.microsoft.com and enter the article number in the Search The Knowledge Base text box.*

AGING AND SCAVENGING RESOURCE RECORDS

Traditionally, the DNS administrator manually added or deleted resource records from DNS zone files as required. With dynamic update, individual computers and services are able to automatically add, update, and delete DNS resource records. For example, the Windows Server 2003 and Windows 2000 DNS Client service register their clients' A and **pointer (PTR) resource records** in DNS at start time and every 24 hours thereafter. Dynamic update ensures that the records are up-to-date and guards against accidental deletion of resource records by the DNS administrator.

Over time, stale resource records accumulate in the DNS database. Records become stale, for example, when computers, especially those of mobile users, abnormally disconnect from the network. Stale records provide outdated and inaccurate information to clients, take up unnecessary space, and can possibly degrade server performance. Windows Server 2003 provides a mechanism to remove these records.

Windows Server 2003 adds a time stamp to dynamically added resource records in primary zones where aging and scavenging are enabled. Records added manually are time stamped with a value of zero, which indicates those records should be excluded from the aging and scavenging process. Since **secondary name servers** receive a read-only copy of the zone data from **primary name servers**, only primary zones are eligible to participate in this process. Servers can be configured to perform recurring scavenging operations automatically, or you can initiate a manual and immediate scavenging operation at the server.

▶ **Initiating Scavenging**

To initiate scavenging, follow these steps:

1. Open the DNS management console.

2. In the console tree, right-click the applicable DNS server, and then click Set Aging/Scavenging For All Zones.

3. In the Server Aging/Scavenging Properties dialog box, select the Scavenge Stale Resource Records check box; set one, none, or both of the following; and then click OK:

   ❏ **No-Refresh Interval**   The time between the most recent refresh of a record time stamp and the moment when the time stamp may be refreshed again.

   ❏ **Refresh Interval**   The time between the earliest moment when a record time stamp can be refreshed and the earliest moment when the record can be scavenged. The refresh interval must be longer than the maximum record refresh period.

4. In the Server Aging/Scavenging Confirmation dialog box, select Apply These Settings To The Existing Active Directory–Integrated Zones, and then click OK.

> **CAUTION**   **Proper Configuration of Aging and Scavenging**   By default, the scavenging mechanism is disabled. You should not enable DNS resource record scavenging unless you are absolutely certain that you understand all the parameters and have configured them correctly. Otherwise, you might accidentally configure the server to delete records that it should retain. If a name is accidentally deleted, not only do users fail to resolve queries for that name, but also a different user can create and own that name, even on zones configured for secure dynamic update.

MANAGING THE DNS RESOLVER CACHE

The DNS resolver is a component of the DNS Client service installed by default with Windows Server 2003. It runs within the **SVCHOST process**.

> **MORE INFO**   **What is SVCHOST?**   See Microsoft Knowledge Base Article 250320, "Description of Svchost.exe in Windows 2000." To find this article, go to *http://support.microsoft.com* and enter the article number in the Search The Knowledge Base text box.

To reduce the amount of traffic to the DNS server or servers, the DNS resolver caches resource records obtained from query responses. These resource records are used to resolve repeated client queries and reduce redundant queries to the DNS server. Each entry in the cache has a specified Time to Live (TTL), typically set by the query response. When the TTL expires, the entry is purged from the cache. When the resolver is unable to answer a query using its own cache, the resolver sends the query to one or more DNS servers configured in the TCP/IP properties of the server. If a **Hosts file** is configured on the client, it is preloaded into the resolver cache.

Practice displaying and purging the resolver cache by doing Exercise 4-3, "Displaying and Purging the Resolver Cache," now.

To view the cache, type the following at a command prompt:

```
ipconfig /displaydns
```

To purge the cache, type the following at a command prompt:

```
ipconfig /flushdns
```

SECURING DNS

DNS is an open **protocol** and is therefore vulnerable to attackers. Windows Server 2003 provides the capability to help prevent a successful attack on your DNS infrastructure through the addition of security features.

This section describes common threats to DNS security and how to determine the level of DNS security in your organization. Default security settings and security features also are discussed.

DNS Security Threats

Table 4-5 describes the typical ways in which a DNS infrastructure is threatened by attackers.

Table 4-5 Common DNS Security Threats

Threat	Description
Footprinting	The process by which DNS zone data, including domain names, computer names, and IP addresses for sensitive network resources, is obtained by an attacker. An attacker commonly begins an attack by using this DNS data to diagram, or footprint, a network. For easy identification, DNS domain and computer names typically indicate the function or location of a domain or computer. An attacker takes advantage of these naming conventions to identify the key network resources on the network.
Denial of service	A *denial of service (DoS) attack* is an assault, usually planned, that seeks to disrupt functionality. A DoS attack overwhelms a network resource with bogus requests that cannot be completed. In so doing, it causes the resource to become so busy attempting to respond to the bogus requests that the resource becomes incapable of servicing legitimate requests. In the context of DNS, a DoS attack is one in which an attacker attempts to overload one or more DNS servers by flooding them with recursive queries. This causes the CPU to constantly operate at 100 percent and will render the DNS server unavailable to legitimate requests.
Data modification	An attempt by an attacker (that has likely completed a DNS footprint attack) to use valid IP addresses in IP packets the attacker has created, thereby giving these packets the appearance of coming from a valid IP address in the network. This is commonly called *IP spoofing*. With a valid IP address (an IP address within the IP address range of a subnet), the attacker can gain access to the network and destroy data or conduct other attacks.
Redirection	When an attacker is able to redirect queries for DNS names to servers under the control of the attacker. One method of redirection involves the attempt to pollute the DNS cache of a DNS server with erroneous DNS data that can direct future queries to servers under the control of the attacker. For example, if a query was originally made, for the name example.microsoft.com, and a referral answer provided a record for a name outside of the microsoft.com domain, such as malicious-user.com, the DNS server would use the cached data for malicious-user.com to resolve a query for that name. Redirection can be accomplished whenever an attacker has writable access to DNS data, such as with nonsecure dynamic updates.

DNS Security Levels

DNS security implementations can be grouped into three levels: low, medium, and high. Review the characteristics of each level to determine which level best describes your current DNS security implementation and which characteristics from each implementation should be added to your DNS implementation.

Low-Level Security Low-level security is a standard DNS deployment without any security precautions configured. Only deploy this level of DNS security in network environments where there is no concern for the integrity of your DNS data or in private networks where there is no threat of external connectivity. Low-level security has the following characteristics:

- If connected to the Internet, the DNS infrastructure of your organization is fully exposed.

- Standard DNS resolution is performed by all DNS servers in your network.

- All DNS servers are configured with root hints that point to the root servers for the Internet.

- All DNS servers permit zone transfers to any server.

- All DNS servers are configured to listen on all of their IP addresses.

- Cache pollution prevention is disabled on all DNS servers.

- Nonsecure dynamic update is allowed for all DNS zones.

- User Datagram Protocol (UDP) and TCP/IP port 53 is open on the firewall for your network for both source and destination addresses.

Medium-Level Security   Medium-level security uses the DNS security features available without running DNS servers on domain controllers and storing DNS zones in Active Directory. Medium-level security has the following characteristics:

- If connected to the Internet, the DNS infrastructure of your organization has limited exposure.

- All DNS servers are configured to use forwarders to point to a specific list of internal DNS servers when they cannot resolve names locally.

- All DNS servers limit zone transfers to servers listed in the NS resource records in their zones.

- DNS servers are configured to listen on specified IP addresses.

- Cache pollution prevention is enabled on all DNS servers.

- Dynamic update is not allowed for any DNS zones.

- Internal DNS servers communicate with external DNS servers through the firewall, with a limited list of source and destination addresses allowed.

- External DNS servers in front of your firewall are configured with root hints that point to the root servers for the Internet.

- All Internet name resolution is performed using proxy servers and gateways.

High-Level Security   High-level security uses the same configuration as medium-level security but also uses the security features available when the DNS Server service is running on a domain controller and DNS zones are stored in Active Directory. In addition, high-level security completely eliminates DNS communication with the Internet. This is not a typical configuration, but it is recommended whenever Internet connectivity is not required. The characteristics of high-level security are as follows:

- The DNS infrastructure of your organization has no Internet communication by internal DNS servers.

- Your network uses an internal DNS root and namespace; all authority for DNS zones is internal.

- DNS servers that are configured with forwarders use internal DNS server IP addresses only.

- All DNS servers limit zone transfers to specified IP addresses.

- DNS servers are configured to listen on specified IP addresses.

- Cache pollution prevention is enabled on all DNS servers.

- Internal DNS servers are configured with root hints pointing to the internal DNS servers hosting the root zone for your internal namespace.

- All DNS servers are running on domain controllers. A **discretionary access control list (DACL)** is configured on the DNS Server service to allow only specific individuals to perform administrative tasks on the DNS server.

- All DNS zones are stored in Active Directory. A DACL is configured to allow only specific individuals to create, delete, or modify DNS zones.

- DACLs are configured on DNS resource records to allow only specific individuals to create, delete, or modify DNS data.

- Secure dynamic update is configured for DNS zones except the top-level and root zones, which do not allow dynamic updates at all.

DNS Objects in Windows Server 2003 Active Directory

In addition to the MicrosoftDNS **container object** in the domain partition that is supported in both Windows 2000 and Windows Server 2003, a MicrosoftDNS container is located in every DNS application directory partition. An *application directory partition* is a new type of directory partition in Windows Server 2003 Active Directory. It can be used by applications to store application-specific data that is of interest in a scope that is smaller than the entire forest or domain. This data can be characterized as either changing frequently (dynamic) or having a short useful lifetime (volatile). For example, Windows Server 2003 DNS can use application directory partitions to store dynamically updated DNS zone data on only those domain controllers that are DNS servers rather than on all domain controllers in the domain, as is required for Windows 2000 **Active Directory–integrated zones**.

The MicrosoftDNS container is the parent object for all zones within the domain or the replication scope, as specified by the DNS application directory partition. A user that does not have read and write permissions on this container is not able to update the zone or create zones or records within zones in that partition.

Each DNS zone is represented in Active Directory by a dnsZone object. Zone objects are the children of a MicrosoftDNS object in the domain or application directory partition. The zone object stores configuration information in the dnsProperty attribute. The DACL on the zone object controls record creation in the zone, and the existing records in the zone may inherit these effects. Zone administration, such as modifying zone parameters, requires a user to have FULL CONTROL permissions on the zone object within the MicrosoftDNS container in Active Directory.

All of the record sets that belong to a single DNS domain name are stored in Active Directory in a single dnsNode object. The access control list (ACL) on this object controls client access.

Securing the DNS Server Service

A DNS Server service may run on a member server or on a domain controller. When the service runs on a domain controller, its security options are far more advanced than the options that are available when it runs on a member server.

Securing a DNS Server that Runs on a Member Server   Table 4-6 describes DNS Server service configuration options that have security implications when the DNS Server service is running on a member server or a domain controller.

Table 4-6   **Security-Related DNS Server Service Settings**

Setting	Description
Interfaces	By default, a DNS Server service that is running on a multi-homed computer is configured to listen for DNS queries using all of its IP addresses. Limit the IP addresses that the DNS Server service listens on, to the IP address that its DNS clients configure as their preferred DNS server.
Secure Against Cache Pollution	The Secure Cache Against Pollution option prevents an attacker from successfully polluting the cache of a DNS server with resource records that were not requested by the DNS server. Changing this default setting will reduce the integrity of the responses provided by the DNS Server service.
Disable Recursion	Recursion can be used by attackers to deny the DNS Server service; therefore, if a DNS server in your network is not intended to receive or perform recursive queries, recursion should be disabled. Note that forwarding is recursive.
Root Hints	If you have an internal DNS root in your DNS infrastructure, configure the root hints of internal DNS servers to point to only the DNS servers hosting your root domain and not the DNS servers hosting the Internet root domain. This will prevent your internal DNS servers from sending private information over the Internet when resolving names.

Active Directory Access Control Settings   The DACL used by the DNS Server service when it is running on a domain controller allows you to control the permissions of the Active Directory users and groups that control the DNS Server service.

> **NOTE**   **Availability of Active Directory Security Features**   The Active Directory security features available to the DNS Server service when it is running on domain controllers are not available when the DNS Server service is running on a Windows Server 2003 member server or the Windows Server 2003 Web Server operating system because these configurations do not host Active Directory.

▶ **Setting the DNS Security Settings for the DNS Server Service**

To set the DNS security settings for the DNS Server service, follow these steps:

1. Open the DNS console.

2. In the console tree, right-click the applicable server, and then click Properties.

3. In the Security tab, modify the list of member users or groups that are allowed to administer the DNS server, and reset their permissions as needed.

NOTE   DNS Server Service Permissions   The security settings determine who can administer the DNS Server service, but they do not affect the DACLs for the zones and resource records hosted on the server.

Securing File-Backed DNS Zones

DNS security for file-backed zones involves the administration of NTFS file system permissions on the zone files stored on the Windows Server 2003 member server.

▶ **Setting Permissions on a File-Backed Zone File**

To set permissions on a file-backed zone file, follow these steps:

1. Open Windows Explorer, and then locate the zone file or DNS folder in which the zone file is located (by default, all DNS zone files are stored in %systemroot%\System32\Dns).

2. Right-click the zone file or folder, click Properties, and then click the Security tab.

3. In the file or folder properties window, do one of the following:

   ❑ To set permissions for a group or user that does not appear in the Group Or User Names box, click Add. Type the name of the group or user you want to set permissions for, and then click OK.

   ❑ To change or remove permissions from an existing group or user, click the name of the group or user.

4. While still in the file or folder properties window, do one of the following:

   ❑ To allow or deny a permission, in the Permissions For *Object* box, select the Allow Or Deny check box.

   ❑ To remove the group or user from the Group Or User Names box, click Remove.

Securing Active Directory–Integrated DNS Zones

Securing Active Directory–integrated zones involves the additional security options of secure dynamic update and access control.

By default, the dynamic updates setting is Secure Only. This default setting is the most secure setting because it prevents an attacker from updating DNS zones, but this setting prevents you from taking advantage of the administrative benefits that dynamic updates provides. Secure dynamic updates restrict DNS zone updates to only those computers that are authenticated and joined to the Active Directory domain where the DNS sever is located and to the specific security settings defined in the DACLs for the DNS zone.

▶ **Allowing Only Secure Dynamic Updates**

To allow only secure dynamic updates, follow these steps:

1. Open the DNS console.

2. In the console tree, right-click the applicable zone, and then click Properties.

3. In the General tab, verify that the zone type selected is Active Directory–Integrated.

4. In Dynamic Updates, click Secure Only.

The DACL used by the DNS Server service when it is running on a domain controller allows you to control the permissions for the Active Directory users and groups that control the DNS zone.

▶ **Setting the DNS Security Settings for the DNS Zone**

To set the DNS security settings for the DNS zone, follow these steps:

1. Open the DNS console.

2. In the console tree, right-click the appropriate zone, and then click Properties.

3. In the General tab, verify that the zone type selected is Active Directory–Integrated.

4. In the Security tab, modify the list of member users or groups that are allowed to securely update the zone, and reset their permissions as needed.

Zone Transfer Security

By default, the Windows Server 2003 DNS Server service allows zone information to be transferred only to servers listed in the NS resource records of a zone. This is a secure configuration, but for increased security, this setting should be changed to the option to allow zone transfers only to specified IP addresses.

▶ **Modifying Zone Transfer Settings**

To modify zone transfer settings, follow these steps:

1. Open the DNS console.

2. Right-click the applicable DNS zone, and then click Properties.

3. In the Zone Transfers tab, do one of the following:

   ❏ To disable zone transfers, clear the Allow Zone Transfers check box.

   ❏ To allow zone transfers, select the Allow Zone Transfers check box.

4. If you allowed zone transfers, do one of the following:

   ❏ To allow zone transfers to any server, click To Any Server.

   ❏ To allow zone transfers to only the DNS servers listed in the Name Servers tab, click Only To Servers Listed On The Name Servers.

   ❏ To allow zone transfers only to specific DNS servers, click Only To The Following Servers, and then add the IP address of one or more DNS servers.

   NOTE   Unsecured Zone Transfer Setting   Changing the zone setting to allow zone transfers To Any Server can expose your DNS data to an attacker attempting to footprint your network.

Securing DNS Resource Records

The access control for DNS resource records stored in Active Directory–integrated zones is managed using DACLs. The DACL applied to a resource record allows you to control the permissions for the Active Directory users and groups that may control the DNS resource record.

▶ **Setting the DNS Security Settings for a DNS Resource Record**

To set the DNS security settings for a DNS resource record, follow these steps:

1. Open the DNS console.

2. In the console tree, click the appropriate zone.

3. In the details pane, right-click the record whose security you want to set, and then click Properties.

4. In the Security tab, modify the list of member users or groups that are allowed to securely update the zone, and reset their permissions as needed.

Securing the DNS Client Service

Whenever possible, specify static IP addresses for the preferred and alternate DNS servers used by a DNS client. If a DNS client is configured to obtain its DNS server addresses automatically, it will obtain them from a Dynamic Host Configuration Protocol (DHCP) server. Although this method of obtaining DNS server addresses is secure, it is only as secure as the DHCP server. By configuring DNS clients with static IP addresses for the preferred and alternate DNS servers, you eliminate one possible avenue of attack.

MONITORING AND TROUBLESHOOTING DNS

In this section, two logging tools and the Replication Monitor are introduced. These tools can be used to both monitor and troubleshoot DNS.

Viewing the DNS Events Log

Windows Server 2003 maintains a separate log for DNS Server events that may be viewed from the Event Viewer and from the DNS console, as shown in Figure 4-8.

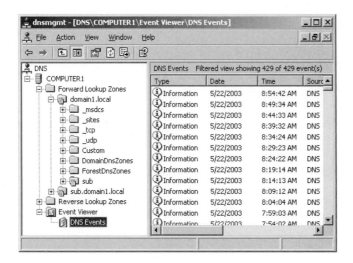

Figure 4-8   Viewing the DNS Events Log

If you have problems with DNS, review the DNS Server Events Log for suspicious events. The graphical user interface (GUI) in Windows Server 2003 has been enhanced (see Figure 4-9) to make it easier to configure the level of logging.

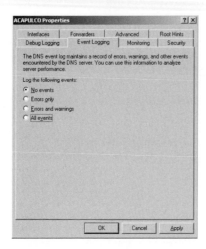

Figure 4-9   Configuring the DNS event logging level

To open the DNS Events Properties dialog box, right-click the DNS Events Log in the DNS console, and then click Properties. The DNS Events Properties dialog box contains a General tab and a Filter tab. The General tab, shown in Figure 4-10, allows you to configure the log display name, log file maximum size, and the action to take when the log reaches its maximum size.

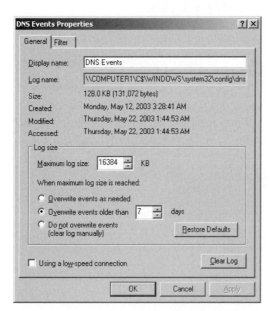

Figure 4-10   The General tab of the DNS Events Properties dialog box

By default, the DNS Events Log displays all DNS events. The Filter tab, shown in Figure 4-11, allows you to restrict events displayed in the DNS Events Log by event type, event source, event ID, date, and other parameters.

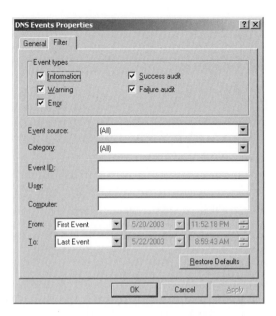

Figure 4-11   Filtering DNS event logging

Troubleshooting DNS with the DNS Debug Log

In addition to the DNS Events Log, the DNS Server service also maintains a separate log used for debugging called the DNS debug log. This *DNS debug log* is a file named Dns.log that is stored in the WINDOWS\System32\Dns folder. In addition, because the native format of the Dns.log file is Rich Text Format (RTF), you should use Microsoft WordPad to view its contents properly. To view the Dns.log file in WordPad, make a copy of the file and then open the copy.

By default, the DNS debug log contains only DNS errors. However, you also can use it to capture DNS packets sent or received by the local DNS server. To enable DNS packet logging, open the DNS Server Properties dialog box and then click the Debug Logging tab. By default, the Log Packets For Debugging check box is cleared and the rest of the options in the tab are unavailable.

However, after you have selected the Log Packets For Debugging check box, as shown in Figure 4-12, you can configure which DNS packets you want captured to the DNS log.

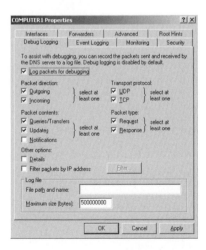

Figure 4-12   Debug logging enabled

In the Debug Logging tab, you can configure the options and values described in Table 4-7.

Table 4-7 **Debug Logging Options, Values, and Descriptions**

Option	Values	Description
Packet Direction	Outgoing	Packets that the DNS server sends are logged in the DNS server log file.
	Incoming	Packets that the DNS server sends are logged in the log file.
Packet Contents	Queries/Transfers	Specifies that packets containing standard queries are logged in the DNS server log file.
	Updates	Specifies that packets containing dynamic updates are logged in the DNS server log file.
	Notifications	Specifies that packets containing notifications are logged in the DNS server log file.
Transport Protocol	UDP	Specifies that packets sent and received over UDP are logged in the DNS server log file.
	TCP	Specifies that packets sent and received over TCP are logged in the DNS server log file.
Packet Type	Request	Specifies that request packets are logged in the DNS server log file.
	Response	Specifies that response packets are logged in the DNS server log file.
Other Options	Details	Logs all packet details. If unchecked, only summary information is logged.
	Filter Packets By IP Address	Provides additional filtering of packets logged in the DNS server log file. This option allows logging of packets that are sent from specific IP addresses to a DNS server or from a DNS server to specific IP addresses.
Log File	File Name	Specifies the name and location of the DNS server log file.
	Log File Maximum Size Limit	Sets the maximum file size for the DNS server log file.

The following output is taken from the Dns.log file and is an example of a query response. Notice the response flag is set to 1 (true) and the PTR resource record in the Answer section.

```
17:19:33 8C8 PACKET  UDP Snd 10.1.1.200     0001 R Q [8085 A DR  NOERROR]
(3)200(1)1(1)1(2)10(7)in-addr(4)arpa(0)
UDP response info at 007AFE40
  Socket = 372
  Remote addr 10.1.1.200, port 4604
  Time Query=157594, Queued=0, Expire=0
  Buf length = 0x0200 (512)
  Msg length = 0x004d (77)
  Message:
    XID       0x0001
    Flags     0x8580
      QR        1 (RESPONSE)
```

```
      OPCODE    0 (QUERY)
      AA        1
      TC        0
      RD        1
      RA        1
      Z         0
      RCODE     0 (NOERROR)
  QCOUNT    1
  ACOUNT    1
  NSCOUNT   0
  ARCOUNT   0
  QUESTION SECTION:
  Offset = 0x000c, RR count = 0
  Name      "(3)200(1)1(1)1(2)10(7)in-addr(4)arpa(0)"
    QTYPE   PTR (12)
    QCLASS  1
  ANSWER SECTION:
  Offset = 0x0029, RR count = 0
  Name      "[C00C](3)200(1)1(1)1(2)10(7)in-addr(4)arpa(0)"
    TYPE    PTR  (12)
    CLASS   1
    TTL     1200
    DLEN    24
    DATA    (8)acapulco(9)contoso01(3)com(0)
  AUTHORITY SECTION:
    empty
  ADDITIONAL SECTION:
    empty
```

CAUTION Enabling DNS Debugging Can Adversely Affect Performance Do not leave DNS debug logging enabled during normal operation because it consumes both processing and hard disk resources. Enable it only when diagnosing and solving DNS problems.

Troubleshooting DNS with Replication Monitor

Replication Monitor (Replmon.exe) is a graphical tool included in the Windows Support Tools that allows you to monitor and troubleshoot Active Directory replication. This feature is essential in monitoring DNS data transfer for Active Directory–integrated zones.

You can use Replication Monitor to perform the following functions:

- Force replication of DNS data throughout various replication scopes.
- Discover when a replication partner fails.
- Display replication topology.
- Poll replication partners and generate individual histories of successful and failed replication events.
- Display changes that have not yet replicated from a given replication partner.
- Monitor replication status of domain controllers from multiple forests.

After you have installed Windows Support Tools, launch Replication Monitor by typing **replmon** at a command prompt (or in the Run dialog box), and then press ENTER. After opening Replication Monitor, you must add at least one server to

monitor. To add a server to monitor, click Monitored Servers, then on the Action
menu, point to Site, click Add Monitored Server, and then follow the wizard
instructions. After adding a server, Replication Monitor looks similar to what is
shown in Figure 4-13.

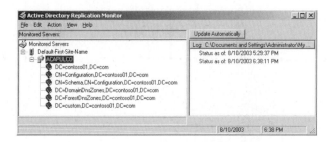

Figure 4-13   Replication Monitor console

After you have added the servers you intend to monitor, you can save this console
configuration as an .ini file and open the file from within Replication Monitor for
subsequent uses.

Directory Partitions and Active Directory–Integrated Zones

For each server listed in the console tree, you can display the Active Directory partitions installed on that server by expanding the associated server icon. Domain
controllers that are DNS servers and that host a single Active Directory–integrated
zone include a replica of five such partitions by default.

The following list describes these five partitions for an Active Directory domain
and DNS zone named contoso01.com:

- **DC=contoso01,DC=com**   The domain partition, which contains objects
  (such as users and computers) associated with the local domain. Each
  domain controller stores a full replica of the domain partition for its local
  domain. In addition, in this partition, DNS data is stored for compatibility
  with Microsoft Windows 2000 DNS servers. To store DNS zone data in the
  domain partition, set the zone replication scope in the DNS console to All
  Domain Controllers In The Domain *domain_name*.

- **CN=Configuration,DC=contoso01,DC=com**   The configuration partition, which contains replication topology and other configuration information that must be replicated throughout the forest. Each domain
  controller in the forest has a replica of the same configuration partition.
  However, this partition does not include DNS zone data.

- **CN=Schema,CD=Configuration,DC=contoso01,DC=com**   The
  schema partition, which contains the classSchema and attributeSchema
  objects that define the types of objects that can exist in the Active Directory forest. Every domain controller in the forest has a replica of the same
  schema partition. However, this partition does not include DNS zone data.

- **DC=DomainDnsZones,DC=contoso01,DC=com**   The built-in application directory partition named DomainDnsZones, which is replicated
  among all Windows Server 2003 domain controllers that are also DNS
  servers in a particular Active Directory domain. To store DNS zone data

in the DomainDnsZones partition, set the zone replication scope in the DNS console to All DNS Servers In The Active Directory Domain *Domain_Name*.

- **DC=ForestDnsZones,DC=contoso01,DC=com**   The built-in application directory partition named ForestDnsZones, which is replicated among all Windows Server 2003 domain controllers that are also DNS servers in an Active Directory forest. To store DNS zone data in the ForestDnsZones partition, set the zone replication scope in the DNS console to All DNS Servers In The Active Directory Forest.

You also can create custom application directory partitions and enlist the domain controllers you choose to store a replica of that partition. In Figure 4-13, Replication Monitor displays such an application directory partition named Custom. To store DNS zone data in a custom application directory partition, set the zone replication scope in the DNS console to All Domain Controllers Specified In The Scope Of The Following Application Directory Partition. Then select the desired application directory partition from the drop-down list.

To find out which Active Directory partition is used to store data for a particular DNS zone, you can either check the DNS zone properties in the DNS console or use the Dnscmd /zoneinfo *ZoneName* command, providing the name of the zone for the *ZoneName* placeholder.

To determine the zone replication scope for a domain named domain1.local, type the following command at a command prompt: **dnscmd /zoneinfo domain1 .local**. Then, look for an entry named Directory Partition in the output. To change zone replication scope, use the /zonechangedirectorypartition switch followed by any of the following switches, as appropriate:

- /domain (for all DNS servers in the domain)
- /forest (for all DNS servers in the forest)
- /legacy (for all domain controllers in the domain)

For example, to set the replication scope of a zone named domain1.local to all DNS servers in the domain, type the following command: **dnscmd /zonechange-directorypartition domain1.local /domain**. If you have proper credentials, you can even use these commands remotely. In this case, simply specify the server name after *dnscmd*.

Forcing Active Directory–Integrated Zone Replication

Once you know the directory partition in which DNS zone information is stored, you can force replication for that zone in Replication Monitor. This procedure can help resolve name resolution problems caused by outdated zone data.

To force Active Directory–integrated zone replication, right-click the appropriate partition in the Replication Monitor console tree, and select Synchronize This Directory Partition With All Servers. The Synchronizing Naming Context With Replication Partners dialog box shown in Figure 4-14 opens.

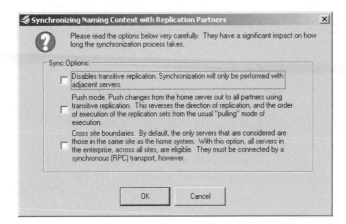

Figure 4-14   Forcing replication

When forcing a replication, you can use this dialog box to replicate only to neighboring servers, to replicate out to all servers on the local site, or to replicate to all servers across sites.

Searching for Replication Errors

DNS errors in Active Directory–integrated zones can result from faulty zone replication. You can use Replication Monitor to search the domain for such replication errors. To do so, on the Action menu, select Domain, and then select Search Domain Controllers For Replication Errors, as shown in Figure 4-15.

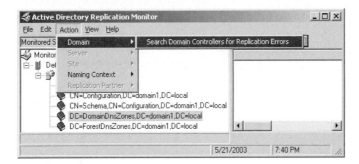

Figure 4-15   Searching for replication errors

As an alternative, you can configure Replication Monitor to send an e-mail to an administrator after a specified number of replication failures. To perform this task, on the View menu, select Options. In the Active Directory Replication Monitor Options dialog box, select the Notify When Replication Fails After This Number Of Attempts option, and then specify the number of failures that you want to trigger an e-mail. Finally, select the Send Mail To check box, and specify an e-mail address in the associated text box.

SUMMARY

- Use tools such as Nslookup, DNSLint, and Dnscmd to manage DNS servers. Use Nslookup in command-line mode or interactive mode to examine the contents of DNS zone files. Use DNSLint to verify the consistency of a particular set of DNS records on multiple DNS servers. Use Dnscmd to help automate the management and updates of existing DNS server configurations.

- DNS and WINS integration is the process in which DNS uses WINS to resolve names to IP addresses. DNS is used to resolve host names and services to IP addresses, and WINS is used to resolve NetBIOS names to IP addresses.

- Use advanced DNS Server settings to disable recursion, increase server interoperability, increase data integrity, and reorder name list responses using round robin and netmask ordering. You also can use advanced settings to secure the cache against pollution, configure name checking, specify from where to load zone data, and enable automatic scavenging of stale records.

- The DNS Client service maintains a local cache, which you can display and purge using Ipconfig.exe.

- Understand various security threats to DNS and prepare for them by assessing the security level of your organization. Based on your assessment, make appropriate configuration changes to restrict dynamic updates, zone transfers, access to file-backed zones, resource records, and the DNS Client service.

- You can use both the DNS Events Log and DNS debug log to monitor and troubleshoot DNS. For example, you can use the DNS debug log to log all dynamic updates received by the server.

EXERCISES

IMPORTANT **Completing All Exercises** If you plan to do any of the textbook exercises in this chapter, you must do all of the exercises in the chapter to return the computer to its original state for the associated Lab Manual labs.

Exercise 4-1: Displaying DNS Zone Information Using Dnscmd

1. Open a command prompt.
2. At the command prompt, type **dnscmd localhost /zoneinfo *zone_name*** (where *zone_name* represents a forward or reverse lookup zone name) and press ENTER.

Exercise 4-2: Integrating DNS and WINS

1. Open the DNS console.
2. In the console tree, right-click the applicable zone, and then click Properties.

3. In the Zone Properties dialog box, click the appropriate tab:

   ❑ Click the WINS tab if the zone is a forward lookup zone.

   ❑ Click the WINS-R tab if the zone is a reverse lookup zone.

4. In the appropriate WINS tab, select the applicable check box to enable the use of WINS resolution:

   ❑ Use WINS Forward Lookup if the zone is a forward lookup zone.

   ❑ Use WINS-R Lookup if the zone is a reverse lookup zone.

5. In the WINS tab, type the IP address of a WINS server that will be used for the resolution of names that are not found in DNS. For a reverse lookup zone, in the WINS-R tab, type a name in the Domain To Append To Returned Name field, if applicable.

6. In the WINS tab, click Add to add the server IP address. For a reverse lookup zone, in the WINS-R tab, click Use WINS-R Lookup.

7. If additional WINS server addresses are used for a forward lookup zone during WINS lookup referral, repeat steps 5 and 6 as needed to add those server addresses to the list.

8. In either the WINS tab or the WINS-R tab, select Do Not Replicate This Record for this WINS record, if applicable.

   CAUTION   **Do Not Replicate WINS Locator Records**   If you are replicating zone data to secondary zones on third-party DNS servers that do not recognize the WINS or WINS-R records, select the Do Not Replicate This Record check box. This prevents the WINS locator records from being replicated to other servers during zone transfers. You would select this option when performing zone transfers to BIND servers, because BIND will not recognize WINS locator records.

9. Optionally, in either the WINS or the WINS-R tab, click Advanced to adjust both the Cache Time-Out value and the Lookup Time-Out value.

10. Optionally, in the WINS-R tab, in the Advanced dialog box, select Submit DNS Domain As NetBIOS Scope.

11. In the *Zone* Properties dialog box, click OK.

Exercise 4-3: Displaying and Purging the Resolver Cache

1. Open a command prompt.

2. At the command prompt, type **ipconfig /displaydns** and press ENTER.

3. At the command prompt, type **ping instructor01** and press ENTER.

4. At the command prompt, type **ipconfig /displaydns** and press ENTER.

5. Scroll through the output to locate the London record.

6. At the command prompt, type **ipconfig /flushdns** and press ENTER.

   A message is displayed saying the DNS resolver cache was successfully flushed.

7. At the command prompt, type **ipconfig /displaydns** and press ENTER.

   Note that the London record is no longer in the DNS resolver cache.

REVIEW QUESTIONS

1. What is the function of round robin in DNS?

2. Which feature takes priority—round robin or netmask ordering?

3. Which of the following are valid reasons to monitor the TTL settings on your DNS servers? Choose all that apply.

   a. Query traffic increases as DNS clients request information that has expired from their cache.

   b. DNS clients may be caching outdated records.

   c. DNS clients may not be able to resolve host names.

   d. Query traffic decreases as DNS clients request information that has expired from their cache.

4. What type of test query can be run from the Monitoring tab of the DNS server properties page?

   a. Recursive query

   b. Simple query

   c. Verbose query

   d. Interval query

5. Which of the following approaches provides the best early warning of a DNS service failure?

   a. Create an alert based on the standard performance counters, and set the threshold to notify you if the counters exceed 95 percent of the recommended threshold.

   b. Create an alert based on the counters that you decide are appropriate indicators of a failure, and set the threshold to notify you when it is 10 percent below the baseline.

   c. Create an alert based on the standard counters, and set the threshold to notify you if the counters exceed 75 percent of the recommended threshold.

   d. Create an alert based on the counters that you decide are appropriate indicators of a failure, and set the threshold to notify you when it is 10 percent above the baseline.

6. You are a systems administrator for Contoso, Ltd. Contoso is planning its DNS zones, and you have been asked to recommend the best way to configure the zones on the company's Microsoft Windows Server 2003 computers.

   You recommend using Active Directory–integrated zones. Why do you recommend this configuration?

   Choose all answers that apply.

   a. DNS data is replicated with Active Directory.

   b. You can configure secure dynamic updates.

   c. The DNS load will be shared because the other domain controllers will become secondary DNS servers.

   d. You can configure a replication scope.

7. You are the administrator for Contoso, Ltd., and have updated the IP address for a host by using the DNS console. Assuming it exists, which of the following types of resource records is associated with the host record and must also be updated?

   a. A resource record

   b. MX resource record

   c. NS resource record

   d. PTR resource record

   e. SOA resource record

   f. SRV resource record

8. A client computer on the internal network of Contoso, Ltd., is unable to connect to a file server. You verify the file server is running and are able to connect to it using another client computer on the same subnet. You suspect the client computer that cannot connect has outdated information in its local cache. Which of the following actions would fix the issue?

   a. At the client computer, run the Ipconfig /flushdns command.

   b. At the file server, run the Ipconfig /flushdns command.

   c. At the file server, run Nslookup.

   d. At the file server, stop and start the DNS Client service.

CASE SCENARIOS

Case Scenario 4-1: Enabling Network Users to Connect to Internet Host Names

You are the network administrator for Contoso, Ltd. The Contoso network consists of a single domain, contoso.com, which is protected from the Internet by a firewall. The firewall runs on a computer named NS1 that is directly connected to the Internet. NS1 also runs the DNS Server service, and its firewall allows DNS traffic to pass between the Internet and the DNS Server service on NS1 but not between the Internet and the internal network. The DNS Server service on NS1 is configured to use round robin. Behind the firewall, two computers are running Windows Server 2003—NS2 and NS3, which host a primary and secondary DNS server, respectively, for the contoso.com zone.

Users on the company network report that, although they use host names to connect to computers on the local private network, they cannot use host names to connect to Internet destinations, such as *www.microsoft.com*.

Which of the following actions requires the least amount of administrative effort to enable network users to connect to Internet host names?

   a. Disable recursion on NS2 and NS3.

   b. Enable netmask ordering on NS1.

   c. Configure NS2 and NS3 to use NS1 as a forwarder.

   d. Disable round robin on NS1.

Case Scenario 4-2: Implementing DNS Updates

You are the system administrator for Contoso, Ltd. The company has grown rapidly over the past year, and currently Contoso is using only a single DNS zone. Recently, the Marketing department has made several requests for DNS changes that were delayed. Users would like the ability to make their own DNS updates.

What should you do to try to address this problem?

a. Create a secondary server in the Marketing department so that users can manage their own zone.

b. Delegate the marketing domain to a DNS server in the Marketing department.

c. Place a domain controller running DNS in the Marketing department so that people in the department can make changes.

d. Upgrade the network infrastructure to improve network performance.

CHAPTER 5
NETWORK SECURITY

Upon completion of this chapter, you will be able to:

- Describe the network security **protocols** used for authorization.

- Assign **user rights** and understand the difference between a user right and a **permission**.

- List and describe the security configuration tools included with Microsoft Windows Server 2003, and understand how the security configuration tools are used to configure security settings. Analyze system security in your Microsoft Windows 2000 network.

- Describe and implement the **principle of least privilege**.

- Implement security baseline settings and audit security settings using security templates.

- Use the **Encrypting File System (EFS)** to encrypt and decrypt files using the Windows graphical user interface (GUI) and the command line.

- Identify and run the Microsoft Baseline Security Analyzer (MBSA) and use the results to increase the level of security on your computers.

Managing and maintaining security are complex tasks; however, several Windows Server 2003 tools make your job easier. As a network professional, you must have a fundamental understanding of how Windows Server 2003 implements security to protect your networks. This means you must understand key security concepts, such as permissions, rights, and the principle of least privilege. In addition to understanding the fundamentals of Windows Server 2003 security, you should also know which tools and procedures could help you effectively secure your network. The tools discussed in this chapter are the Security Configuration And Analysis snap-in, the Security Templates snap-in, MBSA, and the Group Policy snap-in. Procedures include assigning user rights, creating a security baseline, encrypting and decrypting files, and using security templates to apply security policies.

IMPLEMENTING NETWORK SECURITY PROTOCOLS

Network security protocols are used to manage and secure authentication, authorization, confidentiality, integrity, and nonrepudiation. In a Windows Server 2003 network, the major protocols used are **NTLM**, **Internet Protocol Security (IPSec)**, and various subprotocols. Other network communication protocols and security settings support and protect the use of these protocols. Table 5-1 lists the security paradigms and the protocols that support them.

Table 5-1   Network Security Protocol Paradigms

Paradigm	Purpose	Protocols
Authentication	To prove you are who you say you are	Kerberos and NTLM (NTLM is not available by default, but can be configured.)
Authorization	To determine what you can do on the network after you have been authenticated	Kerberos and NTLM
Confidentiality	To keep data secret	**Encryption** components of Kerberos, NTLM, and IPSec (to secure communications other than authentication)
Integrity	To ensure that data received are the same as data sent	Components of Kerberos, NTLM, and IPSec
Nonrepudiation	To determine exactly who sent and received a message	Kerberos and IPSec

This chapter focuses on authorization and confidentiality. Chapter 6, "Securing Network Traffic by Using IPSec," discusses IPSec, which is used for confidentiality, integrity, and nonrepudiation.

MANAGING USER RIGHTS

It is important for you to understand the role user rights and permissions play in authorization and to distinguish the two concepts from each other. *User rights* determine what a user can and cannot do on the system. *Permissions* determine which level of access, if any, a user has to an object. The types of permissions vary by object. Permissions you can grant to use a printer are different from permissions you grant to access files and folders. User rights generally apply to the system as a whole, whereas permissions apply to an individual object. Examples of user rights include the following: backing up files, logging on locally to a computer, and changing the server time. An example of a permission is the Read permission, which, when granted to a user accessing a folder, enables that user to view folder and file attributes. Having only the Read permission does not allow the user to change or delete the folder.

Rights are divided into two types: privileges and logon rights. *Privileges* include the right to run security audits or the right to force a remote system to shut down. *Logon rights* grant the right to connect to a computer. Rights are automatically assigned to the built-in groups in Windows Server 2003, although they can be assigned to individual users as well. To make the administration of rights easier, assign them to groups rather than to individuals. If group membership defines the rights, rights can be removed from a user by simply removing the user from a group. For example, the Backup Operators group is granted the right to back up the system. Consequently, members of the Backup Operators group have this right. If a user is no longer responsible for backing up the system, remove the user from the group. Because rights are assigned to the group rather than to the individual, the removal of the individual from the group ensures that the user no longer derives rights from that group to back up the system, shut down the computer, and so on. The user retains rights to groups for which he or she is a member. If right assignment is applied systematically across groups, you can simply determine a user's rights by examining the user's group memberships.

Users have the rights of the groups to which they are a member. Rights are cumulative. For example, if a user is a member of both the Account Operators and the Backup Operators groups, that user possesses all the rights granted to both groups.

Common User Rights

Common user rights include the following:

- **Allow Log On Locally**   Allows a user to log on to the local computer or to the domain from the computer console

- **Change The System Time**   Allows a user to set the time of the internal clock of a computer

- **Shut Down The System**   Enables a user to shut down a local computer

- **Access This Computer From The Network**   Enables a user to access a computer running Windows Server 2003 from any other computer on the network

- **Allow Log On Through Terminal Services**   Allows a user to log on using a Terminal Services client

The Differences Between Permissions and User Rights

As discussed previously, permissions define the type of access granted to a user or group for an object or object property. For example, you can grant the Read and Write permissions to the Accounting group for a folder named Timesheets. This means that users in the Accounting group can access the Timesheets folder, view its contents, and modify its content.

You can grant permissions to secured objects such as files, printers, other objects in **Active Directory** directory service, and objects in the registry. You can grant permissions to users, security groups, or computers. As with user rights, it is a good practice to grant permissions to groups rather than to individuals.

You can grant permissions to objects for

- Groups, users, and special identities in the domain

- Groups and users in any trusted domains

- Local groups and users on the computer where the object resides

To grant permissions for individual files and folders, Windows Server 2003 requires the **NTFS file system**. The **file allocation table (FAT)** and **FAT32** file systems do not support file-level security. Both NTFS and FAT/FAT32 file systems support security on shared folder resources and network printers.

User Rights Assigned to Built-In Groups

By default, Windows Server 2003 assigns certain rights to built-in groups. The built-in groups include local groups, groups in the Builtin container, and groups in the Users container.

Default User Rights Assigned to Local Groups

User rights are assigned by default to local groups, as listed in Table 5-2.

Table 5-2 **Local Groups and Their User Rights**

Group	User Rights
Administrators	■ Access This Computer From The Network
	■ Adjust Memory Quotas For A Process
	■ Allow Log On Locally
	■ Allow Log On Through Terminal Services
	■ Back Up Files And Directories
	■ Bypass Traverse Checking
	■ Change The System Time
	■ Create A Pagefile
	■ Debug Programs
	■ Enable Computer And User Accounts To Be Trusted For Delegation
	■ Force Shutdown From A Remote System
	■ Increase Scheduling Priority
	■ Load And Unload Device Drivers
	■ Manage Auditing And Security Log
	■ Modify Firmware Environment Variables
	■ Perform Volume Maintenance Tasks
	■ Profile Single Process
	■ Profile System Performance
	■ Remove Computer From Docking Station
	■ Restore Files And Directories
	■ Shut Down The System
	■ Take Ownership Of Files Or Other Objects
Backup Operators	■ Access This Computer From The Network
	■ Allow Log On Locally
	■ Back Up Files And Directories
	■ Bypass Traverse Checking
	■ Restore Files And Directories
	■ Shut Down The System

(continued)

Table 5-2   **Local Groups and Their User Rights**

Group	User Rights
Power Users	■ Access This Computer From The Network ■ Allow Log On Locally ■ Bypass Traverse Checking ■ Change The System Time ■ Profile Single Process ■ Remove Computer From Docking Station ■ Shut Down The System
Remote Desktop Users	■ Allow Log On Through Terminal Services
Users	■ Access This Computer From The Network ■ Allow Log On Locally ■ Bypass Traverse Checking

User Rights Assigned to the Builtin Container

The Builtin container is created by default and contains the Builtin local security groups such as Administrators, Backup Operators, and Guests. The following user rights are assigned to groups in the Builtin container, as listed in Table 5-3.

Table 5-3   **Groups in the Builtin Container and Their User Rights**

Group	User Rights
Account Operators	■ Allow Log On Locally ■ Shut Down The System
Administrators	■ Access This Computer From The Network ■ Adjust Memory Quotas For A Process ■ Back Up Files And Directories ■ Bypass Traverse Checking ■ Change The System Time ■ Create A Pagefile ■ Debug Programs ■ Enable Computer And User Accounts To Be Trusted For Delegation ■ Force A Shutdown From A Remote System ■ Increase Scheduling Priority ■ Load And Unload Device Drivers ■ Allow Log On Locally ■ Manage Auditing And Security Log ■ Modify Firmware Environment Values ■ Profile Single Process ■ Profile System Performance ■ Remove Computer From Docking Station ■ Restore Files And Directories ■ Shut Down The System ■ Take Ownership Of Files Or Other Objects

(continued)

Table 5-3   **Groups in the Builtin Container and Their User Rights** *(continued)*

Group	User Rights
Backup Operators	■ Back Up Files And Directories
	■ Allow Log On Locally
	■ Restore files and directories
	■ Shut Down The System
Pre–Windows 2000 Compatible Access	■ Access This Computer From The Network
	■ Bypass Traverse Checking
Print Operators	■ Allow Log On Locally
	■ Shut Down The System
Server Operators	■ Back Up Files And Directories
	■ Change The System Time
	■ Force Shutdown From A Remote System
	■ Allow Log On Locally
	■ Restore Files And Directories
	■ Shut Down The System

User Rights Assigned to the Users Container

The following user rights are assigned to groups in the Users container, as listed in Table 5-4.

Table 5-4   **Groups in the User Container and Their User Rights**

Group	User Rights
Domain Admins	■ Access This Computer From The Network
	■ Adjust Memory Quotas For A Process
	■ Back Up Files And Directories
	■ Bypass Traverse Checking
	■ Change The System Time
	■ Create A Pagefile
	■ Debug Programs
	■ Enable Computer And User Accounts To Be Trusted For Delegation
	■ Force A Shutdown From A Remote System
	■ Increase Scheduling Priority
	■ Load And Unload Device Drivers
	■ Allow Log On Locally
	■ Manage Auditing And Security Log
	■ Modify Firmware Environment Values
	■ Profile Single Process
	■ Profile System Performance
	■ Remove Computer From Docking Station
	■ Restore Files And Directories
	■ Shut Down The System
	■ Take Ownership Of files Or Other Objects

(continued)

Table 5-4   **Groups in the User Container and Their User Rights**

Group	User Rights
Enterprise Admins (this group only appears in the forest root domain)	■ Access This Computer From The Network ■ Adjust Memory Quotas For A Process ■ Back Up Files And Directories ■ Bypass Traverse Checking ■ Change The System Time ■ Create A Pagefile ■ Debug Programs ■ Enable Computer And User Accounts To Be Trusted For Delegation ■ Force Shutdown From A Remote System ■ Increase Scheduling Priority ■ Load And Unload Device Drivers ■ Allow Log On Locally ■ Manage Auditing And Security Log ■ Modify Firmware Environment Values ■ Profile Single Process ■ Profile System Performance ■ Remove Computer From Docking Station ■ Restore Files And Directories ■ Shut Down The System ■ Take Ownership Of Files Or Other Objects

MORE INFO   *User Rights and Service Account Information*   *See Microsoft Knowledge Base article 325349, "HOW TO: Grant Users Rights to Manage Services in Windows Server 2003." To find this article, go to http://support.microsoft.com and enter the article number in the Search The Knowledge Base text box.*

How to Assign User Rights

In a domain, the easiest way to assign rights is at the domain level using **Group Policy**. Use Active Directory Users And Computers to edit the Group Policy for the domain. For example, suppose you want to assign a set of experienced users the Add Workstations to Domain right. You could create a group called Add Workstations, add those users to the group, and assign the Add Workstations To Domain right to the group. If you do this, each person in the Add Workstations group obtains the right to add workstations to the domain. Typically, administrators add users or groups to built-in groups for which they have already preassigned rights. In some circumstances, a built-in group contains too many or too few rights for a particular user, so you must either create a new group or manually assign rights to this user. To assign rights to users or groups, you add a user or group to the User Rights Assignment policy as described in the following procedure.

> ▶ **Assigning User Rights**
>
> To assign user rights, follow these steps:
>
> 1. Click Start, point to Administrative Tools, and then click Domain Controller Security Policy.
>
> 2. In the console tree, expand Local Policies, and then click User Rights Assignment.
>
> 3. In the details pane, double-click a policy.
>
> 4. Using the properties dialog box of the selected user right, add or remove a group to a user right as needed.

Practice assigning user rights by completing Exercise 5-1, "Assigning User Rights," now.

ADMINISTERING SECURITY PRACTICES

In an enterprise environment, maintaining security can be a daunting task. Windows Server 2003 offers a large number of security features that include an even larger number of security policies and attribute settings that must be configured. Although the large number of features and settings provides a high level of control, it also can make consistently applying an organization's security policy very difficult. The good news is that if you follow practices, such as creating baselines and applying the principle of least privilege, you can ease the pain of administration and still protect your network. This section explains how to do this.

Creating Baselines to Identify Possible Security Events

It is important that you identify the roles each of the computers in your organization fills, and then use those roles to develop security templates to secure each computer. For example, you can create a baseline of security for all of the computers in your organization, no matter what their role. Then, you apply incremental templates specific to those roles, such as a template for database servers, mail servers, file and print servers, and so on. An *incremental template* contains only the settings that are necessary to further secure a server based on its role. The incremental template is combined with the baseline role to provide role-specific security settings. Security templates are discussed in the "Using Security Templates" section later in this chapter.

A security baseline helps you to efficiently and consistently apply security settings across your organization. To help determine whether your security settings are effective, you should enable auditing. *Auditing* is a means by which you can see an attack in progress or by which you can identify a pattern of attack that has occurred over time. For example, you can set the audit policy to create an event each time a logon attempt fails. This would alert you to a hacker who attempts to gain access to the Administrator account by guessing the password. To determine whether this event has occurred, you must view the security audit log.

Viewing and Maintaining the Security Audit Log

The security log details audit information for events specified in your audit policy. Each time an auditable event occurs, it is added to the log file where it can be filtered, sorted, searched, or exported. The security log, along with the application and system logs, can be accessed from **Event Viewer** and can be found in the Computer Management console tree by expanding System Tools, Event Viewer, and then clicking Security.

Each entry in the log contains information about the audited event, including whether the attempt failed or succeeded, the date and time of the event, the event category and ID, and the audited user and computer. Additional information for each entry (shown in Figure 5-1) can be obtained by double-clicking the entry.

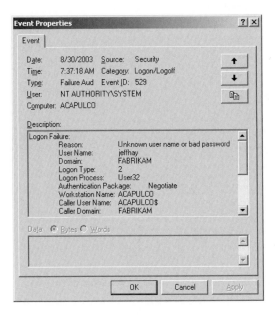

Figure 5-1   Details of a security event

The security log has configurable attributes to define its maximum size. If you audit the system for security-related events, be sure to set the log file large enough to capture the events and to avoid missing events because the log file has reached its maximum size. In addition to the maximum-size attribute, each log file has three options for when the maximum log size is reached, as shown in Figure 5-2 and the following list.

Figure 5-2   Event log size options

- **Overwrite Events As Needed**   If your maximum log file is too small relative to the number of events being logged, you will not be able to see much of the history of events.

- **Overwrite Events Older Than *x* Days**   This option prevents events that are less than a certain number of days (*x*) old from being deleted. Although this ensures a certain number of days of history, it also can result in a full log or the inability to record new events.

Practice setting
an audit policy
and viewing a
security event
by doing
Exercise 5-2,
"Viewing an
Event," now.

■ **Do Not Overwrite Events (Clear Log Manually)**   This option provides
the most history, but also prevents new events from being written to the
log after the log fills.

After reviewing the security log, you can archive it using Event Viewer. Right-click
Security, and then click Save Log File As. Choose a path and file name for the log,
and then click Save.

Applying the Principle of Least Privilege

As you design security policy and grant user rights and permissions, you should
apply the principle of least privilege. This principle states that no user or object
(such as a service) should have more privileges or access to information and
resources than is absolutely necessary.

Applying this principle means that users are thoughtfully placed in groups with
rights and permissions that match each user's responsibilities and authority. It also
means that you have to review rights and permissions regularly to ensure that users
receive the appropriate level of rights or permissions.

The principle of least privilege also applies to system administrators. Although a
system administrator requires access to the entire system, he or she does not
require the same level of access for most day-to-day operations. Logging on as a
user with unlimited access to the system poses a serious security risk to the organization. An administrator logged on with unlimited permissions, who unknow-
ingly launches a malicious program, has far greater potential to damage the system
than a user who is logged on but has limited rights and permissions. For this reason, system administrators should apply the principle of least privilege by using a
user account with limited permissions and by using Administrator privileges only
when absolutely necessary.

One way to accomplish this is by using the Run As feature. The Run As feature can
be used through the context menu, when starting a program (see Figure 5-3),
directly from the command line, or by creating a shortcut.

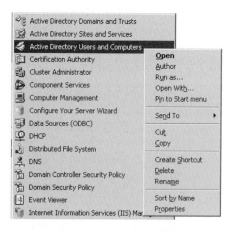

Figure 5-3   Using the Run As feature

The following procedure lists four examples of shortcuts to commonly used administrative tools and instructions for how to create them.

▶ **Creating Shortcuts Using the Run As Command**

To create a shortcut using the Run As command, follow these steps:

1. Right-click the desktop, point to New, and then click Shortcut.

2. In Type The Location Of The Item, type **runas** and the command parameters you want to use. See Table 5-5 for examples.

Table 5-5   **Run As Examples**

To Create a Shortcut to	Target	Description
A command prompt with administrator credentials	**runas /user:*computer-name*\administrator *cmd***	The title bar of the command prompt window indicates the credentials under which the command prompt is running.
Computer Management console with administrator credentials	**runas /user:*computer-name*\administrator "mmc %windir%\ system32\comp-mgmt.msc"**	The Computer Management window provides no indication of the credentials under which it is running. This can cause confusion when you start two or more Computer Management windows in different security contexts.
Active Directory Users And Computers with domain administrator credentials	**runas /user:*domain-name*\administrator "mmc %windir%\ system32\dsa.msc"**	The Active Directory Users And Computers window provides no indication of the credentials under which it is running. This can cause confusion when you start two or more Active Directory Users And Computers windows in different security contexts.
Active Directory Users And Computers in another forest	**runas /netonly /user: *domainname*\UserName "mmc dsa.msc"**	The Active Directory Users And Computers window provides no indication of the credentials under which it is running. This can cause confusion when you start two or more Active Directory Users And Computers windows in different security contexts.

3. Click Next, type a name for the shortcut, and then click Finish.

> **NOTE   The Secondary Logon Service and the Run As Command**   For the Run As command to function, the Secondary Logon service must be running and your credentials must be accepted; Run As will not work with smart cards.

Least Privilege Guidelines

A number of helpful guidelines for applying the principle of least privilege are available, such as the following:

■ Group users by role so that privileges and permissions can be granted by role.

- Configure access control lists (ACLs) for files, folders, registry keys, directory objects, and printers to allow only the precise access a group of users needs.

- Physically protect servers. Allow access only to authorized personnel, and screen this authorization.

- Review audit logs and other logs to find ways to restrict access.

- Use Web proxies to limit user access to external resources.

- Use firewalls to limit access to internal networks.

USING SECURITY TEMPLATES

To manage the large number of security options and configuration settings available to you, Windows Server 2003 provides security templates. Without security templates, it is nearly impossible to manage the thousands of possible settings available for each computer, each role that a computer plays, and the combined roles and settings.

A *security template* is a configuration file that contains all the security attributes of a system. With a single interface, an administrator can generate a security template or a set of templates that reflects the company's security policy as it relates to a particular computer or set of computers and then apply it to a local computer or import it into a **Group Policy Object (GPO)** in Active Directory. When you incorporate the template into a GPO, all computers affected by that object receive the template settings.

Running the Security Templates Snap-In

Security templates can be created and modified with the Security Templates snap-in of the Microsoft Management Console (MMC). To add the snap-in to the MMC, do the following:

1. Click Start, click Run, in the Open box type **mmc,** and then click OK.

2. On the File menu, click Add/Remove Snap-In.

3. In the Add/Remove Snap-In dialog box, click Add.

4. In the Add Standalone Snap-In window, click Security Templates, click Add, and then click Close.

5. In the Add/Remove Snap-In dialog box, click OK.

   The Security Templates snap-in is added to Console Root in the console tree.

6. In the console tree, expand Security Templates and the %systemroot% \Security\Templates folder to display an initial list of templates. These are predefined templates that can be customized for an organization's specific needs. When a new template is created or an existing one is copied, it is added to this list. Select any one of these preloaded policies, and the right pane of the console displays the security areas available for configuration (see Figure 5-4).

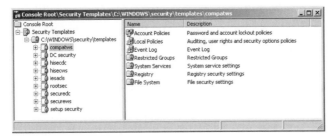

Figure 5-4   Predefined security templates

Each template in the list represents a single .inf file. The snap-in is an interface for modifying these security template files. The files can be found in the following path: %systemroot%\Security\Templates. The following is a small excerpt from the Securews template (Securews.inf), which shows the Account Policies area:

```
[System Access]
;------------------------------------------------------------------------
------------------------
;Account    Policies -  Password Policy
;------------------------------------------------------------------------
------------------------
MinimumPasswordAge = 2
MaximumPasswordAge = 42
MinimumPasswordLength = 8
PasswordComplexity = 1
PasswordHistorySize = 24
ClearTextPassword = 0
LSAAnonymousNameLookup = 0
EnableGuestAccount = 0
```

Examining Template Policies

Each template contains attribute settings for the seven configurable areas of security in Windows Server 2003. Double-click a security area in the right pane of the console or expand the console tree in the left pane to display the specific sections. The sections are as follows:

- **Account Policies**   The Account Policies area includes policies pertaining to user accounts. It contains Password Policy, Account Lockout Policy, and Kerberos Policy.

- **Local Policies**   The Local Policies area includes policies pertaining to who has local or network access to the computer and how events are audited. This area contains Audit Policy, User Rights Assignment, and Security Options.

- **Event Log**   The Event Log area contains attributes that determine how the application, security, and system event logs behave. Log attributes include Maximum Size and Access Restriction. Event logs can be viewed in Event Viewer.

- **Restricted Groups**   The Restricted Groups security setting is for adding members to built-in user groups, which have predefined capabilities, or to other administrator-defined groups that might be privileged.

- **System Services**   The System Services area includes security attributes of all system services on the local computer. System services include file services, print services, network services, and application-specific services, such as Microsoft Exchange System Attendant.

- **Registry**   The Registry area contains security attributes for existing registry keys, including auditing information and the access permissions.

- **File System**   The File System area allows you to configure access permissions and auditing of specific directories and files on the local system.

Using Predefined Templates

The predefined templates supplied by Windows Server 2003 can be used as is, or they can be customized to conform to a more rigorous security requirement. These templates span a range of security levels and represent typical security scenarios for the different types of computers found in a system: workstations, servers, and domain controllers. Table 5-6 shows some of the predefined security templates; they are categorized by security level.

Table 5-6   **Some Predefined Security Templates**

Security Level	Template Name	Description
Secure	securews	Secure workstation or server template
	securedc	Secure domain controller template
Highly secure	hisecws	Highly secure workstation or server template
	hisecdc	Highly secure domain controller template
Compatible	compatws	Compatible workstation or server template
Out of the box	setup security	Out-of-the-box default settings template

Missing from the table are the basic security templates that were included with Microsoft Windows 2000 Server. These templates were removed to ensure that Windows Server 2003 is more secure. In Windows Server 2003, you must choose from more secure (and hence safer) security templates.

Secure Security Templates

Two security templates that enforce a higher level of security are provided: one for the domain controller and one that can be applied to a workstation or server. The Securews and Securedc templates provide a medium level of security by enforcing stricter password and lockout policies and restricting guest access.

Unsuccessful logon events and privilege use, as well as successful and unsuccessful account management and policy changes, are configured for auditing. In addition, the secure domain controller template provides auditing for object and directory service access. Account and local policies also appear in the secure domain controller template. Because the permissions of files, folders, and registry keys are configured securely by default, these security areas are omitted in this template type.

Highly Secure Security Templates

The highly secure templates are actually quite lean and concentrate on the security of communications in native-mode (Windows Server 2003) environments. In short, security attributes are set for digitally signing client-side and server-side communications and for signing and encrypting secure channel data. Because maximum protocol protection is set, however, systems to which these templates are applied will not be able to communicate with machines running Microsoft Windows 95, Microsoft Windows 98, or Microsoft Windows NT. In addition to the fact that there are no Authenticated Users in the Power Users restricted group in the highly secure workstation/server (Hisecws) template, the highly secure workstation/server and domain controller templates are essentially the same.

Compatible Security Template

The goal of the compatible security template is to allow most applications to run successfully without compromising the security levels of Power Users. The compatible security template settings allow members of the local Users group to run only certified Windows applications, whereas only members of the Power Users group and above can run applications that are not certified. Therefore, if your users need to run uncertified applications, you must promote those users to at least Power User status.

Applying Security Templates

Security templates are applied by importing a security template into a GPO. To accomplish this, follow these steps:

1. Choose the target GPO (for example, use Active Directory Users And Computers MMC to link a GPO to an **organizational unit [OU]**, and then edit that GPO).

2. Expand the object, expand Computer Configuration, and then expand Windows Settings.

3. Right-click Security Settings, and then click Import Policy.

4. From the list of .inf files, choose the desired security template, and then click Open.

A number of helpful guidelines for applying the principle of least privilege for security templates are available, such as the following:

- Assign user rights sparingly. Reduce the number of rights you assign as much as possible, especially access and logon rights.

- Enforce a strong password policy to help prevent unauthorized access.

- Use security options to block access and restrict activity.

- Use file and registry ACLs.

- Use the Restricted Groups section to force and limit membership in sensitive groups.

- Use the Services section to disable services and restrict who can manage them.

- Develop a baseline plan for each computer role, and implement templates that are imported into GPOs on representative OUs.

- Apply a comprehensive auditing strategy.

MANAGING ENCRYPTING FILE SYSTEM (EFS)

EFS provides the core file encryption technology for storage of files on an NTFS partition. The EFS encryption technology is public key–based and runs as an integrated system service, which makes it easy to manage, difficult to attack, and transparent to the file owner.

By default, encrypted data is not encrypted when in transit over the network, but only when stored on disk. The exceptions to this are when your system includes IPSec or **Web Distributed Authoring and Versioning (WebDAV)**. IPSec encrypts data while it is transported over a **Transmission Control Protocol/Internet Protocol (TCP/IP)** network. If the file is encrypted before being copied or moved to a WebDAV folder on a server, it will remain encrypted during the transmission and while it is stored on the server.

A user who has ownership of a file or folder can either encrypt or decrypt the file or folder. If a user who attempts to access an encrypted NTFS file has the private key to that file, the user can open the file and work with it transparently as a normal document. A user without the private key is denied access. Encryption and decryption with greater functionality can be accomplished by using the command-line utility Cipher. (Cipher is discussed later in the "Using the Cipher Utility" section.)

Organizations can set policies to recover EFS-encrypted data when necessary. The recovery policy is integrated in the overall Windows Server 2003 security policy. Control of this policy can be delegated to individuals with recovery authority, and different recovery policies may be configured for different parts of the organization. Data recovery discloses only the recovered data, not the key that was used to encrypt the file. Several protections are in place to ensure that data recovery is possible and that no data is lost in the case of total system failure.

EFS allows users to encrypt NTFS files through the use of a strong public key–based cryptographic scheme that encrypts all files in a folder. Users with roaming profiles can use the same private key with trusted remote systems. No administrative effort is needed to begin, and most operations are transparent. Backups and copies of encrypted files also are encrypted if they are on NTFS volumes. Files also remain encrypted if you move or rename them.

You can use EFS to encrypt and decrypt files on remote file servers, but not to encrypt data that is transferred over the network. Windows Server 2003 provides network protocols, such as **Secure Sockets Layer (SSL)** and IPSec, to encrypt data over the network. SSL is a proposed open standard for establishing a secure communications channel to prevent the interception of critical information, such as credit card numbers.

EFS Features

The features of EFS include the following:

- **Transparent encryption**   With EFS, file encryption does not require the file owner to decrypt and reencrypt the file on each use. Decryption and encryption happen transparently when a user reads or writes to a file.

- **Strong protection of encryption keys**   Public key encryption resists all but the most sophisticated methods of attack. Therefore, in EFS, using a **public key** from the user's **X.509 v3 certificate** encrypts the file encryption keys used to encrypt the file. The list of encrypted file encryption keys is stored with the encrypted file and is unique to it. To decrypt the file encryption keys, the file owner supplies a private key, which only the file owner possesses.

- **Integral data recovery system**   The list of file encryption keys is encrypted again by using a recovery agent's public key, and this encrypted list also is stored with the encrypted file. There may be more than one recovery agent, each with a different public key. At least one public recovery key must be present on the system to encrypt a file.

- **Secure temporary files and paging files**   Many applications create temporary files while you edit a document, and these temporary files are left unencrypted on the disk. But because EFS is implemented at the folder level, temporary copies of an encrypted file also are encrypted, provided that all files are on NTFS volumes.

In Windows Server 2003, the file encryption keys reside in the **Windows operating system kernel** and are stored in the nonpaged pool, ensuring that they are never copied to the paging file. This ensures that the paging file cannot be used to access documents that are encrypted with a single key.

Encrypting a File or Folder

To encrypt files or folders, you create an NTFS folder, and then you encrypt it in the Properties dialog box for the folder. In the General tab, click Advanced, and then click Encrypt Contents To Secure Data.

> **NOTE   Encryption and Compression**   Encryption and compression are mutually exclusive. You cannot encrypt files on a compressed volume.

After you encrypt the folder, when you save a file to that folder, the file is encrypted using file encryption keys, which are fast symmetric keys that are designed for bulk encryption. The file is encrypted in blocks, with a different file encryption key for each block. All of the file encryption keys also are encrypted and stored in the Data Decryption Field (DDF) and the Data Recovery Field (DRF). The DDF and DRF are located in the file header.

Practice
encrypting a file
by completing
Exercise 5-3,
"Encrypting a
File," now.

All files and subfolders that you create in an encrypted folder are automatically encrypted, as are any files moved or copied to the encrypted folder. If you move or copy a file from an encrypted folder to an unencrypted folder, the file remains encrypted. Each file has a unique encryption key, which makes it safe to rename files.

Decrypting a File or Folder

When you open an encrypted file, EFS automatically detects an encrypted file and locates a user certificate and the associated private key in the file header. Your private key is applied to the DDF to unlock the list of file encryption keys. This allows the file contents to appear in plaintext.

Practice decrypting a file by completing Exercise 5-4, "Decrypting a File," now.

Access to the encrypted file is denied to anyone else except the owner of the private key, and you cannot share an encrypted file. Only the owner of the file or a recovery agent can decrypt the file. This is true even if administrators change permissions or file attributes, or if they take ownership of the file. Even if you own an encrypted file, you cannot read it unless you have the private key or you are a recovery agent.

Using the Cipher Utility

Windows Server 2003 also includes a command-line utility to provide the greater functionality required for some administrative operations. The Cipher utility has the capability to encrypt and decrypt files and folders from a command prompt by using wildcards. Cipher also can be used to overwrite deleted data.

The format of the Cipher command is as follows:

```
cipher [/e|/d] [/s:folder_name] [/a] [/i] [/f] [/q] [/h] [/k] [path_name [...]]
```

Table 5-7 describes the options that you can use with the Cipher command.

Table 5-7   Cipher Command Options

Option	Description
/e	Encrypts the specified folders. Folders are marked so that files added later will be encrypted.
/d	Decrypts the specified folders. Folders are marked so that files added later will not be encrypted.
/s	Performs the specified operation on the specified folder and all subfolders.
/a	Includes files and folders in the operation.
/i	Continues performing the specified operation, even after errors have occurred. By default, Cipher stops when an error is encountered.
/f	Forces the encryption operation on all specified files, even those that are already encrypted. Files that are already encrypted are skipped by default.
/q	Reports only the most essential information.
/h	Includes hidden files or system files.
/k	Creates a new file encryption key for the user who is running the command. If this option is chosen, Cipher ignores other options.
path_name	Specifies a pattern, file, or folder.

If you run the Cipher command without parameters, it displays the encryption state of the current folder and any files that the folder contains. You can specify multiple file names and use wildcards. You must put spaces between multiple parameters.

To encrypt the C:\Test_files folder, type the following command:

cipher /e test_files

To encrypt files with "cnfdl" in the name, type the following command:

cipher /e /s *cnfdl*

Recovering Encrypted Files

If the owner's private key is unavailable, the recovery agent can open the file using his or her own private key, which is applied to the DRF to unlock the list of file encryption keys. When recovering encrypted files, send the file to the recovery agent's computer rather than using the recovery agent's key at the file's original location. It is not a good security practice to copy a private key onto another computer.

By default, domain administrators are recovery agents. The local administrator is the default recovery agent for stand-alone computers. If additional recovery agents are needed, you must create or obtain certificates, assign users to the certificates, and use Group Policy to designate recovery agents for the certificates.

> **MORE INFO** **About Group Policy** *See Chapter 7, "Introduction to Group Policy," of Planning, Implementing, and Maintaining a Microsoft Windows Server 2003 Active Directory Infrastructure (Microsoft Press, 2004).*

Rotating recovery agents is a good security practice. However, if the agent designation changes, access to the file is denied. It is, therefore, recommended that you keep recovery certificates and private keys until all files that are encrypted with them have been updated.

To recover an encrypted file or folder, a designated recovery agent must perform the following steps:

1. Use Backup or another backup tool to restore a user's backup version of the encrypted file or folder to the computer where the user's file recovery certificate is located.

2. In Windows Explorer, open the Properties dialog box for the file or folder, and then click Advanced in the General tab.

3. Clear the Encrypt Contents To Secure Data check box.

4. Make a backup version of the decrypted file or folder, and return the backup version to the user.

IMPLEMENTING SECURITY CONFIGURATION TOOLS

Windows Server 2003 provides a set of security configuration tools that are designed to ease both the process of securing the network and the ongoing tasks of security analysis and auditing. These tools are MMC snap-ins and command-line tools. They enable you to implement the appropriate security level for your organization and to verify that this level is maintained over time. Security settings include security policies (account and local policies), access control (services, files, and the registry), event logs, group membership (restricted groups), IPSec policies, and public key policies. The security configuration tools include three snap-ins and a command-line tool: the Security Configuration And Analysis snap-in, the Security Templates snap-in, the Group Policy snap-in, and the Secedit command-line tool.

Security Configuration And Analysis Snap-In

Security Configuration And Analysis is an MMC snap-in that enables an administrator to verify and configure current computer settings against one or more security templates stored in a database (shown in Figure 5-5).

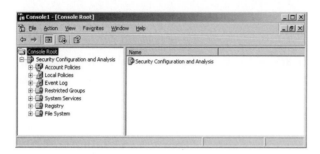

Figure 5-5   Security Configuration And Analysis snap-in

Templates contain settings for each of the system's security attributes. When they have been imported into a Security Configuration And Analysis database, the current settings can be analyzed and configured to match the entire imported template, or they can be individually configured. When all settings have been specified, they can be exported and applied to other computers, thereby greatly simplifying an organization's security policy application process.

Security Configuration And Analysis presents recommendations alongside current system settings and uses icons (see Table 5-8) or remarks to indicate any areas in which the current settings do not match the proposed security level. Security Configuration And Analysis also offers the capability to resolve any discrepancies that analysis reveals (see Figure 5-6).

Table 5-8   Security Configuration And Analysis Icons

Icon	Meaning
Red X	The entry is defined in the analysis database and on the system, but the security setting values do not match.
Green check mark	The entry is defined in the analysis database and on the system, and the security setting values match.
Question mark	The entry is not defined in the analysis database and, therefore, was not analyzed. If an entry is not analyzed, it might not have been defined in the analysis database, or the user who is running the analysis might not have sufficient permission to perform analysis on a specific object or area.
Exclamation point	This item is defined in the analysis database, but it does not exist on the actual system. For example, a restricted group might be defined in the analysis database that does not actually exist on the analyzed system.
No highlight	The item is not defined in the analysis database or on the system.

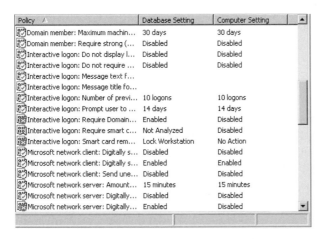

Policy	Database Setting	Computer Setting
Domain member: Maximum machin...	30 days	30 days
Domain member: Require strong (...	Disabled	Disabled
Interactive logon: Do not display l...	Disabled	Disabled
Interactive logon: Do not require ...	Disabled	Disabled
Interactive logon: Message text f...		
Interactive logon: Message title fo...		
Interactive logon: Number of previ...	10 logons	10 logons
Interactive logon: Prompt user to ...	14 days	14 days
Interactive logon: Require Domain...	Enabled	Disabled
Interactive logon: Require smart c...	Not Analyzed	Disabled
Interactive logon: Smart card rem...	Lock Workstation	No Action
Microsoft network client: Digitally s...	Disabled	Disabled
Microsoft network client: Digitally s...	Enabled	Enabled
Microsoft network client: Send une...	Disabled	Disabled
Microsoft network server: Amount...	15 minutes	15 minutes
Microsoft network server: Digitally...	Disabled	Disabled
Microsoft network server: Digitally...	Enabled	Disabled

Figure 5-6   Results of Security Configuration And Analysis

Security Configuration

The Security Configuration And Analysis snap-in can be used to configure local system security by directly modifying settings using the snap-in or by importing and applying security templates, which are created with the Security Templates snap-in, to the GPO for the local computer. In either case, system security settings are configured with the levels specified in the snap-in or by the template.

Security Analysis

By definition, increased security means an increase in complexity and, likely, an increase in problems accessing resources. When a user cannot access a resource because of a security problem, often the most direct solution is to relax security. Although relaxing security can solve the problem quickly, it puts the organization at risk for a security breach. These deviations from security policy often are forgotten and go unnoticed until an attacker breaches security. To avoid this and other situations that result in security gaps, use the Security Configuration And Analysis tool to analyze a computer's security settings against a security template that specifies the proper security settings.

Only through regular inspection and analysis can an administrator ensure that the security level on each network device meets or exceeds acceptable levels. The Security Configuration And Analysis snap-in enables quick review of security analysis results.

Using the Security Configuration And Analysis Snap-In

Administrators can use the snap-in to adjust the security policy and detect security flaws that arise in the system. The Security Configuration And Analysis snap-in enables you to perform the following tasks:

- Analyze system security by comparing existing security settings to settings that are specified in one or more templates.

- Review security analysis results.

- Configure system security by applying one or more templates.

- Edit the base security configuration.

- Import and export a security template.

> **NOTE** Practice using the Security Configuration And Analysis snap-in by completing Exercise 5-5, "Using the Security Configuration And Analysis Snap-In," now.

Secedit Utility

Secedit is a command-line version of the Security Configuration And Analysis snap-in; like its counterpart, Secedit configures and analyzes system security by comparing your current configuration to at least one template. Secedit is useful when you have multiple computers on which security must be analyzed or configured and when you need to perform Secedit tasks during off-hours. The following statement indicates the Secedit syntax (in six parts), and Table 5-9 defines each setting:

```
secedit /configure /db FileName [/cfg FileName ] [/overwrite][/areas Area1
    Area2 ...] [/log FileName] [/quiet]
secedit /analyze /db FileName.sdb [/cfg FileName] [/overwrite] [/log FileName]
    [/quiet]
secedit /import /db FileName.sdb /cfg FileName.inf [/overwrite] [/areas Area1
    Area2 ...] [/log FileName] [/quiet]
secedit /export [/DB FileName] [/mergedpolicy] [/CFG FileName] [/areas Area1
    Area2 ...] [/log FileName] [/quiet]
secedit /validate FileName
secedit /GenerateRollback /CFG FileName.inf /RBK SecurityTemplatefilename.inf
    [/log RollbackFileName.inf] [/quiet]
```

Table 5-9 **Secedit Syntax**

Setting	Description	Comments
configure	Applies security settings from a template	Never use this setting without creating a rollback. Should you find that your template is incorrect or causes problems, a rollback can return most of the security configurations to the way they were.
analyze	Compares settings in a database template to those that are set on the machine	Use this setting to audit security settings for compliance.
import	Imports a template into a database	One use for this setting is to import a security template into a database so that the settings specified in the template can be applied to a system or analyzed against a system.
export	Exports a template from a database	One use for this setting is to build a new template by combining two or more templates. Simply add each template to the database in the order of your choice, and use the Export command to produce an .inf template file.
validate	Validates a template's syntax	One use for this setting is if you have added settings directly to the .inf file.
generate-rollback	Makes a reverse template; that is, a template that removes most of the settings that are applied with a template	Always make one rollback before applying a new template. However, be aware that it does not change ACLs on files and in the registry that might have been set with the template.

(continued)

Table 5-9   **Secedit Syntax**

Setting	Description	Comments
db	Specifies the name of the database file to create or use	You might have to enter the whole path.
cfg	Specifies the name of the template to use	You might have to enter the whole path.
overwrite	Overwrites any existing template in the file with another	Use this setting if you do not want a combined effect when applying a template. If the old template in the file already has been applied, using this setting does not change the those settings that were not overwritten by the new template.
log	Specifies a log file for recording errors	This setting always records errors. By default, if no log file is specified, the system uses WINDOWS\Security\Logs\Scesrv.log.
quiet	Specifies that no data should appear on the screen and no progress comments should be provided to the user	When you use this setting in a script, the logged-on user does not have to know that the program is running.
areas	Applies only the settings as listed in a specific area of the template; ignores other settings	The areas are SECURITYPOLICY, GROUP _MGMT (restricted groups), USER_RIGHTS, REGKEYS, FILESTORE, and SERVICES.
mergedpolicy	Merges and exports domain and local policy	This setting captures all security settings.
rbk	Specifies the name of the security template to be created	This setting is available only with the /generaterollback setting.

Following are some examples of Secedit commands:

- To configure the machine using the foo template:

  ```
  secedit /configure /dbfoo.sdb /cfg foo.inf /logfoo.log
  ```

- To create a rollback template for the foo template:

  ```
  Secedit /generaterollback /cfg foo.inf /rbk foorollback.inf /log
  foorollback.log
  ```

  MORE INFO   Use Gpupdate Instead of Secedit /Refreshpolicy   The Secedit
  /refreshpolicy command has been replaced with the Gpupdate command.

Security Templates Snap-In

The Security Templates snap-in (shown in Figure 5-7) is a tool for creating and assigning security templates for one or more computers. As discussed previously, a *security template* is a physical file representation of a security configuration.

When you import a security template to a GPO, Group Policy processes the template and makes the corresponding changes to the members of that GPO, which can include users or computers.

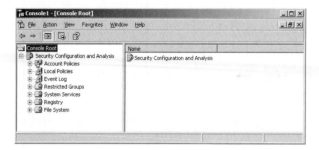

Figure 5-7   Security Templates snap-in

The Security Templates snap-in allows you to perform a variety of tasks, such as the following:

- Customize a predefined security template
- Define a security template
- Delete a security template
- Refresh the security template list
- Set a description for a security template

Group Policy Snap-In

Use Group Policy to define and control how programs, network resources, and the operating system behave for an organization's users and computers. The **Group Policy Object Editor** snap-in (shown in Figure 5-8) uses Active Directory to centralize security configuration. Administrators use the Security Settings folders on the Computer Configuration node and the User Configuration node to set policies that can restrict user access to files and folders, set how many incorrect passwords a user can enter before being locked out, and control user rights, such as which users are able to log on at a domain server.

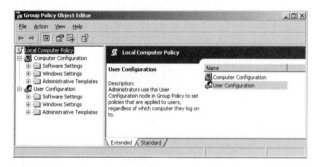

Figure 5-8   Group Policy Object Editor snap-in

Gpupdate

Gpupdate refreshes local group policy settings and Group Policy settings that are stored in Active Directory, including security settings. After you make changes to group policies, you might want the changes to be applied immediately, rather than waiting for the default update interval (90 minutes on domain members and 5 minutes on domain controllers) or restarting the computer. To make this update, run the Gpupdate utility at a command prompt. This command replaces the now obsolete /refreshpolicy option of the Secedit command. The syntax below and Table 5-10 explain the Gpupdate parameters.

```
gpupdate [/target:{computer | user}] [/force] [/wait:Value] [/logoff] [/boot]
```

Table 5-10   Gpupdate Parameters

Parameter	Description
/target:{computer | user}	Processes only the computer settings or the current user settings. Both the computer settings and the user settings are processed by default.
/force	Reapplies all policy settings. The default behavior of Gpupdate is to only apply changed policy settings.
/wait:Value	Number of seconds that policy processing waits to finish. The default is 600 seconds; 0 equals no wait, and −1 equals indefinite wait.
/logoff	Logs off after the refresh has completed. This is required for those Group Policy client-side extensions that do not process on a background refresh cycle but that do process when the user logs on, such as user Group Policy Software Installation and Folder Redirection. This option has no effect if no extensions are called that require the user to log off.
/boot	Restarts the computer after the refresh has completed. This is required for those Group Policy client-side extensions that do not process on a background refresh cycle but that do process when the computer starts up, such as computer Group Policy Software Installation. This option has no effect if no extensions are called that require the computer to be restarted.
/?	Displays help at the command prompt.
/synch	Causes the next foreground policy application to occur synchronously. You can specify this for the user, computer, or both by using the /target parameter. The /force and /wait parameters are ignored when using the /synch parameter.

Using Microsoft Baseline Security Analyzer (MBSA)

MBSA is a powerful tool for checking the security settings of multiple computers. As such, it is the first tool you should use when you want to verify the security status of computers on your network.

▶ **Using MBSA**

To use MBSA, complete the following steps:

1. Download and install the program from the Microsoft Security Web site, which is located at *http://www.microsoft.com/technet/security/tools/Tools/MBSAhome.asp.*

2. Launch the program from the Start menu or the desktop.

3. Click the Scan A Computer hyperlink to scan a single computer, or click the Scan More Than One Computer link to scan multiple computers.

4. Specify the IP address or address range of the computer or computers, specify what you want to look for, and then click Start Scan.

5. Review the results, as shown in Figure 5-9, and then click links to view more detailed information.

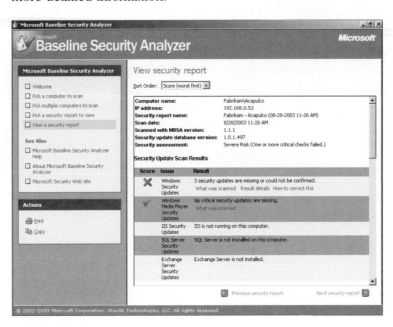

Figure 5-9   Results of MBSA

SUMMARY

■ Windows Server 2003 provides a set of security configuration tools that allows you to configure security settings and perform periodic analysis of the system to ensure that the configuration remains intact or to make necessary changes over time.

■ The principle of least privilege states that you should not give a user or object more privileges or access to information and resources than is absolutely necessary.

■ The Security Configuration And Analysis snap-in allows you to configure and analyze local system security. It reviews and analyzes your system security settings and recommends modifications to the current system settings.

■ The Security Templates snap-in allows you to create and assign security templates for one or more computers.

■ The Group Policy Object Editor snap-in allows you to configure security centrally in the Active Directory store.

EXERCISES

IMPORTANT   *Completing All Exercises*   *If you plan to do any of the textbook exercises in this chapter, you must do all of the exercises in the chapter to return the computer to its original state for the associated Lab Manual labs.*

Exercise 5-1: Assigning User Rights

In this exercise, you will assign the right to Add Workstations To The Domain to the Authenticated Users group.

1. Click Start, point to Administrative Tools, and then click Domain Security Policy.

2. Expand Security Settings, and then expand Local Policies. Click User Rights Assignment.

3. In the details pane, double-click Add Workstations To Domain.

4. In the Add Workstations To Domain Properties dialog box, click Define These Policy Settings.

5. Click Add User Or Group.

6. In the Add User Or Group dialog box, in the User And Group Names box, type **authenticated users**, and then click OK.

Exercise 5-2: Viewing an Event

In this exercise, you will configure audit settings to trigger an event in the audit log, and then you will view it.

To configure auditing, follow these steps:

1. Click Start, point to Administrative Tools, and then click Domain Controller Security Policy.

2. In the Default Domain Controller Security Settings MMC, in the console tree, expand Security Settings, expand Local Policies, and then click Audit Policy.

3. In the details pane, double-click Audit Logon Events.

4. In the Audit Logon Events Properties window, click Define These Policy Settings, click Success, click Failure, and then click OK.

5. Close the Default Domain Controller Security Settings MMC.

6. Click Start, and then click Command Prompt.

7. To force the policy settings to take effect immediately, at the command prompt, type **gpupdate /force**, and then press ENTER.

8. A message is displayed that says the refresh has completed. Close the command prompt.

9. Log off.

10. Attempt to log on using the Administrator account and an incorrect password.

11. Log on as the Administrator using the correct password.

12. Click Start, point to Administrative Tools, and then click Event Viewer.

13. In the Event Viewer MMC, click Security.

14. In the details pane, locate the failed audit that was caused by your unsuccessful attempt to log on as Administrator. Both the failure event and the detail are shown in Figure 5-10.

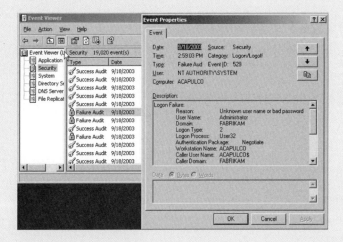

Figure 5-10   Logon failure event

Exercise 5-3: Encrypting a File

In this exercise, you will use Windows Explorer to encrypt a file.

1. Open Windows Explorer.

2. In the folder tree, click Desktop.

3. On the File menu, point to New, and then click Folder.

4. Name the folder My Encrypted Files.

5. At the desktop, on the File menu, point to New, and then click Text Document.

6. Name the text document PasswordFile.txt.

7. Open the text file and add some text.

8. Save and close the text file.

9. Using Windows Explorer, right-click My Encrypted Files, and then click Properties.

10. In the General tab, click Advanced.

11. In the Advanced Attributes window, select Encrypt Contents To Secure Data, and then click OK.

12. To close the My Encrypted Files Properties window, click OK.

   My Encrypted Files is now a different color, which indicates that it is encrypted.

13. Drag the PasswordFile.txt into the My Encrypted Files folder.

14. Open the My Encrypted Files folder.

15. Note that the color of PasswordFile.txt has changed and that it is now encrypted.

Exercise 5-4: Decrypting a File

In this exercise, you will use Windows Explorer to decrypt a file.

1. Open Windows Explorer.

2. Right-click My Encrypted Files, and then click Properties.

3. In the General tab, click Advanced.

4. In the Advanced Attributes window, clear the Encrypt Contents To Secure Data check box, and then click OK.

5. To close the My Encrypted Files Properties window, click OK.

6. In the Custom Attribute Changes dialog box, verify Apply Changes To This Folder, Subfolders, And Files is selected, and then click OK.

   My Encrypted Files and PasswordFile.txt are no longer a different color, indicating they are not encrypted.

Exercise 5-5: Using the Security Configuration And Analysis Snap-In

In this exercise, you will create a Security Configuration And Analysis console, import a security template, and perform an analysis of current computer settings against that template.

1. Click Start, click Run, type **mmc**, and then click OK.

2. On the File menu, click Add/Remove Snap-in.

3. In the Add/Remove Snap-in window, click Add.

4. In the Add Standalone Snap-in dialog box, click Security Configuration And Analysis, click Add, and then click Close.

5. In the Add/Remove Snap-in window, click OK.

6. On the File menu, click Save.

7. In the Save As dialog box, in the File Name box, type **sca**, and then click Save.

Analyzing System Security

To analyze system security, follow these steps:

1. Using the Security Configuration And Analysis MMC, right-click Security Configuration And Analysis, and then click Open Database.

2. In the Open Database window, in the File Name box, type **scadb**, and then click Open.

3. In the Import Template window, click Securedc.inf, and then click Open.

4. In the console tree, right-click Security Configuration And Analysis, and then click Analyze Computer Now.

5. In the Perform Analysis dialog box, click OK to accept the default path for the error log.

6. Expand Security Configuration And Analysis, expand Local Policies, and then click Security Options.

7. In the details pane, review the policies that were analyzed. They display the result of a comparison between actual settings and the database setting.

> **QUESTION**   List some of the configuration settings that are the same in the database and on the computer.

> **QUESTION**   List some of the configuration settings that are different in the database than on the computer.

REVIEW QUESTIONS

1. Which of the following are user rights?

    a. Allow log on locally

    b. Access a share with full control

    c. Open a database file

    d. Back up files and directories

2. An administrator temporarily grants a user rights to log on locally to a domain controller by applying a policy to the domain GPO. The administrator does not add the user to other groups. When the user attempts to log on, Windows Server 2003 displays the following error: "User does not have the right to log on interactively." What is the most likely cause of the problem?

3. You are the system administrator responsible for creating, configuring, and managing GPOs for your organization. The systems engineers present you with a plan, and you must determine whether you can use a default template. Which of the following default Group Policy templates provides the highest default security for clients?

   a. Rootsec

   b. Hisecws

   c. Securews

   d. Compatws

4. You are responsible for creating, configuring, and managing GPOs for your organization. You must determine which settings on the domain controller do not match the security policies that were applied using a specific template. Which of the following tools can you use to determine this?

   a. Domain Security Policy

   b. Security Configuration And Analysis snap-in

   c. Group Policy Management

   d. Active Directory Users And Computers

5. You are the system administrator responsible for creating, configuring, and managing GPOs for your organization. Before you can determine which Group Policy settings you should apply to each GPO, you must determine which types of Group Policy settings you can configure. Which of the following types of Group Policy settings can you configure in an Active Directory environment? Choose all that apply.

   a. Desktop settings

   b. Network connections

   c. Location of computers

   d. Inventory-installed software

   e. Who can log on to a computer and when

CASE SCENARIOS

Case Scenario 5-1: Folder Redirection

You are the system administrator for Contoso, Ltd., and you want to centrally store users' data using folder redirection. Specifically, you want to configure folder redirection of the My Documents folder to each user's existing home directory. Users should have exclusive access to their My Documents data. How will you accomplish your objectives? Choose two answers.

   a. Configure a GPO to set the Folder Redirection policy to redirect to the user's home directory setting, and link it to the appropriate OU.

   b. Configure a GPO to set the Grant The User Exclusive Rights To My Documents setting to Disabled, and link it to the appropriate OU.

   c. Configure a GPO to set the Folder Redirection policy to redirect special OU units.

   d. Configure a GPO to set the Grant The User Exclusive Rights To My Documents setting to Enabled, and link it to the appropriate OU.

Case Scenario 5-2: Auditing

Someone notifies you that users are having a difficult time accessing shared resources on two of the organization's file servers. You decide to review the audit logs for these servers to determine the cause of the issues. When you review the event logs, you discover that the log contains only data from the previous 12 hours. What might be responsible for the lack of data? Choose all that apply.

   a. The maximum size of the event log is too small.

   b. You audited too many events.

   c. The Overwrite Events Older Than [x] Days setting is set to 1 day.

   d. Another administrator manually cleared the event logs.

   e. The relevant events are logged to domain controllers, not member servers.

CHAPTER 6
SECURING NETWORK TRAFFIC WITH IPSEC

Upon completion of this chapter, you will be able to:

■ Identify and explain the major components and concepts of **Internet Protocol security (IPSec)** including security associations, header protocols, **Internet Key Exchange (IKE)**, the role of the IPSec Policy Agent and IPSec driver, and the security negotiation process.

■ Understand the role the **Authentication Header (AH) protocol** and the **Encapsulating Security Payload (ESP) protocol** play in providing confidentiality and authentication.

■ Add or modify IPSec security policies using the IP Security Policy Management console.

■ Determine when to use **Active Directory** directory service or local policies when deploying IPSec.

■ Use tools to manage, monitor, and troubleshoot IPSec. These tools include IP Security Monitor, the IP Security Policy Management console, **Resultant Set of Policy (RSoP)**, **Event Viewer**, Netsh, and the Oakley log.

■ Understand why you would use certificates with IPSec to secure network traffic.

■ Describe the process of certificate enrollment.

■ Configure IPSec to use certificates.

■ Explain the issues associated with **Network Address Translation (NAT)** when using IPSec and identify the methods Microsoft Windows Server 2003 uses to solve those issues.

■ Use Netsh to manage and monitor IPSec.

Whether you have a public presence on the Internet or maintain a private network, securing your data is a core requirement. Much attention is placed on perimeter security and preventing attacks from outside the network. Much less attention is focused on attacks within the network, where an attack is more likely to occur.

A solid security strategy employs many layers of coordinated security. Organizations deploy measures to secure the network perimeter and secure access to resources by instituting authentication and access control; however, securing the actual Internet Protocol (IP) packets and their contents is often overlooked.

This chapter focuses on securing IP traffic by using IPSec. We discuss the purpose and features of IPSec, how to define and deploy IPSec policies, and how to implement IPSec using certificates. After we explain the purpose of IPSec and how to deploy it, we then explain how to manage and monitor IPSec using tools such as the IP Security Monitor, RSoP, Event Viewer, the Oakley log, Netsh, and Netdiag.

THE PURPOSE OF IPSEC

IP, **Transmission Control Protocol (TCP)**, and **User Datagram Protocol (UDP)** headers contain a **checksum** that is used to provide an integrity check for portions of the IP packet. If the data is corrupted, the checksum alerts the receiver. However, because the checksum algorithm is well known, a malicious user can intercept an IP packet, view and modify its contents, recompute the checksums, and forward the packet to its destination all without the knowledge of either the receiver or sender. Because of the limited functionality of the checksum, the destination node is not aware and cannot detect that the packet was modified.

Historically, applications that required security provided it for themselves, leading to a variety of autonomous and incompatible security standards. IPSec is a suite of protocols and cryptographic algorithms that provides security at the Internet layer, regardless of the application sending or receiving data. With IPSec, a single security standard is used and applications need not be modified to use it.

IPSec has two goals:

- To protect the contents of IP packets
- To provide a defense against network attacks through packet filtering and the enforcement of trusted communication

Both goals are met through the use of cryptography-based protection services, security protocols, and dynamic key management. This foundation provides both the strength and flexibility to protect communications between private network computers, domains, sites (including remote sites), extranets, and dial-up clients. It can even be used to block receipt or transmission of specific traffic types.

Protecting Against Security Attacks

IPSec protects data, making it extremely difficult or impossible for an attacker to interpret captured data. IPSec has a number of features that can significantly reduce or prevent the following attacks:

- **Packet sniffing**   A *packet sniffer* is an application or device that can monitor and read network packets. If the packets are not encrypted, a packet sniffer provides a full view of the data inside the packet. Network Monitor is an example of a network sniffer. The ESP protocol in IPSec provides data confidentiality by encrypting the payload of IP packets.

- **Data modification**   The attacker can modify a message in transit and send counterfeit data, which might prevent the receiver from receiving the correct information or might allow the attacker to obtain additional, possibly secure information. IPSec uses cryptography-based keys, shared only by the sending and receiving computers, to create a cryptographic checksum for each IP packet. Any modification to the packet data alters the checksum, which indicates to the receiving computer that the packet was modified in transit.

■ **Identity spoofing**   An attacker falsifies identities (identify spoofing) by using special programs to construct IP packets that appear to originate from valid addresses inside the trusted network. IPSec allows the exchange and verification of identities without exposing that information to interpretation by an attacker. Mutual verification (authentication) is used to establish trust between the communicating systems, and only trusted systems can communicate with each other. After identities are established, IPSec uses cryptography-based keys, shared only by the sending and receiving computers, to create a cryptographic checksum for each IP packet. The cryptographic checksum ensures that only the computers that have knowledge of the keys can send each packet.

■ **Man-in-the-middle attacks**   In this type of attack, someone between the two communicating computers is actively monitoring, capturing, and controlling the data transparently (for example, the attacker might be rerouting a data exchange). IPSec combines mutual authentication with shared, cryptography-based keys to prevent these attacks.

■ **Denial of service attacks (DoS)**   This type of attack prevents the normal use of computers or network resources. Flooding e-mail accounts with unsolicited messages is an example of a DoS attack. IPSec uses IP packet filtering methodology as the basis for determining whether communication is allowed, secured, or blocked. This determination is based on the IP address ranges, IP protocols, or even specific TCP and UDP ports.

UNDERSTANDING IPSEC

Before we can discuss how IPSec works and review the steps for IPSec configuration, you must understand some of the features, terminology, and components of the IPSec framework.

IPSec is an architectural framework that provides cryptographic security services for IP packets. IPSec is an end-to-end security technology. This means that the only nodes aware of the presence of IPSec are the two hosts using IPSec that communicate with each other. Intermediate routers have no knowledge of the security relationship, and they forward the IP packets as they would any others. Each computer handles security at its respective end with the assumption that the medium over which the communication takes place is not secure. Computers that only route data from source to destination are not required to support IPSec. One exception is the firewall-type packet filtering or NAT that occurs between two computers. With this model, IPSec is successfully deployed for the following scenarios:

■ **Local area network (LAN)**   Client/server and peer-to-peer LANs

■ **Wide area network (WAN)**   Router-to-router and gateway-to-gateway WANs

■ **Remote access**   Dial-up clients and Internet access from private networks

Typically, both sides require IPSec configuration, which is called an *IPSec policy*, to set options and security settings that will allow two systems to agree on how to secure traffic between them. The Microsoft Windows 2000, Microsoft Windows XP, and Windows Server 2003 implementations of IPSec are based on industry standards developed by the **Internet Engineering Task Force (IETF)** IPSec working group.

IPSec Security Features

IPSec has many security features designed to meet the goals of protecting IP packets and defend against attacks through filtering and trusted communication. Some of these security features include the following:

- **Automatic security associations**   IPSec uses the **Internet Security Association and Key Management Protocol (ISAKMP)** to dynamically negotiate a mutual set of security requirements between communicating computers. The computers do not require identical policies; they require only a policy that is configured with enough negotiation options to establish a common set of requirements with another computer.

- **IP packet filtering**   This filtering process allows or blocks communications as necessary by specifying address ranges, protocols, or even specific protocol ports.

- **Network layer security**   IPSec exists at the network layer, providing automatic, transparent security for all applications.

- **Peer authentication**   IPSec verifies the identity of the peer computer before any data is sent. IPSec peer authentication for Windows Server 2003 can be based on preshared keys, public keys (such as **X.509 certificates**), or **Kerberos** and Active Directory. Clients must be a member of an Active Directory domain to authenticate using Kerberos.

- **Data origin authentication**   Data origin authentication prevents a malicious user from intercepting packets and posing as the sender. Each packet protected with IPSec contains a cryptographic checksum in the form of a keyed hash. The cryptographic checksum is also known as an Integrity Check Value (ICV) or hash-based message authentication code (HMAC). A *hash* is a one-way cryptographic algorithm that takes an input message of arbitrary length and produces a fixed-length digest. A *keyed hash* includes the secret key in its calculation. The cryptographic checksum ensures that only a computer with knowledge of the shared secret key sent the packet. A malicious user masquerading as the sender cannot calculate a correct cryptographic checksum. If the cryptographic checksum fails, the receiving peer discards the packet.

- **Data integrity**   By including the cryptographic checksum, IPSec protects the data transfer process from unauthorized, undetected modification during transit, ensuring that the information that is received is the same as the information that was sent. A malicious user who modifies the packet contents must also properly update the cryptographic checksum, which is virtually impossible without knowledge of the shared key.

■ **Data confidentiality**   By using conventional secret key encryption techniques, the sent data can be encrypted. This provides data confidentiality. Even if the packet is intercepted and viewed, the interceptor can view only the encrypted data. Without knowledge of the secret key used to encrypt the data, the original data remains hidden. Because the secret key is shared between the sender and the receiver, data confidentiality ensures that the data can be decrypted and disclosed only by the intended receiver.

■ **Anti-replay**   By using a sequence number on each protected packet sent between IPSec peers, a data exchange between IPSec peers cannot be replayed to establish a security relationship or gain unauthorized access to information or resources.

■ **Key management**   Data origin authentication, data integrity, and data confidentiality depend on the shared knowledge of a secret key. If the key is compromised, the communication is no longer secure. To keep malicious users from determining the key through any method except brute force determination (trying all possible key combinations until the key is discovered), IPSec provides a secure way to exchange key information to derive a secret shared key and to periodically change the keys used for secure communications.

New IPSec Features for Windows Server 2003

IPSec is integrated into and can be used to protect network communications for Windows 2000, Windows XP Professional, and Windows Server 2003. A legacy client is available for Microsoft Windows NT 4, Microsoft Windows 98, and Microsoft Windows Millennium Edition (Me). (You can download the legacy client from *http://www.microsoft.com/windows2000/server/evaluation/news/bulletins /l2tpclient.asp.*) New features for Windows Server 2003 IPSec include the following:

■ The IP Security Monitor snap-in improves upon the Ipsecmon tool in Windows 2000. (The snap-in is new in Windows XP Professional and Windows Server 2003.)

■ A stronger cryptographic master key, Diffie-Hellman 2048-bit, is introduced.

■ The Netsh command-line management tool provides convenience, plus many configuration possibilities that are not available from the IP Security Policy Management snap-in.

■ Computer startup security. If configured to use stateful mode, inbound traffic that is sent in response to the outbound traffic is permitted, as is inbound traffic that matches any specific filters that you configure, as well as **Dynamic Host Configuration Protocol (DHCP)** traffic. All other inbound unicast, broadcast, and multicast packets are dropped. The stateful inbound permit filters are discarded after the IPSec service starts and sets persistent IPSec policy.

■ The persistent policy is applied if the local policy or the Active Directory IPSec policy cannot be applied.

■ Only IKE traffic is exempt from traffic filters. This exemption is required to establish secured communication.

■ Certain restrictions determine which computers are allowed to connect by domain, by certificate origin, or by computer group.

■ The name of the **certificate authority (CA)** can be excluded from certificate requests to prevent exposure of information on computer trust relationships such as domain, CA, and company.

■ Logical addressing is applied for local IP configuration—such as DHCP server, **Domain Name System (DNS)**, and **Windows Internet Naming Service (WINS)**—to accommodate dynamic addressing.

■ IPSec functionality over NAT lets ESP packets pass through NATs that allow UDP traffic.

■ Integration with network load balancing has improved, which is good for load balancing IPSec-based **virtual private network (VPN)** services.

■ Support is provided for the RSoP snap-in to view existing IPSec policy assignments.

IPSec Protocols provide security using a combination of protocols including the AH protocol and the ESP protocol. These protocols work independently or in tandem, depending on the need for confidentiality and authentication:

■ AH protocol provides authentication, integrity, and anti-replay for the entire packet (both the IP header and the data payload carried in the packet). It does not provide confidentiality, which means that it does not encrypt the data. The data is readable, but protected from modification. AH uses keyed hash algorithms to sign the packet for integrity.

■ ESP protocol provides confidentiality (in addition to authentication, integrity, and anti-replay) for the IP payload. ESP in transport mode does not sign the entire packet. Only the IP payload (not the IP header) is protected. ESP can be used alone or in combination with AH. For example, when used in combination with AH, the IP payload sent from Computer A to Computer B is encrypted and signed for integrity. Upon receipt, after the integrity verification process is complete, the data payload in the packet is decrypted. The receiver can be certain of who sent the data, that the data is unmodified, and that no one else was able to read it.

IPSec Modes

You can configure IPSec to use one of two modes: transport mode or tunnel mode.

■ **Transport mode**   Use transport mode when you require packet filtering and when you require end-to-end security. Both hosts must support IPSec using the same authentication protocols, must have compatible IPSec filters, and must not cross a NAT interface. Crossing a NAT interface changes the IP address in the header and invalidates the ICV. Figure 6-1 illustrates an example of transport mode.

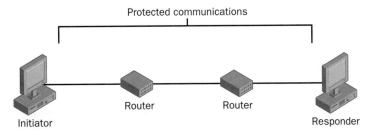

Figure 6-1   Transport mode end-to-end protection

■ **Tunnel mode**   Use tunnel mode for site-to-site communications that cross the Internet (or other public networks). Tunnel mode provides gateway-to-gateway protection. Figure 6-2 illustrates an example of tunnel mode.

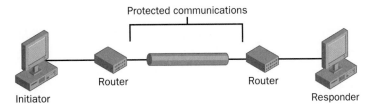

Figure 6-2   Tunnel mode gateway-to-gateway protection

Security Associations

A *security association* (SA) is the combination of security services, protection mechanisms, and cryptographic keys mutually agreed to by communicating peers. The SA contains the information needed to determine how the traffic is to be secured (the security services and protection mechanisms) and with which secret keys (cryptographic keys). Two types of SAs are created when IPSec peers communicate securely: the ISAKMP SA and the IPSec SA.

ISAKMP SA

The ISAKMP SA, also known as the *main mode SA*, is used to protect IPSec security negotiations. The ISAKMP SA is created by negotiating the ciphersuite (a collection of cryptographic algorithms used to encrypt data) used for protecting future ISAKMP traffic, exchanging key generation material, and then identifying and authenticating each IPSec peer. SAs are stored in the Security Association Database (SADB). When the ISAKMP SA is complete, all future SA negotiations for both types of SAs are protected. This is an aspect of secure communications known as *protected ciphersuite negotiation*. Not only is the data protected, but the determination of the protection algorithms negotiated by the IPSec peers is also protected. To break IPSec protection, a malicious user must first determine the ciphersuite protecting the data, which represents another barrier. For IPSec, the only exception to complete protected ciphersuite negotiation is the negotiation of the ciphersuite of the initial ISAKMP SA, which is sent as plaintext.

IPSec SA

The IPSec SA, also known as the *quick mode SA*, is used to protect data sent between the IPSec peers. The IPSec SA ciphersuite negotiation is protected by the ISAKMP SA. No information about the type of traffic or the protection mechanisms is sent as plaintext. For a pair of IPSec peers, two IPSec SAs always exist for each protocol in use: one is negotiated for inbound traffic, and one for outbound traffic. The inbound SA for one IPSec peer is the outbound SA for the other.

Security Parameters Index

For each IPSec session, IPSec peers must track the usage of three different SAs: the ISAKMP SA, the inbound IPSec SA, and the outbound IPSec SA. To identify a specific SA, a 32-bit pseudorandom number known as the **Security Parameters Index (SPI)** is used. The SPI, a field in the IPSec headers, indicates which SA the destination should use and is sent with every packet. The receiver is responsible for providing a unique SPI for each protocol.

The node that initiates an IPSec session is known as the *initiator*. The node that responds to a request to perform IPSec protection is known as the *responder*. The initiator chooses the ISAKMP SA SPI, and each IPSec peer chooses the IPSec SA SPIs for its outbound traffic.

Internet Key Exchange (IKE)

IKE is a standard that defines a mechanism to establish SAs. IKE combines ISAKMP and the Oakley Key Determination Protocol to generate secret key material. **Oakley** is based on the **Diffie-Hellman key exchange** algorithm, which allows two peers to determine a secret key by exchanging unencrypted values over a public network.

The Diffie-Hellman key exchange process derives a secret key known only to the two peers by exchanging two numbers over a public network. A malicious user who intercepts the key exchange packets can view the numbers, but cannot perform the same calculation as the negotiating peers to derive the shared secret key.

The Diffie-Hellman key exchange process does not prevent a man-in-the-middle attack, in which a malicious user between the negotiating peers performs two Diffie-Hellman exchanges, one with each peer. When both exchanges are complete, the malicious user has the secret keys to communicate with both peers. To prevent such an attack, Windows Server 2003 IPSec performs an immediate authentication after the Diffie-Hellman key exchange is complete. If the IPSec peer cannot perform a valid authentication, the security negotiation is abandoned before any data is sent.

Windows Server 2003 IPSec also supports *dynamic rekeying*, the determination of new keying material through a new Diffie-Hellman exchange. Dynamic rekeying is based on an elapsed time (by default, 480 minutes [8 hours]) or the number of data sessions created with the same set of keying material (by default, this number is unlimited).

> **MORE INFO**   **IKE Negotiation Process**   *For more information about the IKE negotiation process, see RFC 2409, "The Internet Key Exchange (IKE)," at http://www.ietf.org/rfc/rfc2409.txt.*

IPSec Policy Agent Service

The purpose of the IPSec Policy Agent is to retrieve policy information and pass it to other IPSec components that require this information to perform security services.

The IPSec Policy Agent is a service that resides on each computer running a Windows Server 2003 operating system, appearing as IPSec Services in the list of system services in the Services console. The IPSec Policy Agent has several responsibilities within the operating system, including the following:

- Retrieves the appropriate IPSec policy (if one has been assigned) from Active Directory (as shown in Figure 6-3) if the computer is a domain member; or it retrieves the IPSec policy from the local registry if the computer is not a member of a domain.

- Polls for changes in policy configuration.

- Sends the assigned IPSec policy information to the IPSec driver.

- If the computer is a member of a domain, policy retrieval occurs when the system starts, at the interval specified in the IPSec policy, and at the default Winlogon polling interval. You can also manually poll Active Directory for policies that use the Gpupdate /target:*computer* command.

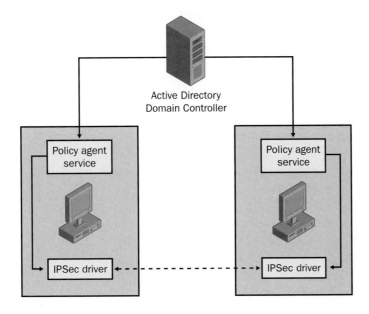

Figure 6-3 The IPSec Policy Agent communicating with IPSec driver

The following are additional aspects of IPSec policy behavior for a computer that is a member of a domain:

- If IPSec policy information is centrally configured for computers that are domain members, the IPSec policy information is stored in Active Directory and cached in the local registry of the computer to which it applies.

- If the computer is temporarily not connected to the domain and policy is cached, new policy information for that computer replaces old, cached information when the computer reconnects to the domain.

- If the computer is a stand-alone computer or a member of a domain that is not using Active Directory for policy storage, IPSec policy is stored in the local registry.

- If there are no IPSec policies in Active Directory or the registry when the IPSec Policy Agent starts automatically at system start time, or if the IPSec Policy Agent cannot connect to Active Directory, the IPSec Policy Agent waits for the policy to be assigned or activated.

IPSec Driver

The IPSec driver receives the active IP filter list from the IPSec Policy Agent, as shown in Figure 6-4. The Policy Agent then checks for a match of every inbound and outbound packet against the filters in the list. IP filters enable network administrators to precisely define which IP traffic is secured. Each IP filter list contains one or more filters, which define IP addresses and traffic types. One IP filter list can be used for multiple communication scenarios. You can access the IP filters using the IP Security Policy Management snap-in. To access the IP filter lists, in the IP Security Policy Management snap-in, right-click the IP Security Policy node, and then click Manage IP Filter Lists And Filter Actions.

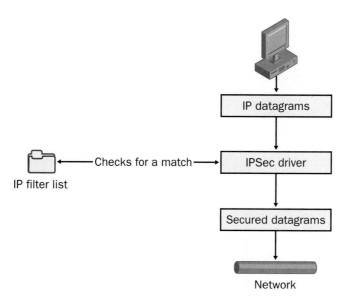

Figure 6-4   IPSec driver checking for IP filter match

When a packet matches a filter, it applies the associated filter action. When a packet does not match any filters, the packet is passed back without modification to the TCP/IP driver to be received or transmitted.

If the filter action permits transmission, the packet is received or sent with no modifications. If the action blocks transmission, the packet is discarded. If the action requires the negotiation of security, main mode and quick mode SAs are negotiated (this is described in the "Security Negotiation Process" section, later in this chapter).

The negotiated quick mode SA and keys are used with both outbound and inbound processing. The IPSec driver stores all current quick mode SAs in a database. The IPSec driver uses the SPI field to match the correct SA with the correct packet.

When an outbound IP packet matches the IP filter list with an action to negotiate security, the IPSec driver queues the packet, and then the IKE process begins negotiating security with the destination IP address of that packet.

After a successful negotiation is completed, the IPSec driver on the sending computer performs the following actions:

1. The IPSec driver receives the SA that contains the session key from the IKE process.

2. The IPSec driver locates the outbound SA in its database and then inserts the SPI from the SA into the header.

3. The IPSec driver signs the packets and encrypts them if confidentiality is required.

4. The IPSec driver sends the packets to the IP layer to be forwarded to the destination computer.

If the negotiation fails, the IPSec driver discards the packet.

When an IPSec-secured inbound packet matches a filter in the IP filter list, the IPSec driver performs the following actions:

1. The IPSec driver receives the session key, SA, and SPI from the IKE process.

2. The IPSec driver locates the inbound SA in its database using the destination address and SPI.

3. The IPSec driver checks the signature and, if required, decrypts the packets.

4. The IPSec driver searches the IP packets for a matching filter in the filter list to ensure that no traffic, other than what was agreed upon during the negotiation, is received.

5. The IPSec driver sends packets to the TCP/IP driver to pass to the receiving application.

When an unsecured IP packet is received, the IPSec driver searches for a matching filter in the filter list. If a match occurs and the filter action for that filter either requires IP Security or blocks the packet, the packet is discarded.

> **NOTE   Match Tunnel Filters First**   The IPSec driver matches all inbound, unsecured packets with the list of filters that specify IPSec tunnels first, and then it matches the packet with all filters that specify end-to-end (transport) filters.

Security Negotiation Process

IPSec processing can be divided into two types of negotiation: main mode negotiation and quick mode negotiation. Figure 6-5 illustrates a high-level overview of the process using Host A and Host B (a more detailed explanation follows):

1. Host A requests secured communications.

2. Main mode (the master key and the IKE SA are established—see the "Main Mode Negotiation" section) negotiations begin and are completed.

3. Quick mode negotiation of an SA pair (inbound and outbound) for application packet transfers is completed.

4. The application packets from Host A are passed by the TCP/IP driver to the IPSec driver.

5. The IPSec driver formats and cryptographically processes the packets and then sends them to Host B using the outbound SA.

6. Secure packets cross the network.

7. The IPSec driver on Host B cryptographically processes the packets arriving on the inbound SA, formats them as normal IP packets, and then passes them to the TCP/IP driver.

8. The TCP/IP driver passes the packets to the application on Host B.

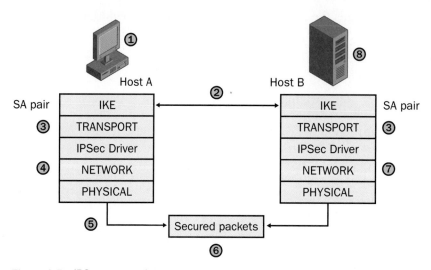

Figure 6-5   IPSec processing

Main Mode Negotiation

Oakley main mode negotiation is used to determine encryption key material and security protection for use in protecting subsequent main mode or quick mode communications. A more detailed main mode negotiation is presented in the following steps:

1. A communication packet is sent from Host A to Host B.

2. The IPSec driver on Host A checks its outbound IP filter lists and concludes that the packets match a filter and that the filter action is Negotiate Security—the packets must be secured.

3. The IPSec driver begins the IKE negotiation process.

4. Host A checks its policy for the main mode settings (authentication, Diffie-Hellman group, encryption, and integrity) to propose to Host B.

5. Host A sends the first IKE message using UDP source port 500 and destination port 500.

6. Host B receives the IKE main mode message that requests secure negotiation and then uses the source IP address and destination IP address of the packet to look up its own IKE filter. The IKE filter provides the security requirements for communications from Host A.

7. If the security settings proposed by Host A are acceptable to Host B, negotiation of the main mode or IKE SA begins.

8. Both computers negotiate options, exchange identities and authenticate them, and generate a master key. The IKE SA is established.

In summary, main mode negotiation creates the ISAKMP SA. The initiator and responder exchange a series of ISAKMP messages to negotiate the ciphersuite for the ISAKMP SA (in plaintext), exchange key determination material (in plaintext), and identify and authenticate each other (in encrypted text).

Quick Mode Negotiation

When main mode negotiation is complete, each IPSec peer has selected a specific set of cryptographic algorithms for securing main mode and quick mode messages, has exchanged key information to derive a shared secret key, and has performed authentication. Before secure data is sent, a quick mode negotiation must occur to determine the type of traffic to be secured and how it will be secured. A quick mode negotiation is also done when a quick mode SA expires.

Quick mode messages are ISAKMP messages that are encrypted using the ISAKMP SA. As noted previously, the result of a quick mode negotiation is two IPSec SAs: one for inbound traffic and one for outbound traffic. The process is as follows:

1. Host A performs an IKE mode policy lookup to determine the full policy.

2. Host A proposes its options (cryptographic, as well as frequency of key changes, and so on) and filters to Host B.

3. Host B does its own IKE mode policy lookup. If it finds a match with the one proposed by Host A, it completes the quick mode negotiation to create a pair of IPSec SAs.

4. One SA is outbound and the other one is inbound. Each SA is identified by an SPI, and the SPI is part of the header of each packet sent. Host A's IPSec driver uses the outbound SA and signs and, if specified, encrypts the packets. If hardware offload of IPSec cryptographic functions is supported by the network card, the IPSec driver just formats the packets; otherwise, it formats and cryptographically processes the packets.

5. The IPSec driver passes the packets to the network adapter driver.

6. The network adapter driver puts the datagrams on the network.

7. The network adapter at Host B receives the (encrypted) packets from the network.

8. The SPI is used to find the corresponding SA. (This SA has the associated cryptographic key necessary to decrypt and process the packets.)

9. If the network adapter is specifically designed to perform encryption and therefore can decrypt the packets, it will do so. It passes the packets to the IPSec driver.

10. Host B's IPSec driver uses the inbound SA to retrieve the keys and processes the packets if necessary.

11. The IPSec driver converts the packets back to normal IP packet format and passes them to the TCP/IP driver, which in turn passes them to the receiving application.

12. IPSec SAs continue processing packets. SAs are refreshed by IKE quick mode negotiation for as long as the application sends and receives data. When the SAs become idle, they are deleted.

IKE main mode is not deleted when idle. It has a lifetime of 8 hours, but this number is configurable (5 minutes to a maximum of 48 hours). Within the configured time frame, new traffic triggers only a new quick mode negotiation. If IKE main mode expires, a new IKE mode is negotiated as necessary.

UNDERSTANDING IPSEC SECURITY POLICIES

Policies are the security rules that define the desired security level, hashing algorithm, encryption algorithm, and key length. These rules also define the addresses, protocols, DNS names, subnets, or connection types to which the security settings will apply.

IPSec policies can be configured to meet the security requirements of a user, group, application, domain, site, or global enterprise. Windows Server 2003 provides the IP Security Policy Management snap-in to create and manage IPSec policies locally or through Group Policy.

Predefined policies are provided for both group and local security configurations. These can be modified to meet specific requirements, or you can create completely new policies. Once a policy is defined, however, to be effective you must assign it. By default, no polices are assigned.

Assigning IPSec Policies

As discussed previously, an IPSec policy is passed from the Policy Agent to the IPSec driver and defines proper procedures for all facets of the protocol—from when and how to secure data to which security methods to use. Several policies can be defined, but only one policy is assigned to a computer at a time. To assign a policy, in Local Security Policy or the appropriate Group Policy console, right-click the IPSec policy, and then click Assign.

To better understand the capabilities of a policy, you must also understand the components of a policy. The components of a policy follow:

- **Tunnel setting**   The IP address of the tunnel endpoint (if using IPSec tunneling to protect the packet destination).
- **Network type**   The type of connection affected by the IPSec policy: all network connections, LAN, or remote access.
- **IP filter**   A subset of network traffic based on IP address, port, and transport protocol. It tells the IPSec driver which outbound and inbound traffic should be secured.
- **IP filter list**   The concatenation of one or more IP filters, which define a range of network traffic.

- **Filter action**   How the IPSec driver should secure network traffic. Pre-defined filter actions include Permit, Request Security (Optional), and Require Security.

- **Authentication method**   One of the security algorithms and types used for authentication and key exchange:

    - ❏ Kerberos

    - ❏ Certificates

    - ❏ Preshared key

Default IPSec Security Policies

You create and configure local IPSec policies by using the IP Security Policies On Local Computer feature, as shown in Figure 6-6. (To access this snap-in, refer to Exercise 6-2, "Configuring IPSec to Use a Certificate," steps 1 through 7.)

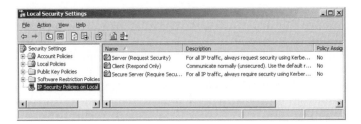

Figure 6-6   IP Security Policies On Local Computer

Use the Client (Respond Only) policy on computers that normally do not send secured data. This policy does not initiate secure communications. If security is requested by a server, the client responds and secures only the requested protocol and port traffic with that server.

The Server (Request Security) policy can be used on any computer—client or server—that needs to initiate secure communications. Unlike the Client policy, the Server policy attempts to protect all outbound transmissions. Unsecured, inbound transmissions are accepted; however, they are not resolved until IPSec requests security from the sender for all subsequent transmissions. This policy requires the Kerberos security protocol.

The strictest of the predefined policies, the Secure Server (Require Security) policy, does not send or accept unsecured transmissions. Clients attempting to communicate with a secure server must use at least the Server predefined policy or an equivalent. Like the Server policy, the Secure Server policy uses Kerberos authentication.

Default Response Rule

The default response rule, activated by default for all policies, is used to ensure that the computer responds to requests for secure communication. If an active policy does not have a rule defined for a computer that requests secure communication, the default response rule is applied and security is negotiated. For example, when Computer A communicates securely with Computer B, and Computer B does not have an inbound filter defined for Computer A, the default response rule is used.

Security methods and authentication methods can be configured for the default response rule. Use the IP Security Policy Management snap-in to modify the default response rule. (To create a console containing the IP Security Policy Management snap-in, refer to Exercise 6-2, "Configuring IPSec to Use a Certificate," steps 1 through 7.)

▶ **Accessing and Modifying the Security Methods for a Filter Action**

1. Open or create a console containing the IP Security Policy Management snap-in.

2. In the console tree, click the node containing the policies you want to modify.

3. In the details pane, double-click the policy you want to modify.

4. In the Rules tab, in the IP Security Rules box, click the rule you want to edit, and then click Edit.

5. In the Filter Action tab, click the filter action you want to modify, and then click Edit.

6. In the Security Methods tab, add, edit, reorder, or remove security methods.

The default response rule has the following characteristics:

- **IP Filter List of <Dynamic>**   The filter list of <Dynamic> indicates that the filter list is not configured, but that filters are created automatically based on the receipt of IKE negotiation packets.

- **Filter Action of Default Response**   The filter action of a policy can be viewed and edited by opening the property page of the corresponding policy using the IP Security Policy Management snap-in. A filter action of Default Response indicates that the action of the filter (Permit, Block, or Negotiate Security) cannot be configured. Negotiate Security will be used.

However, you can configure the following:

- The security methods and their preference order in the Security Methods tab

- The authentication methods and their preference order in the Authentication Methods tab

    NOTE   You Cannot Delete the Default Response Rule   The default response rule cannot be deleted, but it can be deactivated.

▶ **Adding a Policy Setting**

When you select the IP Security Policy Management snap-in to add to a console, you have four options for managing security policies:

- **Local Computer**   Use this option to manage IP Security Policies on the computer on which the console is running.

- **The Active Directory Domain Of Which This Computer Is A Member**   Use this option when you want to manage policies that apply to the entire local domain.

- **Another Active Directory Domain (Use The Full DNS Name Of IP Address)**   Use this option when you want to manage policies that apply to an entire remote domain.

- **Another Computer**   Use this option to manage the policies stored locally on another computer.

To manage Active Directory–based IPSec policies, you must be a member of the Domain Admins group in Active Directory, or you must have been delegated the appropriate authority.

1. Create or open a console containing the IP Security Policy Management snap-in.

2. In the console tree, click IP Security Policies for the location you want to manage (local computer, remote computer, local Active Directory domain, or remote Active Directory domain).

3. On the Action menu, click Create IP Security Policy.

4. On the Welcome To The IP Security Policy Wizard page, click Next.

5. On the IP Security Policy Name page, in the Name box, type a name for the new IP Security policy. If desired, provide a description, and then click Next.

6. To use the default response rule, on the Requests For Secure Communication page, verify that Activate The Default Response Rule is selected, and then click Next.

7. On the Default Response Rule Authentication Method page, select the initial authentication method for the security rule, provide additional information for the method if necessary, and then click Next.

8. On the Completing The IP Security Policy Wizard page, clear the Edit Properties box, and then click Finish.

▶ Modifying a Policy Setting

To modify an existing policy, double-click the policy that you want to modify, select the rule you want to modify, and then click Edit.

▶ Removing a Policy Setting

To remove a policy, click the policy that you want to remove, and on the Action menu, click Delete.

Practice adding an IPSec security policy by completing Exercise 6-1, "Adding an IPSec Security Policy," now.

DEPLOYING IPSEC POLICIES

IPSec policies can be deployed using local policies, Active Directory, or both. Each method has its advantages and disadvantages.

Deploying IPSec Using Local Policies

Only one local **Group Policy Object (GPO)**, often referred to as the *local computer policy*, is stored on a local computer. When using this local GPO, you can store Group Policy settings on individual computers regardless of whether they are members of an Active Directory domain.

On a network without an Active Directory domain (a network that lacks a Windows 2000 or Windows Server 2003 domain controller), the local GPO settings determine IPSec behavior because they are not overwritten by other GPOs. The local GPO can be overwritten by GPOs associated with sites, domains, or **organizational units (OUs)** in an Active Directory environment.

The settings of a local IPSec policy are added to the persistent policy if a persistent policy has been configured. If an Active Directory–based IPSec policy is assigned and the computer is connected to an Active Directory domain, the settings of the Active Directory–based policy are applied instead.

You should use the local policy in the following two scenarios:

- You have no Active Directory infrastructure in place, or you have a very small number of computers that need to use IPSec.

- You do not want to centralize the organization's IPSec strategy.

Persistent Policies

Permanent IPSec polices are known as *persistent* policies. You can configure persistent policies to extend existing Active Directory–based or local IPSec policies, override Active Directory–based or local IPSec policies, and enhance security during computer startup. Persistent policies enhance security by providing a secure transition from computer startup to Active Directory–based IPSec policy enforcement. Persistent policies, if configured, are stored in the local registry. You can update a persistent policy at any time, as long as the IPSec service is running. However, changes in persistent policy are not active immediately. You must restart the IPSec service to load the new persistent policy settings.

If you have configured Active Directory–based policies, you can use a persistent policy as a tool to require that traffic to Active Directory always be secured by IPSec, including the retrieval of Active Directory–based IPSec policies. When an Active Directory–based or local policy is applied, those policy settings are added to the persistent policy settings.

Deploying IPSec Using Active Directory

To deploy IPSec policies using Active Directory, assign IPSec policies to the target GPO of a site, domain, or OU. Assign the policies to a GPO that propagates to all computer accounts affected by that GPO.

Use the IP Security Policy Management console or the Netsh command to manage an Active Directory–based policy. The IP Security Policy Management console is discussed in the "Adding a Policy Setting" procedure. See the "Managing and Monitoring IPSec" section later in this chapter for more information about the Netsh command.

An Active Directory–based policy overrides any local IPSec policy that is assigned and adds to the persistent IPSec policy that has already been applied by the IPSec Policy Agent, if a persistent policy has been configured. If there is a conflict between a persistent IPSec policy and either a domain or local policy, the persistent policy settings prevail.

When assigning an IPSec policy in Active Directory, consider the following:

■ You can assign the list of all IPSec policies at any level in the Active Directory hierarchy. However, only a single IPSec policy can be assigned at a specific level in Active Directory.

■ An OU inherits the policy of its parent OU unless policy inheritance is explicitly blocked or policy is explicitly assigned.

■ IPSec policies from different OUs are never merged.

■ An IPSec policy that is assigned to an OU in Active Directory takes precedence over a domain-level policy for members of that OU.

■ An IPSec policy that is assigned to the lowest-level OU in the domain hierarchy overrides an IPSec policy that is assigned to a higher-level OU for member computers of that OU.

■ The highest possible level of the Active Directory hierarchy should be used to assign policies to reduce the amount of configuration and administration required.

You should use Active Directory to deploy policies if your enterprise meets the following criteria:

■ An Active Directory infrastructure is in place.

■ You use a substantial number of computers that must be grouped for IPSec assignment.

■ You want to centralize the organization's IPSec strategy.

Deployment in a Mixed Environment

You can deploy IPSec in an environment in which you have computers that are members of a domain and that receive their IPSec policy through an Active Directory group policy, in addition to computers that are not members of a domain and that receive their IPSec policy through a local group policy. Regardless of how the IPSec policies are received, two computers that must communicate with each other can negotiate with each other using the rules defined in their IPSec policies.

IMPLEMENTING IPSEC USING CERTIFICATES

IPSec relies on mutual authentication to provide secure communications. Because IPSec is an industry standard, this authentication can occur between systems that do not share a centralized Kerberos protocol authentication infrastructure. X.509 certificates provide another means of authentication for IPSec that is standards based and can be used if a trusted **public key infrastructure (PKI)** is in place. This section describes how you can use public key certificates for authentication to provide trust and secure communication on your network.

X.509 Certificates

An *X.509 certificate*, which is also called a digital certificate, is an electronic credential that is commonly used for authentication and secure exchange of information on open networks, such as the Internet, extranets, and intranets.

A certificate securely binds a public key to the entity that holds the corresponding private key. For example, you can encrypt data for a recipient with the recipient's public key, trusting that only the recipient has the private key that is required to decrypt the data.

A *certificate issuer*, called a certificate authority (CA), digitally signs certificates. The certificates can be issued for a user, a computer, or a service, such as IPSec.

A certificate contains the following information:

- The public cryptographic key from the certificate subject's public and private key pair
- Information about the subject that requested the certificate
- The user or computer's X.500 distinguished name
- The e-mail address of the certificate's owner
- Details about the CA
- Expiration dates
- A hash of the certificate contents to ensure authenticity (digital signature)

One of the main benefits of certificates is that hosts no longer have to maintain a set of passwords for individuals who must be authenticated as a prerequisite to access. Instead, the host merely establishes trust in a CA and that CA issues certificates.

The Role of a CA

A CA is responsible for authenticating and validating the keys for encryption, decryption, and authentication. After a CA verifies the identity of a key holder, the CA distributes the public keys by issuing X.509 certificates. A CA can issue certificates for specific functions, such as securing e-mail or securing IPSec, in addition to general-purpose certificates.

Using a Certificate with IPSec

If you choose to use a certificate for authentication, you must select a CA, which is usually the root CA for your installed computer certificate. You cannot leave the Use A Certificate From This Certification Authority (CA) field blank.

▶ **Configuring IPSec to Use a Certificate**

To configure IPSec to use a certificate, follow these steps:

1. Create an IP Security Management snap-in containing IP Security policies, or open a saved console file that contains IP Security policies.

2. Double-click the policy that you want to modify.

3. In the *Policy* Properties dialog box (where *Policy* is the name of the IP Security policy), double-click the IPSec security rule that you want to modify.

4. In the Edit Rule Properties dialog box, in the Authentication Methods tab, click Add, or, if you reconfigure an existing method, click the authentication method, and then click Edit.

5. Select Use A Certificate From This Certificate Authority (CA), and then click Browse.

6. In the Select Certificate dialog box, click the appropriate CA, and then click OK.

7. In the Authentication Method tab, click OK.

8. In the Edit Rule Properties dialog box, click OK.

9. In the *Policy* Properties dialog box, click OK.

Practice configuring IPSec to use a certificate by completing Exercise 6-2, "Configuring IPSec to Use a Certificate," now.

USING NAT WITH IPSEC

NAT is a widely-used translation process that allows a network with private addresses to access information on the Internet. A common scenario is a company that has only a few publicly routable IP addresses and distributes private IP addresses to its internal resources.

The translation of addresses, TCP ports, or UDP ports for NAT to connect users to the Internet invalidates the security services of IPSec. Specifically, address and port translation causes the following problems for ESP-based IPSec traffic:

- For ESP-protected packets, the TCP and UDP ports are encrypted and therefore cannot be translated.

- ISAKMP messages calculate hashes and signatures based on SA information, which includes IP addresses. Translating the IP address invalidates the hash or signature.

    NOTE   IKE over NAT   To allow IKE negotiation and ESP-encapsulated packets to work over NAT, Windows Server 2003 IPSec supports IPSec NAT Traversal (NAT-T). NAT-T is especially useful when making Layer Two Tunneling Protocol (L2TP)/IPSec connections from a VPN client that is behind NAT.

MANAGING AND MONITORING IPSEC

Windows Server 2003 provides several tools you can use to manage and monitor IPSec, including the IP Security Monitor, RSoP, Event Viewer, the Oakley log, Netsh, and Netdiag.

Using IP Security Monitor

In Windows 2000, IP Security Monitor is implemented as an executable program (Ipsecmon). In Windows XP and Windows Server 2003, IP Security Monitor is implemented as a **Microsoft Management Console (MMC)** and includes enhancements that allow you to do the following:

- Monitor IPSec information for your local computer and for remote computers.

- View details about active IPSec policies including the name, description, date last modified, store, path, OU, and Group Policy object name.

- View main mode and quick mode generic filters and specific filters.

- View main mode and quick mode statistics. (For information about the statistics displayed in IP Security Monitor, see Main Mode and Quick Mode statistics in IP Security Monitor.)

- View main mode and quick mode security associations.

- View main mode IKE policies.

- View quick mode negotiation policies.

- Customize refresh rates, and use DNS name resolution for filter and SA output.

- Search for specific main mode or quick mode filters that match any source or destination IP address, a source or destination IP address on your local computer, or a specific source or destination IP address.

Using IP Security Monitor to Monitor IPSec Traffic

If an IPSec policy is active, you can use IP Security Monitor (shown in Figure 6-7) to examine the policy and its operations. You can monitor IPSec only on computers running the Windows XP or Windows Server 2003 operating system. To monitor IPSec on a computer running Windows 2000, use the Ipsecmon command at a command prompt. Information that you can obtain includes the following:

- The name of the active IPSec policy

- Details about the active IPSec policy

- Quick mode statistics

- Main mode statistics

- Information about active SAs

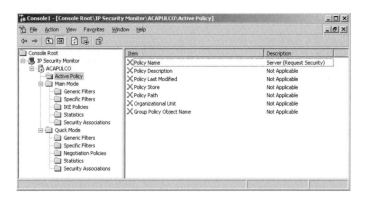

Figure 6-7   IP Security Monitor

Understanding Main Mode and Quick Mode Statistics in IP Security Monitor

Viewing IPSec statistics is simply a matter of expanding the server node, expanding the main mode node or the quick mode node, and then selecting the Statistics node. Understanding what each statistic means is more difficult. Table 6-1 describes the most common main mode statistics. (Table 6-2 describes the most common quick mode statistics.) In Table 6-1, several statistics appear to be related to quick mode. They are related, but they are initialized during the main mode IKE negotiation process, hence their inclusion as part of the main mode statistics table.

Table 6-1 **IPSec Main Mode Statistics**

Statistic	Description
Active Acquire	Number of pending requests for IKE negotiation for SAs between IPSec peers.
Active Receive	Number of IKE messages queued for processing.
Acquire Failures	Number of failed outbound requests that occurred to establish the SA since the IPSec service started.
Receive Failures	Number of errors found in the IKE messages received since the IPSec service last started.
Send Failures	Number of errors that occurred when sending IKE since the IPSec service last started.
Acquire Heap Size	Number of successive outbound requests to establish SAs.
Receive Heap Size	Number of IKE messages in IKE receive buffers.
Authentication Failures	Number of authentication failures that occurred since the IPSec service last started. If you cannot make an IPSec connection, check to see whether authentication failures increase during an attempt. If they do increase, authentication is the issue. Check to see that shared secrets match, peers are members of the domain, and certificates are correct.
Negotiation Failures	Number of main mode negotiation failures since the IPSec service last started. Attempt to communicate and see whether negotiation failures increase. If they do increase, check the authentication and security method settings for unmatched or incorrect configuration.
Invalid Cookies Received	The total number of cookies that could not be matched with an active main mode SA since the IPSec service was last started. A *cookie* is a value contained in a received IKE message that is used to help identify the corresponding main mode SA.
Total Acquire	The total number of requests that have been submitted to IKE since the IPSec service was last started to establish an SA. This number includes acquires that result in soft SAs.
Total Get SPI	The total number of requests that have been submitted by IKE to the IPSec driver to obtain a unique SPI since the IPSec service was last started. The SPI matches inbound packets with SAs.
Key Additions	The total number of outbound quick mode SAs that have been added by IKE to the IPSec driver since the IPSec service was last started.
Key Updates	The total number of inbound quick mode SAs that have been added by IKE to the IPSec driver since the IPSec service was last started.
Get SPI Failures	The total number of failed requests that have been submitted by IKE to the IPSec driver to obtain a unique SPI since the IPSec service was last started.
Key Addition Failures	The total number of failed outbound quick mode SA addition requests that have been submitted by IKE to the IPSec driver since the IPSec service was last started.

(continued)

Table 6-1   **IPSec Main Mode Statistics**

Statistic	Description
Key Update Failures	The total number of failed inbound quick mode SA addition requests that have been submitted by IKE to the IPSec driver since the IPSec service was last started.
ISADB List Size	The number of main mode state entries. This number includes successfully negotiated main modes, main mode negotiations in progress, and main mode negotiations that failed or expired and have not yet been deleted.
Connection List Size	The number of quick mode negotiations that are in progress.
IKE Main Mode	The total number of successful SAs that have been created during main mode negotiations since the IPSec service was last started.
IKE Quick Mode	The total number of successful SAs that have been created during quick mode negotiations since the IPSec service was last started.
Soft Associations	The total number of SAs formed with computers that have not responded to main mode negotiation attempts since the IPSec service was last started. Although these computers did not respond to main mode negotiation attempts, IPSec policy allowed communications with the computers. Soft SAs are not secured by IPSec.
Invalid Packets Received	The total number of invalid IKE messages that have been received since the IPSec service was last started. This number includes IKE messages with invalid header fields, incorrect payload lengths, and incorrect values for the responder cookie. Invalid IKE messages are commonly caused by retransmitted IKE messages or an unmatched preshared key between the IPSec peers.

Table 6-2 describes the most common quick mode statistics.

Table 6-2   **IPSec Quick Mode Statistics**

Statistic	Description
Active Security Association	Number of quick mode SAs.
Offloaded Security Associations	Number of quick mode SAs offloaded to hardware. Some network adapters process cryptography data themselves to increase overall performance.
Pending Key Operations	Number of key exchange operations in progress.
Key Additions	Number of keys for quick mode SAs successfully added since the computer started.
Key Deletions	Number of keys for quick mode SAs successfully deleted since computer started.
Rekeys	Number of successful rekey operations for quick mode.
Active Tunnels	Number of active tunnels.
Bad SPI Packets	Number of packets with incorrect SPI since the computer was last started. The SPI might have expired and an old packet just arrived. This will likely be larger if rekeying is frequent and there is a large number of SAs. Might indicate a spoofing attack.
Packets Not Decrypted	Number of packets that could not be decrypted since the computer was last started. A packet might not be decrypted if it fails a validation check.

Table 6-2   **IPSec Quick Mode Statistics**

Statistic	Description
Packets Not Authenticated	Number of packets for which data could not be verified (for which the integrity hash verification failed) since the computer was last started. Increases in this number might indicate an IPSec packet spoofing or a modification attack or packet corruption by network devices.
Packets With Replay Detection	Number of packets containing an invalid sequence number since the computer was last started. Detection increases might mean network problems or a replay attack.
Confidential Bytes Sent	Number of bytes sent using the ESP protocol since the computer was last started.
Confidential Bytes Received	Number of bytes received using the ESP protocol (excluding non-encrypted ESP) since the computer was last started.
Authenticated Bytes Sent	Number of authenticated bytes sent using the AH protocol or the ESP protocol since the computer was last started.
Authenticated Bytes Received	Number of authenticated bytes received using the AH protocol or the ESP protocol since the computer was last started.
Transport Bytes Sent	Number of bytes sent using IPSec transport mode since the computer was last started.
Transport Bytes Received	Number of bytes received using IPSec transport mode since the computer was last started.
Bytes Sent In Tunnels	Number of bytes sent using the IPSec tunnel mode since the computer was last started.
Bytes Received In Tunnels	Number of bytes received using the IPSec tunnel mode since the computer was last started.
Offloaded Bytes Sent	Number of bytes sent using hardware offload since the computer last started.
Offloaded Bytes Received	Number of bytes received using hardware offload since the computer was last started.

Using RSoP

In addition to viewing the policies with the IP Security Monitor, you can use RSoP to determine the IPSec policies that are assigned but that are not applied to IPSec clients. The RSoP snap-in displays only detailed IPSec policy settings. It shows the filter rules, filter actions, authentication methods, tunnel endpoints, and the connection type for the policy that is applied.

Using Event Viewer

You can use Event Viewer to view the following IPSec-related events (see Figure 6-8):

- IPSec Policy Agent events in the audit log
- IPSec driver events in the system log
- IKE events in the audit log
- IPSec policy change events in the audit log

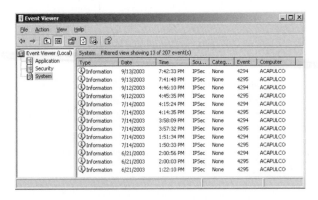

Figure 6-8   Event Viewer filtered for IPSec events

> **CAUTION**   **Increasing the Size of the Event Log**   If you enable audit logging, you can cause event logs to quickly fill with events. If you audit for a large number of events, be sure to increase the size of the event logs to cope with this.

Using the Oakley Log

You can use the Oakley log to view details of the SA establishment process. The Oakley log is enabled in the registry; it is not enabled by default. To enable the Oakley log, set the HKEY_LOCAL_MACHINE\System\CurrentControlSet\Services \PolicyAgent\Oakley\EnableLogging registry setting to 1.

The Oakley log records all ISAKMP main mode or quick mode negotiations. A new Oakley log file is created each time the IPSec Policy Agent is started, and the previous version of the Oakley log file is saved as Oakley.log.sav.

Using Netsh

Netsh is a native Windows Server 2003 command-line scripting tool that you can use to display or modify the local or remote network configuration of a computer running Windows Server 2003. You can run Netsh from a batch file or from the command prompt. The Netsh commands for IPSec can be used to configure IPSec policies only on computers running members of the Windows Server 2003 family.

> **MORE INFO**   **Netsh Commands for IPSec**   For a complete list of Netsh IPSec commands, in the Windows Server 2003 Help And Support Center, click Tools, click Command Line Reference, and then navigate to and click Netsh Commands For Internet Protocol Security (IPSec).

To set the Netsh IPSec context, type the word **static** or **dynamic** at the Netsh IPSec prompt. A *context* is a specified set of commands arranged within a hierarchy. For example, to access commands available within the IPSec context, type **ipsec** at the Netsh prompt (netsh>). After you have selected a context, you can use the Netsh commands to produce a policy or to monitor IPSec activity. Two modes are possible. *Static mode* allows you to create, modify, and assign policies without affecting the active IPSec policy. *Dynamic mode* allows you to display the active state and immediately implement changes to the active IPSec policy. Dynamic

Netsh commands affect the service only when it runs. If it is stopped, dynamic policy settings are discarded.

> **CAUTION** **Making Dynamic Mode Changes Immediately** If you must immediately initiate a change to IPSec processing, dynamic mode is very useful because commands issued in that mode are implemented immediately (except when a service must be stopped and restarted). However, dynamic mode is also a mixed blessing. If you make a mistake in dynamic mode, you do not have the opportunity to discover it before implementing the change; therefore, you could accidentally create an incorrect configuration without warning.

Using Netsh to Monitor IPSec

You can use Netsh to monitor the current IPSec session. Monitoring consists of either displaying policy information, obtaining diagnostics and logging IPSec information, or both. Any information you can find with the IP Security Monitor snap-in, you can find with Netsh. To obtain syntax information for Netsh, at the command prompt, type **netsh /?**, and then press ENTER.

Displaying IPSec Policy Information

To find out what the current IPSec policy is, use the Show command. If you choose to use the Show All command, a lot of information will be returned, as displayed in Figure 6-9 (note that this is only part of the information that would be displayed).

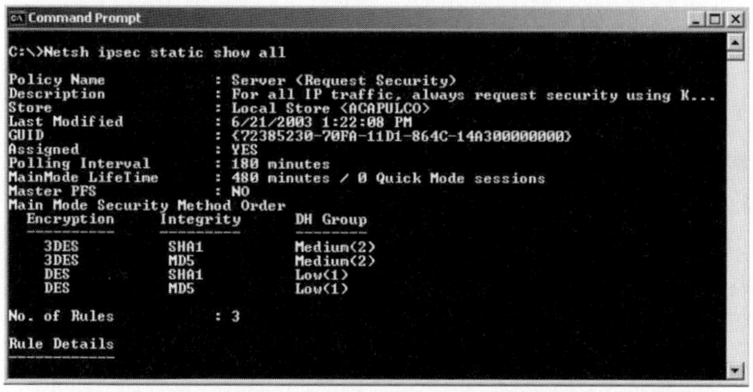

Figure 6-9 Initial output from Show All command

Because of the potentially large amount of available information, it is useful to view only a portion of the IPSec configuration information. Several Show commands are available to do this, some of which are listed in Table 6-3. You can enter all of the commands from the Netsh IPSec dynamic or the Netsh IPSec static context or, with modification, from the command line.

Table 6-3 **Netsh IPSec Show Static Commands**

Operation	Command
To display a specific filter list, use...	**show filterlist name =*filterlistname***
To display the policy assigned to the specified GPO, use...	**show gpoassignedpolicy name =*name***
To display a specific policy, use...	**show policy name =*policyname***
To display a specific rule, use...	**show rule name =*rulename***

Obtaining Diagnostic IPSec Information

One of the steps in diagnosing IPSec problems—or just establishing that the policy is working like you think it should—is to obtain information about the current policy. The Show commands described in Table 6-3 provide that information. The information that each command reveals identifies the settings in the policy. For example, the Show Filterlist command lists the information in the policies filter list.

Some examples of the Show command syntax are illustrated in Table 6-4. In Table 6-5, in the commands, the equal sign is part of the command and the italicized words are replaced by a value as indicated.

Table 6-4   **Descriptions of Show Command Syntax**

Command	Description
show config	Displays IPSec configuration and boot time behavior.
show mmsas	Displays information on the IPSec main mode SA. You can see the source and destination addresses. When used with the Resolvedns=yes switch, the names of the computers are also displayed.
show qmsas	Displays information about the IPSec quick mode SAs.
show stats	Displays the IKE main mode statistics, IPSec quick mode statistics, or both. The statistics are the same ones as those described in Table 6-2.

In addition to Show commands, you can use several dynamic mode Netsh IPSec diagnostic commands to obtain diagnostic information, such as those listed in Table 6-5.

Table 6-5   **Dynamic Mode Netsh IPSec Diagnostic Commands**

Command	Description
set config property= ipsecdiagnostics value=*value*	Can be set with a value of 0 to 7, which indicates the level of IPSec diagnostic logging. The default is 0, which means logging is disabled. The level 7 causes all logging to be performed. The computer must be restarted for logging to begin.
set config property= ipsecloginterval value=*value*	Indicates how frequently in seconds the IPSec events are sent to the system event log. The range of the value parameter is 60 to 86,400 with a default of 3600.
set config property= ikelogging value=*value*	Can be set with a value of 0 or 1 to determine whether IKE (Oakley) logging will occur. This command produces a log with a copious amount of information. You must understand the Requests for Comments (RFCs) at the expert level to completely understand the Oakley logs.
set config property= strongcrlcheck value=*value*	Determines whether **certificate revocation list (CRL)** checking is used. If the value is 0, CRL checking is disabled. If 1 is the value, certificate validation fails only if the certificate is revoked. Level 2 fails if any CRL check error occurs. A CRL check fails if the CRL cannot be located on the network. You can make other diagnostic efforts by modifying the current policy to reduce security. For example, if you change authentication to Shared Secret on both computers instead of Kerberos or Certificates, you eliminate the possibility that the problem is related to authentication.

Practice displaying IPSec information using Netsh by completing Exercise 6-3, "Using Netsh to Display IPSec information," now.

Using Netdiag

Netdiag is a command-line tool that you can use to display IPSec information and test and view the network configuration. Netdiag is available for Windows Server 2003, Windows 2000, and Windows XP. However, it must be installed in a different way for each operating system. For Windows Server 2003, Netdiag is installed with the Windows Server 2003 Support Tools. For Windows 2000, Netdiag is included with the Windows 2000 Resource Kit tools that you can also download from the Internet. It is also available on the Windows XP Installation CD-ROM and is installed by running Setup from the Support\Tools folder.

You can obtain general network diagnostic information (but not IPSec information) by using the Netdiag command. For example, entering **netdiag /v /l** provides the IP configuration and routing configuration for a computer, tests WINS and DNS name resolution, reports the build version of the computer and the hotfixes that are installed, tests the validity of domain membership, verifies contacts by member computers with their domain controllers, and checks trust relationships. All of this information is useful when you must eliminate general networking problems before you attempt to diagnose IPSec issues.

> **NOTE   Use Netsh Instead of Netdiag**   The Netdiag tool is available for Windows Server 2003; however, the Netdiag /test:ipsec option has been removed. Use the Netsh command instead. Use Netdiag with earlier versions of the Windows operating system. To remotely examine the IPSec policy of a computer running Windows XP or Windows 2000, consider using a remote desktop session and the Netdiag tool.

SUMMARY

■ IPSec is the standard method of providing security services for IP packets.

■ ESP protocol provides confidentiality (in addition to authentication, integrity, and anti-replay) for the IP payload, while the AH protocol provides authentication, integrity, and anti-replay for the entire packet.

■ Two types of SAs are created when IPSec peers communicate securely: the ISAKMP SA and the IPSec SA.

■ To negotiate SAs for sending secure traffic, IPSec uses IKE, a combination of ISAKMP and the Oakley Key Determination Protocol. ISAKMP messages contain many types of payloads to exchange information during SA negotiation.

■ Main mode negotiation is used to establish the ISAKMP SA, which is used to protect future main mode and all quick mode negotiations.

■ Quick mode negotiation is used to establish the IPSec SA to protect data.

■ Certificates provide a means of authentication between systems that do not share a centralized Kerberos protocol authentication infrastructure.

■ You can use Netsh IPSec static mode to create and assign IPSec policies, add a persistent policy, and change other configuration features.

EXERCISES

IMPORTANT   Complete All Exercises   If you plan to do any of the textbook exercises in this chapter, you must do all of the exercises to return the computer to its original state in preparation for the subsequent Lab Manual labs.

Exercise 6-1: Adding an IPSec Security Policy

1. Click Start, point to Administrative Tools, and then click Domain Controller Security Policy.

2. In the console tree, expand Security Settings, and then click IP Security Policies On Active Directory.

3. On the Action menu, click Create IP Security Policy.

4. On the Welcome To The IP Security Policy Wizard page, click Next.

5. On the IP Security Policy Name page, in the Name box, type **security policy example**, and then click Next.

6. On the Requests For Secure Communication page, verify that Activate The Default Response Rule is selected, and then click Next.

7. On the Default Response Rule Authentication Method page, verify Active Directory Default (Kerberos V5 Protocol) is selected, and then click Next.

8. On the Completing The IP Security Policy Wizard page, click Finish.

Exercise 6-2: Configuring IPSec to Use a Certificate

To configure IPSec to use a certificate, follow these steps:

1. Click Start, click Run, type **mmc** in the Open box, and then click OK.

2. In the Console1 window, on the File menu, click Add/Remove Snap-In.

3. In the Add/Remove Snap-In window, click Add.

4. In the Add Standalone Snap-In window, click IP Security Policy Management, and then click Add.

5. In the Select Computer Or Domain window, verify Local Computer is selected, and then click Finish.

6. In the Add Standalone Snap-In window, click Close.

7. In the Add/Remove Snap-In window, click OK.

8. In the console tree, click IP Security Policies On Local Computer.

9. In the details pane, double-click Security Policy Example (the one you created in Exercise 6-1).

10. In the Security Policy Example Properties window, double-click the default response rule.

11. In the Edit Rule Properties dialog box, in the Authentication Methods tab, click Add.

12. Select Use A Certificate From This Certification Authority (CA), and then click Browse.

13. In the Select Certificate dialog box, click Microsoft Root Certificate Authority, and then click OK.

14. In the New Authentication Method Properties window, click OK.

15. In the Edit Rule Properties window, click OK.

16. In the Security Policy Example Properties window, click OK.

Exercise 6-3: Using Netsh to Display IPSec Information

1. Open a command prompt.

2. At the command prompt, type **netsh**, and then press ENTER.

   The prompt changes to netsh>.

3. At the command prompt, to enter the IPSec static context, type **ipsec static**, and then press ENTER.

4. At the command prompt, to view information about the Security Policy Example IPSec policy, type **show policy "security policy example"**, and then press ENTER.

5. To display the rule associated with the Security Policy Example IPSec policy, at the command prompt, type **show rule all "security policy example"**, and then press ENTER.

   Note the listing of the certificate you added in Exercise 6-2.

REVIEW QUESTIONS

1. Which of the following most accurately describes the functionality of the Client (Respond Only) default policy rule?

   a. The client will respond only to requests secured by IPSec.

   b. The client will respond to unsecured requests, but will respond by using IPSec.

   c. The client will respond to unsecured requests with an unsecured response, but will respond to secure requests with a secure response.

   d. The client will respond to a server only if it can perform a reverse lookup on the IP address of the server.

2. Fabrikam, Inc., recently joined two servers to its Active Directory domain. After joining the servers to the domain, the company no longer is able to communicate on the network. You suspect that applying the IPSec policies caused the problem. Which tool would you use to determine whether your suspicion is correct?

   a. Network Monitor

   b. The security log in Event Viewer

   c. Resultant Set of Policies (RSoP)

   d. IP Security Monitor

3. You wish to determine whether a quick mode association is currently in place. Which of the following tools can you use to make that determination?

   a. RSoP

   b. Event Viewer

   c. Oakley log file

   d. IP Security Monitor

4. IPSec can be used to secure communications between two computers. Which of the following would be good reasons to use IPSec? Choose all that apply.

   a. Examine Kerberos tickets

   b. Block transfer of specific protocol packets

   c. Allow transfer of packets with a destination TCP port of 23 from any computer to the host computer

   d. Permit one user to use Telnet to access the computer, while denying another user

5. What is a good reason for assigning an IPSec policy using Netsh instead of using Group Policy?

   a. Using Netsh is the only way to apply a policy that can be used to permit a user's computer to be used for a telnet session with another computer while blocking all other telnet communications.

   b. Using Netsh is more easily implemented than Group Policy when multiple machines must be configured.

   c. You can apply Netsh even if the computers are not joined in a domain, whereas Group Policy can work only in a domain.

   d. You can use Netsh to create a persistent policy if Group Policy cannot be used.

6. Netsh is used to create and assign an IPSec policy for a stand-alone server running Windows Server 2003. One of the commands used is executed from the Netsh IPSec static context. It follows:

```
Add rule name="SMTPBlock" policy="smtp" filterlist="smtp computerlist"
filteraction="negotiate smtp" description="this rule negotiates smtp"
```

   Why is the policy not working?

   a. The policy is set with the wrong IP addresses.

   b. Each policy specifies a different encryption algorithm.

   c. A stand-alone server does not have a Simple Mail Transfer Protocol (SMTP) service; therefore, the policy is unassigned.

   d. The policy uses Kerberos for authentication and the computer is not a member of a domain.

7. You wish to set up a tool for maintenance and monitoring of IP policies on remote hosts in your domain. You add the IP Security Monitor and IP Security Policy Management snap-ins to an MMC. However, when you try to add the host 192.168.0.100 to the IP Security Monitor, you get the error message shown in Figure 6-10.

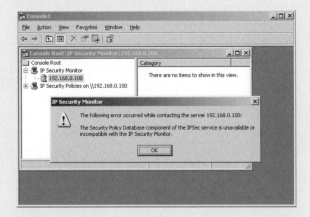

Figure 6-10   IPSec console error message

How can you manage and monitor IPSec on 192.168.0.100?

    a. You cannot do so. The host 192.168.0.100 is a legacy host that does not support IPSec.

    b. The host 192.168.0.100 is not part of the domain. You must join the host to your domain if you want to use IP Security Monitor.

    c. Only IPSec policies that use your authentication can be managed and monitored using IP Security Monitor. You must assign such a policy to 192.168.0.100.

    d. You should use legacy Ipsecmon.

    e. You cannot add a computer using its IP address. You must use the computer's DNS host name.

8. During the testing of the IPSec policies, the workstation you use as a test computer works correctly and the traffic is encrypted; however, when you resume testing after making some changes on one of the servers, the workstation can no longer communicate with that server. The policy that you set on the server requires you to use Kerberos as the authenticating protocol. What is the most likely cause of the communication issue?

    a. Your workstation lost its connection to a domain controller.

    b. Your workstation lost its connection to the CA.

    c. The IPSec Policy Agent lost communication with the domain controller and must be restarted.

    d. You must reapply the server's IPSec policy.

CASE SCENARIOS

Case Scenario 6-1: Securing Communications

You administer a Windows Server 2003 Active Directory domain. All client PCs are in a top-level OU called Clients, and all server PCs (apart from domain controllers) are in a top-level OU called Servers. The domain controllers are in their default OU. The Secure Server (Require Security) default IPSec policy has been assigned to all servers, including domain controllers. The Client (Respond Only) default IPSec policy has been assigned to all clients. All client PCs are Windows 2000 Professional hosts.

Management is concerned that the client computers in the Research department do not securely communicate with each other and with other clients. Only four such machines exist. On one of them, you create a custom policy that requires secure communications. You export it to a file and import it into the other three client machines in the Research department. You assign the policy on all four machines.

Next, you use the IP Security Monitor console on one of the machines and find that no SAs are set up between the Research department hosts or between these machines and clients in other departments. You capture traffic using Network

Monitor and discover that unencrypted traffic is passing between the Research clients. What is the first step you should take to solve the problem?

a. Change the authentication method on the custom policy to use a preshared key.

b. Change the encryption algorithm from Triple DES (3DES) to Data Encryption Standard (DES).

c. Create an OU.

d. Move the Research department computer accounts into the Servers OU.

Case Scenario 6-2: Troubleshooting IPSec

Your company does not use a domain structure; it uses workgroups. The Research workgroup has six clients running Windows XP Professional, four clients running Windows 2000 Professional, and two stand-alone servers running Windows Server 2003. Communication between hosts in this workgroup must be secure. A member of your support staff configures and assigns an IPSec security policy on all hosts in the Research workgroup. All hosts can ping each other by IP address, but the Research department staff cannot access files on the servers from their client PCs.

You log on to one of the servers using the local administrator account, you access the Security Settings node within Local Computer Policy, and you enable success and failure auditing for logon events. You open Event Viewer and locate a failure audit event 547 in the security log. The failure reason given is, "Failed to obtain Kerberos server credentials for the ISAKMP/ERROR_IPSEC_IKE service." What is the most likely cause of the problem?

a. The default response rule is not activated.

b. Kerberos has been specified as the initial authentication method.

c. The 3DES encryption algorithm has been specified, and it cannot be used on the clients running Windows 2000.

d. The incorrect policy has been assigned.

CHAPTER 7

IMPLEMENTING AND MANAGING SOFTWARE UPDATE SERVICES

Upon completion of this chapter, you will be able to:

- Configure **Windows Update** and **Automatic Updates**, and explain the difference between the two.

- Explain the purpose and benefits of deploying Microsoft Software Update Services (SUS) in your organization.

- Implement SUS in your organization.

- Manage SUS by synchronizing, approving, and distributing update packages.

- Configure client computers to use SUS using **Group Policy** or the registry.

- Monitor the SUS server using logs and the SUS Administration Web page.

Traditionally, system administrators and users kept systems up-to-date by frequently checking the Microsoft Windows Update Web site or the Microsoft Security Web site for software updates. Administrators manually downloaded available updates, tested the updates in their environment, and then distributed the updates manually or with traditional software distribution tools. In a less favorable scenario, users on a corporate network were left to select, download, and install their own updates. These scenarios resulted in difficult processes for the system administrator and a potentially unreliable, insecure system for the user.

This chapter introduces SUS, a tool for managing and distributing software updates that resolve known security vulnerabilities or otherwise improve performance of Microsoft Windows 2000, Microsoft Windows XP, and Microsoft Windows Server 2003 operating systems. This chapter briefly discusses Windows Update and Automatic Updates. The primary focus is on the SUS concepts: hardware and software requirements; installing, managing, and monitoring SUS; and how to configure SUS client computers.

WHAT DOES AN UPDATE INCLUDE?

Updates can include security fixes, critical updates, and critical drivers. These updates resolve known security vulnerabilities and stability issues in Windows 2000, Windows XP, and Windows Server 2003 operating systems.

The following are categories for the Windows operating system updates:

- **Critical updates** Security fixes and other important updates that keep computers current and networks secure. A computer that is missing one or more critical updates should be considered a security risk, unstable, or both.

- **Recommended downloads** The latest Windows and Microsoft Internet Explorer service packs and other important updates.

- **Windows tools** Utilities and other tools that are provided to enhance performance, facilitate upgrades, and ease the burden on system administrators.

- **Internet and multimedia updates** Includes Internet Explorer upgrades and patches, upgrades to Microsoft Windows Media Player, and similar updates.

- **Additional Windows downloads** Updates for desktop settings and other Windows operating system features.

- **Multilanguage features** Menus and dialog boxes, language support, and Input Method Editors for a variety of languages.

- **Documentation** Deployment guides and other software-related documents are also available.

OVERVIEW OF SUS

SUS is a free product that provides a means of aggregating, testing, deploying, and providing notification of updates to client computers in your organization. SUS can be deployed as a single server or as multiple servers to provide greater testing capabilities and load balancing.

Dynamic notification of updates to Windows client computers does not require that client computers have Internet access. SUS extends current Microsoft Windows Update technologies and provides a solution to the previously discussed problem of managing and distributing critical Windows updates. This software updates Windows 2000, Windows XP, and Windows Server 2003 operating systems.

The SUS solution comprises the following components:

- **A content synchronization service** A server-side component on your organization's intranet that retrieves the latest critical updates from the Windows Update Web site. As new updates are added to Windows Update, the SUS server automatically downloads and stores them based on an administrator-defined schedule, or the administrator can manually download them.

- **An internal Windows Update server**   This user-friendly server acts as the virtual Windows Update server for client computers. It contains the synchronization service and administrative tools for managing updates. It uses Hypertext Transfer Protocol (HTTP) to service requests for approved updates by the client computers that are connected to it. This server can also host critical updates (an example of a critical update is a security patch necessary to close a known vulnerability in the operating system) downloaded from the synchronization service and refer client computers to those updates.

- **Automatic Updates on computers (desktops or servers)**   A Windows feature that can be set up to automatically check for updates that are published on Windows Update. SUS uses this Windows feature to publish administrator-approved updates on an intranet. You can configure the Windows operating system to install updates on a schedule.

The administrator can test and approve updates from the public Windows Update site before deploying them on the corporate intranet. Recall that deployment takes place on a schedule that the administrator creates. If multiple servers run SUS, the administrator controls which clients access particular servers that run SUS. Administrators enable this level of control through Group Policy in an Active Directory environment or through registry keys.

SUS AND OTHER SOFTWARE-DISTRIBUTION TECHNOLOGIES

SUS is designed to quickly deliver critical updates for computers that run Windows 2000 and later operating systems inside your corporate firewall. It is not intended to serve as a replacement to your enterprise software-distribution solution, such as Microsoft Systems Management Server (SMS) or Group Policy–based software distribution. Many customers today use solutions such as SMS for complete software management, including responding to security and virus issues. SMS customers should continue using these solutions. In addition to providing administrative controls that are critical for medium-sized and large organizations, advanced solutions such as SMS provide the capability to deploy all software throughout an enterprise. SUS is a focused solution; organizations that do not already have patch management solutions in place but that desire to more closely manage the update process should use this solution.

WINDOWS UPDATE AND AUTOMATIC UPDATES

Windows Update and Automatic Updates are two separate components designed to work together to keep Windows operating systems updated and secure. The following sections discuss each of these components.

Windows Update

Windows Update is a Microsoft Web site that works with Automatic Updates to provide timely, critical, and noncritical system updates (see Figure 7-1). Updates include security patches, updated drivers, and other recommended files. Windows

Update scans your system to determine which updates your system is missing and provides a list of available downloads. Windows Update also maintains a history of the files you have downloaded.

Figure 7-1   Windows Update Web site

In addition to the downloads for your own system, the **Windows Update Catalog** provides updates for other systems. Windows Update Catalog is a Web site that lists hardware and software designed for use with Windows XP, Microsoft Windows 2000 Server products, and products in the Windows Server 2003 family. You can use this site to help you decide whether to purchase a particular device or program and to evaluate whether a particular computer would support an upgraded operating system, as well as to help you make similar decisions about hardware and software.

Practice using the Windows Update Web site by completing Exercise 7-1, "Using the Windows Update Web Site," now.

Although using Windows Update and Windows Update Catalog is helpful, it is still a manual process that does not scale well to hundreds or thousands of computers.

Automatic Updates

Automatic Updates enables you to obtain critical software updates by automatically interacting with the Windows Update Web site. Automatic Updates can inform you when Windows updates are available and enable you to specify how and when you want to update Windows operating systems. These updates can include everything from critical updates to enhancements.

Automatic Updates includes a range of options for how to update Windows operating systems. For example, you can set Windows to automatically download and install updates on a schedule that you specify. Or you can choose to have Windows notify you whenever it finds updates available for your computer. Windows can then download the update in the background while you continue to work uninterrupted. After the download is complete, a balloon message and an icon appear in the notification area to alert you that the updates are ready to be installed (see Figure 7-2). When you click the icon or message, Automatic Updates quickly guides you through the installation process. Depending on the type of update and the configuration of your system, you might have to restart your computer after certain components are installed.

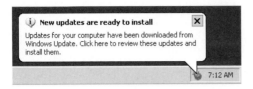

Figure 7-2   Automatic Updates notification

If you choose not to install a specific update that has been downloaded, Windows deletes its files from your computer. If you change your mind later, you can download it and all declined updates by clicking Declined Updates in the Automatic Updates tab, which is shown in Figure 7-3. If any of the updates you previously declined still apply to your computer, they will appear the next time Windows notifies you of available updates.

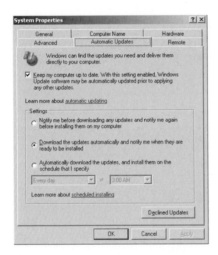

Figure 7-3   Automatic Updates tab of System Properties

Following are the operating systems that ship with Automatic Updates:

- Microsoft Windows 2000 Professional (Service Pack 3 and later)
- Microsoft Windows 2000 Server (Service Pack 3 and later)
- Microsoft Windows 2000 Advanced Server (Service Pack 3 and later)
- Microsoft Windows XP Professional
- Microsoft Windows XP Home Edition
- Microsoft Windows Server 2003 family of operating systems

Automatic Updates has been enhanced to support SUS. This enhancement adds the following features to the Windows XP Automatic Updates client:

- Approved content download from a SUS server
- Scheduled content download and installation
- The ability to configure all Automatic Updates options by using Group Policy Object Editor or by editing the registry
- Support for systems without a local administrator logged on

SUS-compatible Automatic Updates can be obtained from one of the following sources:

Practice viewing
and configuring
Automatic
Updates by
completing
Exercise 7-2,
"Enabling
Automatic
Updates," now.

- Software Update Services 1.0 Service Pack 1 or later

- A stand-alone setup package (Microsoft Installer [MSI] package, available from *http://www.microsoft.com/windows2000/downloads/recommended /susclient/default.asp*)

- Microsoft Windows 2000 Service Pack 3 or later

- Microsoft Windows XP Service Pack 1 or later

- Microsoft Windows Server 2003 family of operating systems

INSTALLING AND CONFIGURING SUS

To install SUS, your system must meet certain hardware and software requirements. You should also understand the impact of related components, such as **Internet Information Server (IIS) Lockdown**, and potential application compatibility issues.

Hardware Requirements

The minimum configuration for a server running SUS is as follows:

- Pentium III 700-megahertz (MHz) or a higher processor

- 512 megabytes (MB) of RAM

- 6 gigabytes (GB) of free hard disk space for setup and security packages

This configuration supports approximately 15,000 clients using one server running SUS.

> **MORE INFO**   **Planning Enterprise-Level SUS Deployment**   For additional information about how to deploy SUS in an enterprise environment with thousands of clients and various sites and **wide area network (WAN)** links, see the "Deploying Microsoft Software Update Services" white paper, and refer to the section, "Planning a Software Update Services Deployment." You can download the white paper from http://www.microsoft.com/windowsserversystem/sus/susdeployment.mspx.

Software Requirements

SUS runs on the Windows 2000 Server operating system with Service Pack 2 or later and on machines running Windows Server 2003. SUS must be installed on an NTFS file system partition. The system partition on your server must also use the **NTFS file system**. SUS 1 Service Pack 1 adds the capability to install SUS on a domain controller and on computers running Microsoft Small Business Server 2000.

Required Applications

To install SUS on machines running Windows Server 2003, you must first install IIS 6 or add the Application Server role using the Manage Your Server page. A default installation provides all necessary IIS components for SUS. However, if you wish to minimize the IIS installation, you should install the following components before installing SUS:

- Common Files

- Internet Information Services Manager

- World Wide Web Service

- Internet Explorer 5.5 or later

Installing IIS Lockdown

When you install SUS on a computer that runs Windows 2000 Server or Small Business Server 2000 with Service Pack 1, the setup utility automatically installs IIS Lockdown 2. This includes installing and configuring IIS URL Scanner 2.5. Because Windows Server 2003 already includes all the security benefits provided by IIS Lockdown, IIS Lockdown is not installed on Windows Server 2003 computers.

If you previously installed IIS Lockdown or URL Scanner, the SUS setup utility does not attempt to install the IIS Lockdown tool again; no IIS Lockdown tool settings are modified; and none of the information in the **IIS metabase** (the IIS configuration database) is deleted. This functionality is new for SUS Service Pack 1.

> **NOTE** **IIS Lockdown Settings Persist**   When you uninstall SUS, the settings applied by IIS Lockdown are not removed, thus leaving your server in a more secure state. Refer to the SUS Deployment Guide to understand all of the IIS Lockdown settings that continue to apply after you have uninstalled SUS.

Because the default installation option for IIS on computers running Windows Server 2003 already includes all of the security work performed by the IIS Lockdown tool, the SUS setup utility does not install IIS Lockdown on those computers. However, the SUS setup utility does enable Asp.dll by setting the following property in the IIS metabase:

```
ISAPIRestrictionList: = "0", "asp.dll"
```

This setting disables all script mappings other than Asp.dll. This means that only Asp.dll will process scripts. For example, files with the extension .htr are used for Web-based password resets. Files with an .htr extension are mapped the Ism.dll to perform this function. By setting the ISAPIRestrictionList property to zero, .htr files are no longer mapped to the Ism.dll and Web-based password resets are disabled. If your server requires only mappings to Asp.dll, you should reduce your risk of attack on other services, such as Web-based password resets, by disabling them.

> **MORE INFO**   **IIS Lockdown Tool**   For additional information about the IIS Lockdown tool and the Windows Security Toolkit CD, visit *http://www .microsoft.com/security*.

Application Compatibility Issues

The ideal situation is to dedicate a server to run SUS; however, if this is not feasible, you can still run other services on the same server as SUS—but you must verify that no compatibility issues with the other applications and SUS exist.

Specifically, you must determine whether any applications depend on a specific IIS configuration or whether they are incompatible with certain configurations of the IIS URL Scanner, a tool that protects IIS from improperly formatted HTTP requests.

▶ **How to Install SUS 1 with Service Pack 1**

To install SUS 1 with Service Pack 1, perform the following steps:

1. Download SUS at *http://www.microsoft.com/windows2000/windowsupdate /sus/default.asp*.

2. Click the Download Software Update Services With Service Pack 1 link.

3. On the Change Language Box On The Software Update Services Server 1.0 With Service Pack 1 page, select the appropriate language, and then click Download.

4. Click Save in the File Download window.

   The SUS installation files are included in a package named Sus10sp1.exe. (This file is approximately 33 MB in size.)

5. In the Save As dialog box, specify a path, and then click Save.

6. Navigate to the path specified in the previous step, and then double-click Sus10sp1.exe.

7. On the Welcome To The Microsoft Software Update Services Setup Wizard page, click Next.

8. On the End-User License Agreement page, click I Accept The Terms In The License Agreement, and then click Next.

9. On the Choose Setup Type page, click Typical.

10. On the Ready To Install page, note the Uniform Resource Locator (URL) to which Automatic Updates should be configured (for example, **http://computer.xx**), and then click Install.

    SUS is installed with the default settings.

11. On the Completing The Microsoft Software Update Services Setup Wizard page, note the URL of the Administration Web site (for example, **http://computer.xx/SUSAdmin)**, and then click Finish.

    In the Administrative Tools folder, SUS setup adds a shortcut to the administration Web pages.

As shown in Figure 7-4, the SUS Administration Web site opens in Internet Explorer. You are now ready to configure and use SUS.

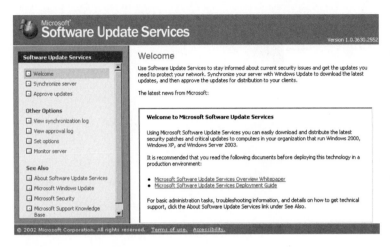

Figure 7-4   The SUS Administration Web page

HOW SUS WORKS

SUS has three main components:

- Windows Update Synchronization Service, which downloads content to your server that runs SUS

- A Web site hosted on a IIS server that services update requests from Automatic Updates clients

- A SUS Administration Web page

The SUS server performs two primary functions:

- Synchronizing content with the public Windows Update site

- Approving content for distribution to your organization

Both functions are performed using the SUS Administration Web page. Synchronization can be scheduled or executed immediately. When packages have been downloaded, the system administrator selects packages to release to clients and clicks Approve. Clients are configured to use specific SUS distribution points to retrieve approved packages.

SUS Distribution Points

A server that runs SUS can be synchronized from the public Windows Update servers, from another server running SUS, or from a manually configured content distribution point. SUS servers can download and store content locally, or they can use the content on the Windows Update Web site.

In Figure 7-5, Server A and Server B both run SUS. Server A synchronizes content over the Internet from the public Windows Update servers. Server A is a *parent server*; that is, a server configured to store content locally. Server B is also configured to store content locally; however, rather than synchronizing with the Windows Update site, it is configured to synchronize content from Server A. Server B is therefore a *child server* of Server A.

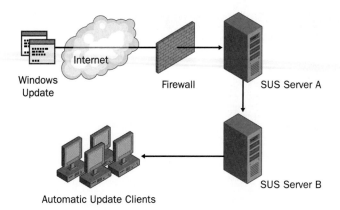

Figure 7-5   SUS server-to-server synchronization

To successfully synchronize Server A and Server B:

- Both Server A and Server B must be configured to save updates locally.

- Server A must be configured to support all the locales that Server B might request on the Set Options page.

- Server B must specify Server A as its synchronization server (see Figure 7-6).

Figure 7-6   Specifying a local synchronization server

- Server B must support only locales that Server A supports.

Synchronizing from another server that runs SUS, or a manually configured content distribution point, is useful in the following scenarios:

- You have multiple servers running SUS in your organization and you do not want all of the servers to access the Internet to synchronize content.

- You have sites that do not have Internet access.

- You want to have the ability to test content in a test environment and push the content to your production environment.

- You want to provide redundancy in case of server failure.

Creating Distribution Points

When you install SUS, a content distribution point is automatically created on that server. When you synchronize the server, its content is updated from the Windows Update download servers. The content distribution point is a virtual directory in IIS named Content. A *virtual directory* is a friendly name, or alias, either for a physical directory on your server hard drive that does not reside in the home directory or for the home directory on another computer. Because an alias is usually shorter than the path of the physical directory, it is more convenient for users to type. Downloaded content is stored in the physical location that is specified in the virtual directory (by default, SUS\Content) unless you choose to maintain content on Microsoft.com; in this case, the content distribution point is empty.

You can also manually create a content distribution point on a server running IIS 5 or later without installing the entire SUS server. To create the distribution point, copy content from the Content folder from an existing SUS server connected to the Internet to a manually created content distribution point.

▶ Creating a Manual Content Distribution Point Using IIS 6

To create a manual content distribution point, follow these steps:

1. Verify that the required IIS components are installed.

2. Using Microsoft Windows Explorer, create a folder named Content.

3. Copy all content from the SUS\Content\Cabs directory from the source server running SUS to the Content directory on the manual distribution point server.

4. Copy the following files under the default Web site's virtual root (VROOT):

   ❑ *Root of the SUS Web site*\Aucatalog1.cab

   ❑ *Root of the SUS Web site*\Aurtf1.cab

   ❑ *Root of the SUS Web site*\Approveditems.txt

5. Click Start, point to Administrative Tools, and then click Internet Information Services (IIS) Manager.

6. In the console tree, expand Web Sites, right-click Default Web Sites, point to New, and then click Virtual Directory.

7. On the Welcome To The Virtual Directory Creation Wizard page, click Next.

8. In the Alias box on the Virtual Directory Alias page, type **content**, and then click Next.

9. In the Path box, on the Web Site Content Directory page, type ***path*\content\cabs** (where *path* is the path you used to create the folder in step 2), and then click Next.

10. On the Virtual Directory Access Permissions page, verify that Read And Run Scripts (Such As ASP) is selected, and then click Next.

11. On the You Have Successfully Completed The Virtual Directory Creation Wizard page, click Finish.

When you have successfully created the manual distribution point folder and virtual root, you must synchronize the manual distribution point with an existing SUS server.

▶ Synchronizing a Manually Created Content Distribution Point

To synchronize a manually created content distribution point, follow these steps:

1. On the server hosting the manual distribution point, open the SUS Administration Web site (http://servername/SUSAdmin).

2. In the Software Update Services panel, click Set Options.

3. In the Select Where You Want To Store Updates, click Save The Updates To A Local Folder. Select or clear package locales as desired.

4. In the Select Which Server To Synchronize Content From, click Synchronize From A Local Software Update Services Server; type the name of the parent SUS server (**http://servername**) in the text box.

5. To synchronize only approved updates, select Synchronize List Of Approved Items Updated From This Location (Replace Mode), and then click Apply.

6. In the Software Update Services panel, click Synchronize Server, and then click Synchronize Now.

NOTE   You Cannot Change Content Distribution Point Port   Both automatically and manually configured content distribution points must use port 80. You cannot use any port other than 80 for a content distribution point.

MANAGING SUS

After completing installation and the initial download, you must manage both the server and the client. Server management includes reviewing and changing configuration options, automatically or manually synchronizing the server, viewing the update status, and backing up and restoring the server. Client management includes controlling download and installation behavior and configuration for Active Directory and non–Active Directory environments.

Server Management

The five main administrative tasks for SUS are these:

- Initial server configuration and postinstallation

- Synchronization (manual and automatic) of content between the public Windows Update service and the server that runs SUS

- Selection and approval of synchronized content to be published to computers that run the Automatic Updates client

- Backing up and restoring the SUS server

- Monitoring server status and logs (discussed in the "Monitoring SUS" section later in this chapter)

These administrative tasks are performed through a series of Web pages that are hosted on the server that runs SUS; this server can be accessed over a corporate intranet using Internet Explorer 5.5 or a later version (see Figure 7-4). For this version of SUS, there is no user interface (UI) for managing multiple servers as a set.

Initial Server Configuration

Configuration options include the following:

- Choice of whether the update files are hosted on the Internet Windows Update service or locally on your server that runs SUS.

- Proxy-server information for the server to access the Internet.

- Options for handling previously approved content. This is important if previously approved content is changed on the Windows Update service.

- The list of client languages you would like to support.

▶ **Manually Synchronizing the SUS Server**

Follow these steps to manually synchronize the SUS server:

1. Open the SUS Administration Web page.

2. In the Software Update Services panel, click Synchronize Server.

3. In the details pane, click Synchronize Now.

   Updates are downloaded to the local SUS server. After the synchronization is finished, the list of updates you can approve appears on the Approve Updates page (see Figure 7-7).

4. For more information about current or past synchronizations and the specific update packages that were downloaded, click View Synchronization Log in the Software Update Services panel.

▶ **Automatically Synchronizing the SUS Server**

Follow these steps to set a schedule for synchronizations to occur automatically:

1. Open the SUS Administration Web page.

2. In the Software Update Services panel, click Synchronize Server.

3. In the details pane, click Synchronization Schedule.

4. In the Schedule Synchronization dialog box, click Synchronize Using This Schedule.

5. In the At This Time dialog box, select the time to synchronize.

6. In the Following Day(s) section, select either Daily or Weekly. If Weekly, select the day or days on which to perform synchronization.

7. In the Number Of Synchronization Retries To Attempt On A Scheduled Synchronized Failure box, select the number of retries, and then click OK.

   NOTE **Customize Retry Interval** If a scheduled synchronization is not successful, by default SUS tries again three times at 30-minute intervals. You can use the Schedule Synchronization dialog box to customize the number of retries performed during an automatic synchronization. To display the Schedule Synchronization dialog box, in the Software Update Services panel, click Synchronize Server, and then in the details pane, click Synchronization Schedule.

Approving Content

One of the chief purposes of deploying a SUS server is to control which updates clients receive and when they receive them. As described earlier, part of this distribution process approves each update. Although you can configure SUS to automatically approve every update that is downloaded from the Windows Update Web site, this is not recommended. The recommended practice is to test updates before approving and distributing them throughout your organization.

As shown in Figure 7-7, status is displayed on the top-right corner of each update description.

Figure 7-7   Updates awaiting approval

The different status types are as follows:

- **New**   This indicates that the update was downloaded recently. The update has not been approved and therefore will not be offered to any client computers that query the server.

- **Approved**   This means that an administrator has approved the update and it will be made available to client computers that query the server.

- **Not Approved**   This indicates that the update has not been approved and will not be made available to client computers that query the server.

- **Updated**   This indicates that the update has been changed during a recent synchronization.

- **Temporarily Unavailable**   An update stored locally is in the Temporarily Unavailable state if one of the following is true:

  - ❑   The associated update package file required to install the update is not available.

  - ❑   A dependency that is required by the update is not available.

To obtain more information about a particular update, click Approve Updates in the navigation bar, and then click the Details link under the update name.

The Details page includes the following information:

- The **.cab files** that are associated with the package
- The locale(s) for each .cab file
- The operating system(s) required for each .cab file
- A link to the actual .cab file that was used to install the package and any command-line setup options that must be used to install the package
- An optional link to the Read More page about the update in the Info column

Backing Up the SUS Server

As with any infrastructure server, you should back up the SUS server. Over time, a large number of updates will be downloaded, tested, approved, or deferred. A system failure that does not have a backup in place results in many lost hours of work.

To back up a SUS server, you must back up the following three items:

- The IIS metabase
- The Web site directory containing the administration site
- The SUS content directory

▶ **Backing Up the IIS Metabase**

The IIS management console is used to back up the IIS metabase as follows:

1. Start the IIS management console, and then click the server to back up.

2. On the Action menu, select All Tasks, and then click Backup/Restore Configuration.

3. In the Configuration Backup/Restore dialog box, a number of automatic backups have already been created. Click Create Backup.

4. In the Configuration Backup dialog box, in the Configuration Backup Name box, type a name for the configuration backup, and then click OK.

5. Verify that the backup is listed in the Configuration Backup/Restore dialog box, and then click Close.

▶ **Backing Up the SUS Web Site and Content Directory**

After creating the IIS metabase backup, use file backup software, such as the Backup Utility for Windows (Ntbackup.exe), to back up the data. Perform the following steps to back up the SUS Web site and content directory:

1. Click Start, click All Programs, select Accessories, select System Tools, and then click Backup.

2. If the Backup Wizard appears, click Advanced Mode.

3. In the Backup tab, select the following folders:

   ❏ C:\Inetpub\Wwwroot (default Web site)

   ❏ C:\Sus

   ❏ %windir%\System32\Inetsrv\Metaback (IIS metabase) (%windir% is a system environment variable that refers to the Windows directory, typically C:\Windows.)

4. In the Backup Destination box, select a backup destination.

5. In the Backup Media Or File Name box, specify a file name or backup medium.

6. Click Start Backup.

7. In the Backup Job Information dialog box, click Start Backup.

> **NOTE Creating a Regular Backup** You should create regular backups because new content is often synchronized to the server that runs SUS. The IIS metabase contains information about all updates provided through SUS; therefore, you should create a new backup of the metabase using the IIS console before running Ntbackup to back up the data to media.

▶ **Restoring the SUS Server**

The following procedure should be used to restore the SUS server. The restore results in exactly the same state of the SUS server at the time of the last backup. This procedure assumes that you are running IIS 6, that you are restoring onto the same operating system that was installed when the failure occurred, and that the name of the computer has not changed since the last SUS backup.

1. Restore SUS to the same directory in which it was originally installed.

2. Start the Windows Backup Utility, and then select the Restore And Manage Media tab.

   You might have to catalog the backup before the Windows Backup Utility will display the backup set data. To catalog the media, in the console tree, expand the backup media, right-click the backup data (for example, C:), and then click Catalog.

3. Select the data to restore the following:

   ❏ The SUS content directory (typically C:\Sus)

   ❏ The IIS site that contains the SUSAdmin and AutoUpdate virtual directories (included in C:\Inetpub\Wwwroot)

   ❏ The IIS metabase backup (by default, %systemroot%\System32 \Inetsrv\Metaback)

4. In the Restore Files To box, select Original Location, click Start Restore, and then click OK.

   After restoring the data, you must restore the IIS metabase.

5. To restore the IIS metabase, start Internet Information Services (IIS) Manager.

6. On the Action menu, select All Tasks, and then click Backup/Restore Configuration.

7. In the Backup/Restore Configuration dialog box, select the backup configuration you just restored using the Windows Backup Utility, click Restore, and then answer Yes in the IIS Manager dialog box.

8. A dialog box will appear indicating that the restore was successful. Click OK.

9. To verify successful restoration, open the SUS Administration Web site and verify that the previous settings are displayed in the Set Options and the previously approved updates appear in the Approve Updates page.

Client Management

To use the SUS software, client computers must be running the updated Automatic Updates client. A newer version of the Automatic Updates client is necessary for some machines running Windows 2000 and Windows XP to use SUS. You must install Automatic Updates only on computers running Windows 2000 with Service Pack 2 (or earlier) or Windows XP without Service Pack 1. Computers running Windows Server 2003 need not download the newer version. You can download the Automatic Updates client from *http://www.microsoft.com/windows2000/downloads /recommended/susclient/default.asp.*

After you have installed the newer client, if necessary, you must configure Automatic Updates and specify the download behavior.

Configuration Options
There are several ways to configure Automatic Updates:

- By using a wizard that is automatically displayed 24 hours after Automatic Updates is initially installed.

- By using the Automatic Updates Configuration properties page in the System tool in Control Panel (as shown previously in Figure 7-3). You can also display this page in Windows XP by displaying the System properties.

- By using Group Policy.

- By configuring registry entries.

After you have determined how you will configure Automatic Updates, you can control how updates are downloaded and installed. Specifically, you can choose from the following:

- To be notified before updates are downloaded and again before the downloaded updates are installed

- For updates to be downloaded automatically and for the administrative user to be notified before updates are installed

- For updates to be downloaded automatically and installed based on the specified schedule

Download Behavior
Automatic Updates downloads updates based on the configuration options that the administrative user selected. It uses the **Background Intelligent Transfer Service (BITS)** to perform the download using idle network bandwidth. If Automatic Updates is configured to notify the user of updates that are ready to install, it checks to see whether a user with administrative privileges is logged on to the computer. If so, the user is notified. If not, the computer defers notification until a user with privileges logs on. As shown in Figure 7-8, Automatic Updates displays

the available updates to install when a logged-on administrator clicks the balloon or notification area icon. The administrative user must then click the Install button to allow the installation to proceed. If the update requires a restart of the computer to complete the installation, a message is displayed that states that a restart is required. Until the system is restarted, Automatic Updates defers detection of additional updates.

Figure 7-8   The Ready To Install dialog box

Configuration Options in an Active Directory Environment

The SUS installation package includes a policy template file—Wuau.adm—that contains the Group Policy settings described previously. The System.adm file on machines running Windows 2000 Service Pack 3, Windows Server 2003, and Windows XP Service Pack 1 also includes these policies. These settings can be loaded into Group Policy Object Editor for deployment.

Configure Automatic Updates Policy   If you configure clients by using Group Policy, the Group Policy settings override user-defined settings; the ability to configure Automatic Updates options on the client is disabled. The Configure Automatic Updates Group Policy setting (which can be accessed by opening the Group Policy Object Editor in Computer Configuration\Administrative Templates \Windows Components\Windows Update, then double-clicking Configure Automatic Updates in the details pane) specifies whether this computer receives security updates and other important downloads through Automatic Updates (see Figure 7-9).

When enabled, the Configure Automatic Updates policy also specifies the download and installation behavior, which can be one of the following three options:

- **Notify For Download And Notify For Install**   This option notifies a logged-on user with administrative privileges before the download and before the update installation.

- **Auto Download And Notify For Install**   This option automatically begins downloading updates and then notifies a logged-on administrative user before installing the updates.

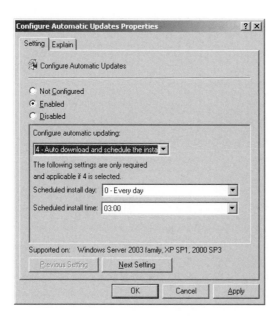

Figure 7-9   The Group Policy setting to configure Automatic Updates service

- **Auto Download And Schedule The Install**   Typically, if Automatic Updates is configured to perform a scheduled installation, the recurring scheduled installation day and time are also set.

Following are possible options for scheduled installation days and times:

- **Day**   Every Day and Every Sunday through Every Saturday
- **Time**   12 A.M. to 11 P.M. in 24-hour format (00:00 to 23:00)

> **NOTE**   **Remind Me Later Is Disabled**   Setting the policy to perform scheduled installations disables the Remind Me Later button in the Ready To Install Update dialog box.

If the Configure Automatic Updates policy is disabled, Automatic Updates does not perform any system updating, and you must go to the Windows Update site to download and manually install any available updates.

Specify Intranet Microsoft Update Service Location   This policy specifies which intranet server to use for detecting updates. You can access this setting in Group Policy Object Editor in Computer Configuration\Administrative Templates \Windows Components \Windows Update by double-clicking Specify Intranet Microsoft Update Service Location in the details pane. You must set both of the following values to configure this policy setting (see Figure 7-10):

- Set The Intranet Update Service For Detecting Updates
- Set The Intranet Statistics Server

The expected value for each of these settings is a URL (such as ***http://computerxx***), and both settings can be the same server.

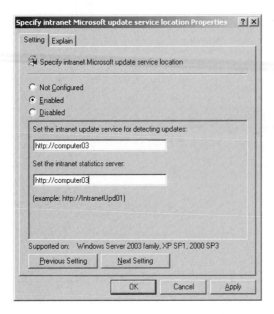

Figure 7-10   Specify Intranet Microsoft Update Service Location

If you specify a server running SUS and specify a Web server for collecting statistics, computers running Automatic Updates send success or failure information about the download and installation status to the Web server's log files.

Reschedule Automatic Updates Scheduled Installations   Use the Reschedule Automatic Updates Scheduled Installations setting (you can access this setting in Group Policy Object Editor in Computer Configuration\Administrative Templates \Windows Components \Windows Update by double-clicking Reschedule Automatic Updates Scheduled Installations in the details pane) to specify how much time (in minutes) to wait before proceeding with a previously missed scheduled installation. The waiting period begins after system startup. For this policy to be effective, the Configure Automatic Updates policy must be enabled (see Figure 7-11).

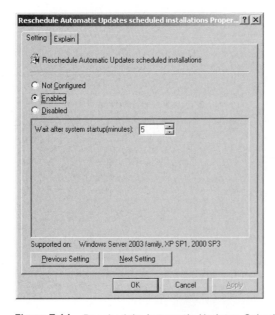

Figure 7-11   Reschedule Automatic Updates Schedule Installation

No Auto-Restart For Scheduled Automatic Updates Installations   This setting (you can locate this setting in Group Policy Object Editor in Computer Configuration \Administrative Templates \Windows Components \Windows Update by double-clicking No Auto-Restart For Scheduled Automatic Update Installations in the details pane) specifies that to complete a scheduled installation, Automatic Updates waits for a user to restart the computer rather than causing the computer to restart automatically. If this policy is set to Enabled, Automatic Updates does not restart a computer automatically, though, depending on the type of update, you might be asked to restart the computer (see Figure 7-12). As mentioned previously, Automatic Updates cannot detect future updates until the restart occurs. If this policy is Disabled or Not Configured, Automatic Updates notifies the user that the computer will automatically restart in 5 minutes to complete the installation. This policy also requires that the Configure Automatic Updates policy be enabled.

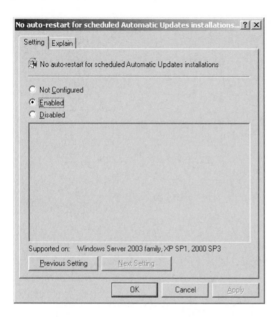

Figure 7-12   No Auto-Restart For Scheduled Automatic Updates Installations

Configuration Options in a Non–Active Directory Environment

An administrator can set registry settings to configure Automatic Updates in an environment without Active Directory directory service. The following settings are added to the registry of each Windows client at this location:

```
HKEY_LOCAL_MACHINE\Software\Policies\Microsoft\Windows\WindowsUpdate\AU
```

- **NoAutoUpdate**   Range = 0|1. 0 = Automatic Updates is enabled (default); 1 = Automatic Updates is disabled.

- **AUOptions**   Range = 2|3|4. 2 = notify of download and installation; 3 = auto download and notify of installation; and 4 = auto download and scheduled installation. All options notify the local administrator.

- **ScheduledInstallDay**   Range = 0|1|2|3|4|5|6|7. 0 = Every day; 1 through 7 = the days of the week from Sunday (1) to Saturday (7).

- **ScheduledInstallTime**   Range = n, where n = the time of day in 24-hour format (0–23).

- **UseWUServer**   Set this to 1 to enable Automatic Updates to use the SUS server, as specified in the WUServer value.

To determine to which SUS server your clients and servers go for their updates, place the following two settings in the registry at this location:

`HKEY_LOCAL_MACHINE\Software\Policies\Microsoft\Windows\WindowsUpdate`

- **WUServer**   Sets the Windows Update intranet server by HTTP name (for example, http://intranetSUS)

- **WUStatusServer**   Sets the Windows Update intranet statistics server by HTTP name (for example, http://intranetSUS)

MONITORING SUS

A server-monitoring Web page is provided so you can view the status of updates for target computers. These statuses are stored in the server's memory and might have to be refreshed occasionally.

Most SUS tasks involve synchronizing and approving updates. The two logs that are available to SUS administrators are the synchronization log and the approval log. Both logs are **Extensible Markup Language (XML)** files and are stored in an administrator-accessible folder on the server.

Monitor Server Page

SUS keeps information about available updates in the metadata cache. The *metadata cache* is an in-memory database that SUS uses to manage updates. The cache includes metadata that identifies and categorizes updates and information about update applicability and installation. The Monitor Server page gives the administrator a view of the current contents of the metadata cache.

Using the information from the Monitor Server page, the administrator can tell how many updates are available for each of the products on the network. SUS refreshes the metadata cache each time the administrator performs synchronization. The Monitor Server page also indicates the last date and time when the metadata cache was updated.

SUS retrieves text files that contain the information for the metadata cache. These text files are loaded into the metadata cache during synchronization and then are saved to disk. Although the text files are automatically loaded into the metadata cache during synchronization, the administrator can also refresh the cache manually.

Synchronization Logs

Each server that runs SUS maintains a synchronization log to keep track of the content synchronizations it has performed. This log contains the following synchronization information (see Figure 7-13):

- Time of last synchronization
- Synchronization success and failure notifications

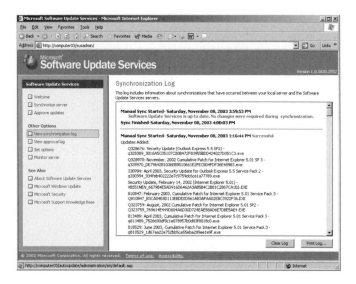

Figure 7-13   SUS synchronization log

- If scheduled synchronization is enabled, the time of the next synchronization

- A list of newly downloaded or updated packages since the last synchronization

- A list of update packages that failed synchronization

- The type of synchronization that was performed (manual or automatic)

The log can be accessed from the navigation pane of the administrator's SUS user interface. You can also access this file directly by using any text editor. The file name is History-Sync.xml, and it is stored in the *Location of SUS Website*\AutoUpdate \Administration directory.

Approval Logs

An approval log is maintained on each server that runs SUS to track approved and unapproved content (see Figure 7-14).

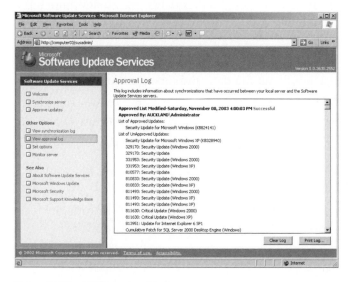

Figure 7-14   SUS approval logs

This log contains the following information:

- A record of each time the list of approved packages was changed
- The list of items that changed
- The new list of approved items
- A record of who made this change; that is, the server administrator or the synchronization service

The log can be accessed from the navigation pane in the administrative user interface. You can also access this file directly using a text editor. The file name is History-Approve.xml, and it is stored in the *Location of SUS Website* \AutoUpdate\Administration directory.

Server Event Log Messages

The synchronization service generates an event log message for each synchronization the server performs and for when the synchronization service encounters any major errors. Event log messages are also generated whenever the list of approved updates on the server changes.

> **MORE INFO** **List of Server Event Log Messages** *See the SUS deployment guide for a complete list of event log messages generated by SUS.*

Client Event Log Messages

The Automatic Updates client writes events to the system event log to notify users of operations that are being performed. Following are the possible events it writes:

- **Unable to connect** The Automatic Updates client cannot connect to the update service (Windows Update or the server running SUS) and therefore cannot download and install updates according to the set schedule. The Windows operating system continues to try to establish a connection (Event ID 16).

- **Install ready—no recurring schedule** The event lists downloaded updates that are ready to install. To install the updates, an administrator must log on to the computer and use the notification area icon to install the updates (Event ID 17).

- **Install ready—recurring schedule** The event lists downloaded updates that are ready to install and the date and time for the scheduled installation of those updates (Event ID 18).

- **Install success** The event lists successfully installed updates (Event ID 19).

- **Install failure** The event lists updates that failed to install (Event ID 20).

- **Restart required—no recurring schedule** You must restart the computer to complete the installation of the listed updates (Event ID 21).

- **Restart required—recurring schedule** The computer will be restarted within 5 minutes to complete the installation of the listed updates (Event ID 22).

SUMMARY

- SUS is a tool used to manage and distribute software updates that fix known security vulnerabilities or otherwise improve the performance of Microsoft operating systems.

- Updates can include items such as security fixes, critical updates, and critical drivers.

- Windows Update is a Microsoft Web site that works with Automatic Updates to provide timely critical and noncritical system updates.

- Automatic Updates enables you to automatically interact with the Windows Update Web site.

- SUS has three main components:

   - A synchronization service called Windows Update Synchronization Service that downloads content to your server running SUS

   - An IIS Web site that services update requests from Automatic Updates clients

   - A SUS Administration Web page

- SUS server management includes reviewing and changing configuration options, automatically or manually synchronizing the server, viewing update status, and backing up and restoring the server.

- You can configure Automatic Updates through the Automatic Updates configuration page, Group Policy, and by configuring registry entries.

- Because SUS tasks most often involve synchronizing and approving updates, administrators can use two logs (the synchronization log and the approval log) to monitor SUS server operation.

EXERCISES

IMPORTANT   Completing All Exercises   If you plan to do any of the textbook exercises in this chapter, you must do all of the exercises in the chapter to return the computer to its original state for the associated Lab Manual labs.

Exercise 7-1: Using the Windows Update Web Site

IMPORTANT   Procedure Steps May Vary   Depending on the browser security level, the following steps may vary.

1. Start Internet Explorer.

2. In the Address bar, type **http://windowsupdate.microsoft.com**, and then click Go.

3. On the Welcome To Windows Update page, click Scan For Updates.

4. Review the list of updates that is suggested for your computer, if any.

   Review the three categories: critical updates and service packs, operating system–specific files, and driver updates.

5. Under Other Options in the Windows Update pane, click View Installation History, and then review the list of items, if any.

6. In the Windows Update pane, click Personalize Windows Update.

7. On the Personalize Your Windows Update Experience page, select Display The Link To The Windows Update Catalog Under See Also, and then click Save Settings.

8. In the Windows Update pane, click Windows Update Catalog.

9. On the Welcome To Windows Update Catalog page, click Find Updates For Microsoft Windows Operating Systems.

10. In the Operating Systems box of the Microsoft Windows page, click Windows Server 2003 Family.

11. In the Language box, verify that English is selected.

12. Click Advanced Search Options to display additional search options.

13. Clear all options except Critical Updates And Service Packs, and then click Search.

14. In the search results box, click Critical Updates And Service Packs.

15. Select a small security update, and then click Add.

16. Click Go To Download Basket.

17. On the Download Basket page, browse to your My Documents folder, and then click Download Now.

18. If a license agreement page is displayed, click Accept.

   After the download completes, your Windows Update Catalog Download History is displayed.

Exercise 7-2: Enabling Automatic Updates

1. Click Start, right-click My Computer, and then click Properties.

2. In the System Properties window, click Automatic Updates.

3. Verify that Keep My Computer Up To Date is selected.

4. Under Settings, click Automatically Download The Updates, And Install Them On The Schedule That I Specify; in the day drop-down box, select Every Saturday, verify that the time box displays 3:00 A.M., and then click OK.

REVIEW QUESTIONS

1. You are the system administrator for Contoso, Ltd., and you have been given the responsibility of managing security patches and other updates to operating systems that already have a SUS-compatible version of Automatic Updates installed. Although you want the ability to approve updates, you do not want to store them all locally. How can you accomplish this?

2. You want to obtain critical updates and security fixes for your PC that runs Windows XP Professional. You access the Windows Update site. However, you cannot find the Windows Update Catalog under See Also in the left pane. What is the problem?

    a. You have not installed and configured SUS.

    b. You have not installed and configured Automatic Updates.

    c. Transmission Control Protocol (TCP) port 80 is blocked for incoming traffic on the firewall at your Internet service provider (ISP).

    d. You must configure the Windows Update site.

3. You administer your company's Windows Server 2003 Active Directory domain. All client PCs run Windows XP Professional. Company policy states that employees cannot download software or software updates from the Internet. Software must be installed or upgraded on client machines automatically through Group Policy. As the domain administrator, you have been exempted from this policy so that you can download operating system upgrades, security fixes, virus definitions, and Microsoft utilities from the Windows Update site. You then want these upgrades, fixes, and so forth to be installed automatically on other users' PCs when these users log on to the domain. What should you do after you have downloaded the software?

    a. Install and configure SUS on your PC.

    b. Install Automatic Updates on the client computers.

    c. Create a Windows installer package.

    d. Configure Remote Installation Services (RIS) to distribute the software.

4. You are the system administrator for Contoso, Ltd., and you have deployed SUS. You open the SUS Administration Web page and perform a synchronization that downloads several new updates. On the Approve Updates page, you notice that the updates are already approved even though you have not yet approved them. What is the most likely reason the updates are already approved?

5. You have just finished installing SUS and realize that there is not enough disk space to store all the updates locally. How can you configure SUS to solve this problem? Select the best answer.

    a. Compress the drive.

    b. Configure the SUS server to store the updates on the client computers.

    c. Configure the SUS server to download only 80 percent of the available disk free space.

    d. Configure the SUS server to use the Microsoft update site rather than to store updates locally.

6. You have deployed a SUS server; however, several clients running Windows XP (no service pack) and Windows 2000 Service Pack 2 are unable to use the SUS server. What is the most likely reason for this problem?

7. You have set up a second SUS server. You want to configure this server to download only approved updates from another server. How can you configure the second SUS server to only download approved items from a local server?

8. You are troubleshooting SUS client issues and want to check event log messages. Which log should you examine to find SUS client messages?

   a. Application log

   b. Security log

   c. System log

   d. Directory Service log

CASE SCENARIOS

Case Scenario 7-1: Need for SUS

You are the systems administrator for Contoso, Ltd., and you are seeking a way to keep all workstations and servers updated with the latest security patches, driver updates, and recommended updates from Microsoft. You are considering deploying SUS.

A colleague asked you why, since everyone in the company already has an operating system with Automatic Updates enabled, is a SUS server still necessary?

Which of the following answers are valid responses to your colleague's question?

   a. Although Automatic Updates keeps systems updated, you cannot rely on users to consistently accept and install updates.

   b. Relying on individual users to individually download and install updates from the Internet causes increased external network traffic relative to downloading updates from an internal SUS server.

   c. It is a recommended practice to test updates before deploying them. Allowing individuals to deploy their own updates without first testing the updates could be problematic.

   d. A SUS server will automatically update clients running Microsoft Windows 95, a practice that Automatic Updates does not support.

Case Scenario 7-2: Stage and Test Updates

You are deploying SUS in your organization. Several workstations in your organization run a non-Microsoft application that was negatively impacted in the past after downloading certain updates. As a result, many of the users of that application have disabled the update feature and are reluctant to participate in the SUS server deployment. How should you design your deployment plan so that you can stage and test updates before distributing them to the rest of the organization?

CHAPTER 8
CONFIGURING ROUTING BY USING ROUTING AND REMOTE ACCESS

Upon completion of this chapter, you will be able to:

■ Configure a Microsoft Windows Server 2003 to act as a **local area network (LAN)** router.

■ Configure and troubleshoot dial-up and **virtual private network (VPN)** remote access.

■ Understand how **Network Address Translation (NAT)** works and how to configure it.

■ Manage **routing protocols**, **routing tables**, and routing ports.

■ Describe how a routing table routes packets, and view the routing table using the command prompt and the Routing And Remote Access console.

■ Configure and manage **packet filters**.

■ Configure **demand-dial routing**, and describe when demand-dial routing is most appropriate.

■ Configure Routing and Remote Access policies to permit or deny access.

■ Centralize network access authentication and polices using **Remote Authentication Dial-In User Service (RADIUS)** and **Internet Authentication Service (IAS)**.

■ Differentiate between and select the most appropriate form of remote access authentication.

Routing, or the process of transferring data across an **internetwork** from one LAN to another, provides the basis for the Internet and nearly all network communication. It plays a key role in every organization that is connected to the Internet or that has more than one network segment. Routing can be complex, but if you understand some key concepts—such as authentication, authorization, **static routing**, and policies—you can effectively configure, monitor, and troubleshoot routing and remote access for your organization. Windows Server 2003 Routing and Remote Access offers the following features:

■ Connects LAN segments (subnets) within a corporate network

■ Connects branch offices to corporate intranets and shares resources as if all the computers are connected to the same LAN

- Provides **remote computers** with access to corporate network resources

- Provides multiprotocol **unicast** routing for **Internet Protocol (IP)** and the **AppleTalk protocol**

- Uses industry-standard unicast IP routing protocols:

  - ❏ **Open Shortest Path First (OSPF)**

  - ❏ **Routing Information Protocol (RIP)** versions 1 and 2

- Provides IP multicast services (**Internet Group Management Protocol [IGMP]** router mode and IGMP proxy mode) that enable the forwarding of IP multicast traffic

- Uses IP NAT services to simplify the connection of small office or home office (SOHO) networks to the Internet

- Employs a simple packet-filtering service (basic firewall) that can be enabled for any public interface—even one that is also configured for NAT

- Uses demand-dial routing over dial-up **wide area network (WAN)** links

- Provides VPN support with the **Point-to-Point Tunneling Protocol (PPTP)** and the **Layer Two Tunneling Protocol (L2TP)** over **Internet Protocol Security (IPSec)**, referred to as **Layer Two Tunneling Protocol/ Internet Protocol Security (L2TP/IPSec)**

- Provides industry-standard support for a **Dynamic Host Configuration Protocol (DHCP) relay agent** for IP

OVERVIEW OF WINDOWS SERVER 2003 ROUTING AND REMOTE ACCESS

Most enterprise networks employ several common network devices: **hubs**, **switches**, and **routers**. This chapter focuses on the routing capabilities of Windows Server 2003. Before examining that topic, let's review these three network devices and clearly identify the role of the router.

A *hub* (sometimes called a repeater) operates at **Open Systems Interconnection (OSI) reference model** layer 1. Because a hub operates at layer 1 (the physical level), it does not process the data it receives; instead, it simply receives the incoming signal and re-creates it for transmission on all of its ports. Using a hub extends the size of a network by joining multiple segments together into a larger segment. The hub is invisible to all nodes on a LAN on which it is deployed.

> **MORE INFO** *OSI Layers*   *For more information about OSI layers, see Network+ Certification Training Kit, Second Edition (Microsoft Press, 2003).*

Unlike a hub, a *switch* examines the destination and source address of an incoming **frame** and forwards the frame to the appropriate port according to the destination address. Most switches operate at OSI layer 2 (the data-link layer).

Switches have multiple parallel data paths. They use temporary, or virtual, connections to connect source and destination ports for the time it takes to forward the frame (a segment of data on a network). The virtual connection is terminated after the frame has been sent from the source to the destination. Switches are fast and inexpensive; they are typically used to segment a LAN into many smaller segments, which can thereby increase the speed of an existing network.

As its name suggests, a *router* determines routes: where to send network packets based on the addressing in the packet. Routers operate at OSI layer 3 (the network layer), which is at the packet level rather than the frame level. Because routers operate at this level, they are referred to as layer 3 devices. Layer 3 software, such as IP or **Internetwork Packet Exchange (IPX)**, generates the packets.

Routers can be used as follows:

- To link networks over extended distances or WANs. WAN traffic often travels over multiple routes, and the routers choose the fastest or cheapest route.

- To connect dissimilar LANs, such as an **Ethernet** LAN, to a **Fiber Distributed Data Interface (FDDI)** backbone.

  NOTE Gateways and Routers   Although the terms *gateway* and *router* are often used interchangeably. Technically, a *gateway* is a device that translates between networks of different architectures, such as NetWare and Microsoft Windows. A *router* is a device that sends packets between two or more network segments as necessary using IP addresses.

One of the many roles that Windows Server 2003 can play is that of a network router. Using Windows Server 2003 instead of a hardware router can often provide cost, management, and functionality advantages over a physical router device. This is caused in large part by the integration of its routing capability with the rest of the operating system features, such as Group Policy, security, and tools such as the **Microsoft Management Console (MMC)**.

Routing Examples

You can use routers in many different *topologies* (the physical layout of the network) and network configurations. When you configure a server running Routing and Remote Access as a router, you can specify the following:

- The protocols to be routed (IP or AppleTalk) by the router

- Routing protocols (RIP, OSPF, IGMP, and Dynamic Host Configuration Protocol [DHCP] Relay) for each protocol to be routed

- LAN or WAN media (network adapters, modems, or other dial-up equipment)

Simple Routing Scenario

Figure 8-1 shows a simple network configuration with a server running Routing and Remote Access and connecting two LAN segments (LAN Segment 1 and LAN Segment 2). In this configuration, the router joins the two segments; routing protocols are not necessary because there is only one router. Because the router is connected to both networks for which it would have to route packets, there is no need to create static routes. Static routes need not be added manually because the router is directly connected to all the networks to which it needs to route packets.

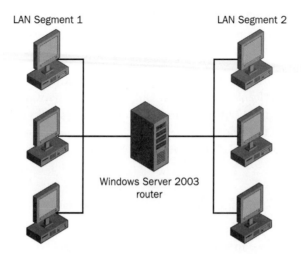

Figure 8-1   Two network segments connected by a router

Multiple-Router Scenario

Figure 8-2 shows a more complex router configuration. In this scenario, three networks (LAN Segments 1, 2, and 3) are connected by two routers (Routers 1 and 2).

Router 1 is directly connected to Segments 1 and 2, and Router 2 is directly connected to Segments 2 and 3. Router 1 must notify Router 2 that Segment 1 can be reached through Router 1, and Router 2 must notify Router 1 that Segment 3 can be reached through Router 2. This notification is automatically communicated if routing protocols such as RIP and OSPF are used. Without routing protocols, the network administrator must manually configure routing tables for the different segments to reach each other by adding static routes. Static routes are often the best option for small, simple networks; however, they are difficult to implement in larger networks, and static routes do not automatically adapt to changes in the internetwork topology.

When routing is configured properly and a user on Segment 1 wants to communicate with a user on Segment 3, the user's computer on Segment 1 forwards the packet to Router 1. Router 1 then forwards the packet to Router 2. Router 2 then forwards the packet to the user's computer on Segment 3.

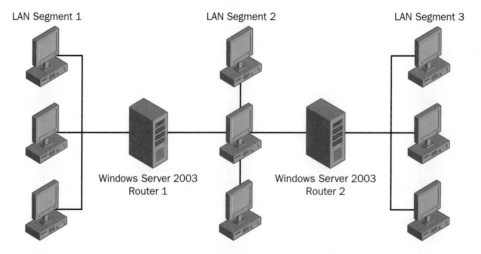

Figure 8-2   Three network segments connected by two routers

CONFIGURATION OPTIONS FOR REMOTE ACCESS SERVERS

As shown in Figure 8-3, the Routing And Remote Access Server Setup Wizard presents you with a configuration page from which you can select services. The final option on the list is Custom Configuration. Use this option if you are capable of manually configuring the server and if none of the services match your routing and remote access needs exactly.

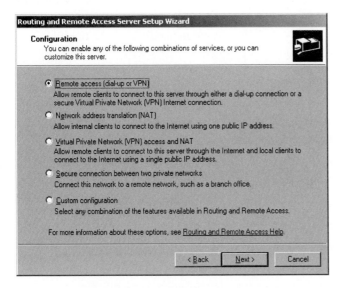

Figure 8-3   Options for routing and remote access

There are several options available to you when configuring remote access:

- **Remote Access (Dial-Up Or VPN)**   This option enables remote clients to connect to the server by using either a dial-up connection or a secure VPN.

- **Network Address Translation (NAT)**   This option enables internal clients to connect to the Internet using a single, external IP address.

- **Virtual Private Network (VPN) Access And NAT**   This option configures NAT for the internal network and configures VPN connections.

- **Secure Connection Between Two Private Networks**   This option is useful when, for example, setting up a router-to-router VPN.

- **Custom Configuration**   As noted previously, you use this option when none of the service combinations meet your exact needs.

Configuring Dial-Up Remote Access

Dial-up remote access, also called dial-up networking, enables remote computers that have a modem to connect to the organization's network as if the remote computers were connected locally, although at slower data transfer speeds. Windows Server 2003 **remote access servers** can connect to clients that run Windows Server 2003, Microsoft Windows XP Professional, Microsoft Windows NT, Microsoft Windows 95, Microsoft Windows 98, Microsoft Windows for Workgroups, MS-DOS, or Apple Macintosh. Typically, the client connects through a standard phone line—**Plain Old Telephone Service (POTS line)**, **Integrated Services Digital Network (ISDN)**, **digital subscriber line (DSL)**, cable, **X.25**, or **Asynchronous Transfer Mode (ATM)** link.

To enable multiple dial-up users to connect to your network simultaneously, you must have a modem bank (also called modem-pooling equipment), appropriate connections to the local telecommunications provider, and a means of connecting the modem bank (such as an adapter installed on the computer that runs Windows Server 2003). After you have installed the hardware according to the manufacturer's instructions, do the following:

1. Click Start, point to Administrative Tools, and then click Routing And Remote Access.

2. In the console tree, right-click the server, and then click Configure And Enable Routing And Remote Access.

3. On the Welcome To Routing And Remote Access Server Setup Wizard page, click Next.

4. On the Configuration page, click Remote Access (Dial-Up Or VPN), and then click Next.

5. On the Remote Access page, select the Dial-Up check box, and then click Next.

6. If your server has more than one network interface, on the Network Selection page, click the interface to which you wish to assign remote clients, and then click Next.

7. On the IP Address Assignment page, select either Automatically (to use a DHCP server to assign addresses) or From A Specified Range Of Addresses (addresses are supplied by the routing and remote access server), and then click Next.

8. In the Managing Multiple Remote Access Servers dialog box, select the option to not use a RADIUS server.

9. Click Next, and then click Finish. The Routing and Remote Access service starts and initializes automatically.

Troubleshooting Dial-Up Remote Access Connections

After you have completed the installation of your modem bank and the configuration of Routing and Remote Access, use the following checklist to troubleshoot dial-up remote access connections if problems arise:

- Verify that the Remote Access Server option is selected in the server properties General tab in the Routing And Remote Access console.

- If you have configured a static address pool, verify that the pool is large enough to accommodate the maximum number of concurrent client connections.

- If you have configured the remote access server to assign addresses through a DHCP server, verify that the address scope defined at the

DHCP server is large enough to accommodate the address block size specified in the registry key InitialAddressPoolSize located at HKEY_LOCAL_ MACHINE\SYSTEM\CurrentControlSet\Services\RemoteAccess \Parameters\Ip.

- Verify that enough modem devices are configured in the Ports node (which can be accessed by expanding the server node and then clicking Ports) to accommodate the maximum number of concurrent client connections.

- Verify that the dial-up client, the remote access server, and the remote access policy are configured to use at least one common authentication protocol.

- Verify that the dial-up client, the remote access server, and the remote access policy are configured to use at least one common encryption strength.

- Verify that the dial-up remote access connection has the appropriate permissions through the user account's dial-in properties and remote access policies.

- Verify that the remote access server (or RADIUS server) computer is a member of the RAS and IAS Servers security group in the local domain.

- Verify that the remote access policy profile's settings do not conflict with the remote access server properties.

- Verify that, if Microsoft Challenge Handshake Authentication Protocol version 1 (MS-CHAPv1) is used as the authentication protocol, the user password does not exceed 14 characters.

Configuring VPNs

Another means of connecting remote users is by using a VPN, which is an extension of a private network across a public network, such as the Internet. Like dial-up remote access, after the user is connected to the organization's network, it is as if the user is physically located at a computer that is local to the organization (with, however, slower data transfer speeds).

Because a VPN can be established using the Internet, your organization's network can be accessed globally. Accessing your network can be done quickly, cheaply, and safely across the world. Dedicated private lines are not required, and security can be configured at very high levels.

When Not to Use a VPN

Although VPNs are versatile and provide solutions to many different connectivity challenges, such as branch offices, telecommuters, and traveling employees, the following are situations in which a VPN does not provide the best solution:

- When performance at any price is the primary concern

- When most traffic is synchronous, as in voice and video transmissions

- When using an application with unusual protocols that are not compatible with TCP/IP

In these situations, you should consider a dedicated private line.

How VPNs Work

In a VPN, both ends of the connection make a link to a public internetwork, such as the Internet. The link can take the usual forms: a regular telephone line, an ISDN line, or a dedicated line of some sort. Rather than sending a packet as the originating node produces it, the VPN uses a tunneling protocol to encapsulate the packet in an additional header. The header provides routing information so that the encapsulated data can traverse the intermediate internetwork. The data is encrypted for privacy; if packets are intercepted, they cannot be unencrypted without encryption keys.

A VPN enables a remote user in Missouri, for example, to establish a dial-up connection with any Internet service provider (ISP) and, through that connection, to make a direct connection to a server on the company network in Texas. It is quick, cheap, and easy to set up. A VPN enables traveling employees, telecommuters in home offices, and employees in branch offices to connect to the main network at a company's headquarters. Each component connects to the ISP through a different type of communications channel, but they are all part of the same VPN.

Just as remote users can connect to their corporate network by utilizing an intermediate internetwork, two routers can also establish connection the same way. Figure 8-4 shows an example of a VPN: a connection between two routers.

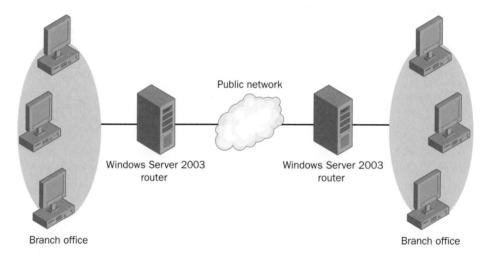

Figure 8-4   A router-to-router VPN

Components of a VPN

A VPN connection in Windows Server 2003 consists of the following components:

- A VPN server
- A VPN client
- A VPN connection (the portion of the connection in which the data is encrypted)

- A VPN tunnel (the portion of the connection in which the data is encapsulated). The following two tunneling protocols provide this service and are installed with Routing and Remote Access:

  ❑ **Point-to-Point Tunneling Protocol (PPTP)**   An extension of the Point-to-Point Protocol (PPP) that was in use for many years, PPTP was first used in Windows NT 4.

  ❑ **Layer Two Tunneling Protocol (L2TP)**   An Internet Engineering Task Force (IETF) standard tunneling protocol that is used to encapsulate Point-to-Point Protocol (PPP) frames for transmission over TCP/IP, X.25, frame relay, or Asynchronous Transfer Mode (ATM) networks. LT2P combines the best features of PPTP, which was developed by Microsoft, and the Layer 2 Forwarding (L2F) protocol, which was developed by Cisco Systems. You can implement L2TP with IPSec to provide a secure, encrypted VPN solution.

> **MORE INFO**   VPN Protocol Information   For more information about the VPN protocols, see Request for Comments (RFC) 2637, "Point-to-Point Tunneling Protocol," and RFC 2661, "Layer Two Tunneling Protocol." Both can be looked up at http://www.rfc-editor.org/rfcsearch.html.

Configuring NAT

Implemented by Windows Server 2003 Routing and Remote Access service, NAT is a protocol that enables private networks to connect to the Internet. The NAT protocol translates internal, private IP addresses to external, public IP addresses, and vice versa. This process reduces the number of IP addresses required by an organization and thereby reduces the organization's IP address acquisition costs because private IP addresses are used internally and then translated to public IP addresses to communicate with the Internet. The NAT process also protects private networks from unauthorized access by hiding private IP addresses from public networks. The only IP address that is visible to the Internet is the IP address of the computer running NAT.

> **MORE INFO**   NAT Information   For more information about NAT, see the RFC 3022, "Traditional IP Network Address Translator (Traditional NAT)," and RFC 1631, "The IP Network Address Translator (NAT)," at http://www.ietf.org/rfc.html.

How NAT Works

When NAT is used to connect a private network user to a public network, the following process occurs (see Figure 8-5):

1. The user's IP on the client computer creates an IP packet with specific values in the IP and **Transmission Control Protocol (TCP)** or **User Datagram Protocol (UDP)** headers. The client computer then forwards the IP packet to the computer running NAT.

2. The computer running NAT changes the outgoing packet header to indicate that the packet originated from the NAT computer's external address, but the computer running NAT does not change the destination; it then sends the remapped packet over the Internet to the Web server.

3. The external Web server receives the packet and sends a reply to the computer running NAT.

4. The computer running NAT receives the packet and checks its mapping information to determine the destination client computer. The computer running NAT changes the packet header to indicate the private address of the destination client, and then sends the packet to the client.

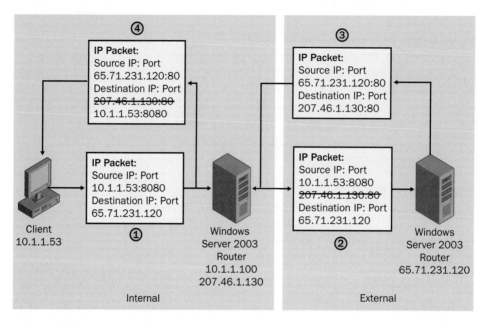

Figure 8-5   The NAT process

▶ **Configuring a Server to Use NAT**

Follow these steps to configure a server to use NAT:

1. Open the Routing And Remote Access console.

2. In the console tree, right-click the server, then click Configure And Enable Routing And Remote Access.

3. On the Routing And Remote Access Server Setup Wizard Welcome page, click Next.

4. On the Configuration page, click Custom Configuration, and then click Next.

5. On the Custom Configuration page, click NAT And Basic Firewall, and then click Next.

6. On the Completing The Routing And Remote Access Server Setup Wizard Page, click Finish.

7. When you are prompted to start the Routing and Remote Access service, click Yes.

8. In the console tree, expand the server node, expand IP Routing, right-click NAT/Basic Firewall, and then click New Interface (see Figure 8-6).

9. In the New Interface For Network Address Translation (NAT) dialog box, click the interface you wish to use, and then click OK.

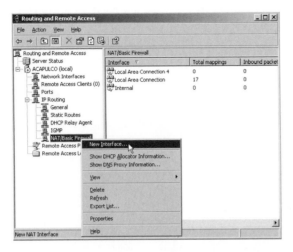

Figure 8-6   Constructing a new interface for NAT

10. On the Network Address Translation Properties page for your interface, configure the following properties, and then click OK:

   a. Select Public Interface Connected To The Internet.

   b. Select the Enable NAT On This Interface check box.

   c. If your network does not already have a firewall in place, select the Enable A Basic Firewall On This Interface check box.

   d. If desired, restrict traffic based on packet attributes by configuring Inbound Filters and Outbound Filters.

   e. In the Address Pool tab, add the pool of addresses assigned by your ISP and restrict one or more for specific computers.

   f. In the Services And Ports tab, select the services to which users will have access. When you select a service, a properties dialog box opens and requests the private IP address to which packets arriving on this service should be sent.

   g. In the ICMP tab, designate requests for information to which the server will respond.

SELECTING A ROUTING PROTOCOL

To successfully forward packets to networks to which they are not directly connected, a router must have routing table entries for these networks. In a small network where routes change infrequently, manually configuring static routes in the routing table is sufficient. Consider using RIP for small networks where routes change frequently or for medium-sized networks. For larger networks, consider using OSPF.

Using Static Routes

A static-routed IP environment is best suited to small, single-path, static IP internetworks. By definition, static-routed networks do not use routing protocols such as RIP or OSPF to communicate routing information between routers. For best results, the internetwork should be limited to fewer than 10 subnets with an easily predicted traffic pattern (such as arranged consecutively in a straight line; see

Figure 8-7). Of course, a static-routed IP environment is appropriate only as long as the routes in the environment remain the same.

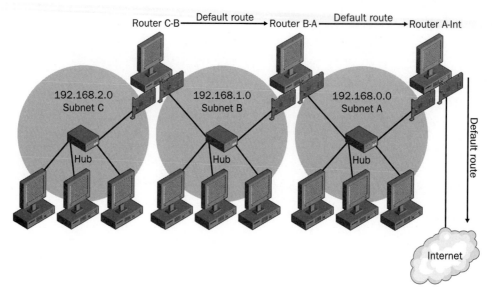

Figure 8-7 A static network with predictable traffic pattern

In Figure 8-7, Router C-B can see all computers on Subnets C and B. When Router C-B receives a packet that is destined for an address outside Subnet C or B, it forwards this packet along the default route to Router B-A. Because all computers outside of Subnets B or C lie in the direction of the default route, static routes do not need to be added to the routing table on Router C-B. However, for Router B-A, which sees all computers on Subnets B and A, the computers on Subnet C do not lie in the direction of the default route. If Router B-A receives a packet that is destined for Subnet C, it incorrectly forwards the packet to Router A-Int unless instructed to do otherwise. Adding a static route to the routing table on Router B-A (as shown in Figure 8-8) allows Router B-A to properly direct traffic destined for Subnet C toward Router C-B.

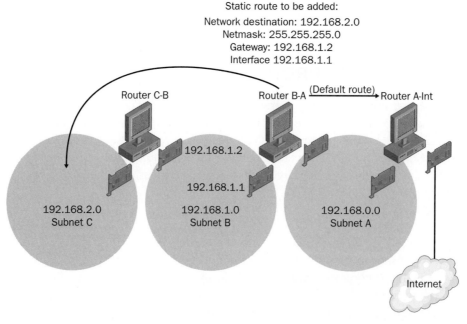

Figure 8-8 Adding a static route

Using Dynamic Routes

Windows Server 2003 includes the following four routing protocols that can be added to the Routing and Remote Access service:

- **RIP**   Designed for exchanging routing information within a small to medium-sized network. Enables routers to determine the appropriate paths along which to send traffic.

- **OSPF**   Designed for exchanging routing information within a large or very large network. Enables routers to determine appropriate paths along which to send traffic.

- **IGMP Router And Proxy**   Used for multicast forwarding.

- **DHCP Relay Agent**   Also considered a routing protocol in Routing and Remote Access; this service relays DHCP information between DHCP servers to provide an IP configuration to computers on different subnets.

▶ **Adding a Routing Protocol**

To add a routing protocol, follow these steps:

1. In the Routing And Remote Access console, expand the server, expand IP Routing, right-click General, and then click New Routing Protocol (see Figure 8-9).

Figure 8-9   The New Routing Protocol dialog box

2. In the New Routing Protocol dialog box, select the appropriate routing protocol, and then click OK.

MANAGING ROUTING TABLES

The *routing table* (see Figure 8-10) contains entries called routes that provide directions toward destination networks or hosts. The IP routing table serves as a decision tree that enables IP to decide the interface and gateway through which it should send the outgoing traffic. The routing table contains many individual routes; each route consists of a destination, network mask, gateway interface, and metric. The routing table is parsed from the most specific to the most general, so the packet is sent to the first gateway whose routing table entry matches the packet's destination. If two routes are identical, the route with the lowest metric (cost) is chosen over the route with the higher metric. In the case of a tie, one of the routes is arbitrarily selected. Four types of routes exist:

- **Directly attached network routes**   Routes for subnets to which the node is directly attached. For directly attached network routes, the Gateway column can either be blank or can contain the IP address of the interface on that subnet. If the address is local, delivery requires little additional effort. Address Resolution Protocol (ARP) resolves the IP address into a hardware address, which is typically a Media Access Control (MAC) address for the destination Ethernet card.

- **Remote network routes**   Routes for subnets that are available across routers and that are not directly attached to the node. For remote network routes, the Next-Hop field is a local router's IP address. If the address is remote, the next step is to determine the gateway through which to reach the remote address. In a network with only a single router acting as an external connection, no determination needs to be made. In any network with more than one router, determining which gateway to use requires routing table consultation.

- **Host routes**   A route to a specific IP address. Host routes allow routing to occur on a per–IP address basis. For host routes, the network ID is a specific IP address, and the network mask is 255.255.255.255.

- **Default route**   The default route is used when a more specific network or host route is not found. The default route destination is 0.0.0.0 with the network mask 0.0.0.0. The next-hop address of the default route is typically the node's default gateway.

ACAPULCO - IP Routing Table						
Destination	Network mask	Gateway	Interface	M..	Protocol
0.0.0.0	0.0.0.0	192.168.0.1	Local Area Connection 4	20	Network management
0.0.0.0	0.0.0.0	65.71.231.1	Local Area Connection	20	Network management
65.71.231.0	255.255.255.0	65.71.231.130	Local Area Connection	20	Local
65.71.231.130	255.255.255.255	127.0.0.1	Loopback	20	Local
65.255.255.255	255.255.255.255	65.71.231.130	Local Area Connection	20	Local
127.0.0.0	255.0.0.0	127.0.0.1	Loopback	1	Local
127.0.0.1	255.255.255.255	127.0.0.1	Loopback	1	Local
192.168.0.0	255.255.255.0	192.168.0.82	Local Area Connection 4	20	Local
192.168.0.82	255.255.255.255	127.0.0.1	Loopback	20	Local
192.168.0.255	255.255.255.255	192.168.0.82	Local Area Connection 4	20	Local
224.0.0.0	240.0.0.0	192.168.0.82	Local Area Connection 4	20	Local
224.0.0.0	240.0.0.0	65.71.231.130	Local Area Connection	20	Local
255.255.255.255	255.255.255.255	192.168.0.82	Local Area Connection 4	1	Local
255.255.255.255	255.255.255.255	65.71.231.130	Local Area Connection	1	Local

Figure 8-10   IP Routing table–GUI version

Viewing the IP Routing Table

You can view the IP routing table by using the Routing And Remote Access console or the command prompt. In the Routing And Remote Access console, expand the IP Routing node, right-click the Static Routes node, and then click Show IP Routing Table (see Figure 8-10).

Practice viewing
the IP routing
table by
completing
Exercise 8-1,
"Viewing the IP
Routing Table,"
now.

To view the routing table from the command prompt, at the command prompt, type **route print**, and then press ENTER (see Figure 8-11).

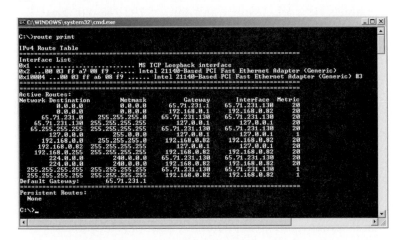

Figure 8-11   Viewing the routing table from a command prompt

Reading the IP Routing Table

Routers use routing tables to determine where to send packets. When IP packets are sent to an IP router, the router reads the destination address of the packet and compares that destination address to the entries in the routing table. One of these entries is used to determine the interface to which to send the packet and the gateway to which the packet will be sent next. As shown previously in Figure 8-11, each routing table entry includes the five columns, which are described here:

- **Network Destination**   The router compares the destination address of every received IP packet to entries in this column. Entries in this column that are common to most routing tables include the following:

  - 0.0.0.0 represents the default route, which is used when no other matches are found in the routing table.

  - 127.0.0.0 points to the loopback address of 127.0.0.1, which corresponds to the local machine.

  - 224.0.0.0 entries refer to a separate multicast route.

  - *w.x.y*.255 represents a broadcast address. Broadcast addresses include specific subnet broadcast addresses, such as 192.168.0.255.

  - 255.255.255.255 is the limited broadcast address, which is general for all networks and routers.

- **Netmask**   The subnet mask that is applied to the destination IP address when matching it to the value in the Destination field. This information is important because the largest match determines the route or table entry that is applied to the packet. For instance, suppose the router whose routing table is shown in Figure 8-11 receives two packets, the first destined for the address 192.168.0.82 and the second destined for the address 192.168.0.87. Both packets match the seventh routing table entry (192.168.0.0) because the netmask value of 255.255.255.0 signifies that the first three octets (plus a 0 for the fourth octet) match the table's network destination value of 192.168.0.0. The eighth entry (192.168.0.82) has a netmask of 255.255.255.255, which signals that all four octets must match the table's network destination value of 192.168.0.82. The fourth octet of the second address is 87 which does not match the fourth octet of the eighth routing table entry which is 82. Therefore, only the first packet matches the eighth entry (192.168.0.82). The seventh entry (192.168.0.0) is therefore applied to the first packet because this entry represents the largest match in the routing table. In this manner, the seventh entry is applied to the second packet because, aside from the default route, that entry represents the packet's only match in the routing table.

■ **Gateway**   When a particular route or table entry is applied to a packet, the gateway value determines the next address or hop for which that packet is destined. For example, according to the routing table shown in Figure 8-11, an IP packet with a destination such as 206.73.118.5 (which matches only the default route of 0.0.0.0) would next be forwarded to the gateway address of 65.71.231.130. In Figure 8-11, two default routes are displayed because the computer has two network interfaces. Note that the gateway value for the default route is the same as the default gateway address configured in TCP/IP properties.

■ **Interface**   When a particular route (table entry) is applied to a packet, the interface value specified in that route determines which local network interface is used to forward the packet to the next hop. For example, in Figure 8-11, an IP packet with a destination of 131.107.23.101 matches only the default route. According to the routing table, such a packet is sent through the interface 65.71.231.130 toward the default gateway address.

■ **Metric**   This column indicates the cost of using a route. If separate routes (entries) match an IP packet's destination address equally, the metric is used to determine which route is applied. Lower metrics have precedence over higher metrics. For the routing protocol RIP, the number of hops before the network destination determines the metric. However, you can use any algorithm to determine the metric if you are configuring a route manually.

Configuring the IP Routing Table

The IP routing table can be viewed from the command line and by using the Routing And Remote Access console. To configure the routing table, use the Route command line utility. The Route utility syntax is as follows:

```
route [-f] [-p] [Command [Destination] [mask Netmask]
[Gateway] [metric Metric]] [if Interface]]
```

Table 8-1 lists the available commands, their functions, and an example of how to use each command. Type **route /?** at the command prompt for additional usage information.

Table 8-1 **Route Command-Line Utility Commands**

Command	Function	Example
Print	Displays the routing table.	`route print`
Add	Adds a route to the routing table. By default, routes do not persist (they are discarded) when the system reboots. Use the -p switch to make a route persist across system restarts. Persistent routes are stored in the registry location HKEY_LOCAL_MACHINE\SYSTEM \CurrentControlSet\Services\Tcpip \Parameters\PersistentRoutes.	`route add -p 10.0.0.1` `mask 255.0.0.0 192.168.0.1`
Change	Use the Change command to modify an existing route.	`route change 10.0.0.1` `mask 255.255.0.0 10.27.0.25`
Delete	Deletes an existing route. To delete a route, you need only provide the IP address of the route.	`route delete 10.0.0.1`

▶ **Adding a Route to the Routing Table**

To add a route to the routing table, using the Route command:

1. Open a command prompt.

2. At the command prompt, type **route add *IP_address* mask *subnet_mask_address next_hop_destination_address***.

PACKET FILTERING

Packet filtering prevents certain types of network packets from being sent or received across a router. A *packet filter* is a TCP/IP configuration setting that is designed to allow or deny inbound or outbound packets. Packet filters can restrict traffic for a particular interface by source address, destination address, direction, or protocol type.

The packet-filtering feature in Routing and Remote Access is based on exceptions. You can set packet filters per interface and configure them to do one of the following actions:

- Pass through all traffic except packets prohibited by filters
- Discard all traffic except packets allowed by filters

In Windows Server 2003, packet filters occur in two types: input filters and output filters. *Input filters* restrict traffic entering into an interface from the immediately attached network. *Output filters* restrict traffic being sent from an interface onto the immediately attached network. Figure 8-12 presents an example of an input filter denying all packets except those destined for TCP port 1723 and IP address 207.46.22.1.

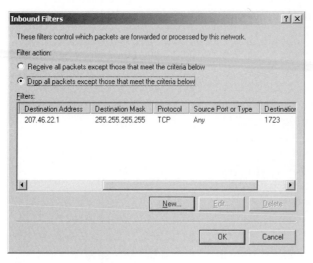

Figure 8-12   Packet filter example

Creating Packet Filters

You create packet filters in the Routing And Remote Access console through the IP Routing node. Within the IP Routing node, select either the General node or the NAT/Basic Firewall node. Packet filters are then configured through the properties page of the appropriate interface, which is listed in the details pane. Note that the NAT/Basic Firewall node allows you to create packet filters for external interfaces only, whereas the General node allows you to create packet filters for any interface.

▶ **Creating a Packet Filter**

To create a packet filter, follow these steps:

1. Open the Routing And Remote Access console.

2. In the console tree, expand IP Routing, and click the General node.

3. In the details pane, right-click the interface on which you want to add a filter, and then click Properties. The interface Properties dialog box opens, as shown in Figure 8-13.

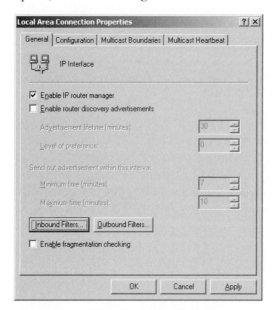

Figure 8-13   Configuring packet filters

4. In the General tab, click either Inbound Filters or Outbound Filters.

5. In the Inbound Filters dialog box or the Outbound Filters dialog box, click New.

6. In the Add IP Filter dialog box, type the settings for the filter, and then click OK (see Figure 8-14 for an example).

Figure 8-14   Adding an IP filter

7. In Filter Action, select the appropriate filter action, and then click OK.

8. Click OK to close the Filters Properties dialog box.

> **NOTE Defining Packet Filters**   You can also define packet filters in a remote access policy profile. Remote access policies, which are discussed later in the "Applying Remote Access Policies" section later in this chapter, allow you to apply rules and restrictions to specific remote access connections. By defining packet filters at the remote access policy level, you can apply different levels of access restrictions to different users.

CONFIGURING DEMAND-DIAL ROUTING

Routing and Remote Access also includes support for *demand-dial routing* (also known as dial-on-demand routing). When the router receives a packet, the router can use demand-dial routing to initiate a connection to a remote site. The connection becomes active only when data is sent to the remote site. The link is disconnected when no data has been sent over the link for a specified amount of time. Because demand-dial connections for low-traffic situations can use existing dial-up telephone lines instead of leased lines, demand-dial routing can significantly reduce connection costs.

You can use demand-dial filters to specify which types of traffic are allowed to create the connection. Demand-dial filters are separate from IP packet filters, which you configure to specify which traffic is allowed into and out of an interface after the connection is made.

The first step in deploying demand-dial routing is to configure a demand-dial interface on each computer you wish to function as a demand-dial router. You can configure these interfaces by using the Demand-Dial Interface Wizard when you initially set up Routing and Remote Access or as an option after the Routing and Remote Access service has already been configured and enabled.

If you have previously configured and enabled the Routing and Remote Access service without demand-dial functionality, you must enable this functionality before you create any demand-dial interfaces.

To enable demand-dial functionality, select the LAN And Demand-Dial Routing option in the General tab of the Routing and Remote Access Server Properties dialog box, as shown in Figure 8-15.

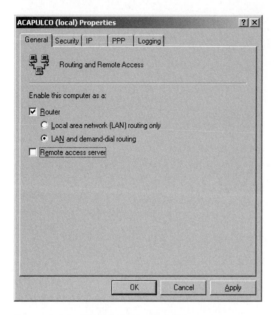

Figure 8-15 Enabling demand-dial routing

Testing Demand-Dial Connections

After enabling LAN and demand-dial routing and after configuring the demand-dial interfaces, you can test whether a demand-dial connection works correctly by using either manual or automatic testing.

Manual Testing

By manually testing a demand-dial connection, you are testing whether the PPP link can be established. Manual testing verifies that the configuration of the authentication methods, encryption, user credentials, and address for the demand-dial interface are valid.

▶ **Manually Testing a Demand-Dial Interface**

To manually connect a demand-dial interface, follow these steps:

1. In the Routing And Remote Access snap-in, expand the appropriate server, and then click Routing Interfaces.

2. In the details pane, right-click the appropriate demand-dial interface.

3. Click Connect.

4. After the demand-dial connection is made, the Connection Status column of the demand-dial interface changes from Disconnected to Connected.

Automatic Testing

By automatically testing a demand-dial connection, you are testing whether the demand-dial connection is automatically initiated when traffic that matches a configured route is sent to the demand-dial router.

To test for an automatic connection, verify that the demand-dial interface being tested is in a disconnected state. Next, generate network traffic for a location that exists across the demand-dial connection. One easy way to generate IP traffic is to use the Ping or Tracert commands.

For the Ping and Tracert commands, the first attempt might fail because of the connection establishment delay. However, the first packet sent across the interface causes the demand-dial interface to connect; subsequent use of the testing utility is successful after the initial connection is made. One way to see the connection process from an application viewpoint is to use the Ping command with the -t parameter to continue sending Internet Control Message Protocol (ICMP) Echo messages until interrupted. You see "Request timed out" messages until the demand-dial connection is made, after which you see the replies.

Troubleshooting Demand-Dial Routing

The following sections give troubleshooting tips to help you isolate the configuration or infrastructure problem that causes the demand-dial routing problem when these issues arise:

- On-demand connection does not occur automatically
- Cannot make a demand-dial connection

On-Demand Connection Does Not Occur Automatically

If an on-demand connection does not occur automatically, verify the following:

- The correct static routes exist and are configured with the appropriate demand-dial interface.
- For the static routes that use a demand-dial interface, the Use This Route To Initiate Demand-Dial Connections check box is selected.
- The demand-dial interface is not in a disabled state. To enable the interface, right-click the demand-dial interface, and then select Enable.
- The dial-out hours for the demand-dial interface on the calling router are not preventing the connection attempt.
- The demand-dial filters for the demand-dial interface on the calling router are not preventing the connection attempt.

Cannot Make a Demand-Dial Connection

If your system cannot make a demand-dial connection, verify the following for both the calling and answering routers:

- The Routing and Remote Access service is running on both the calling and answering routers.
- Routing is enabled with LAN and demand-dial routing on both the calling and answering routers.

- The dial-up ports being used on both the calling router and the answering router are configured to allow demand-dial routing connections (inbound and outbound).

- At least one of the dial-up ports on both the calling and answering routers remains unconnected.

- The calling and answering routers, in conjunction with a remote access policy, are enabled to use at least one common authentication method.

AUTHORIZING REMOTE ACCESS CONNECTIONS

After the credentials submitted with the remote access connection are authenticated, the connection must be authorized. Remote access authorization consists of two steps:

1. The dial-in properties of the user account are verified.

2. The first matching remote access policy listed in the Routing And Remote Access console is applied.

Configuring Dial-In Properties of the User Account

Dial-in properties, which apply to both direct dial-up and VPN connections, are configured in the Dial-In tab of the User Account Properties dialog box. If a user is dialing in to a domain, a user account that corresponds to the name sent through the dial-up connection must already exist in the domain. Dial-in properties for this account can thus be configured in the Active Directory Users And Computers console.

If the user is dialing in to a stand-alone server, however, the account must already exist as a user account in the answering server's local **Security Accounts Manager (SAM) database**. SAM is a Windows service used during the logon process. SAM maintains user account information, including groups to which a user belongs. Dial-in properties for this account can thus be configured in the Local Users And Groups console in Computer Management.

Figure 8-16 shows the Dial-In tab of the user account properties, which is described in the next section.

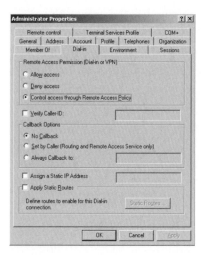

Figure 8-16   Configuring user dial-in properties

In all server environments except Active Directory domains, for which the functional level is Windows 2000 mixed, the Control Access Through Remote Access Policy option is enabled by default. You can set the remote access permission for user accounts to any one of the following three levels:

- **Control Access Through Remote Access Policy** This particular option neither blocks nor allows dial-up access for the user. Instead, it specifies that the user's access permissions be determined by first matching the remote access policy applied to the connection. (By default, remote access policies block all remote access connections.)

- **Deny Access** When you select the Deny Access option, dial-up access for the user account is blocked, regardless of other settings or policies that are applied to the account.

- **Allow Access** When you select the Allow Access option, dial-up remote access for the user account is permitted, thereby overriding the remote access permission setting in remote access policies. Note that the Allow Access setting does not always prevent remote access policies from blocking remote access; a remote access policy can still restrict the account's remote access through the remote access policy profile. For example, dial-up hours specified in a remote access policy profile might prevent a user account from connecting in the evening hours, even when the Allow Access option has been set for the user account's dial-in properties. However, the Allow Access option specifies that the Deny Remote Access Permission setting in remote access policies is ignored.

    IMPORTANT   **Mixed-Mode Remote Access Permissions**   By default, Active Directory domains in Windows Server 2003 are installed at the Windows 2000 mixed-mode domain functional level. In this server environment, only Allow Access and Deny Access remote access permissions are available for user accounts. In this case, the Allow Access setting is the default and is the equivalent of the Control Access Through Remote Access Policy setting in all other server environments. At this functional level, there is no setting that allows you to override user-level remote access permissions in remote access policies.

Verifying Caller ID

If the Verify Caller ID check box is selected, the server verifies the caller's phone number; if the phone number does not match the configured phone number, the connection attempt is denied. The caller, the phone system between the caller and the server, and the remote access server must support caller ID. On a computer running the Routing and Remote Access service, caller ID support consists of call-answering equipment that provides caller ID information and the appropriate Windows driver to pass the information to the Routing and Remote Access service. If you configure a caller ID phone number for a user and you do not have support for the passing of caller ID information from the caller to the Routing and Remote Access service, connection attempts are denied.

Exploring Callback Options

By default, this setting is configured as No Callback. If the Set By Caller option is selected, the server calls the caller back at a number specified by the caller. If the Always Call Back To option is selected, an administrator must specify a number that the server always uses during the callback process. The callback feature requires that **Link Control Protocol (LCP)** extensions are enabled in Routing and Remote Access server properties. (They are enabled by default.)

Assigning a Static IP Address

You can configure the Assign A Static IP Address setting to assign a specific IP address to a user when a connection is made.

Applying Static Routes

You can use the Apply Static Routes setting to define a series of static IP routes that is added to the routing table of the server that runs the Routing and Remote Access service when a connection is made.

APPLYING REMOTE ACCESS POLICIES

A *remote access policy* is a set of permissions or restrictions that is read by a remote access authenticating server that applies to remote access connections. Remote access permissions were simple to understand and implement in Windows NT 4 and Windows NT 3.51. Remote access permissions were granted directly on the user's account using User Manager or the Remote Access Administration utility. Although this was simple and easy to understand, it only worked well when a small number of users required permission for remote access.

In Windows Server 2003 and Windows 2000, remote access authorization is more complicated and consequently requires more effort to understand; however, it is also much more powerful and can be precisely configured to meet the security and access needs of both small and very large organizations.

As mentioned previously, authorization is determined by a combination of the dial-in properties for the user account and the remote access policies. With remote access policies, connections can be authorized or denied based on user attributes, group membership, the time of day, the type of connection being requested, and many other variables.

> **NOTE**   **Authentication Versus Authorization**   *The concepts of authorization and authentication are often blurred or misunderstood. Authentication is the process of verifying that an entity or object is who or what it claims to be. Examples include confirming the source and integrity of information, such as verifying a digital signature or verifying the identity of a user or computer. Authorization is the process that determines what a user is permitted to do on a computer system or network. Naturally, authorization occurs only after successful authentication.*

CONFIGURING A REMOTE ACCESS POLICY

A *remote access policy*, which is a rule for evaluating remote connections, consists of three components: the conditions, remote access permission, and the profile:

- **Conditions**   Remote access policy conditions are one or more attributes that are compared to the settings of the connection attempt. If there are multiple conditions, all of the conditions must match the connection attempt's settings for it to match the policy.

■ **Remote access permissions**   If all conditions of a remote access policy are met, the If A Connection Request Matches The Specified Conditions setting is applied, thereby granting or denying the remote access permission. Remember that remote access permission is also granted or denied for each user account. The user account remote access permission overrides the policy remote access permission. When a user account's remote access permission is set to the Control Access Through Remote Access Policy option, the policy remote access permission determines whether the user is granted access. Granting access through either the user account permission setting or the policy permission setting is simply the first step in accepting a connection. The connection attempt is subject to the settings of both the user account dial-in properties and policy profile properties. If the connection attempt does not match the user account's settings or policy profile properties, the connection attempt is rejected.

■ **Profile**   After a connection has been authorized, a set of properties contained in the remote access policy profile is applied. The set of properties, explained later in this section, includes the following (see Figure 8-17):

  ❑ Dial-In Constraints

  ❑ IP

  ❑ Multilink

  ❑ Authentication

  ❑ Encryption

  ❑ Advanced

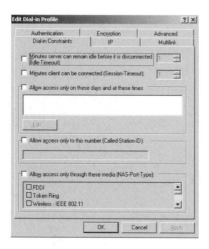

Figure 8-17   Dial-In Profile settings

By default, Routing and Remote Access is configured with the following two policies:

■ **Connections To Microsoft Routing And Remote Access Server**   This policy contains only one condition: MS-RAS-Vendor Matches "^311$" (see Figure 8-18). This means that the policy applies only when the version of the RADIUS client is ^311$. Any client besides a RADIUS client with a version of "^311$" will not match this condition and will attempt to match to the second policy.

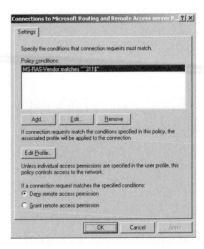

Figure 8-18   Default remote access policy Properties page

■ **Connections To Other Access Servers**   This policy is configured to match every incoming connection regardless of network access server type; however, because the first policy matches all connections to Routing and Remote Access, only connections to other remote access servers read and match the policy when the default policy order is not changed. Unless the first policy is deleted or the default policy order is rearranged, this second policy can be read only by RADIUS servers.

As shown in Figure 8-19, you can view currently configured remote access policies in the Routing And Remote Access console by selecting the Remote Access Policies node in the console tree.

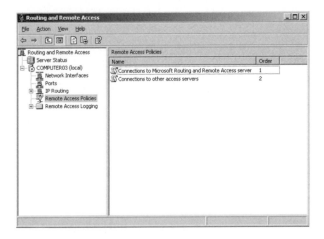

Figure 8-19   Routing And Remote Access console

Remote access policies are unique to each local machine, but not unique to Routing and Remote Access. After they have been created, they can be read either by Routing and Remote Access or by a RADIUS server configured on the local machine. Similarly, you cannot remove remote access policies by simply disabling Routing and Remote Access. Rather, remote policies are written to the local hard disk and are stored until they are specifically deleted from either the Routing And

Remote Access console or the Internet Authentication Service console (the administrative tool for RADIUS servers).

By default, two remote access policies are preconfigured in Windows Server 2003. The first default policy is Connections To Microsoft Routing And Remote Access Server, which is configured to match every remote access connection to the Routing and Remote Access service. When Routing and Remote Access is reading this policy, the policy naturally matches every incoming connection. However, when a RADIUS server is reading the policy, network access might be provided by a non-Microsoft vendor; consequently, this policy does not match those connections.

The second default remote access policy is Connections To Other Access Servers. This policy is configured to match every incoming connection, regardless of network access server type; however, because the first policy matches all connections to Routing and Remote Access, only connections to other remote access servers read and match the policy when the default policy order is unchanged. Unless the first policy is deleted or the default policy order is rearranged, only RADIUS servers can read this second policy.

Policy Conditions

Each remote access policy is based on policy conditions that determine when the policy is applied. For example, a policy might include a condition that Windows-Groups matches FABRIKAM\Telecommuters; this policy would then match a connection for which a user who belongs to the Windows global security group Telecommuters. Figure 8-20 shows such a policy.

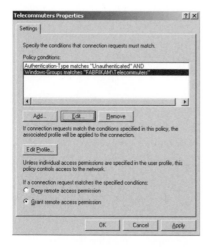

Figure 8-20   Conditions matching dial-up telecommuters

Clicking the Add button opens the Select Attribute dialog box, which allows you to add a new category for a remote access policy condition. For example, the NAS-IP-Address attribute allows a RADIUS server to distinguish remote access clients that connect through a particular remote access server (as distinguished by IP address). Figure 8-21 shows the Select Attribute dialog box and its associated set of configurable attributes.

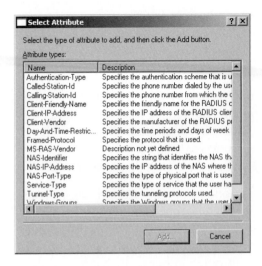

Figure 8-21   Policy condition attributes

By clicking the Add button in the Select Attribute dialog box, you can open a dialog box that allows you to configure the condition for a specific attribute. For example, as shown in Figure 8-22, the Authentication-Type dialog box opens if you click the Add button when the Authentication-Type attribute is selected. This dialog box allows you to choose which remote access connections, as specified by authentication protocol, match the policy. In the example, the policy is configured to match unauthenticated connections. Similarly, you can specify the particular elements for any attribute you choose to serve as a policy's conditions.

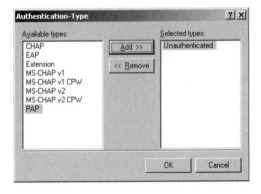

Figure 8-22   Examples of policy condition elements

> **NOTE** **Remote Policy Condition and Global Security Groups**   Only membership in global security groups can serve as a remote policy condition. You cannot specify membership in universal or domain local security groups as the condition for a remote access policy.

Remote Access Permission

Every remote access policy specifies whether the connection matching the policy is allowed or denied. These permission settings correspond to the Grant Remote Access Permission option and the Deny Remote Access Permission option, respectively, as shown previously in Figure 8-20. Remember that the Allow Access option (outside of Windows 2000 mixed-mode domains) or the Deny Access option (in the dial-in properties for an individual user account) usually overrides this setting.

Policy Profile

A remote access policy profile consists of a set of dial-up constraints and properties that can be applied to a connection. You can configure a remote access policy profile by clicking the Edit Profile button in the policy Properties page, as shown in Figure 8-20. Clicking this button opens the Edit Dial-In Profile dialog box, which is shown in Figure 8-23. By default, the policy profile is not configured; consequently, no additional restrictions or properties are applied to the connection.

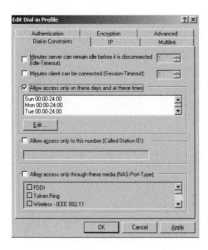

Figure 8-23   A configured dial-up remote access policy profile

The following sections describe the six tabs that are found in the policy profile.

- **Dial-In Constraints**   This tab allows you to set the following dial-up constraints:
    - ❏ Minutes Server Can Remain Idle Before It Is Disconnected
    - ❏ Minutes Client Can Be Connected
    - ❏ Allow Access Only On These Days And At These Times
    - ❏ Allow Access Only To This Number
    - ❏ Allow Access Only Through These Media
- **IP**   You can set IP properties that specify IP address assignment behavior. You have the following options:
    - ❏ Server Must Supply An IP Address.
    - ❏ Client May Request An IP Address.
    - ❏ Server Settings Determine IP Address Assignment (the default setting).
    - ❏ Assign A Static IP Address. The assigned IP address is typically used to accommodate vendor-specific attributes for IP addresses.

You can also use the IP tab to define IP packet filters that apply to remote access connection traffic.

- **Multilink** You can set **multilink** properties that enable multilink and determine the maximum number of ports (modems) that a multilink connection can use.

  Additionally, you can set Bandwidth Allocation Protocol (BAP) policies that determine BAP usage and specify when extra BAP lines are dropped. The multilink and BAP properties are specific to the Routing and Remote Access service. By default, multilink and BAP are disabled.

  The Routing and Remote Access service must have multilink and BAP enabled for the multilink properties of the profile to be enforced.

- **Authentication** You can set authentication properties to both enable the authentication types that are allowed for a connection and specify the **Extensible Authentication Protocol (EAP)** type that must be used. Additionally, you can configure the EAP type. By default, MS-CHAP and MS-CHAP version 2 are enabled. In Windows Server 2003, you can specify whether users can change their expired passwords by using MS-CHAP and MS-CHAP v2 (this is enabled by default).

  The Routing and Remote Access service must have the corresponding authentication types enabled for the authentication properties of the profile to be enforced.

- **Encryption** Windows Server 2003 supports two general methods for the encryption of remote access connection data: Rivest-Shamir-Adleman (RSA) RC4 and Data Encryption Standard (DES). RSA RC4 is the family of algorithms used in **Microsoft Point-to-Point Encryption (MPPE)**, the encryption type used with the MS-CHAP or Extensible Authentication Protocol-Transport Layer Security (EAP-TLS) authentication protocols in both dial-up and PPTP-based VPN connections. DES is the general encryption scheme most commonly used with IPSec, the security standard used with L2TP authentication protocol in VPNs. (VPNs, PPTP, and L2TP/IPSec are discussed in the section "Components of a VPN" earlier in this chapter.)

As shown in Table 8-2, both MPPE and IPSec support multiple levels of encryption.

Table 8-2 **Encryption Types**

Encryption Type	Level of Encryption Supported
MPPE Standard	40-bit, 56-bit
MPPE Strong	128-bit
IPSec DES	56-bit
IPSec Triple DES	168-bit

The settings in the Encryption tab in a remote access policy profile (shown in Figure 8-24) allow you to specify allowable encryption levels independently of encryption type. However, the nature of each encryption level varies with the encryption scheme used.

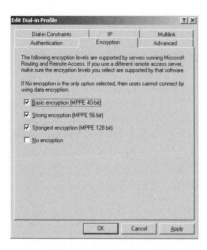

Figure 8-24   The remote access policy profile Encryption tab

There are four encryption options available in the Encryption tab:

■ **Basic Encryption (MPPE 40-Bit)**   For dial-up and PPTP-based VPN connections, MPPE is used with a 40-bit key. For L2TP/IPSec VPN connections, 56-bit DES encryption is used.

■ **Strong Encryption (MPPE 56-Bit)**   For dial-up and PPTP VPN connections, MPPE is used with a 56-bit key. For L2TP/IPSec VPN connections, 56-bit DES encryption is used.

■ **Strongest Encryption (MPPE 128-Bit)**   For dial-up and PPTP VPN connections, MPPE is used with a 128-bit key. For L2TP/IPSec VPN connections, 168-bit Triple DES encryption is used.

■ **No Encryption**   This option allows unencrypted connections that match the remote access policy conditions. Clear this option to require encryption.

■ **Advanced**   You can set advanced properties to specify the series of RADIUS attributes that the IAS server returns for evaluation by the **network access server (NAS)**/RADIUS client. Only RADIUS servers use these settings, which are not read by Routing and Remote Access.

MANAGING NETWORK ACCESS AUTHENTICATION AND POLICIES

After the dial-up client calls the remote access server and the necessary IP addresses are assigned, the credentials that were submitted with the connection must be authenticated. Authentication is the process of validating—through verification of a password or of alternative credentials, such as a certificate or smart card—that users are in fact who they claim to be. Remote access authentication precedes domain logon authentication; if a dial-up user attempts to log on to a domain remotely, the dial-up connection must be authenticated, authorized, and established before normal domain logon occurs.

To log on to a domain through a dial-up connection, select the Log On Using Dial-Up Connection check box in the Log On To Windows dialog box. After you type in your username and password and click OK, the Network Connections dialog box appears. From the Choose A Network Connection drop-down list, select the network connection you have configured for dial-up remote access, and then click Connect.

The dial-up connection is attempted; remote access authentication and authorization follow. Typically, the username, domain, and password configured for the connection match those that you submit for domain logon; however, these two sets of credentials are configured and authenticated separately.

A remote access connection is established if the credentials of the dial-up connection are successfully authenticated and the remote access connection is authorized. Normal domain logon follows; the credentials you enter in the Log On To Windows dialog box are submitted to a domain controller for domain authentication.

> **NOTE   Local and Remote Verification**   If users are dialing in to a stand-alone, remote access server that is not a member of a domain, they must first log on to their local computers or local domains before attempting to connect to the remote server. In this case, the remote computer's verification of the credentials sent with the dial-up connection is the only required authentication before the connection is authorized and established. These credentials must be stored in the answering server's local SAM before the user connects.

Performing Authentication Through RADIUS

You can configure remote access authentication to be performed through Windows authentication or a RADIUS server. In Windows authentication, when the remote user attempts to dial up a workgroup computer, the NAS authenticates the connection by verifying the username and password in the server's own local security database. When the remote user attempts to dial in to a domain, the NAS forwards the authentication request to a domain controller. However, when you configure a RADIUS server to authenticate remote access connections, the NAS passes both the authentication and authorization responsibility to a central server running IAS.

You choose this authentication method in one of two places: on the Managing Multiple Remote Access Servers page of the Routing And Remote Access Server Setup Wizard (as shown in Figure 8-25), or in the Security tab of the Server Properties dialog box in the Routing And Remote Access console (as shown in Figure 8-26). Note that, if you wish to use Windows authentication instead of a RADIUS server in the wizard, you should select the option No, Use Routing And Remote Access To Authenticate Connection Requests.

Choosing Authentication Protocols

To authenticate the credentials submitted by the dial-up connection, the remote access server must first negotiate a common authentication protocol with the remote access client. Most authentication protocols offer some measure of security so that user credentials cannot be intercepted. Authentication protocols in Windows clients and servers are assigned a priority based on this security level.

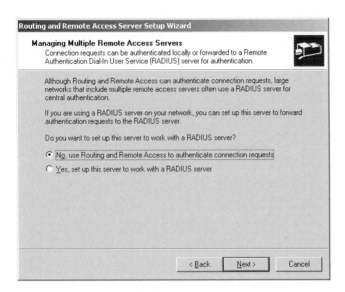

Figure 8-25   Choosing a remote access authentication method using the Routing And Remote Access Server Setup Wizard

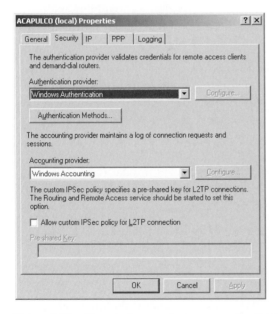

Figure 8-26   Choosing a remote access authentication method using the Security tab

The authentication protocol chosen for a remote access connection is always the most secure of those enabled in the client connection properties, the remote access server properties, and the remote access policy that is applied to the connection. By default, that protocol is MS-CHAP v2 for all remote access clients and servers running either Windows 2000, Windows XP, or the Windows Server 2003 family.

Following is a complete list of the authentication protocols supported by Routing and Remote Access in Windows Server 2003 (listed in order from most secure to least secure):

■ **EAP-TLS**   A certificate-based authentication that is based on EAP, an extensible framework that supports new authentication methods.

EAP-TLS is typically used in conjunction with smart cards. It supports encryption of both authentication data and connection data. Note that stand-alone servers do not support EAP-TLS; the remote access server that runs Windows Server 2003 must be a member of a domain.

- **MS-CHAP v2**   A mutual authentication method that offers encryption of both authentication data and connection data. A new cryptographic key is used for each connection and each transmission direction. MS-CHAP v2 is enabled by default in Windows 2000, Windows XP, and Windows Server 2003.

- **MS-CHAP v1**   A one-way authentication method that offers encryption of both authentication data and connection data. The same cryptographic key is used in all connections. MS-CHAP v1 supports older Windows clients, such as Windows 95 and Windows 98.

- **Extensible Authentication Protocol-Message Digest 5 Challenge Handshake Authentication Protocol (EAP-MD5 CHAP)**   A version of CHAP (see the following bullet) that is ported to the EAP framework. EAP-MD5 CHAP supports encryption of authentication data through the industry-standard MD5 hashing scheme and provides compatibility with non-Microsoft clients, such as those running Mac OS X. It does not support the encryption of connection data.

- **Challenge Handshake Authentication Protocol (CHAP)**   A generic authentication method that offers encryption of authentication data through the MD5 hashing scheme. CHAP provides compatibility with non-Microsoft clients. The group policy that is applied to accounts using this authentication method must be configured to store passwords using reversible encryption. (Passwords must be reset after this new policy is applied.) It does not support encryption of connection data.

- **Shiva Password Authentication Protocol (SPAP)**   A weakly encrypted authentication protocol that offers interoperability with Shiva remote networking products. SPAP does not support the encryption of connection data.

- **Password Authentication Protocol (PAP)**   A generic authentication method that does not encrypt authentication data. User credentials are sent over the network in plaintext. PAP does not support the encryption of connection data.

- **Unauthenticated access**   Not an authentication protocol, but a configuration option that—when set on the NAS and remote access policy is applied to the connection—allows remote access connections to connect without submitting credentials. Can be used to troubleshoot or test remote access connectivity. Unauthenticated access does not support the encryption of connection data.

Table 8-3 provides information to help you map your requirements to the appropriate protocol.

Table 8-3   **Selecting an Authentication Protocol**

Requirement	Select
Encrypted authentication support for Windows 95, Windows 98, Microsoft Windows Millennium Edition (Me), or Windows NT 4 remote access clients (native support)	MS-CHAP v1
Encrypted authentication support for Windows 95, Windows 98, Windows Millennium Edition (Me), or Windows NT 4 remote access clients (with the latest Dial-Up Networking upgrade)	MS-CHAP v2 (VPN only for Windows 95)
Encrypted authentication support for certificate-based **public key infrastructure (PKI)**, such as those used with smart cards (when the remote access server is a member of a Windows 2000 server or Windows Server 2003 domain)	EAP-TLS
Encrypted authentication support for other Windows 2000, Windows XP, and Windows Server 2003 remote access clients	MS-CHAP v2
Mutual authentication (client and server always authenticate each other)	EAP-TLS and MS-CHAP v2
Support for encryption of connection data	MS-CHAP v1, MS-CHAP v2, and EAP-TLS
Encrypted authentication report for remote access clients that use other operating systems	CHAP and EAP-MD5 CHAP
Encrypted authentication report for remote access clients running Shiva LAN Rover software	SPAP
Unencrypted authentication when the remote access clients do not support any other protocol	PAP
Authentication credentials are not supplied by the remote access client	Unauthenticated access

SUMMARY

- By using the Routing and Remote Access service, Windows Server 2003 can be configured as a router and remote access server. A significant advantage of using Windows Server 2003 in this manner is that it is integrated with Windows features such as Group Policy and the Active Directory directory service. The Routing And Remote Access console is the principal tool used for configuring and managing this service.

- Routing and Remote Access can be automatically configured for several options: Remote Access (Dial-Up or VPN), Network Address Translation (NAT), Virtual Private Network (VPN) Access And NAT, and Secure Connection Between Two Private Networks. Or, if none of the standard options match your requirements, you can also manually configure Routing and Remote Access.

- Without dynamic routing protocols such as RIP and OSPF, network administrators must add static routes to connect to non-neighboring subnets when those subnets do not lie in the same direction as the default route.

- Routers read the destination addresses of received packets and route those packets according to directions that are provided by routing tables. In Windows Server 2003, you can view the IP routing table through the Routing And Remote Access console or through the Route Print command.

- Windows Server 2003 provides extensive support for demand-dial routing, which is the routing of packets over physical point-to-point links, such as analog phone lines and ISDN, and over virtual point-to-point links, such as PPTP and L2TP. Demand-dial routing allows you to connect to the Internet, connect branch offices, or implement router-to-router VPN connections.

- The remote access connection must be authorized after it is authenticated. Remote access authorization begins with the user account's dial-in properties; the first matching remote access policy is then applied to the connection.

- The Microsoft implementation of a RADIUS server is IAS. Use a RADIUS server to centralize remote access authentication, authorization, and logging. When you implement RADIUS, multiple Windows Server 2003 computers running the Routing and Remote Access service forward access requests to the RADIUS server. The RADIUS server then queries the domain controller for authentication and applies remote access policies to the connection requests.

EXERCISE

IMPORTANT **Completing All Exercises**   If you plan to do any of the textbook exercises in this chapter, you must do all of the exercises in the chapter to return the computer to its original state for the associated Lab Manual labs.

Exercise 8-1: Viewing the IP Routing Table

In this exercise, you will view the IP routing table at the command prompt.

1. Open a command prompt.

2. At the command prompt, type **route print**, and then press ENTER.

   QUESTION   What is the Netmask for the 10.1.0.0 Network Destination?

REVIEW QUESTIONS

1. You are the network administrator for Fabrikam, Inc. Fabrikam's network consists of several subnets. Current network users require access to only the company intranet and other internal company resources such as file shares and printers. Fabrikam, Inc., recently hired a team of developers who will be joining your network and whose connectivity requirement you must support. Which of the following options would require you to implement a routing solution for the new developer team? Choose all that apply.

   a. The developer team needs corporate connectivity, but its test applications must be isolated from the rest of the network.

   b. The developer team uses Internet access to connect to the corporate network.

   c. The developer team does not require Internet access, and its test applications do not require corporate connectivity.

   d. Source code repositories must be encrypted when stored and accessed across the network.

2. You are the network administrator for Fabrikam, Inc. Fabrikam's network consists of several subnets. Current network users require access to only the company intranet and other internal company resources such as file shares and printers. Fabrikam, Inc., recently hired a team of developers who will be joining your network and whose connectivity requirements you must support. Which of the following options would require you to determine a packet-filtering solution for the new developer team? Choose all that apply.

   a. The developer team needs full corporate connectivity, but its test applications must be isolated to only specific test computers.

   b. The developer team needs corporate connectivity, but its test applications must be completely isolated from users on the rest of the network.

   c. The developer team does not require Internet access, and its test applications do not require corporate connectivity.

   d. The developer team uses a predetermined unique protocol to test its applications.

3. Over the past several weeks, users have intermittently complained that they were unable to connect to the VPN server. You examine the network logs and determine that each of the complaints occurred when network usage was peaking. You have ruled out addressing as the cause. What is the most likely reason for the intermittent access problems?

4. You have configured your remote access server to distribute addresses to remote access clients through a DHCP server. However, you find that your remote access clients assign themselves with only APIPA addresses. Name two possible causes of this scenario.

5. Fabrikam, Inc., recently deployed smart cards to employees who require remote access to the corporate network. Which authentication protocol must you use to support the use of smart cards?

6. Fabrikam, Inc., management wants to ensure that data transferred during remote access are encrypted. Which authentication protocols provide data encryption?

7. You have recently created a new domain in a Windows Server 2003 network, and the domain functional level is Windows 2000 mixed. How is the Allow Access setting in the dial-in properties of a user account different in this environment from that in other server environments?

8. You are troubleshooting a failed remote access connection. You verify that the user account's dial-in properties are set to Allow Access and that the first matching remote access policy is set to Grant Remote Access Permission. The client still cannot connect. What should you check next?

CASE SCENARIOS

Case Scenario 8-1: Phone Number Authentication

Fabrikam, Inc., has 10 vendors that must access the company network. For security reasons, Fabrikam wants these 10 vendors to be authenticated only by their phone numbers when dialing into the network. Because they are going to be authenticated by their phone numbers, Fabrikam does not want them to be required to enter a username or password for authentication. How can you implement this configuration?

Case Scenario 8-2: Single-Credential Entry

You are a networking consultant for Fabrikam, Inc., which has already configured a PPTP-type VPN. Although users are not having trouble connecting, they must type their usernames and passwords twice. You have been asked to configure the system so users have to type their passwords only once to connect to the company domain. How can you allow users to avoid typing in their credentials in both the Log On To Windows screen and the VPN connection dialog box? Which authentication protocols can be used over this VPN connection?

CHAPTER 9

MAINTAINING A NETWORK INFRASTRUCTURE

Upon completion of this chapter, you will be able to:

■ Use the Networking tab in Task Manager to view network activity.

■ Monitor network traffic.

■ Find and set alerts using the Performance console.

■ Capture specific data using the version of Network Monitor included with Microsoft Windows Server 2003.

■ Troubleshoot connectivity to the Internet.

■ Troubleshoot server **services** using the Service utility and Event Viewer.

■ Use service recovery options to diagnose and resolve service-related issues.

■ Diagnose and resolve issues related to **service dependency**.

Simply stated, there are two approaches to maintaining your network: the reactive approach and the proactive approach. After implementation of your network design is complete and you have verified your network works properly, the reactive approach means that you will "wait and see" what problems arise. A proactive approach doesn't wait for problems to arise. A proactive approach to network management is preventative and makes use of tools such as Task Manager, the Performance console, Network Monitor, the network connection Repair feature, and Netdiag. Proactive system administrators use these tools to help spot potential and actual networking issues without wasting time guessing what the problems might be because they lack historical data. They do this by systematically monitoring, logging, and analyzing the network's data.

This chapter discusses three tools that can help you proactively troubleshoot network problems. First, you explore the simple and helpful networking tools in Task Manager. The second tool you examine is the Performance console (formerly called the Performance Monitor), which provides a much deeper look into system performance measurement. Finally, you explore some of the advanced capturing features found in Network Monitor.

USING THE NETWORKING TAB IN TASK MANAGER

Task Manager provides an aggregated view of key information about the local computer. It combines networking information, application information, running processes, key performance counters, and connected users all into one application view. When running, Task Manager also places a small histogram (bar graph) in the notification area to display real-time processor utilization.

Task Manager is most useful for immediate feedback on the status of a local computer. For example, the performance of the local computer degrades sharply and you want to determine which application or applications are utilizing the processor the most. To make this determination, you can display Task Manager, click Processes, and then sort by the CPU column. Doing so displays the processes in descending order of the percentage of the processor's time they consume. In other words, the application using the most processing time is displayed first. Task Manager also displays the amount of memory each **process** uses. To access Task Manager (Taskmanager.exe), press CTL+ALT+DEL, and then click Task Manager.

Task Manager has the same capability for quickly assessing the amount of bandwidth used by each of the network connections on the local machine. Figure 9-1 shows the Networking tab and the percentage of total bandwidth utilization. The Networking tab provides an overview of the use of each of your network connections. You can also determine other data—such as whether the link is operational or unplugged—by looking at the State column. Finally, in the Link Speed column, you can see what speed the link is.

The scale on the left is the percentage used, and it automatically changes scale depending on how much the link is used. Note carefully the scale in Figure 9-1, which ranges from 0 percent to 1 percent. Using this scale, if network usage spikes to the top of the chart, only 1 percent of the total bandwidth is being used.

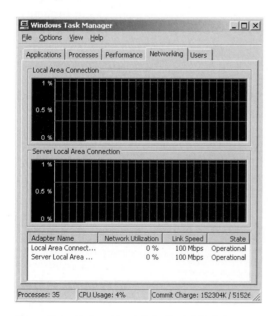

Figure 9-1   Networking tab in Task Manager

Filtering Network Traffic

If you receive reports that the server is not responding fast enough to reads or writes, you might want to isolate the view of the network traffic. Indeed, you can choose to show and highlight the total traffic (the default), or you can choose to show and highlight the bytes sent or bytes received, as shown in Figure 9-2.

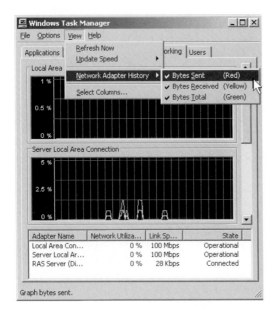

Figure 9-2   Filtering by direction of network flow

Filtering allows you to select the directions of network traffic you want to monitor. For example, if you are troubleshooting a server that is not responding quickly to writes, you can temporarily ignore the bytes sent. Conversely, if you troubleshoot a server that is not responding quickly to reads, you can temporarily ignore the bytes received.

Choosing Columns

As you saw in Figure 9-1, you can obtain an overview of some important state data, such as link speed. However, the Networking tab can also be a useful tool to determine which types of traffic are coming across the interface. Your view of what's going on is greatly enhanced by means of a network **counter**, an exposed piece of information, sometimes called a *data point*, which you can access to see the current status. If you determine the value of an available data point over time, you are sampling the data.

You can choose to add more counters in the overview by clicking the View menu, clicking Select Columns, and then selecting the additional information you want to display from the Select Columns dialog box, which is shown in Figure 9-3.

Although many different counters are available, only a few of them are necessary for any one troubleshooting session. Table 9-1 shows some of the most useful counters for troubleshooting network performance.

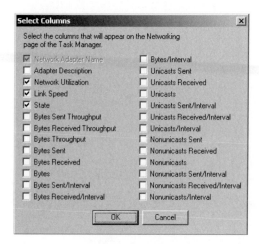

Figure 9-3   Available columns

Table 9-1   **Troubleshooting Using Performance Counters**

Property	Description
Network Adapter Name	The name of the network adapter. This check box is always selected. If you have multiple network adapters, you will see multiple listings.
Link Speed	The speed of the network interface. If you suspect a bottleneck, verify that this number is the maximum speed of the network. Sometimes, the network card receives a signal from the router to fall back to a slower speed (typically 100 megabits per second [Mbps] falls back to 10 Mbps).
Bytes/Interval	The rate at which bytes are sent and received on the network adapter during the polling time interval (by default every 2 seconds). As with many counters, a baseline (a reference point taken during normal operations) is very helpful in analyzing this value.
Unicasts/Interval	The number of unicast datagrams received during the polling time interval (by default every 2 seconds). Data indicated by the counter are directed traffic and not broadcast traffic, which might be seen in the next counter, Nonunicasts/Interval.
Nonunicasts/Interval	The number of broadcast and multicast datagrams received during the polling time interval (by default every 2 seconds). If this counter has data, your interface might be dealing with background or broadcast traffic. A high value in this counter may indicate problems on your network that aren't specifically related to the server that receives the traffic.

Practice using
Task Manager by
completing
Exercise 9-1,
"Displaying Task
Manager," now.

USING THE PERFORMANCE CONSOLE

Task Manager is an effective tool for taking a snapshot of the local server's network performance; the Performance console provides detailed information necessary for in-depth analysis, logging capabilities, and alerts, which are useful for early warnings of possible system issues. Use the Performance console instead of Task Manager when you need

- Access to more performance counters
- The ability to send alert **triggers** based on specific criteria

▶ **Starting the Performance Console**

You can start the Performance console in various ways. One of the simplest methods is to open the Start menu, select Run, type **perfmon.exe**, and then click OK. Performance Monitor automatically starts with three of the most used counters, as shown in Figure 9-4.

- **Pages/Sec**   Shows how often memory pages are being swapped in and out of random access memory (RAM) to disk. High-sustained values here can indicate that there is not enough RAM.

- **Avg. Disk Queue Length**   Monitor this counter to see how many system requests are waiting for disk access. The number of waiting input/output (I/O) requests should be sustained at no more than 1.5 to 2 times the number of spindles making up the physical disk.

- **% Processor Time**   Shows how much the processor is being used. High, sustained values can indicate that the processor is not fast enough or there might not be enough RAM.

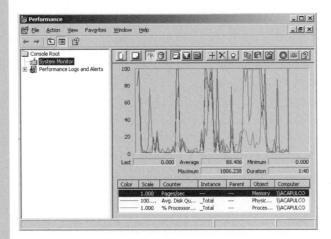

Figure 9-4   Performance console with the default counters loaded

Adding Network Counters

The Performance console is capable of sampling a huge range of performance counters—many more than Task Manager. These networking and non-networking components fall into several categories, as shown in Figure 9-5.

> **NOTE   Available Categories**   The categories available to you can vary based on the server software that is installed.

Figure 9-5   Categories of counters for monitoring performance

Our focus is on monitoring the networking items. The following list describes the key networking performance objects:

- **Network Interface**   This object contains some of the same counters as the Task Manager counter; however, it also contains counters for monitoring specific details about packets on the network.

- **TCPv4**   This object contains counters related to Transmission Control Protocol (TCP) version 4 connections.

- **TCPv6**   This object contains counters related to TCPv6 connections.

- **NBT Connection**   The NBT Connection performance object consists of counters that measure the rates at which bytes are sent and received over the network basic input/output system (NetBIOS) over TCP/IP (NetBT or NBT) protocol, which provides NetBIOS support for the Transmission Control Protocol/Internet Protocol (TCP/IP) protocol suite.

- **RAS Port**   This category is helpful if you have **virtual private network (VPN)** or other Remote Access Service (RAS) connections set up. With VPNs and RAS, you can choose to troubleshoot your connection problems based on specific ports. You can check the errors on a **port** or on other counters, such as the Percent Compression Out.

- **RAS Total**   This object contains counters that show the overall aggregated RAS performance, as opposed to the RAS Port object, which helps with a specific port.

Using the Performance Console to Create Alerts

As you have already seen, using counters to monitor the real-time performance of your system is a very powerful feature of the Performance console. Another useful capability for system administrators is creating alerts.

Alerts are like tripwires that are set to notify you when a system exceeds a specific threshold or boundary. For example, you can set an alert to

notify you when your system has less than 20 percent total free disk space
remaining.

You create alerts in the Performance Logs And Alerts snap-in in the Performance console. Right-click Alerts, and then select New Alert Settings, as shown
in Figure 9-6.

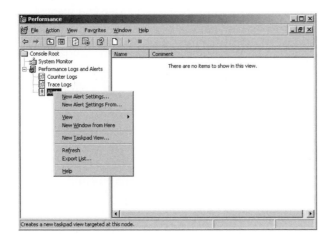

Figure 9-6   Setting up new alerts

Name the alert based on the type of counter or counters you want to monitor, and
then select the counters. When you click the Add button, as shown in Figure 9-7,
you can choose the different performance objects (such as PhysicalDisk) and then
pick a specific counter (such as % Disk Time). Sometimes you might want to
choose more than one counter to trigger an alert. For example, you might choose
to receive a notification if both the network bandwidth is heavy and if high numbers of errors are generated.

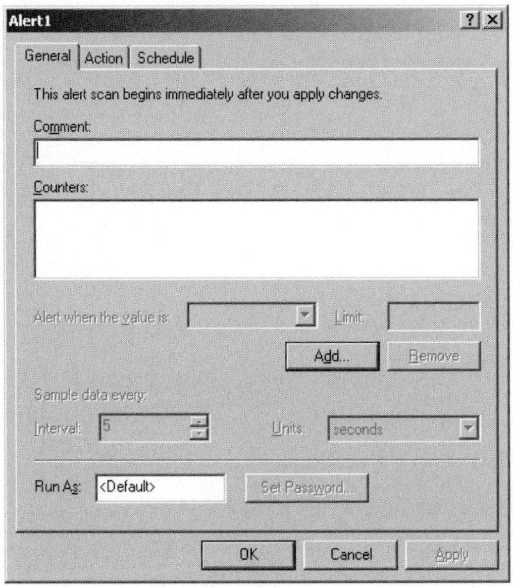

Figure 9-7   Adding an alert

Before you choose how you want the alert reported, you must set several options
in the General tab to specify how you want to sample the counters.

The following list describes some of the parameters you can configure in the General tab:

- **Comment**   Although the alert has a name, you can also give it a comment to help you or others recall what the purpose of the alert is and to whom the alert goes.

- **Alert When The Value Is**   This allows you to specify whether you want to trigger the alert when it's under the Limit value or over the Limit value.

- **Limit**   You can specify the value of the counter to be monitored. When the value goes over or under this limit (based on the selection in Alert When The Value Is), the alert is triggered.

- **Interval**   You can set how often the Performance console queries the system for what you want to monitor. The system doesn't continuously monitor for the counters you want; instead, sample data is collected at intervals during a specified amount of time. For example, you can set an interval of 5 seconds and collect data for 10 minutes. That means a snapshot of counters you have selected will be taken every 5 seconds for 10 minutes. The longer the interval, the less accurate the sample is because it is being sampled less often. The shorter the interval, the more accurate the sample is, but the more the processor is used to obtain the sample.

- **Units**   You can specify the units in time to collect samples. For instance, you might not want to sample every 5 seconds; instead, you might want to sample every 30 seconds. Again, if you reduce the frequency of sampling, or reduce the **sampling rate**, you will use fewer processor cycles, but your samples will provide less information because there are fewer of them.

- **Run As**   You can sample the counters by selecting either the System account or another account of your choice. However, for monitoring network-related counters, the System account has access to what it needs to perform the work.

  NOTE   Using Comment and Run As for All Counters   If two or more counters are being monitored, you must select each counter and set the Alert When The Value Is, Limit, Interval, and Units fields. The Comment field and Run As field are used for all counters in an alert.

After you set these parameters, select the Action tab, as shown in Figure 9-8.

The Action tab specifies what happens after an alert is triggered. A multitude of options let you know that the counter's criteria have been met. These options are as follows:

- **Log An Entry In The Application Event Log**   Selecting this option puts an event in the event log, which you can see using Event Viewer. A notice of the counter, value, and limit are part of the log entry, as shown in Figure 9-9.

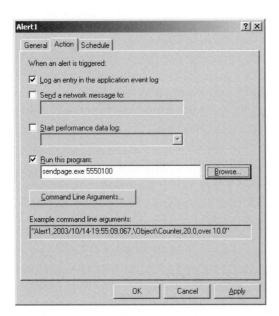

Figure 9-8 Specify how you want to handle the notification of your trigger with the Action tab

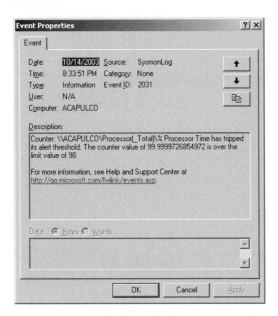

Figure 9-9 An example of an event that is based on triggers

■ **Send A Network Message To**   Selecting this option sends the equivalent of a Net Send command (Net Send sends messages to other users or computers on the network) with the alert's message to the computer specified in the field. For messages to be sent, the Alerter service must be started on the machine on which you are doing the monitoring. For messages to be received, the Messenger service must also be started on the receiving computer.

NOTE   Manually Enabling Services   The Alerter service and Messenger service do not run on a newly installed Windows Server 2003 server; you must manually change the state from Disabled to Automatic and ensure that the services are running.

- **Start Performance Data Log**   You can configure the alert system to start by writing additional counters to a log file. These counters can be reviewed later. You must preset the log file using the Counter Logs node in the Performance Logs And Alerts node. This option is useful when you want to start a log only when the system being monitored exhibits certain characteristics, such as monitoring the paging file when the available disk space falls below 15 percent.

- **Run This Program**   Use this setting to execute a program after one or more of the counters you set has exceeded its threshold. Use this option to specify a paging application, a batch file, or, if necessary, to shut down the system using the built-in Shutdown command.

Use the Schedule tab to automate starting and stopping the alert. For example, you might want to set the alert to operate during peak network usage, such as when the majority of users logs on to the network. You might also set the alert to operate during off-peak times, such as in the early morning hours. If you do not specify a schedule, or if you specify a manual start of the alert, you can start the alert by right-clicking it and then selecting Start, as shown in Figure 9-10.

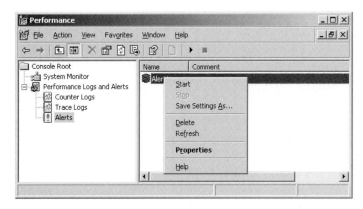

Figure 9-10   Starting alerts manually

MONITORING NETWORK TRAFFIC BY USING NETSTAT

One tool you can use to help monitor your traffic is a command-line utility called Netstat. Netstat provides information about existing network connections of a computer running TCP/IP and network activity statistics. For example, if you want to determine on which ports a system is listening for connections, you can run the Netstat -a command. Running this command displays the existing connections and listening ports.

After you have determined which ports are listening for connections, you might want to close a specific port, but before you close it, you should determine which application or applications might be using it. To make this determination, open a command prompt and type **netstat -o**, and then press ENTER. This command displays the protocol, the local inbound port that is open, the connection from or to the other computer, and the port uses, as shown in Figure 9-11.

Figure 9-11   Using Netstat -o to show the processes and ports used on a server

In this example, notice that the last entry shows Acapulco and a computer at 192.168.16.20 communicating over port 3389. In this instance, you can see that the **process identifier (PID)** is 660. Use the Processes tab in Windows Task Manager to determine which process has been assigned ID 660. By default, the Processes tab does not display the PIDs of processes. You view the PIDs by opening the View menu, selecting Select Columns, and then selecting PID (Process Identifier; not selected by default), as shown in Figure 9-12.

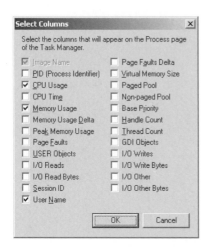

Figure 9-12   Configuring Task Manager to show the PID

If you select the PID column, you will see a display that is similar to the one shown in Figure 9-13.

Match the PID and the process to determine which process or application has the port open. If the PID belongs to the Svchost process, you must take an additional step to determine which services are aggregated in the Svchost process. To display the list of aggregated services, open a command prompt and type **tasklist /svc**. In the current example, the Svchost process with the PID of 660 provides services for TermService (Terminal Services). **Terminal Services** uses port 3389 for communications. Using this method, you can find applications and services that are associated with open ports before closing the ports.

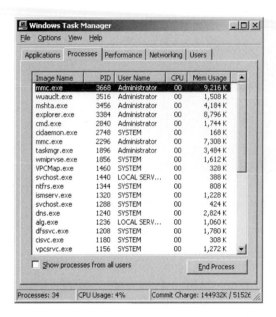

Figure 9-13   Using Task Manager to see the PID of each process

USING WINDOWS SERVER 2003 NETWORK MONITOR

Windows Server 2003 includes Network Monitor Lite (use the Windows Component Wizard to install Network Monitor), which is a powerful tool; however, a more powerful version of the Network Monitor tool is available in Microsoft Systems Management Server. To determine whether you are using the Lite version of Network Monitor (part of the Network Monitor), on the Help menu, click About. The information in the Network Monitor dialog box will indicate which version you are running. The two main differences between the standard version and the Lite version of Network Monitor are these:

■ The Lite version of Network Monitor can capture only traffic sent to or from its own network interface; whereas the standard version of Network Monitor runs in *promiscuous mode*, which means it can capture 100 percent of the network traffic available to the network interface.

■ The standard version of Network Monitor enables you to see where other instances of Network Monitor are running. This information is useful when you set up multiple monitoring stations across your network and then use a central monitoring point to collect the data. Because sensitive data can be captured and examined using this tool, knowing who uses a version of the tool in promiscuous mode helps to maintain a secure network environment. To determine who is running Network Monitor, select Identify Network Monitor Users on the Tools menu, as shown in Figure 9-14.

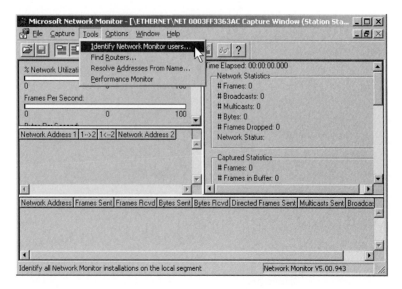

Figure 9-14   Tracking other Network Monitor instances

▶ **Installing Network Monitor Lite**

To Install Network Monitor Lite, follow these steps:

1. Open Control Panel.

2. Double-click Add Or Remove Programs.

3. In the Add Or Remove Programs window, click Add/Remove Windows Components.

4. In the Windows Components Wizard, click Management And Monitoring Tools, and then click Details.

5. Select the Network Monitor Tools check box, and then click OK.

6. In the Windows Components window, click Next.

7. On the Windows Setup screen, click Finish.

Using Network Monitor Triggers

Network Monitor's main function is to capture packets as they cross the network. However, watching Network Monitor in real time as it waits for a problem to appear is obviously impractical. As discussed previously, you can set triggers to alert you when certain conditions are met. To configure a trigger, start Network Monitor, and from the Capture menu, select Trigger. The Capture Trigger dialog box opens, as shown in Figure 9-15.

By default, none of the triggers are active. You can set up a trigger to alert you based on the size of the buffer or patterns found in the capture, or both the buffer space and pattern. For example, you can configure the trigger to notify you when the buffer space is 25 percent, 50 percent, 75 percent, or 100 percent full.

> **NOTE**   **Network Monitor Buffer**   During the capture process, Network Monitor copies the frames that match your capture filter to a temporary capture file called a buffer file. You can specify both the size and location of this file; when the buffer reaches its maximum size, each new frame causes the oldest frame to be overwritten.

Figure 9-15   Configuring a trigger to alert you to specific conditions

Because a full buffer results in overwritten frames, you may want to be notified when the buffer is 75 percent full so that you can save the buffer to a file. You might also decide to use the Pattern Match feature (selected in Figure 9-15), which allows you to type in a hexadecimal or American Standard Code for Information Interchange (ASCII) representation of what you want to find. For example, you could look for any instance of a string of characters, and then, by using the Execute Command Line option, have a message sent to you that says the text string was found.

TROUBLESHOOTING INTERNET CONNECTIVITY

One of the more common network troubleshooting issues is a loss of connectivity to the Internet. There are several links in the chain of connectivity from a client to the Internet. If one of the links is broken, the user will not be able to connect to the Internet. As the system administrator, you must choose how to troubleshoot a loss of Internet connectivity for each situation.

There are two basic approaches to troubleshooting the loss of Internet connectivity: inside out and outside in. The inside-out approach starts at the innermost point, the client, and troubleshoots to the public network. Outside in takes the opposite approach: it starts outside of the organization's firewall or router and troubleshoots to the client. Both approaches have merit and should be used when appropriate.

When a single user complains that "the Internet is down," generally the more efficient approach is inside out. Although you have no indication of what might be causing the loss of connectivity, you do know that only one user from the network has an issue. Therefore, you should use the inside-out approach and start by gathering more information from the user. You should also determine whether other users on the same subnet can access the Internet. If other users can access the Internet, the most likely cause of the loss of connectivity is misconfiguration of the user's computer or some other issue directly related to that client computer. If the entire subnet, or more than one subnet, cannot access the Internet, an outside-in approach is probably more efficient.

Identifying the Specific Networking Issue

At the client, you take a number of simple steps to narrow down the issue. First, you can determine the computer's IP configuration by opening a command prompt and typing **ipconfig /all**. Review the output of this command, and verify the following:

- The computer has a valid IP address and subnet mask.

- The default gateway specified for the computer is correct.

- There is at least one **Domain Name System (DNS)** server listed.

- If the computer should be configured for **Dynamic Host Configuration Protocol (DHCP)**, verify that the DHCP Enabled attribute displays Yes.

- The computer does not have an IP address in the range 169.254.0.0 to 169.254.255.255, unless you intend to use Automatic Private IP Addressing (APIPA).

After you have verified the IP configuration, you can also determine whether the issue is related to name resolution.

Identifying Connectivity Issues

To verify whether the problem is a name resolution issue, ping a different network host, as shown in Figure 9-16.

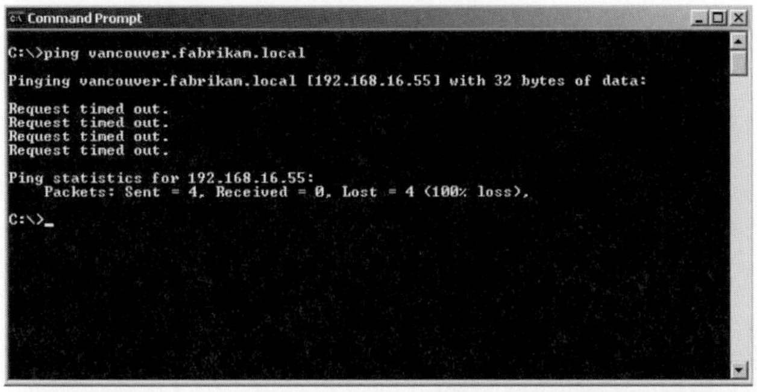

Figure 9-16   Results of a network ping showing DNS responds, but the packets are not finding the destination

The response from the Ping command is helpful. Although the response to pinging vancouver.fabrikam.local is "Request Timed Out," you know that name resolution is not the issue because the correct IP address for vancouver.fabrikam.local is in the brackets. This means that the host name was correctly resolved to an IP address. For this situation, you should focus on connectivity issues that are not related to name resolution.

The next most logical tool to use is PathPing, which shows you each route between the client and the target and helps you determine which link does not pass the packet on to the next destination. The following is an example of how you would use PathPing to trace the path to Mail01. To save time, the -n switch is used to prevent PathPing from attempting to resolve the IP addresses of intermediate routers to their names.

```
D:\> pathping -n mail01

Tracing route to mail01 [10.54.1.196]
over a maximum of 30 hops:
  0  172.16.87.35
  1  172.16.87.218
  2  192.168.52.1
  3  192.168.80.1
  4  10.54.247.14
  5  10.54.1.196

Computing statistics for 125 seconds...
              Source to Here   This Node/Link
Hop  RTT     Lost/Sent = Pct  Lost/Sent = Pct  Address
  0                                                172.16.87.35
                                0/ 100 =  0%   |
  1   41ms     0/ 100 =  0%     0/ 100 =  0%   172.16.87.218
                               13/ 100 = 13%   |
  2   22ms    16/ 100 = 16%     3/ 100 =  3%   192.168.52.1
                                0/ 100 =  0%   |
  3   24ms    13/ 100 = 13%     0/ 100 =  0%   192.168.80.1
                                0/ 100 =  0%   |
  4   21ms    14/ 100 = 14%     1/ 100 =  1%   10.54.247.14
                                0/ 100 =  0%   |
  5   24ms    13/ 100 = 13%     0/ 100 =  0%   10.54.1.196
Trace complete.
```

Identifying Name Resolution Issues

If you received the response shown in Figure 9-17, you should consider examining the inability to resolve host names to IP addresses as the cause of the client's problems.

Figure 9-17   Ping request results showing DNS unable to resolve the requested host name

In Figure 9-17, there is no indication that the client can resolve stlouis.fabrikam.local to an IP address. If you suspect this is a name resolution issue and you know the IP address of stlouis.fabrikam.local, type **ping *ip_address*** (where *ip_address* is the IP address of stlouis.fabrikam.local). If you receive a successful reply to your Ping command, the issue is most likely name resolution. To resolve the problem, check the DNS server configuration, the Windows Internet Naming Service (WINS) servers, and, if applicable, check the local host file and Lmhost file.

To determine whether the DNS server has the correct address for a specific host, use Nslookup. For example, at the command prompt, type **nslookup stlouis .fabrikam.local**, and then press ENTER. Running this command will display the IP address provided to the client by the default DNS server.

MORE INFO **Nslookup Primer** *An excellent primer on Nslookup is Microsoft Knowledge Base article 200525, "Using Nslookup.exe." To find this article, go to http://support.microsoft.com and enter the article number in the Search The Knowledge Base text box.*

If you suspect DNS name resolution issues for names beyond the scope of this particular server, or if name resolution issues exist for names outside of your organization, you should next check the DNS server. First, make sure the DNS server is forwarding to the next logical place based on your network design. You perform this task by verifying the configuration of the Forwarders tab, as shown in Figure 9-18.

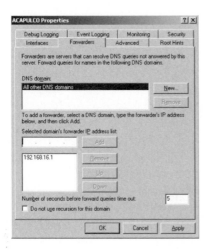

Figure 9-18 Ensuring that the forwarders are set up correctly

Typically, the DNS server forwards to a server with more knowledge of the network layout or directly to the Internet service provider (ISP). If this is not the case, you must adjust the settings in the Forwarders tab.

Additionally, verify that the server itself is responding to requests and that it can also respond to tests on servers to which it forwards information. In the example shown in Figure 9-19, the server does respond to resolution requests; however, it is unable to get any resolution from servers to which it forwards requests.

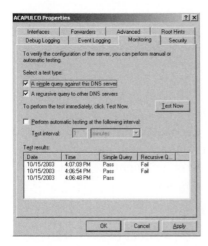

Figure 9-19 Failure of the recursive query, usually indicating a forwarding problem

Practice
verifying the
configuration of
DNS forwarding
by completing
Exercise 9-2,
"Verifying the
Configuration
of DNS
Forwarding,"
now.

This failure could indicate that the name resolution problem does not occur on your servers, but on servers on which your servers rely.

Using the Repair Feature

The Repair feature in Windows Server 2003 enables you to perform many tasks in one step. You can find this feature in the Support tab while inspecting the status of a network adapter, as shown in Figure 9-20.

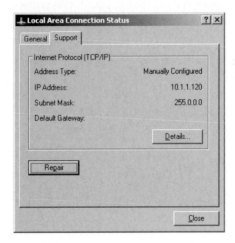

Figure 9-20   Using the Repair button to perform a multitude of configuration resets

Clicking the Repair button initiates many actions as if they were each typed on the command line. The commands are performed in the order listed in Table 9-2.

Table 9-2   Repair Actions

Repair Button Action	Description
Ipconfig /renew	Attempts to renew the DHCP lease
Arp -d *	Flushes the Address Resolution Protocol (ARP) cache
Nbtstat -R	Reloads the NetBIOS cache
Nbtstat -RR	Sends the NetBIOS computer name to WINS for an update
Ipconfig /flushdns	Flushes the DNS cache
Ipconfig /registerdns	Registers the name with the DNS server

> **MORE INFO**   **Repair Button Information**   You can learn more about the Repair button in Microsoft Knowledge Base article 289256, "A Description of the Repair Option on a Local Area Network or High-Speed Internet Connection." To find this article, go to http://support.microsoft.com and enter the article number in the Search The Knowledge Base text box.

Verifying the DHCP Server

If the client computer does not receive an IP address, a default gateway, and at least a primary DNS server address, the client will not be able to access the Internet. The following are some reasons the DHCP information might not be delivered to the client:

- A router blocks the **Bootstrap Protocol (BOOTP)**.
- The DHCP relay agent does not exist on segments without BOOTP relay.

- Addresses are not available in the DHCP scope.

- The DHCP server might not be functioning.

While you inspect the DHCP server, you should also verify the validity of the IP address, subnet mask, default gateway, and the DNS servers that are delivered to the client.

If some clients are able to connect to the Internet and others are not, and you determine that client computers configured for DHCP obtain configuration information from separate scopes, a rogue DHCP server might exist. A *rogue DHCP server* is an unauthorized DHCP server on your network. Usually rogue DHCP servers are set up for testing purposes; however, they can unintentionally distribute addressing and configuration information to clients, which can prevent clients from accessing the Internet.

If DHCP servers are not authorized, they automatically shut down. Use the Dhcploc tool, which is found in Windows Server 2003 Support Tools, to discover DHCP servers that should not be authorized or other DHCP servers that need not be authorized, such as older Microsoft DHCP servers or non-Microsoft DHCP servers. Dhcploc can be configured to send alerts when rogue DHCP servers are identified.

You might be asked to troubleshoot connections to the Internet that start from wireless machines. In some cases, you might want to bridge a single wireless access point (WAP) with multiple and varying connection topologies, as shown in Figure 9-21.

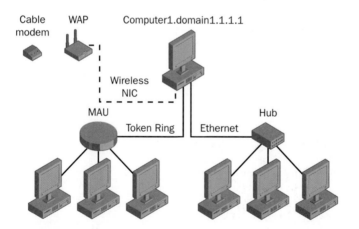

Figure 9-21   Example network that can leverage network bridging

Bridging Multiple Networks

In Figure 9-21, an Internet connection is joined to a single WAP. The WAP then communicates with the wireless **network interface card (NIC)** in the server. In addition, the server has an **Ethernet** connection and a **Token Ring** connection attached to other networks.

When you enable network bridging on this connection, all points that enter the server (wireless, Token Ring, and Ethernet) appear on the same network. Hence, they can all share the wireless connection and get out to the Internet. To create a **network bridge**, hold down the CTRL key as you click the multiple connections on the server. Then right-click, and select Bridge Networks, as shown in Figure 9-22.

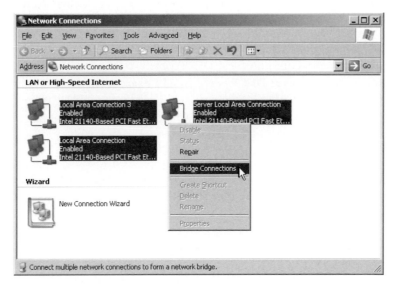

Figure 9-22   Selecting multiple networks, and then right-clicking to bridge them

When you configure network bridging, you allow traffic from the wireless, Ethernet, and Token Ring NIC to share the same network space. Hence, a single wireless NIC can be the outbound gateway to disparate networks.

To troubleshoot bridged connectivity to the Internet, take the following steps:

■ In the properties in the General tab of the bridged connection, verify that all networks are indeed bridged.

■ The bridge should have its own IP address. Verify this by typing **ipconfig /all** at the command prompt. If the bridge does not have its own IP address, remove the bridge and re-create it.

■ Check the physical connectivity among the segments on the bridge.

Using Netdiag

Netdiag is a command-line tool that performs a series of tests to help the system administrator isolate networking and connectivity problems.

To help you understand how Netdiag works, consider the following scenario. You are the system administrator for Fabrikam, Inc., and a user has complained that she cannot connect to a network resource. You investigate and encounter only a "Network path not found" error message and no other information. Although you suspect the DNS server you have trouble with is down, you decide to run Netdiag to get a quick report from a wide range of network tests. At the command line, you type **netdiag**, and then press ENTER.

When executed in this scenario, Netdiag performs tests on each NIC, and it performs a set of global tests. The tests on the NICs are performed in the following order:

1. Netcard queries test

2. Ipconfig test

3. Autoconfiguration test (APIPA)

4. Default gateway test

5. NetBT name test

6. WINS Service test

Netdiag performs the set of global tests in the following order:

1. Domain membership test

2. NetBT transports test

3. Autoconfiguration address test (APIPA)

4. IP loopback ping test

5. Default gateway test

6. NetBT name test

7. Winsock test

8. DNS test

9. Redir and Browser test

10. Domain controller discovery test

11. Domain controller list test

12. Trust relationship test

13. Kerberos test

14. The Lightweight Directory Access Protocol (LDAP) test

15. Bindings test

16. Wide area network (WAN) configuration test

17. Modem configuration test

18. IP security test

In the following Netdiag output sample, the results of these tests show that the network adapter protocol, bindings, and IP address tests succeed. The DNS ping test fails and reports that the DNS server cannot be contacted.

```
Computer Name: RKSRVR-2
DNS Host Name: rksrvr-2.reskita.microsoft.com
System info : Windows 2000 Server (Build 2467)
Processor : x86 Family 6 Model 6 Stepping 0, GenuineIntel
List of installed hotfixes : Q147222

Netcard queries test . . . . . . . : Passed
[WARNING] The net card 'Intel(R) PRO/100+ Management Adapter' may not be working.

Per interface results:
    Adapter : Local Area Connection
        Netcard queries test . . . : Passed
        Host Name. . . . . . . . . : rksrvr-2
        IP Address . . . . . . . . : 10.10.1.51
        Subnet Mask. . . . . . . . : 255.255.255.0
        Default Gateway. . . . . . :
        Dns Servers. . . . . . . . : 10.10.1.77
        AutoConfiguration results. . . . . . : Passed
```

```
              Default gateway test . . . . : Skipped
                  [WARNING] No gateways defined for this adapter.
              NetBT name test. . . . . . : Passed
              WINS service test. . . . . : Skipped
                  There are no WINS servers configured for this interface.
          Adapter : Local Area Connection 2
              Netcard queries test . . . : Failed
              NetCard Status:            DISCONNECTED
                  Some tests will be skipped on this interface.
              Host Name. . . . . . . . . : rksrvr-2
              Autoconfiguration IP Address : 169.254.74.217
              Subnet Mask. . . . . . . : 255.255.0.0
              Default Gateway. . . . . :
              Dns Servers. . . . . . . :

Global results:
Domain membership test . . . . . . : Passed
NetBT transports test. . . . . . . : Passed
    List of NetBt transports currently configured:
        NetBT_Tcpip_{A2D04C22-3BB8-4FA0-B7DA-414DC1DD08A7}
        NetBT_Tcpip_{56079E37-8246-4712-8B36-F503FF6F9873}
    2 NetBt transports currently configured.
Autonet address test . . . . . . . : Passed
IP loopback ping test. . . . . . . : Passed
Default gateway test . . . . . . . : Failed
    [FATAL] NO GATEWAYS ARE REACHABLE.
    You have no connectivity to other network segments.
    If you configured the IP protocol manually then
    you need to add at least one valid gateway.
NetBT name test. . . . . . . . . . : Passed
Winsock test . . . . . . . . . . . : Passed
DNS test . . . . . . . . . . . . . : Failed
          [WARNING] Cannot find a primary authoritative DNS server for the name
              'bdover.reskita.microsoft.com.'. [ERROR_TIMEOUT]
              The name 'bdover.reskita.microsoft.com.' may not be registered in DNS
  .
      [WARNING] The DNS entries for this DC cannot be verified right now on DNS
 server 10.10.1.77, ERROR_TIMEOUT.
      [FATAL] No DNS servers have the DNS records for this DC registered.
Redir and Browser test . . . . . . : Passed
    List of NetBt transports currently bound to the Redir
        NetBT_Tcpip_{A2D04C22-3BB8-4FA0-B7DA-414DC1DD08A7}
        NetBT_Tcpip_{56079E37-8246-4712-8B36-F503FF6F9873}
    The redir is bound to 2 NetBt transports.
    List of NetBt transports currently bound to the browser
        NetBT_Tcpip_{A2D04C22-3BB8-4FA0-B7DA-414DC1DD08A7}
        NetBT_Tcpip_{56079E37-8246-4712-8B36-F503FF6F9873}
    The browser is bound to 2 NetBt transports.
DC discovery test. . . . . . . . . : Passed
DC list test . . . . . . . . . . . : Passed
Trust relationship test. . . . . . : Failed
    Secure channel for domain 'RESKITA' is to '\\a-dcp.reskita.microsoft.com'.
    [FATAL] Cannot set secure channel for domain 'RESKITA' to PDC emulator. [ERR
OR_NO_LOGON_SERVERS]
Kerberos test. . . . . . . . . . . : Passed
LDAP test. . . . . . . . . . . . . : Passed
    [WARNING] Failed to query SPN registration on DC 'a-
dcp.reskita.microsoft.com'.
    [WARNING] Failed to query SPN registration on DC 'a-
dc1.reskita.microsoft.com'.
    [WARNING] Failed to query SPN registration on DC 'a-
dc3.reskita.microsoft.com'.
Bindings test. . . . . . . . . . . : Passed
```

```
WAN configuration test . . . . . . : Skipped
    No active remote access connections.
Modem diagnostics test . . . . . . : Passed
IP Security test . . . . . . . . . : Passed
    Service status  is: Started
    Service startup is: Automatic
    IPSec service is available, but no policy is assigned or active
    Note: run "ipseccmd /?" for more detailed information

The command completed successfully
```

With this information, the administrator knows that either the DNS server address is incorrect or the DNS server does not respond. Because the DNS address is also displayed as output, you can easily verify whether it is correct.

After the problem is isolated, the administrator can perform additional troubleshooting to determine why the DNS server is down.

TROUBLESHOOTING SERVER SERVICES

When a server runs, you might think it is OK to relax, when in fact, you must continue to be vigilant. This section explores how to troubleshoot services to keep the server running smoothly.

Determining Service Dependency

Windows Server 2003, like other Microsoft servers, is made up of a collection of processes, each of which performs a specific task. Sometimes, these tasks run as services. A service can run either in the foreground—requiring user interaction—or in the background—requiring no interaction. Often, services run in the background and require little to no user interaction to perform the specified job. An example of a background service is Net Logon, which is responsible for authenticating users and services.

To determine which services are installed and running, on the Start menu, right-click My Computer, click Manage, expand Services And Applications, and then click Services. An example of a list of services is shown in Figure 9-23.

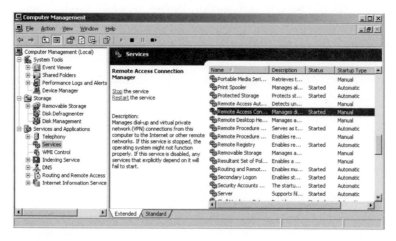

Figure 9-23   Services node showing the status of all the services

Services can be in one of three possible states: started, stopped, or paused. Three possible methods exist to configure a service for starting:

- **Automatic**   The service starts automatically when the system is restarted.

- **Manual**   The service does not start automatically when the system is restarted, but it will start if it is manually started or if another process calls upon this service.

- **Disabled**   The service will not start automatically when the system is restarted; the service will not start even if another process calls upon this service to start or if a user attempts to start it manually.

Some services depend on other services to start. This concept is called a *service dependency*. Therefore, if just one service does not work properly, it could have a cascading effect throughout the entire server. Using the Services console, if you take a closer look at the Remote Access Connection Manager service (double-click the service and then select the Dependencies tab), you can see the services it depends on to start, as well as the services that depend on it to start. This is shown in Figure 9-24.

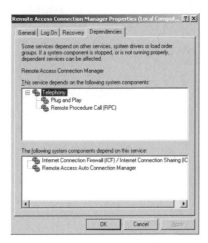

Figure 9-24   The Dependencies tab showing the dependency interaction

In this case, you can see that the Remote Access Connection Manager service relies on the Telephony service, which relies on both the Plug And Play service and the **Remote Procedure Call (RPC)** service running. If the Remote Access Connection Manager service is not running, neither the Internet Connection Firewall/Internet Connection Sharing (ICF/ICS) service nor the Remote Access Auto Connection Manager service will start.

Using Service Recovery Options

Most of the services that are installed by Windows Server 2003 run under the Local System context; that is, the special **Local System account** controls when the service should be started and stopped. However, additionally loaded services (usually these are loaded by Microsoft or third-party applications) run under potentially different contexts. Often, when the service is being loaded, the administrator is asked for specific credentials under which the service is run. Instead of providing the service unobstructed access to the system by means of the special System account, the service is restricted to the capabilities of the user account specified by the administrator. Sometimes this account is a local user to the computer (say, a local administrator account); other times, the account has fewer privileges. The level of access required depends on the requirements of the application and the services it installs.

The best approach, however, is to provide to the account only the least amount of access that is required. For instance, if the service account could start with a local user account, you should not necessarily make the account a local administrator account simply because it is going to be used to control a service. Consult your installation documentation for specific rights required for each application you plan to load.

Occasionally, after you install a new application that installs new services, the new application's services might not start. You can see whether the service is started and any errors associated with the service if it did not start by inspecting Computer Manager or by viewing the System event log, as shown in Figure 9-25.

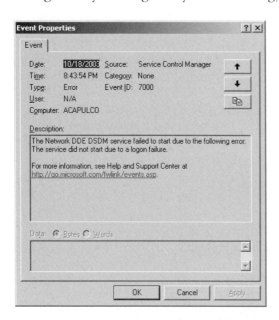

Figure 9-25   Network DDE DSDM service failed to start

If you determine that the error is a logon failure, you must investigate the reasons for the failure. There are many possible reasons why the failure has occurred including the following:

■ The user name for the account has been renamed, deleted, disabled, or it is otherwise invalid.

■ The password for the account has expired and must be reset.

■ The account specified to run the service has not been granted the Log On As A Service right.

To address these problems, first, in the service itself, inspect the Log On tab (as shown in Figure 9-26) to ensure that the account information provided is correct based on the application's specifications.

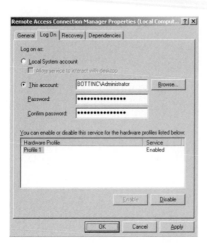

Figure 9-26   Using the Log On tab to ensure that the account information for the service is correct

After you verify the name of the account and the password, you should also ensure that the account has been granted the Log On As A Service right. If you use a domain account to run the service, you should inspect the Default Domain Controller policy. To perform this task, on the Start menu, point to Administrative Tools, and then click Domain Controller Security Policy. In the left pane, under the Local Policies node, double-click User Rights Assignment, and in the right pane, select Log On As A Service, as shown in Figure 9-27.

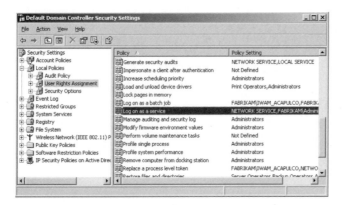

Figure 9-27   Ensuring that the service is granted the Log On As A Service right

Ensure that the domain account you want to use is specified in the Policy Setting and attempt to restart the service.

If the account you want to use is on a stand-alone machine that runs Windows Server 2003, run the Gpedit utility. Then expand Local Computer Policy, Computer Configuration, Windows Settings, Security Settings, Local Policies, and finally, select User Rights Assignment. Locate the Log On As A Service right and ensure that the account you want to use is listed.

Windows Server 2003 has many options if a service fails to start because of the reasons described previously. If a service fails, events are logged to the server where the service is loaded. However, you can choose to take a more proactive approach to service management.

If you select the Recovery tab of the service, several options enable you to specify behavior after a service fails, as shown in Figure 9-28.

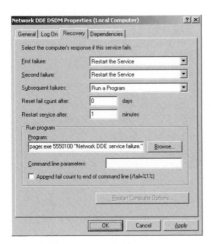

Figure 9-28   Setting behavior in the Recovery tab

If a service fails, you have four choices:

- Take No Action
- Restart The Service
- Run A Program
- Restart The Computer

A single service failure might be an anomaly. That is, the service could have failed to load initially because another service it depended on had not yet been started. This situation can occur for a number of reasons including temporary slow disk access or another service must finish writing to a log file before fully starting. Hence, because that other service was not fully started, this service could have requested to start, recognized that a service it depended on was not started, and simply missed the opportunity to start. Therefore, on the first failure, you are advised to restart the service.

Practice
configuring
services by
completing
Exercise 9-3,
"Configuring
Services," now.

However, if the service fails multiple times, you could try to restart it again, run a program to let you know that the service has not started, or restart the computer to see whether the timing dependency has disappeared.

SUMMARY

- After completing your network implementation, it is very important to proactively maintain your Windows Server 2003 network.

- The Task Manager Networking tab is a quick way to view network activity. You can add columns to the networking page to view more information.

- Use the Performance console to monitor real-time activity, configure alerts, and create performance logs. The Performance console provides more detailed analysis of system resource usage through the use of counters, which can be used to locate bottlenecks. The Performance console alerts allow you to send a notification after a trigger has been set off.

- Use Netstat to help monitor network traffic, and execute the Netstat -o command to determine the PID of a process that has opened a port. Use Task Manager to show the process that matches the PID.

- There are two versions of Network Monitor: Lite and standard. The Lite version of Network Monitor can capture only traffic sent to or from its own network interface; whereas the standard version of Network Monitor runs in promiscuous mode, which means it can capture 100 percent of the network traffic available to the network interface. The standard version of the Network Monitor tool can be found in Systems Management Server (SMS) and can capture traffic between any computers on the local segment. Network Monitor enables you to capture specific packets from your network to analyze network activity. You can configure Network Monitor to trigger an alert when specific patterns are matched or a specific amount of buffer space is used.

- When troubleshooting Internet connectivity, check the client's IP settings, DNS settings, and forwarder settings.

- If a problem is related to DNS, you must ensure that the client has the correct DNS server information. If so, first use the Nslookup command to verify that the server correctly returns what you expect. Then verify the DNS server's **forwarders**.

- The network adapter's Repair button performs a myriad of tests and functions that can resolve connectivity problems.

- Network bridging makes multiple networks appear as one network.

- Some services depend on each other to start. You can check dependencies in a service's Dependencies tab. The service recovery options allow you to restart the service, run a program, or restart the computer after single or multiple service failures. When troubleshooting service failures, you should check the username, password, and the Log On As A Service right. You can configure the recovery options to inform you when a service has failed to start.

EXERCISES

IMPORTANT   Complete All Exercises   If you plan to do any of the textbook exercises in this chapter, you must do all of the exercises to return the computer to its original state in preparation for the subsequent Lab Manual labs. You need DNS installed to do Exercise 9-2, "Verifying the Configuration or DNS Forwarding." If DNS is not installed, refer to Exercise 3-1 in this textbook, "Adding the DNS Server Role," to install DNS.

Exercise 9-1: Displaying Task Manager

In this exercise, you use Task Manager to display the list of running processes and to view network activity.

1. Log on as Administrator, press CTL+ALT+DEL, and then click Task Manager.

2. Click the Networking tab.

3. On the View menu, click Select Columns.

4. Select the following counters, and then click OK:

   ❑ Network Utilization

   ❑ Link Speed

   ❑ State

   ❑ Unicasts/Interval

   ❑ Nonunicasts/Interval

5. To open a command prompt, click Start, click Run, type **cmd**, and then click OK.

6. At the command prompt, type **ping *instructor_computer*** (where *instructor_computer* is the IP address of the instructor computer).

7. View the Networking tab.

   You should see activity on the connection over which the ping was sent.

Exercise 9-2: Verifying the Configuration of DNS Forwarding

In this exercise, you use the Monitoring tab in DNS to verify that forwarding is working.

NOTE   To Install DNS   If DNS is not installed, refer to Exercise 3-1 in this textbook, "Adding the DNS Server Role," to install DNS before beginning this exercise.

1. Verify you are logged on as Administrator.

2. Click Start, point to Administrative Tools, and then click DNS.

3. Select and right-click *Your_Computer* (where *Your_Computer* is the name of your computer), and then click Properties.

4. On the *Your_Computer* Properties page, in the Monitoring tab, click Select A Recursive Query To Other DNS Servers.

5. Click Test Now. A response is displayed in the Test Results box.

Exercise 9-3: Configuring Services

In this exercise, you configure service dependency and recovery options.

1. Click Start, right-click My Computer, and then click Manage.

2. Expand Services And Applications, and then click Services.

3. Double-click the ClipBook service.

4. On the ClipBook Properties page, change the Startup Type from Disabled to Automatic, and then click Apply.

5. Click Start to attempt to start the service.

   An error states, "Could not start the ClipBook service on Local Computer. Error 1068: The dependency service or group failed to start." Click OK.

6. In the Dependencies tab, view the services on which ClipBook depends.

   Note that the Network DDE and Network DDE DSDM services must be started because the ClipBook service relies on them. Close the ClipBook Properties page by clicking OK.

7. Locate the Network DDE DSDM service, and double-click it to view its properties.

8. Change the Startup Type from Disabled to Automatic, and click Apply.

9. Click Start to start the service. Click OK to close the Network DDE DSDM Properties page.

10. Now locate the Network DDE service, and double-click it to view its properties. Change the Startup Type from Disabled to Automatic, and then click Apply.

11. Click Start to start the service. Click OK to close the Network DDE Properties page.

12. Right-click the ClipBook service, and click Start to start the ClipBook service.

    The ClipBook service starts.

13. Stop and disable Network DDE, Network DDE DSDM, and ClipBook services.

REVIEW QUESTIONS

1. You receive a report that a user's computer is responding slowly to user network requests. You want a quick way to see which type of network traffic the server is receiving. You use Network Monitor. You want to see whether any general broadcast traffic is being sent. Which counter should you enable?

   a. Nonunicasts/Interval

   b. Unicasts/Interval

   c. Bytes Sent/Interval

   d. Bytes Received/Interval

2. You set up Performance Logs And Alerts to send a message to ComputerB to notify an operator when the network bandwidth utilization on ComputerA reaches a certain level. However, ComputerB never receives the message sent from ComputerA. What must you do to enable messages to be sent by ComputerA and received by ComputerB? Choose all that apply.

   a. On ComputerA, start the Messenger service.

   b. On ComputerA, start the Alerter service.

   c. On ComputerB, start the Messenger service.

   d. On ComputerB, start the Alerter service.

3. You suspect that a virus has infected your computer, which runs Windows Server 2003. You believe this virus transmits data from your server over the network using a specific port. You want to determine which process is using a specific port.

   Which command should you run?

   a. Nbtstat -RR

   b. Nbtstat -r

   c. Netstat -a

   d. Netstat -o

4. A user in the branch office reports that he cannot use Microsoft Internet Explorer to open a commonly used Web site on the Internet. At your client computer in the main office, you are able to ping the target address. What should you do to troubleshoot this problem? Choose all that apply.

   a. From the user's client computer, ping the destination address.

   b. From the user's client computer, use the Network Repair feature.

   c. From the DNS server, perform a simple query test.

   d. From the DNS server, perform a recursive query test.

5. A user in the branch office reports that he cannot use Internet Explorer to view a commonly used Web site on the Internet. At your client computer in the main office, you run Nslookup to verify the target address and receive the correct address. At the user's client computer, you also run Nslookup, but the address returned is incorrect. What should you do to troubleshoot this problem? Choose all that apply.

   a. Verify that the client is using the correct DNS servers.

   b. Run Ipconfig /flushdns.

   c. Run Ipconfig /registerdns.

   d. Run Ipconfig /renew.

6. You install a new application, which reports that it is installing a service on the computer. However, when you attempt to run the application for the first time, it cannot start. You inspect the event log to determine the nature of the problem. You receive an error that states, "The service did not start due to a logon failure." Which of the following steps should you take to troubleshoot this problem?

   a. Verify the service has been configured to start automatically.

   b. Change the password to the same name as the account.

   c. Verify the correct password has been supplied on the properties
   page of the service.

   d. Verify the account has been granted administrative rights.

7. You install a new application on a member server. The application
   reports that it is installing a service on the computer. The installation for
   the service requests a username and password to run the service. You
   provide the name DOMAIN1\Service1. However, when you attempt to
   run the application for the first time, it is unable to start. You suspect that
   the account has not been given appropriate rights to start the service.
   What do you do?

   a. On the member server, grant the Service1 account the Log On As A
   Service right.

   b. In the domain, grant the Service1 account the Log On As A Service
   right.

   c. On the member server, grant the Service1 account the Log On As A
   Batch Job right.

   d. In the domain, grant the Service1 account the Log On As A Batch
   Job right.

8. A user complains that after she rebooted her computer, she no longer has
   access to the Internet. You examine her network settings and see that she
   has an IP address in the wrong network subnet and that her default gateway is actually part of a test network. You suspect a rogue DHCP server.
   Which tool should you use to locate the DHCP server?

   a. Ipconfig

   b. Dhcploc

   c. Netdiag

   d. Netstat

CASE SCENARIO

Case Scenario 9-1: Using Diagnostic Tools

You are the network administrator for Fabrikam, Inc. Users and other administrators report issues on the network. You must decide which diagnostic tool will most
appropriately solve the problem.

Five different help desk issues are described. For each issue, determine which tool
is appropriate. Choose from the following tools. Provide a reason to justify each of
your choices. You might not need to use all of the possible answer choices.

The troubleshooting tools are as follows:

■ The standard version of Network Monitor

■ The Lite version of Network Monitor

- Netstat
- Ping
- The testing feature in the DNS Monitoring tab
- The Network Repair button
- Network bridging
- Service configurations

1. A user in Arkansas reports that he cannot browse the Internet. You ask him to ping the local gateway, and after doing so, he does not receive a successful reply from the local gateway. Other users on the network do not have the same problem.

2. All users in the company report that they cannot browse the Internet, although the users receive replies when they ping the external resources by IP address. Access to company resources is not affected.

3. A network administrator in Delaware wants to know the best way to implement a new segment on the network with a different physical topology. She doesn't want to buy a hardware router.

4. A network administrator in Delaware reports that a third-party service on a server refuses to start. He has tried to restart the service several times, but it does not start.

5. An administrator in a remote office thinks her server might have been infected with a virus or a Trojan horse program. A specific port appears to be open. How can the administrator determine which process uses which port?

GLOSSARY

A *See* address (A) resource record.

access control list (ACL) A list of security protections that apply to an entire object, a set of the object's properties, or an individual property of an object. There are two types of access control lists: discretionary access control lists (DACLs) and system access control lists (SACLs).

ACL *See* access control list (ACL).

Active Directory The Windows-based directory service. Active Directory directory service stores information about objects on a network and makes this information available to users and network administrators. Active Directory gives network users access to permitted resources anywhere on the network using a single logon process. It provides network administrators with an intuitive, hierarchical view of the network and a single point of administration for all network objects.

Active Directory–integrated zone A Domain Name System (DNS) zone that is stored in Active Directory directory service so that it can use multimaster replication and Active Directory security features.

address pool The addresses within a Dynamic Host Configuration Protocol (DHCP) scope range of addresses that are available for leased distribution to clients.

Address Resolution Protocol (ARP) A Transmission Control Protocol/Internet Protocol (TCP/IP) network layer protocol responsible for resolving Internet Protocol (IP) addresses into media access control (MAC) addresses. Address Resolution Protocol (ARP) is defined in Request for Comments (RFC) number 826.

address (A) resource record A resource record used to map a Domain Name System (DNS) domain name to a host Internet Protocol version 4 (IPv4) address on the network.

AH *See* Authentication Header (AH).

American National Standards Institute (ANSI) A voluntary, nonprofit organization of business and industry groups that formed in 1918 for the development

and adoption of trade and communication standards in the United States. ANSI is the American representative of ISO (International Organization for Standardization). Among its many concerns, ANSI has developed recommendations for the use of programming languages including FORTRAN, C, and COBOL and for various networking technologies.

American Standard Code for Information Interchange (ASCII) A coding scheme that uses seven or eight bits to assign numeric values up to 256 characters, including letters, numerals, punctuation marks, control characters, and other symbols. ASCII was developed in 1968 to standardize data transmission among disparate hardware and software systems and is built into most minicomputers and all PCs. ASCII is divided into two sets: 128 characters (standard ASCII) and a 256-character version (extended ASCII).

ANSI *See* American National Standards Institute (ANSI).

APIPA *See* Automatic Private IP Addressing (APIPA).

AppleTalk protocol The set of network protocols on which AppleTalk network architecture is based. The AppleTalk protocol is installed with Services for Macintosh to help users access resources on a network.

ARP *See* Address Resolution Protocol (ARP).

ASCII *See* American Standard Code for Information Interchange (ASCII).

Asynchronous Transfer Mode (ATM) A high-speed, connection-oriented protocol used to transport many different types of network traffic. ATM packages data in a 53-byte, fixed-length cell that can be switched quickly between logical connections on a network.

ATM *See* Asynchronous Transfer Mode (ATM).

Authentication Header (AH) A header that provides authentication, integrity, and anti-replay for the entire packet (the Internet Protocol [IP] header and the data payload carried in the packet).

Authentication Header protocol
See Authenthentication Header (AH).

Automatic Private IP Addressing (APIPA)   A Transmission Control Protocol/Internet Protocol (TCP/IP) feature in Windows products that automatically configures a unique Internet Protocol (IP) address from the range 169.254.0.1 to 169.254.255.254 and a subnet mask of 255.255.0.0 when the TCP/IP protocol is configured for dynamic addressing and a Dynamic Host Configuration Protocol (DHCP) server is not available. The APIPA range of IP addresses is reserved by the Internet Assigned Numbers Authority (IANA), and IP addresses within this range are not used on the Internet.

Automatic Updates   A Windows feature that can be set up to automatically check for updates published on the Microsoft Windows Update Web site. Software Update Services (SUS) uses this Windows feature to publish administrator-approved updates on an intranet.

Background Intelligent Transfer Service (BITS)   A service that asynchronously transfers files in the foreground or background, controls the amount of resources used for transfers to preserve the responsiveness of other network applications, and automatically resumes file transfers after network disconnects and machine restarts.

Applications use the BITS application programming interface (API) to create transfer jobs and to monitor the progress of jobs in the transfer queue. The BITS API is included in the Microsoft Platform Software Development Kit (SDK).

Berkeley Internet Name Domain (BIND)   A popular software tool for administering and maintaining the Domain Name System (DNS) on UNIX platforms. BIND was originally written for Berkeley Software Distribution (BSD) UNIX and is currently maintained by the Internet Software Consortium. Because most versions of UNIX include some port of BIND, it is the most popular DNS server used by Internet service providers (ISPs) for administering and maintaining DNS for the Internet. The DNS Server services on Microsoft Windows NT and Microsoft Windows 2000 are Request for Comments (RFC)–compliant implementations of DNS and are compatible with BIND.

BIND   *See* Berkeley Internet Name Domain (BIND).

BITS   *See* Background Intelligent Transfer Service (BITS).

BOOTP   *See* Bootstrap Protocol (BOOTP).

Bootstrap Protocol (BOOTP)   A protocol used primarily on Transmission Control Protocol/Internet Protocol (TCP/IP) networks to configure diskless workstations. Request for Comments (RFC) 951 and 1542 define this protocol. Dynamic Host Configuration Protocol (DHCP) is a later boot configuration protocol that uses this protocol. The Microsoft DHCP service provides limited support for BOOTP service.

CA   *See* certification authority (CA).

.cab files   Stands for cabinet file and is a single cabinet file that stores multiple compressed files. These files are commonly used in software installation and to reduce the file size and the associated download time for Web content.

canonical name (CNAME) resource record   A resource record used to map an alternate alias name to a primary canonical Domain Name System (DNS) domain name used in the zone.

certificate   A digital document that is commonly used for authentication and to secure information on open networks. A certificate securely binds a public key to the entity that holds the corresponding private key. Certificates are digitally signed by the issuing certification authority (CA), and they can be issued for a user, a computer, or a service.

certificate revocation list (CRL)   A document maintained and published by a certification authority that lists certificates that have been revoked.

certification authority (CA)   An entity responsible for establishing and vouching for the authenticity of public keys belonging to subjects (usually users or computers) or other certification authorities. Activities of a certification authority can include binding public keys to distinguished names through signed certificates, managing certificate serial numbers, and certificate revocation.

checksum   A calculated value that is used to test data for the presence of errors that can occur when data is transmitted or when it is written to disk. The checksum is calculated for a given chunk of data by sequentially combining all the bytes of data with a series of arithmetic or logical operations. After the data is transmitted or stored, a new checksum is calculated in the same way using the (possibly faulty) transmitted or stored data. If the two checksums do not match, an error has occurred, and the data should be transmitted or stored again. Checksums cannot detect all errors, and they cannot be used to correct erroneous data.

class   An administrative feature that allows you to group Dynamic Host Configuration Protocol (DHCP) clients logically according to a shared or common need. For example, you can define or use a user class to allow similar DHCP leased configurations for all client computers in a specific building or site location.

CNAME   *See* canonical (CNAME) resource record.

container object   An object that can logically contain other objects. For example, a folder is a container object.

counter   A representation of an object found in the system. You monitor counters for performance reasons and to help you determine whether processes are running smoothly.

CRL   *See* certificate revocation list (CRL).

DACL   *See* discretionary access control list (DACL).

default gateway   A device on a Transmission Control Protocol/Internet Protocol (TCP/IP) internetwork that can forward Internet Protocol (IP) packets to another network, usually a router. In an internetwork, a given subnet might have several router interfaces that connect it to other, remote subnets. One of these router interfaces is usually selected as the default gateway of the local subnet. When a host on the network wants to send a packet to a destination subnet, it consults its internal routing table to determine whether it knows which router to forward the packet to in order to have it reach the destination subnet. If the routing table does not contain any routing information about the destination subnet, the packet is forwarded to the default gateway (one of the routers with an interface on the local subnet). The host assumes that the default gateway knows what to do with any packets that the host itself does not know how to forward.

demand-dial routing   Routing that makes dial-up connections to connect networks based on need—such as a branch office with a modem that dials and establishes a connection only when there is network traffic between offices.

DHCP   *See* Dynamic Host Configuration Protocol (DHCP).

DHCP audit log file   A Dynamic Host Configuration Protocol (DHCP) audit log file is a log of service related events that occur on a DHCP server. Examples of such events are the stopping and starting of the service, verifications and authorizations, and the leasing, renewal, and denial of Internet Protocol (IP) addresses.

DHCP client   A host on a Transmission Control Protocol/Internet Protocol (TCP/IP) internetwork that is capable of having its Internet Protocol (IP) address information dynamically assigned using Dynamic Host Configuration Protocol (DHCP). The term "DHCP client" can also describe the software component on a computer that is capable of interacting with a DHCP server to lease an IP address.

DHCP client reservation   A process for configuring a Dynamic Host Configuration Protocol (DHCP) server so that a particular host on the network always leases the same Internet Protocol (IP) address. You can create a client reservation on a DHCP server if you want the server to always assign the same IP address to a specific machine on the network. You might do this to assign IP addresses to servers on the network because the IP addresses of servers should not change. (If they do, client machines might have difficulty connecting with them.) An alternative and more common way to assign a client reservation to a server is to manually assign a static IP address to the server.

DHCP lease   The duration for which a Dynamic Host Configuration Protocol (DHCP) server loans an Internet Protocol (IP) address to a DHCP client.

DHCP options   Additional Internet Protocol (IP) address settings that a Dynamic Host Configuration Protocol (DHCP) server passes to DHCP clients. When a DHCP client requests an IP address from a DHCP server, the server sends the client at least an IP address and a subnet mask value. Additional information can be sent to clients if you configure various DHCP options. You can assign these options globally to all DHCP clients, to clients belonging to a particular scope, or to an individual host on the network.

DHCP relay agent   A Transmission Control Protocol/Internet Protocol (TCP/IP) host that is configured to allow a single Dynamic Host Configuration Protocol (DHCP) server to lease Internet Protocol (IP) address information to DHCP clients on remote subnets. DHCP relay agents make it unnecessary to maintain a separate DHCP server on every subnet in an internetwork. You can configure Windows NT and Windows 2000 servers to operate as DHCP relay agents.

DHCP server   A server that dynamically allocates Internet Protocol (IP) addresses to client machines using the Dynamic Host Configuration Protocol (DHCP). DHCP servers perform the server-side operation of the DHCP protocol. The DHCP server is responsible for answering requests from DHCP clients and leasing IP addresses to these clients.

DHCP servers should have static IP addresses. A DHCP server gives DHCP clients at least two pieces of Transmission Control Protocol/Internet Protocol (TCP/IP) configuration information: the client's IP address and the subnet mask. Additional TCP/IP settings can be passed to the client as DHCP options.

Diffie-Hellman key exchange   A cryptographic mechanism that allows two parties to establish a shared secret key without having any pre-established secrets between them. Diffie-Hellman is frequently used to establish the shared secret keys that are used by common applications of cryptography, such as Internet Protocol security (IPSec). It is not normally used for data protection.

digital subscriber line (DSL)   A special communication line that uses modulation technology to maximize the amount of data that can be sent over conductive wires. DSL is used for connections between telephone switching stations and a subscriber, rather than between switching stations.

directory partition replicas   Active Directory objects are logically divided into sets of objects called "directory partitions" (also called "naming contexts"). A directory partition replica is a copy of a set of directory objects in one directory partition as it exists on a specific domain controller. During the process of replication, updates to replicas are synchronized among the domain controllers that store replicas of the same directory partitions. When replication occurs, all current updates to a replica on one domain controller are transferred to the corresponding replica on another domain controller. If more than one replica is shared by the two domain controllers, all updates that apply are replicated.

discretionary access control list (DACL)   The part of an object's security descriptor that grants or denies permission to specific users and groups to access the object. Only the owner of an object can change permissions granted or denied in a DACL; thus, access to the object is at the owner's discretion.

domain namespace   A subset of the Domain Name System (DNS) namespace bounded by a particular domain name. The root of the DNS namespace branches out to a relatively small number of top-level domains such as .com, .org, and .edu. Private companies can register a domain name in one of these top-level domains and then subdivide their branch of the DNS namespace as they desire. This subdivision of the DNS namespace is bounded by the domain name and is called the "domain namespace." For example, a company named Fabrikam might register the domain name fabrikam.com, and then the company might create three new subdomains under it named sales.fabrikam.com, support.fabrikam.com, and hq.fabrikam.com. Specific servers and router interfaces exposed to the Internet might then be given specific DNS addresses to uniquely identify them in the DNS namespace. If you want to locate a particular node in the DNS namespace, you query a name server. The process of locating a particular DNS node and resolving its fully qualified domain name (FQDN) into its associated Internet Protocol (IP) address is called "name resolution."

Domain Name System (DNS)   A hierarchical, distributed database that contains mappings of DNS domain names to various types of data, such as Internet Protocol (IP) addresses. DNS enables the location of computers and services by user-friendly names, and it also enables the discovery of other information stored in the database.

DNS   *See* Domain Name System (DNS).

DNS domain   Any tree or subtree in the Domain Name System (DNS) namespace. Although the names for DNS domains often correspond to Active Directory domains, DNS domains should not be confused with Active Directory domains.

DNS dynamic update   An update to the Domain Name System (DNS) standard that permits DNS clients to dynamically register and update their resource records in zones.

DNS namespace   The entire namespace in Domain Name System (DNS) starting at the root and branching out to a relatively small number of top-level domains (TLDs), such as .com, .org, and .edu. Private companies can register a domain name in one of these TLDs and then subdivide their branch of the DNS namespace as they desire. For example, a company named Fourth Coffee might register the domain name fourthcoffee.com and then create three new subdomains under it named sales.fourthcoffee.com, support.fourthcoffee.com, and hq.fourthcoffee.com. Specific servers and router interfaces exposed to the Internet might then be given specific DNS addresses to uniquely identify them in the DNS namespace. An address in the DNS namespace, called an "fully qualified domain name (FQDN)," maps to a unique node on the Internet. An example might be widgets.support.fourthcoffee, which might map to the address 10.15.6.133. Names of domains, subdomains, and individual hosts are maintained on name servers located at various points across the Internet or within large private internetworks. If you want to locate a particular node in the DNS namespace, you query a name server. The process of locating a particular DNS node and resolving its FQDN into its associated Internet Protocol (IP) address is called "name resolution."

DNS server   A server that maintains information about a portion of the Domain Name System (DNS) database and that responds to and resolves DNS queries.

DNS zone   Also called a "zone of authority," a subset of the Domain Name System (DNS) namespace that is managed by a name server. This administrative unit can consist of a single domain, or it can be a domain that is combined with a number of subdomains. The concepts of a zone and a DNS domain are related: each zone is anchored in a specific domain known as the zone's "root domain."

DSL   *See* digital subscriber line (DSL).

Dynamic Host Configuration Protocol (DHCP)   A standard Internet protocol that enables the dynamic configuration of hosts on an Internet Protocol (IP) internetwork. DHCP is an extension of the Bootstrap Protocol (BOOTP).

EAP   *See* Extensible Authentication Protocol (EAP).

EFS   *See* Encrypting File System (EFS).

Encapsulating Security Payload (ESP)   An Internet Protocol security (IPSec) protocol that provides confidentiality, in addition to authentication, integrity, and anti-replay. ESP can be used alone, in combination with Authentication Header (AH), or nested with the Layer Two Tunneling Protocol (L2TP). ESP does not normally sign the entire packet unless it is being tunneled. Ordinarily, just the data payload is protected, not the Internet Protocol (IP) header.

Encrypting File System (EFS)   A feature in Microsoft Windows Server 2003 that enables users to encrypt files and folders on an NTFS volume disk to keep them safe from intruders.

encryption   The process of disguising a message or data to hide its substance.

ESP   *See* Encapsulating Security Payload (ESP).

Ethernet   The most popular network architecture for local area networks (LANs). Ethernet was originally developed by Xerox in the 1970s and was proposed as a standard by Xerox, Digital Equipment Corporation (DEC), and Intel in 1980. A separate standardization process for Ethernet technologies, known as "Project 802," was established in 1985 in the Institute of Electrical and Electronics Engineers (IEEE) 802.3 standard. The International Organization for Standardization (ISO) then adopted the IEEE standard, thereby making it a worldwide standard for networking. Because of its simplicity and reliability, Ethernet is by far the most popular networking architecture in use today. It is available in three different speeds:

- 10 megabits per second (Mbps), which is simply called "Ethernet"

- 100 Mbps, which is called "Fast Ethernet"
- 1000 Mbps or 1 gigabit per second (Gbps), which is an emerging standard called "Gigabit Ethernet"

event logging The process of recording an audit entry in the audit trail whenever certain events occur, such as the following events: services starting and stopping, users logging on and off, and users accessing resources.

Event Viewer A component you can use to view and manage event logs, gather information about hardware and software problems, and monitor security events. Event Viewer maintains logs about program, security, and system events.

Extensible Authentication Protocol (EAP) An extension to the Point-to-Point Protocol (PPP) that allows for arbitrary authentication mechanisms to be employed for the validation of a PPP connection.

Extensible Markup Language (XML) A meta-markup language that provides a format for describing structured data. This facilitates more precise declarations of content and more meaningful search results across multiple platforms. In addition, XML enables a new generation of Web-based data-viewing and manipulation applications.

FAT *See* file allocation table (FAT).

FAT32 A derivative of the file allocation table (FAT) file system. FAT32 supports smaller cluster sizes and larger volumes than FAT, which results in more efficient space allocation on FAT32 volumes.

FDDI *See* Fiber Distributed Data Interface (FDDI).

Fiber Distributed Data Interface (FDDI) A high-speed network technology that conforms to the Open Systems Interconnection (OSI) reference model for networking and the American National Standards Institute (ANSI) standard X3T9, which runs at 100 megabits per second (Mbps) over fiber-optic cabling. It is often used for network backbones in a local area network (LAN) or metropolitan area network (MAN).

file allocation table (FAT) A file system used by MS-DOS and other Windows operating systems to organize and manage files. The file allocation table is a data

structure that Windows creates when you format a volume using the FAT or FAT32 file systems. Windows stores information about each file in the file allocation table so that it can retrieve the file later.

forwarder A Domain Name System (DNS) server designated by other internal DNS servers to be used to forward queries for resolving external or offsite DNS domain names. Forwarders are useful for reducing name resolution traffic and speeding DNS name queries for large private Transmission Control Protocol/Internet Protocol (TCP/IP) internetworks that are connected to the Internet. They also are used to resolve name queries when a firewall between your network and the Internet prevents clients in your network from directly querying name servers located at your Internet service provider (ISP) or elsewhere on the Internet. In this case, a typical location for the forwarder is on the bastion host. (The bastion host is the host running the proxy server or application-layer gateway application.)

forward lookup A Domain Name System (DNS) query for a DNS name.

forward lookup zone *See* forward lookup; zone.

FQDN *See* fully qualified domain name (FQDN).

frame A segment of data on a network or telecommunications link, generally consisting of a header with preamble (Start of Frame flag), destination and source addresses, data payload, and usually some form of error-checking information. Frames are assembled and generated by the data-link layer and physical layer of the Open Systems Interconnection (OSI) reference model. This assembly process is called "framing." In other words, packets from the network layer are encapsulated by the data-link layer into frames. Data segments generated by higher layers of the OSI model are generally referred to as packets, but the term "packet" is also sometimes used to include frames.

fully qualified domain name (FQDN) A Domain Name System (DNS) name that has been stated to indicate its absolute location in the domain namespace tree. In contrast to relative names, an FQDN has a trailing period (.) to qualify its position to the root of the namespace (host.example.microsoft.com.).

GPO   *See* Group Policy Object (GPO).

Group Policy   The infrastructure in Active Directory directory service that enables directory-based configuration of user and computer settings, including security and user data. You use Group Policy to define configurations for groups of users and computers. You can specify policy settings for registry-based policies, security, software installation, scripts, folder redirection, remote installation services, and Internet Explorer maintenance. The Group Policy settings that you create are contained in a Group Policy Object (GPO). By associating a GPO with selected Active Directory system containers—sites, domains, and OUs—you can apply the GPO's policy settings to the users and computers in those Active Directory containers. To create an individual GPO, use the Group Policy Object Editor. To manage GPOs across an enterprise, you can use the Group Policy Management console.

Group Policy Object (GPO)   A collection of Group Policy settings. GPOs are essentially the documents created by the Group Policy Object Editor. GPOs are stored at the domain level, and they affect users and computers that are contained in sites, domains, and OUs. In addition, each computer has exactly one group of policy settings stored locally, which is called the "local Group Policy Object."

Group Policy Object Editor   The MMC snap-in that is used to edit Group Policy Objects (GPOs).

hash   A one-way cryptographic algorithm that takes an input message of arbitrary length and produces a fixed-length digest. Two hash algorithms used by Windows Server 2003 are Secure Hash Algorithm 1 (SHA1) and Message Digest 5 (MD5).

host   Any device on a Transmission Control Protocol/Internet Protocol (TCP/IP) network that has an Internet Protocol (IP) address. Examples include servers, workstations, network interface print devices, and routers. The terms "node" and "host" are often used interchangeably in this regard.

Sometimes the term "host" means a device on a TCP/IP network that can both receive data and initiate contact with other devices. For example, a computer configured as a Simple Mail Transfer Protocol (SMTP) host receives e-mail messages and forwards them to their destination.

Hosts file   A text file that provides a local method for resolution of fully qualified domain names (FQDNs) into their respective Internet Protocol (IP) addresses on a Transmission Control Protocol/Internet Protocol (TCP/IP) network. Hosts files are an alternative to Domain Name System (DNS) servers for name resolution on TCP/IP networks. They are used mainly on small networks or when maintaining a DNS server is impractical.

hub   A common connection point for devices in a network. Typically used to connect segments of a local area network (LAN), a hub contains multiple ports. When data arrives at one port, it is copied to the other ports so that all segments of the LAN can see the data.

IAS   *See* Internet Authentication Service (IAS).

IETF   *See* Internet Engineering Task Force (IETF).

IGMP   *See* Internet Group Management Protocol (IGMP).

IIS   *See* IIS metabase; Internet Information Server (IIS) Lockdown.

IIS metabase   A database that stores all of the configuration settings for Internet Information Server (IIS). The metabase is similar to the registry that stores all of the configuration settings for Windows Server.

IKE   *See* Internet Key Exchange (IKE).

in-addr.arpa domain   A special top-level Domain Name System (DNS) domain reserved for mapping of Internet Protocol (IP) addresses to DNS host names, which is the reverse of the mapping used for standard DNS name resolution.

in-addr.arpa zone   *See* in-addr.arpa; reverse lookup; zone.

Integrated Services Digital Network (ISDN)   A digital phone line used to provide higher bandwidth. ISDN in North America is typically available in two forms: Basic Rate Interface (BRI), which consists of 2 B channels at 64 kilobits per second (Kbps) and a D channel at 16 Kbps, and Primary Rate Interface (PRI), which consists of 23 B channels at 64 Kbps and a D channel at 64 Kbps. The phone company must install an ISDN line at both the calling and the called "sites."

International Telecommunication Union-Telecommunication Standardization Sector (ITU-T)   The standardization division of the International Telecommunication Union, formerly called "Comité Consultatif International Télégraphique et Téléphonique (CCITT)." The ITU-T (also abbreviated ITU-TSS) develops communications recommendations for all analog and digital communications.

Internet Authentication Service (IAS)   The Microsoft implementation of a Remote Authentication Dial-In User Service (RADIUS) server and proxy, which provides authentication and accounting for network access.

Internet Engineering Task Force (IETF)   An international community of networking engineers, network administrators, researchers, and vendors whose goal is to ensure the smooth operation and evolution of the Internet. The Internet Engineering Task Force (IETF) receives its charter from the Internet Society (ISOC), and its daily operations are overseen by the Internet Architecture Board (IAB).

The work of the IETF is performed by a number of working groups that are dedicated to such aspects of the Internet as routing, operations and management, transport, security, applications, and user services. These working groups interact primarily through mailing lists and are managed by area directors who belong to the Internet Engineering Steering Group (IESG). Some working groups develop extensions and newer versions of familiar protocols such as Hypertext Transfer Protocol (HTTP), Lightweight Directory Access Protocol (LDAP), Network News Transfer Protocol (NNTP), Point-to-Point Protocol (PPP), and Simple Network Management Protocol (SNMP). Others develop new protocols such as the Common Indexing Protocol, Internet Open Trading Protocol, and the Internet Printing Protocol (IPP).

The working groups produce documents called "Internet Drafts," which have a life span of six months, after which they must be deleted, updated, or established as a Request for Comments (RFC) document.

Internet Group Management Protocol (IGMP)   A protocol used by Internet Protocol version 4 (IPv4) hosts to report their multicast group memberships to any immediately neighboring multicast routers.

Internet Information Server (IIS) Lockdown   A security tool that provides templates for the major IIS-dependent Microsoft products. The IIS Lockdown Wizard works by turning off unnecessary features, thereby reducing vulnerabilities that are available to attackers. To provide defense-in-depth, or multiple layers of protection against attackers, URL Scanner has been integrated into the IIS Lockdown Wizard with customized templates for each supported server role.

Internet Key Exchange (IKE)   A protocol that establishes the security association and shared keys necessary for two parties to communicate by using Internet Protocol security (IPSec).

Internet Protocol (IP)   A routable protocol in the Transmission Control Protocol/Internet Protocol (TCP/IP) protocol suite that is responsible for IP addressing, routing, and the fragmentation and reassembly of IP packets.

Internet Protocol Security (IPSec)   A set of industry-standard, cryptography-based protection services and protocols. IPSec protects the protocols in the Transmission Control Protocol/Internet Protocol (TCP/IP) protocol suite, and it protects Internet communications by using Layer Two Tunneling Protocol (L2TP).

Internet Security Association and Key Management Protocol (ISAKMP)   A framework for managing keys within Internet Protocol Security (IPSec).

internetwork   A network (usually Transmission Control Protocol/Internet Protocol, or TCP/IP) that consists of multiple networks joined by routers. More generally, an internetwork is any network that consists of smaller networks joined in any fashion using bridges, switches, routers, and other devices. For example, an Internet Protocol (IP) internetwork could consist of a mix of Windows NT or Windows 2000 and UNIX machines distributed over different subnets, connected with standard IP routers from Cisco Systems or another vendor. An Internetwork Packet Exchange (IPX) internetwork could be a set of networks that use Novell NetWare clients and servers running IPX that are connected using IPX-enabled routers.

Internetwork Packet Exchange (IPX) A network protocol native to NetWare that controls addressing and routing of packets within and between local area networks (LANs). IPX does not guarantee that a message is complete (no lost packets).

IP *See* Internet Protocol (IP).

IPSec *See* Internet Protocol Security (IPSec).

IPX *See* Internetwork Packet Exchange (IPX).

ISAKMP *See* Internet Security Association and Key Management Protocol (ISAKMP).

ISDN *See* Integrated Services Digital Network (ISDN).

iterative query A query made to a Domain Name System (DNS) server for the best answer the server can provide without seeking further help from other DNS servers. Iterative queries are also called "nonrecursive queries."

ITU-T *See* International Telecommunication Union-Telecommunication Standardization Sector.

Kerberos V5 authentication protocol An authentication mechanism used to verify user or host identity. The Kerberos V5 authentication protocol is the default authentication service. Internet Protocol security (IPSec) can use the Kerberos protocol for authentication.

lame delegation A lame delegation occurs when one server delegates a zone to a server that is not authoritative for that zone.

LAN *See* local area network (LAN).

Layer Two Tunneling Protocol (L2TP) An industry-standard Internet tunneling protocol that provides encapsulation for sending Point-to-Point Protocol (PPP) frames across packet-oriented media. For Internet Protocol (IP) networks, L2TP traffic is sent as User Datagram Protocol (UDP) messages. In Microsoft operating systems, L2TP is used in conjunction with Internet Protocol Security (IPSec) as a virtual private network (VPN) technology to provide remote access or router-to-router VPN connections. Request for Comments (RFC) 2661 describes L2TP.

Layer Two Tunneling Protocol/ Internet Protocol Security (L2TP/ IPSec) A virtual private network (VPN) connection method that provides session authentication, address encapsulation, and strong encryption of private data between remote access servers and clients. L2TP provides address encapsulation and user authentication, and Internet Protocol Security (IPSec) provides computer authentication and encryption of the L2TP session.

LCP *See* Link Control Protocol (LCP).

L2TP *See* Layer Two Tunneling Protocol (L2TP).

L2TP/IPSec *See* Layer Two Tunneling Protocol/Internet Protocol Security (L2TP/IPSec).

leaf object An element in the directory hierarchy that is the endpoint of a branch and cannot contain other objects like containers can. An example of a leaf object is a mailbox in the directory of Microsoft Exchange Server, which is found within the Recipients container. You can view and manage objects in the Exchange directory hierarchy using the Exchange Administrator tool.

The term "leaf object" can also describe an endpoint of a branch in Active Directory directory service of Windows 2000 and Windows Server 2003. Leaf objects (or terminal objects) are found in containers such as organizational units (OUs), and they cannot contain other directory objects. You can view and manage objects in Active Directory using the Microsoft Management Console (MMC) and by installing snap-ins, such as Active Directory Users And Computers or Active Directory Sites And Services.

Link Control Protocol (LCP) A subprotocol within the Point-to-Point Protocol (PPP) protocol suite that is responsible for link management. LCP operates at the data-link layer (layer 2) of the Open Systems Interconnection (OSI) reference model for networking and is considered a data-link layer protocol. During the establishment of a PPP communication session, LCP establishes the link, configures PPP options, and tests the quality of the line connection between the PPP client and PPP server. LCP automatically handles encapsulation format options and varies packet sizes over PPP communication links.

local area network (LAN) A communications network that connects a group of computers, printers, and other devices that are located within a relatively limited area (such as a building). A LAN enables any connected device to interact with any other device on the network.

Local System account   A predefined local account that is used to start a service and provide the security context for that service. The name of the account is NT AUTHORITY\System. This account does not have a password, and any password information that you supply is ignored. The Local System account has full access to the system, including the directory service on domain controllers. Because the Local System account acts as a computer on the network, it has access to network resources.

MAC address   *See* Media Access Control (MAC) address.

Media Access Control (MAC) address   A unique 6-byte (48-bit) address that is usually permanently burned into a network interface card (NIC) or other physical-layer networking device and that uniquely identifies the device on an Ethernet-based network. A MAC address is also known as an "Ethernet address," a hardware address, a physical address, or a PHY address.

Microsoft Management Console (MMC)   A framework for hosting administrative tools called "snap-ins." A console might contain tools, folders, or other containers, World Wide Web pages, and other administrative items. These items are displayed in the left pane of the console, or the console tree. A console has one or more windows that can provide views of the console tree. The main MMC window provides commands and tools for authoring consoles. The authoring features of MMC and the console tree itself might be hidden when a console is in User Mode.

Microsoft Point-to-Point Encryption (MPPE)   A 128-bit key or 40-bit key encryption algorithm using Rivest-Shamir-Adleman (RSA) RC4. MPPE provides for packet confidentiality between the remote access client and the remote access or tunnel server, and it is useful where Internet Protocol Security (IPSec) is not available. MPPE 40-bit keys are used to satisfy current North American export restrictions. MPPE is compatible with Network Address Translation (NAT).

MMC   *See* Microsoft Management Console (MMC).

MPPE   *See* Microsoft Point-to-Point Encryption (MPPE).

multicasting   The process of sending a message simultaneously to zero or more destinations on a network.

multicast scope   A range of multicast group Internet Protocol (IP) addresses in the Class D address range that are available to be leased or assigned to multicast Dynamic Host Configuration Protocol (DHCP) clients by DHCP.

Multilink   The combination of bandwidth of two or more physical communications links into a single logical link to increase remote access bandwidth and throughput by using remote access Multilink. Based on the Internet Engineering Task Force (IETF) standard Request for Comments (RFC) 1990, Multilink combines analog modem paths, Integrated Services Digital Network (ISDN) B channels, and mixed analog and digital communications links on both client and server computers. This increases Internet and intranet access speed and decreases the amount of time users are connected to a remote computer.

name resolution   The process of translating an Internet Protocol (IP) address, which is necessary in Transmission Control Protocol/Internet Protocol (TCP/IP) communications, into a name that users can remember and identify more easily (and vice versa). Name resolution can be provided by software components such as Domain Name System (DNS) or Windows Internet Naming Service (WINS).

name server (NS) resource record   A resource record that is used in a zone to designate the Domain Name System (DNS) domain names for authoritative DNS servers for the zone.

NAS   *See* network access server (NAS).

NAT   *See* Network Address Translation (NAT).

NetBIOS   *See* network basic input/output system (NetBIOS).

NetBIOS name   A 16-byte name for a networking service or function on a machine running Windows Server 2003. Network basic input/output system (NetBIOS) names are a more friendly way of identifying computers on a network than network numbers and are used by NetBIOS-enabled services and applications.

network access server (NAS)   The device that accepts Point-to-Point Protocol (PPP) connections and places clients on the network that the NAS serves.

Network Address Translation (NAT)   An Internet Protocol (IP) translation process that allows a network with private addresses to access information on the Internet.

network basic input/output system (NetBIOS)   An application programming interface (API) that is used by programs on a local area network (LAN). NetBIOS provides programs with a uniform set of commands for requesting the lower-level services required to manage names, conduct sessions, and send datagrams between nodes on a network.

network bridge   A connection that makes multiple, disparate networks act as one network.

network ID   A number used to identify the systems that are located on the same physical network, which is bounded by routers. The network ID should be unique to the internetwork.

network interface card (NIC)   An adapter card that plugs into the system bus of a computer and allows the computer to send and receive signals on a network. A NIC is also known as a "network adapter card" or simply a "network card."

NIC   *See* network interface card (NIC).

node   A general term for a network device that has a specific physical or logical address or that can recognize addresses. Nodes can be computers, repeaters, bridges, or other devices on a network that can transmit, receive, or process signals. Another name for a node, especially on Ethernet networks, is a station.

Other common meanings for the term "node" include the following:

- A domain or subdomain in the namespace of Domain Name System (DNS)

- An object in the console hierarchy of Microsoft Management Console (MMC)

- In Microsoft Cluster Server (MSCS) terminology, an independent computer system running Windows NT Server or Enterprise Edition that is a member of a cluster

noncontiguous namespace   A namespace based on different Domain Name System (DNS) root domain names, such as that of multiple trees in the same forest.

NS resource record   *See* name server (NS) resource record.

NTFS file system   An advanced file system that provides performance, security, reliability, and advanced features that are not found in any version of file allocation table (FAT). For example, NTFS guarantees volume consistency by using standard transaction logging and recovery techniques. If a system fails, NTFS uses its log file and checkpoint information to restore the consistency of the file system. NTFS also provides advanced features, such as file and folder permissions, encryption, disk quotas, and compression.

NTFS permissions   The settings that administrators apply to access control entries (ACEs) for managing access to files and folders under the NTFS file system. The Take Ownership permission is an example of an NTFS permission.

NTLM authentication protocol   A challenge/response authentication protocol. The NTLM authentication protocol is supported in Windows 2000, Microsoft Windows XP, and the Windows Server 2003 family, but it is not the default. It is the default authentication protocol for earlier versions of Windows.

Oakley   A protocol used by Internet Protocol Security (IPSec) for exchanging keys securely. Oakley uses the Diffie-Hellman algorithm.

Open Shortest Path First (OSPF)   A routing protocol used in medium-sized and large networks. This protocol is more complex than Routing Information Protocol (RIP), but it allows better control and is more efficient in propagating routing information.

Open Systems Interconnection (OSI) reference model   A networking model introduced by the International Organization for Standardization (ISO) to promote multivendor interoperability. OSI is a seven-layered conceptual model that consists of the application, presentation, session, transport, network, data-link, and physical layers.

organizational unit (OU)   An Active Directory container object used in domains. An OU is a logical container into which users, groups, computers, and other OUs are placed. It can contain objects only from its parent domain. An OU is the smallest scope to which a Group Policy Object (GPO) can be linked or over which administrative authority can be delegated.

OSI *See* Open Systems Interconnection (OSI) reference model.

OSPF *See* Open Shortest Path First (OSPF).

OU *See* organizational unit (OU).

packet filtering Process that prevents certain types of network packets from being sent or received. This can be employed for security reasons (to prevent access by unauthorized users) or to improve performance by disallowing unnecessary packets from traveling over a slow connection.

permissions Settings that you establish for a resource to control which users and groups can access the resource and what degree of access they have. Permissions are implemented at several levels in Microsoft Windows operating systems and other Microsoft BackOffice applications. Permissions are implemented in Microsoft systems using discretionary access control lists (DACLs), which are attached to the object they control.

Examples of permission types include the following:

- Shared folder permissions. Can be applied to shared folders on Windows systems to control access to network shares by users

- NTFS permissions. Can be applied to files and folders on NTFS for both local and network control of access to the resources

- Print permissions. Can be assigned to printers to control who can manage printers, manage documents, or print documents

- Active Directory permissions. Can be assigned to objects within the Active Directory directory service of Windows 2000 using Active Directory Users And Computers

- Exchange permissions. Can be assigned to objects in the Microsoft Exchange Server directory hierarchy to control who can administer different parts of an Exchange organization using the Exchange Administrator program

- Public folder permissions. Can be assigned using Microsoft Outlook to files in public folders to control who can read, edit, or delete those files

PID *See* process identifier (PID).

PKI *See* public key infrastructure (PKI).

Plain Old Telephone Service (POTS line) The basic analog telecommunications service provided by a local telco. POTS was the only type of telephone service until the 1970s.

pointer (PTR) resource record A Domain Name System (DNS) resource record used in a reverse lookup zone to map an Internet Protocol (IP) address to a DNS name.

Point-to-Point Tunneling Protocol (PPTP) PPTP is a virtual private network (VPN) protocol implemented at layer 2 in the Open Systems Interconnection (OSI) model. PPTP encapsulates VPN data inside Point-to-Point Protocol (PPP) frames, which are then further encapsulated in Internet Protocol (IP) datagrams for transmission over a transit IP internetwork such as the Internet. This means that users can remotely run applications that depend on particular network protocols.

port In Transmission Control Protocol/Internet Protocol (TCP/IP) networking, the endpoint of a logical connection between two hosts on an internetwork. Ports are identified by port numbers. A port identifies a unique process for which a server can provide a service or the client can access a service. Ports can be Transmission Control Protocol (TCP) ports or User Datagram Protocol (UDP) ports, depending on the type of service supported.

In general networking terminology, a port is a connector that attaches cables or peripherals to a computer—for example, a parallel port for connecting a printer to a computer or a serial port for connecting a serial mouse or modem to a computer. Connectors on networking components, such as hubs or routers, are also sometimes called "ports," although a better term for a connector on a router is a "router interface."

POTS line *See* Plain Old Telephone Service (POTS line).

PPTP *See* Point-to-Point Tunneling Protocol (PPTP).

primary name server A name server that maintains its own local Domain Name System (DNS) database of resource records. A primary name server has a master copy of resource records for each zone over which it has authority. These records are stored locally on the name server in the form of a text file called the "zone file." All changes to the resource records for a zone must be made on the primary name server.

primary zone   A zone file that contains the master copy of the Domain Name System (DNS) database file.

principle of least privilege   The security guideline that says users should have the minimum privileges necessary to perform required tasks. This helps to reduce the risk of security compromise and, upon compromise, reduces the potential impact. In practice, a user runs within the security context of a normal user. When a task requires additional privileges, the user can use a tool such as Run As to start a specific process with those additional privileges or to log on as a user with the necessary privileges.

process   The virtual address space and the control information necessary for the execution of a program.

process identifier (PID)   A numerical identifier that uniquely identifies a process while it runs. Use Task Manager to view PIDs.

protocol   A set of rules and conventions for sending information over a network. These rules govern the content, format, timing, sequencing, and error control of messages exchanged among network devices.

proxy server   A firewall component that manages Internet traffic to and from a local area network (LAN) and that can provide other features, such as document caching and access control. A proxy server can improve performance by supplying frequently requested data, such as a popular Web page, and it can filter and discard requests that the owner does not consider appropriate, such as requests for unauthorized access to proprietary files.

PTR   *See* pointer (PTR) resource record.

public key   The nonsecret half of a cryptographic key pair that is used with a public key algorithm. Public keys are typically used when encrypting a session key, verifying a digital signature, or encrypting data that can be decrypted with the corresponding private key.

public key infrastructure (PKI)   The laws, policies, standards, and software that regulate or manipulate certificates and public and private keys. In practice, it is a system of digital certificates, certification authorities (CAs), and other registration authorities that verify and authenticate the validity of each party involved in an electronic transaction. Standards for PKI are still evolving, even though they are being widely implemented as a necessary element of electronic commerce.

RADIUS   *See* Remote Authentication Dial-In User Service (RADIUS).

RARP   *See* Reverse Address Resolution Protocol.

recursive query   One of the two process types (iterative and recursive) used for Domain Name System (DNS) name resolution. In this process, a resolver (a DNS client) requests that a DNS server provide a complete answer to a query that does not include pointers to other DNS servers. When a client makes a query and requests that the server use recursive resolution to answer, it effectively shifts the workload of resolving the query from the client to the DNS server. If the DNS server supports and uses recursive resolution, it contacts other DNS servers as necessary (using iterative queries on behalf of the client) until it obtains a definitive answer to the query. This type of resolution allows the client resolver to be small and simple.

recursive resolution   One of the two process types (iterative and recursive) for DNS name resolution. In this process, a resolver (a DNS client) will request that a DNS server provide a complete answer to a query that does not include pointers to other DNS servers. When a client makes a query and requests that the server use recursive resolution to answer, it effectively shifts the workload of resolving the query from the client to the DNS server. If the DNS server supports and uses recursive resolution, it contacts other DNS servers as necessary (using iterative queries on behalf of the client) until it obtains a definitive answer to the query. This type of resolution allows for a small and simple client resolver.

remote access server   A Microsoft Windows–based computer that runs the Routing and Remote Access service and is configured to provide remote access.

Remote Authentication Dial-In User Service (RADIUS)   A security authentication protocol based on a client/server model and widely used by Internet service providers (ISPs). RADIUS is the most popular means of authenticating and authorizing dial-up and tunneled network users. The Routing and Remote Access service that ships with the Windows Server 2003 family includes RADIUS. A RADIUS server, named Internet Authentication Service (IAS), is included in Windows Server 2003, Standard Edition; Windows Server 2003, Enterprise Edition; and Windows Server 2003, Datacenter Edition.

remote computer   A computer that you can access only by using a communications line or a communications device, such as a network card or a modem.

Remote Procedure Call (RPC)   A message-passing facility that allows a distributed application to call services that are available on various computers on a network. Used during remote administration of computers.

Request for Comments (RFC)   An official document of the Internet Engineering Task Force (IETF) that specifies the details for protocols included in the Transmission Control Protocol/Internet Protocol (TCP/IP) family.

resolver   Domain Name System (DNS) client programs used to look up DNS name information. Resolvers can be either a small stub (a limited set of programming routines that provide basic query functionality) or larger programs that provide additional lookup DNS client functions, such as caching.

resource record   A standard Domain Name System (DNS) database structure containing information used to process DNS queries. For example, an address (A) resource record contains an Internet Protocol (IP) address corresponding to a host name. Most of the basic resource record types are defined in Request for Comments (RFC) 1035, but additional resource record types have been defined in other RFCs and are approved for use with DNS.

Resultant Set of Policy (RSoP)   A feature that simplifies Group Policy implementation and troubleshooting. RSoP uses Windows Management Instrumentation (WMI) to determine how policy settings are applied to users and computers. RSoP has two modes: logging mode and planning mode. Logging mode determines the resultant effect of policy settings that have been applied to an existing user and computer based on a site, domain, and organizational unit. Planning mode simulates the resultant effect of policy settings that are applied to a user and computer.

Reverse Address Resolution Protocol (RARP)   A protocol for resolving Internet Protocol (IP) addresses into Media Access Control (MAC) addresses.

reverse lookup   The process of a resolver querying a name server to resolve a host's Internet Protocol (IP) address into its associated fully qualified domain name (FQDN). This is the reverse of the usual host name resolution process, in which a resolver queries a name server to resolve a host name into its associated IP address. Reverse name lookups use a special domain called in-addr.arpa.

reverse lookup zone   *See* reverse lookup; zone.

RFC   *See* Request for Comments (RFC).

RIP   *See* Routing Information Protocol (RIP).

root hints   Domain Name System (DNS) data stored on a DNS server that identifies the authoritative DNS servers for the root zone of the DNS namespace. The root hints are stored in the file Cache.dns, which is located in the %systemroot%\System32\Dns folder.

round robin   A simple mechanism Domain Name System (DNS) servers use to share and distribute loads for network resources. Round robin is used to rotate the order of resource records returned in a response to a query when multiple resource records of the same type exist for a queried DNS domain name.

router   Hardware that helps local area networks (LANs) and wide area networks (WANs) achieve interoperability and connectivity and that can link LANs that have different network topologies (such as Ethernet and Token Ring). Routers match packet headers to a LAN segment and choose the best path for the packet, thereby optimizing network performance.

routing   The process of forwarding a packet through an internetwork from a source host to a destination host.

Routing Information Protocol (RIP)   An industry-standard, distance vector routing protocol used in small to medium-sized Internet Protocol (IP) and Internetwork Packet Exchange (IPX) internetworks.

routing protocol   Any of several protocols that enable the exchange of routing table information between routers. Typically, medium- to large-sized Transmission Control Protocol/Internet Protocol (TCP/IP) internetworks implement routing protocols to simplify the administration of routing tables.

routing tables   An internal table that a computer or router uses to determine which router interface to send packets to based on their destination network addresses. Microsoft Windows platforms automatically build their own routing tables, which are used to determine whether to forward specific packets to the local network segment, a near-side router interface, or the default gateway for the segment.

RPC   *See* Remote Procedure Call (RPC).

RSoP   *See* Resultant Set of Policy (RSoP).

SACL   *See* system access control list (SACL).

SAM database   *See* Security Accounts Manager (SAM) database.

sampling (or sample) rate   The frequency at which a counter is checked to see whether specific criteria are met. The faster a counter is sampled, the more detailed the response. However, the slower a counter is sampled, the less the central processing unit (CPU) must be used.

scope   A range of Internet Protocol (IP) addresses that are available to be leased or assigned to Dynamic Host Configuration Protocol (DHCP) clients by the DHCP service.

secondary name server   A name server that downloads its Domain Name System (DNS) database of resource records from a master name server. The master name server can be either a primary name server or another secondary name server. Primary name servers get their resource records from local files called "zone files." Secondary name servers do not maintain local zone files—they obtain their resource files over the network from master name servers by a zone transfer, which occurs when a secondary name server polls a master name server and determines that there are updates to the DNS database that must be downloaded. This means that the

DNS administrator has to maintain only a single set of DNS resource records (on the primary name server), which simplifies DNS administration.

Secondary name servers are used in DNS to provide redundancy and load balancing for name resolution. On Berkeley Internet Name Domain (BIND) implementations of DNS, secondary name servers are often referred to as slave name servers.

A name server can be a primary name server for one zone and a secondary name server for a different zone. In other words, name servers are defined as primary or secondary on a per-zone basis.

secondary zone   A file containing a read-only replica of the primary zone file.

Secure Sockets Layer (SSL)   A proposed open standard for establishing a secure communications channel to prevent the interception of critical information, such as credit card numbers. Primarily, it enables secure electronic financial transactions on the World Wide Web, although it is designed to work on other Internet services as well.

Security Accounts Manager (SAM) database   The database of user and group account information that is stored on a domain controller in a Windows NT–based network. The SAM database is also known as the "domain directory database," or sometimes simply the "directory database."

The SAM database occupies a portion of the Windows NT registry. All user accounts, group accounts, and resource definitions such as shares and printers have their security principals defined in the SAM database. Because the entire SAM database must reside in a domain controller's random access memory (RAM), it cannot exceed approximately 40 megabytes (MB) in Windows NT, which equals approximately 40,000 user accounts, or 26,000 users and Windows NT workstations combined.

The master copy of the SAM database is stored on the primary domain controller (PDC). Periodic directory synchronization ensures that backup domain controllers (BDCs) have an accurate replica of this master database, so BDCs can also be used for logons and pass-through authentication of users attempting to access network resources.

Security Parameters Index (SPI)   A unique, identifying value in the security association (SA) used to distinguish among multiple SAs existing at the receiving computer.

security template   A physical file representation of a security configuration that can be applied to a local computer or imported to a Group Policy Object (GPO) in the Active Directory directory service. When you import a security template to a GPO, Group Policy processes the template and makes the corresponding changes to the members of that GPO, which can be users or computers.

Server Message Block (SMB)   A high-level file-sharing protocol jointly developed by Microsoft, IBM, and Intel for passing data between computers on a network. Microsoft Windows and OS/2 use SMB. Many UNIX operating systems also support it.

SMB is used between clients and servers to do the following:

- Open and close connections between client redirectors and shared network resources

- Locate, read, and write to files shared on a server

- Locate and print to print queues that are shared on a server

service dependency   A relationship between services in which one service requires that other services are started before it can start.

services   Programs, routines, or processes that perform a specific system function to support other programs, particularly at a low (close to the hardware) level. When services are provided over a network, they can be published in the Active Directory directory service, facilitating service-centric administration and usage. Some examples of services are the Security Accounts Manager service, the File Replication service, and the Routing and Remote Access service.

SMB   *See* Server Message Block (SMB).

SPI   *See* Security Parameters Index (SPI).

static routing   A routing mechanism that is handled by the Internet Protocol (IP) and that depends on manually configured routing tables. Routers that use static routing are called "static routers." Static routers are generally used in smaller networks that contain only a couple of routers or when security is an issue. Each static router must be configured and maintained separately because static routers do not exchange routing information with each other.

stub zone   A copy of a zone that contains only the resource records required to identify the authoritative Domain Name System (DNS) servers for that zone. A DNS server that hosts a parent zone and a stub zone for one of the parent zone's delegated child zones can receive updates from the authoritative DNS servers for the child zone.

subnet mask   A number that, when compared with a network address number, will block out all but the necessary information. For example, in a network that uses XXX.XXX.XXX.YYY and where all computers within the network use the same first address numbers, the mask will block out XXX.XXX.XXX and use only the significant numbers in the address, YYY.

superscope   An administrative grouping feature that supports a Dynamic Host Configuration Protocol (DHCP) server's ability to use more than one scope for each physical interface and subnet. Superscopes are useful under the following conditions: if more DHCP clients must be added to a network than were originally planned, if an Internet Protocol (IP) network is renumbered, or if two or more DHCP servers are configured to provide scope redundancy and fault-tolerant design DHCP service for a single subnet. Each superscope can contain one or more member scopes (also known as "child scopes").

SVCHOST process   A generic host process name for services that are run from dynamic-link libraries (DLLs). The Svchost.exe file is located in the %systemroot%\System32 folder. At startup, Svchost.exe checks the services portion of the registry to construct a list of services that it needs to load. Multiple instances of Svchost.exe can run at the same time. Each Svchost.exe session can contain a grouping of services so that separate services can be run depending on how and where Svchost.exe is started. This allows for better control and debugging.

switch   In the context of controlling data flow within a network, the term "switch" is also used to describe a data-link-layer device that routes frames between connected networks. Data flow switches include the following:

- Local area network (LAN) switches. Used to route Ethernet frames over a Transmission Control Protocol/Internet Protocol (TCP/IP) internetwork. Also called "Ethernet switches."

- Asynchronous Transfer Mode (ATM) switches. Used to switch ATM cells at high speeds over an ATM network.

In the context of high-speed Ethernet networks, the term "switch" usually refers to an Ethernet switch. Thus, the phrase "routers and switches" is understood to mean "routers and Ethernet switches."

The term "switch" can also refer to a device used at a telco central office (CO) for establishing connections in circuit-switched services or forwarding packets in packet-switched services.

system access control list (SACL) The part of an object's security descriptor that specifies which events are to be audited per user or group. Examples of auditing events are file access, logon attempts, and system shutdowns.

TCP *See* Transmission Control Protocol (TCP/IP).

TCP/IP *See* Transmission Control Protocol/Internet Protocol (TCP/IP).

Terminal Services The underlying technology that enables Remote Desktop, Remote Assistance, and Terminal Server.

TLD *See* top-level domain (TLD).

Token Ring The Institute of Electrical and Electronics Engineers (IEEE) 802.5 standard that uses a token-passing technique for Media Access Control (MAC). Token Ring supports media of both shielded and unshielded twisted-pair wiring for data rates of 4 megabits per second (Mbps) and 16 Mbps.

top-level domain (TLD) Domain names that are rooted hierarchically at the first tier of the domain namespace. They are directly under the root (.) of the Domain Name System (DNS) namespace. On the Internet, top-level domain names such as .com and .org are used to classify and assign second-level domain names (such as microsoft.com) to individual organizations and businesses according to their organizational purpose.

Transmission Control Protocol (TCP) *See* Transmission Control Protocol/Internet Protocol (TCP/IP).

Transmission Control Protocol/Internet Protocol (TCP/IP) A set of networking protocols widely used on the Internet that provides communications across interconnected networks of computers with diverse hardware architectures and various operating systems. TCP/IP includes standards for how computers communicate and conventions for connecting networks and routing traffic.

triggers Actions taken when sampled counters are set to go off. Triggers are typically set when a counter rises above a certain value or drops below a certain value.

UDP *See* User Datagram Protocol (UDP).

unicast An address that identifies a specific, globally unique host.

user class An administrative feature that allows Dynamic Host Configuration Protocol (DHCP) clients to be grouped logically according to a shared or common need. For example, a user class can be defined and used to allow similar DHCP leased configuration for all client computers in a specific building or site location.

User Datagram Protocol (UDP) A Transmission Control Protocol (TCP) complement that offers a connectionless datagram service that guarantees neither delivery nor correct sequencing of delivered packets (much like Internet Protocol [IP]).

user rights Tasks that a user is permitted to perform on a computer system or domain. There are two types of user rights: privileges and logon rights. An example of a privilege is the right to shut down the system. An example of a logon right is the right to log on to a computer locally. Administrators assign both types of rights to individual users or groups as part of the security settings for the computer.

vendor class An administrative feature that allows Dynamic Host Configuration Protocol (DHCP) clients to be identified and leased according to their vendor and hardware configuration type. For example, assigning a vendor class of HP to a printer vendor such as Hewlett-Packard would allow all Hewlett-Packard printers to be managed as a single unit so they could all obtain a similar DHCP leased configuration.

virtual private network (VPN) The extension of a private network that encompasses encapsulated, encrypted, and authenticated links across shared or public networks. VPN connections can provide remote access and routed connections to private networks over the Internet.

VPN   *See* virtual private network (VPN).

WAN   *See* wide area network (WAN).

WebDAV   *See* Web Distributed Authoring and Versioning (WebDAV).

Web Distributed Authoring and Versioning (WebDAV)   An application protocol related to Hypertext Transfer Protocol (HTTP) 1.1 that allows clients to transparently publish and manage resources on the World Wide Web.

wide area network (WAN)   A communications network that connects geographically separated computers, printers, and other devices. A WAN enables any connected device to interact with any other device on the network.

Windows Internet Naming Service (WINS)   A software service that dynamically maps Internet Protocol (IP) addresses to computer names (network basic input/output system [NetBIOS] names). This enables users to access resources by name instead of requiring them to use IP addresses that are difficult to recognize and remember.

Windows operating system kernel   The core (also called the "kernel") of the Windows Server 2003 operating system. Code that runs as part of the kernel does so in privileged processor mode and has direct access to system data and hardware.

Windows Update   A Microsoft Web site that works with Automatic Updates to provide timely critical and noncritical system updates. Updates include security patches, updated drivers, and other recommended files.

Windows Update Catalog   A Web site that lists hardware and software that is designed for use with Windows XP, Windows 2000 Server products, and products in the Windows Server 2003 family. You can use this site to help you decide whether to purchase a particular device or program and help you evaluate whether a particular computer would support an upgraded operating system, as well as for similar hardware and software decisions.

WINS   *See* Windows Internet Naming Service (WINS).

X.25   A packet-switching protocol for wide area network (WAN) connectivity that uses a public data network (PDN) that parallels the voice network of the Public Switched Telephone Network (PSTN). The current X.25 standard supports synchronous, full-duplex communication at speeds of up to 2 megabits per second (Mbps) over two pairs of wires; however, most implementations are 64-kilobits-per-second (Kbps) connections using a standard DS0 link.

X.25 was developed by common carriers in the early 1970s and approved in 1976 by the CCITT, the precursor of the International Telecommunication Union (ITU). X.25 was designed as a global standard for a packet-switching network and was originally designed to connect remote, character-based terminals to mainframe hosts. The original X.25 standard operated at only 19.2 Kbps, but this was generally sufficient for character-based communication between mainframes and terminals.

X.509 v3 certificate   Version 3 of the International Telecommunication Union-Telecommunication (Standardization Sector) (ITU-T) recommendation X.509 for certificate syntax and format. This is the standard certificate format used by Windows certificate-based processes.

An X.509 certificate includes the public key and information about the person or entity to which the certificate is issued, information about the certificate, plus optional information about the certificate authority (CA) issuing the certificate.

XML   *See* Extensible Markup Language (XML).

zone   In a Domain Name System (DNS) database, a manageable unit of the DNS database that is administered by a DNS server. A zone stores the domain names and data of the domain with a corresponding name, except for domain names stored in delegated subdomains.

zone transfer   The process of copying information from the zone file on one Domain Name System (DNS) server to another DNS server.

zone file   A file on a name server that contains information that defines the zone that the name server manages. The zone file is a text file consisting of a series of resource records that form the Domain Name System (DNS) database of the name server. These records identify which name server is responsible for a given zone, timing parameters for zone transfers between name servers, IP address to host name mappings for hosts within the domains over which the zone file is authoritative, and so on.

INDEX

Symbol

% Processor Time performance counter,
283

A

A records (address resource records), 76
 registering, 123
 updating, 33
access control list (ACL), 38
 least privilege principle for, 156
Account Operators group, user rights
 assignment to, 149
Account Policies section, in security
 templates, 157
Acquire Failures statistic (IPSec main
 mode), 199
Acquire Heap Size statistic (IPSec main
 mode), 199
Active Acquire statistic (IPSec main
 mode), 199
Active Directory
 access control settings, 128
 DHCP server authorization, 13, 16
 DNS objects in, 127
 DNSLint to troubleshoot, 113
 for IPSec deployment, 194
 loading zone data on startup from, 122
Active Directory Users And Computers, 32
 creating shortcut to, 155
 dial-in properties, 262
 Group Policy, 151
Active Directory–integrated zone, 69–70
 DNS notification in, 94
 forcing replication, 137
 forward lookup zone, 70
 in Replication Monitor, 136
 reverse lookup zone, 70
 security, 129
Active queue length counter, 52
Active Receive statistic (IPSec main
 mode), 199
Active Security Association statistic
 (IPSec quick mode), 200
Active Tunnels statistic (IPSec quick
 mode), 200

Add command (Route utility), 257
Add Or Remove Programs, 291
Add/Remove Snap-in dialog box, 156
address pools in DHCP scope, 17
Address Resolution Protocol (ARP), 2,
 254
 broadcasting for default gateway, 9
address resource records (A records), 76
 registering, 123
 updating, 33
administrator, logon as, 154
Administrators group
 default user rights, 148
 user rights assignment to, 149
.aero domain, 64
aging DNS resource records, 123
AH protocol, 182
Alerter service, enabling, 287
alerts in System Monitor, DHCP
 performance, 53
aliases for FQDN, 77
 Ls command to display, 112
Allow Access option for user accounts,
 263
American Standard Code for Information
 Interchange (ASCII), 121
anti-replay, IPSec and, 181
APIPA (Automatic Private IP
 Addressing), 4, 10, 54, 293
 disabling, 54
 troubleshooting, 55
application directory partition, 127
 in Replication Monitor, 136
Application Event Log, entry addition for
 alert, 286
Application layer, in OSI reference
 model, 4
Application Server role, 218
applications, rights required, 303
approval logs, 235
ARP (Address Resolution Protocol), 2, 254
 broadcasting for default gateway, 9
ARPANET, name resolution, 62
ASCII (American Standard Code for
 Information Interchange), 121

SYSTEM REQUIREMENTS

To complete the exercises in this textbook, get the most out of the Supplemental Course Materials CD-ROM, and install the Microsoft Windows Server 2003 evaluation software, you will need a computer equipped with the following minimum configuration:

- Microsoft Windows Server 2003, Enterprise Edition. (A 180-day evaluation edition of Windows Server 2003, Enterprise Edition is included on the CD-ROM.)

- Microsoft PowerPoint or Microsoft PowerPoint Viewer. (PowerPoint Viewer is included on the Supplemental Student CD-ROM.)

- Microsoft Word or Microsoft Word Viewer. (Word Viewer is included on the Supplemental Student CD-ROM.)

- Microsoft Internet Explorer 5.01 or later.

- Minimum CPU speed: 133 MHz for x86-based computers and 733 MHz for Itanium-based computers. (733 MHz is recommended.)

- Minimum RAM: 128 MB. (256 MB is recommended.)

- Disk space for setup: 1.5 GB for x86-based computers and 2.0 GB for Itanium-based computers.

- Display monitor capable of 800 x 600 resolution or higher.

- CD-ROM drive.

- Microsoft mouse or compatible pointing device.

Uninstall Instructions

The time-limited release of Microsoft Windows Server 2003, Enterprise Edition, will expire 180 days after installation. If you decide to discontinue the use of this software, you will need to reinstall your original operating system. You might need to reformat your drive.